COMMUNICATION
PATHWAYS

second edition

Joseph M. Valenzano III

Melissa A. Broeckelman-Post

Erin Sahlstein Parcell

FOUNTAINHEAD
PRESS

Editorial director: Christina Bruer
Developmental and managing editor: Amy Salisbury-Werhane
Book and cover design: Ellie Moore

Image sources: Shutterstock, Alamy, and Getty Images, unless otherwise credited

Copyright © 2016, 2019 Fountainhead Press

ISBN: 978-1-68036-942-7

Printed in the United States of America.

DEDICATIONS

For my son, Connor, whose smile and laughter remind me that every day is a joyful blessing.

Joseph M. Valenzano III

For my nieces, nephews, and others yet to come: may you learn to communicate in ways that help to make the world a kinder and gentler place.

Melissa A. Broeckelman-Post

For my husband Drew and daughter Lucy, who support me in my work and bring so much happiness to my life.

Erin Sahlstein Parcell

CONTENTS

PREFACE

Communication is woven into our daily lives, and often we do not stop to think how complicated and challenging effectively communicating with others can be. Nevertheless, it is through communication that we add color, interest, and energy to our lived experiences. Without communication we could not share ideas, solve problems, build relationships, establish and maintain families, or express our emotions. Put simply, communication makes us human.

The basic communication course is too often the only exposure students have to training in communication, and even that class often focuses exclusively on public speaking. This course and this book do not focus on public speaking alone, but rather several different contexts and situations in which you will need to effectively communicate with others. To do this, the book is divided into several parts.

In the first part you will encounter the basic principles of communication and how it functions. You will learn about models of communication, how different cultural experiences result in different styles of communication, and the role of perception in the communication process. In addition to discussions of the models and principles that serve as the foundation for understanding communication, this book uniquely includes a chapter devoted to illustrating the concept of dialogic communication. We view dialogic communication as so important that we revisit how to engage in it in every subsequent chapter.

The first part also includes chapters that discuss the role of language in communication, how our nonverbal communication can influence the meaning in any message, and the complex purpose listening serves in the process of understanding and interpreting meaning.

The second significant part of this book considers communication in interpersonal contexts. This is, by far, the most common situation in which we communicate with others. The relationships we form, no matter how short- or long-lived they may be, serve as our tethers to other people and help us form communities. We discuss how we use communication to create and develop these bonds with others, how we maintain relationships (and how we don't), and pay special attention to the intimate relationships in our lives and the role communication plays in them.

Yet another chapter that sets this book apart is the chapter in which we cover mediated relationships. Today we use various media to develop and maintain relationships with people in ways we never could before. From Facebook and Pinterest to Skype and Facetime, we now have tools to communicate with people that allow us to overcome historical challenges to maintaining relationships, like distance and time.

The third part of the book turns the focus to public speaking. These chapters focus on introducing some basic elements of delivering a formal presentation, with a focus on how to do so to facilitate understanding and encourage dialogue. We cover things like delivery, organization, the basics of explaining information, and the persuasive process.

The fourth part of the book addresses communication in a third and final context: small groups. Often in your academic and professional lives you will be asked to work in groups with others, and the success of those groups depends upon effective communication. We also spend a chapter discussing leadership and the role communication plays for leaders in organizations and groups. Finally, we discuss interviewing, with a focus on job interviews and how to successfully present yourself in these very important moments.

Throughout the book you will also notice some short stories in boxes set apart from the main text. In these "Mediated Moments" we use contemporary examples from television, literature, and movies to illustrate key components of a given chapter. We believe these will help make content easier to understand and identify in our daily lives. The other consistent sidebars in the text are called "Dialing Diversity," and these short vignettes illustrate how communication concepts and principles play out differently within diverse groups.

New to this second edition are vignettes we have termed "Engaging Ethics" in each chapter. These boxes provide tough pragmatic questions to very real ethical dilemmas and events that have either occurred or could feasibly happen to you. Additionally, we have streamlined content on certain theories and approaches throughout the book, and we updated several of the boxes in each chapter. We feel these meaningful adjustments retain the style, purpose, and content of the book while enhancing the reader's ability to take away important key points from each chapter.

We believe this book addresses a gap in the current offerings for "survey" communication courses by tying communication in different contexts together through a focus on dialogue. Examples of poor communication abound in society today, with people talking over each other, arguing vociferously, and not respecting or even trying to understand the positions taken by others. We hope our focus on dialogic communication in multiple contexts provides the tools necessary for students to become more dialogic communicators.

Sincerely,

Joseph M. Valenzano, III
Melissa A. Broeckelman-Post
Erin Sahlstein Parcell

1

THE BASICS OF COMMUNICATION

As the world around us becomes increasingly accessible, communication skills become more important than ever. Whether we are speaking with family over dinner, going out on a first date, working with a sales team to market a product, delivering a graduation address, or using technology to interact with friends across long distances, the one constant in all our days is communication. It is important to develop good communication skills so that we maximize our ability to be successful in all our endeavors with other people.

People often believe they know how to communicate well and that the same style or mode of communication works in every scenario. With our increasingly complex and digital world, this is simply not the case. Communication skills, like any other skill, require practice and continual development. In this chapter, we introduce you to the basic principles of communicating in any context so that as we progress through the book you begin to see how these principles work to inform how we adapt our communication in a variety of situations. We will begin with briefly describing the various reasons why and how we communicate in today's global world. We will then discuss some common myths about communication and what people erroneously believe it can do. Finally, we will explain models for when communication works and discuss what makes a person a competent communicator.

WHY WE COMMUNICATE

A quick answer to why we communicate could very well be "to get something done"; however, as we will see in this section of the chapter, there are more reasons that drive us to interact with others than simply accomplishing tasks. In fact, there are five fundamental motives that drive our need to communicate with others. These needs all feed into some level of noted psychologist Abraham Maslow's hierarchy of needs (see Figure 1.1).[1] His model shows that people first need to fill physiological needs, such as food and sleep, before then seeking safety for themselves and their family. Once these two needs are met, they move on to filling their needs to love and to belong to a group, which in turn allow them to seek out a way to fill their needs for self-esteem and confidence. Finally, they seek to fill their moral needs through what Maslow calls self-actualization. Maslow's hierarchy demonstrates that for communication to be successful and fulfilling, it needs to be driven by a purpose.

FIGURE 1.1   Maslow's Hierarchy of Needs

Physical Needs

Communication enhances our physical and mental health. This fact is what undergirds such programs as cancer support groups, Alcoholics Anonymous, and even suicide help lines. People can feel better when they talk to other people, because in doing so they feel connected to the world around them. For example, according to the American Cancer Society, research indicates that participation in support groups can help reduce stress, tension, and fatigue, while also potentially helping patients achieve greater tolerance for the grueling treatment they are undergoing.[2]

The benefits of communication on a person's health are rooted in the fact that we are social beings. Sometimes it is as if we cannot survive without social contact, something German Emperor Frederick II proved in a grossly unethical experiment in the thirteenth century. In an effort to determine what language children would speak without being exposed to any language, he took 50 newborns and had nurses feed and clean them, but not speak or otherwise hold them. All of the infants eventually died.[3] In more current and less dangerous research, scholars have shown how important human contact, especially touch, is to newborns. In fact, more recent work has demonstrated that talking to babies, even at very early ages, helps them develop language skills.[4] Contact and communication are clearly directly related to health for children and adults, and help people fill their physiological and safety needs.

Instrumental and Task Needs

Despite the health benefits provided by interacting with others, communication also often results in the fulfillment of practical needs. For example, without communication we could not exchange phone numbers, relay sales figures, share a diagnosis with a patient, or even build a bridge.

From ordering dinner, to calling emergency services, we use communication to complete important tasks that allow us to remain safe and even find food. The role communication plays in completing everyday tasks is as important as the benefits it accords our health and well-being. Without communication, we most assuredly would not be able to survive, but since we have survived, we can look to the other needs communication fills in our lives.

Relational Needs

In addition to personal health and safety, we need companionship with others. This companionship helps us receive and give affection to others, as well as find ways to relax and escape from the stresses of life. These are things made possible through connection to other people, which would not be possible without communication. Communication is how we establish and maintain relationships with other people.

In today's global, digital world, there are myriad ways in which we can create relationships with others. There are the traditional avenues, such as face-to-face communication with our neighbors, classmates, and colleagues, and we can also maintain relationships at a distance, thanks to the telephone, video chat programs like Skype and FaceTime, and social media sites like Facebook, Instagram, and Pinterest, just to name a few. Furthermore, we can create relationships with people we have never met in person using these same digital media.

Despite the abundance of communication tools, sometimes the more connected we are, the less connected to other people we feel. This is precisely the worry that has been raised by several scholars and cultural experts. For example, MIT professor Sherry Turkle delivered a *TED* Talk titled, "The Innovation of Loneliness," where she argued our increased use and reliance on social media and electronic communication has created an atmosphere where we feel more isolated from each other.[5] The medium of the computer has created a barrier preventing us from truly learning how to relate with other people. Nevertheless, communication helps us fulfill our need to develop and maintain relationships with others, despite the challenges some forms of communication may present in doing so.

Identity Needs

Our conversations with others help shape how we see ourselves. The resulting communication thus provides us with how others understand us, and also provides us the language to define how we present ourselves to other people. Our identities are always in a state of flux, changing based on how new people see us, and how we choose to interact with them. This constant feedback allows us to adapt our self-images based on the different contexts in which we find ourselves.

MEDIATED MOMENTS

The Artist Formerly Known As Prince

One of the more popular and successful musicians in recent years, the late artist Prince changed his name to a symbol in 1993 during a dispute with his record label, Warner Bros. Appearing before the press with the word "slave" written on his face, Prince declared his new "name" and explained its meaning:

> The first step I have taken toward the ultimate goal of emancipation from the chains that bind me to Warner Bros. was to change my name from Prince to the Love Symbol [⚥]. Prince is the name that my mother gave me at birth. Warner Bros. took the name, trademarked it, and used it as the main marketing tool to promote all of the music that I wrote. The company owns the name Prince and all related music marketed under Prince. I became merely a pawn used to produce more money for Warner Bros...

> I was born Prince and did not want to adopt another conventional name. The only acceptable replacement for my name, and my identity, was the Love Symbol, a symbol with no pronunciation, that is a representation of me and what my music is about. This symbol is present in my work over the years; it is a concept that has evolved from my frustration; it is who I am. It is my name.

In this statement, Prince publicly announced the symbol he would be referred to as from that point on. He tied it to his sense of self and what he believed he represented. Since people could not verbalize the symbol, they referred to him as "The artist formerly known as Prince." This action by the famous artist shows how close the tie is between communication and our identity, and it depicts how communication can work to fulfill those needs.

For example, you define yourself differently and communicate differently with your parents than you do with your friends from school. In turn, you define yourself differently and speak differently with your college friends than you do with your friends from high school. Our identities shift based on what we let people see in us, what we choose to hide, and even what we do not know we are sharing or presenting to others. Later, in the chapter on perception and the self, we will explore self-esteem in greater detail, but for now it is enough to say we use communication to construct our self-image.

Spiritual Needs

In the 2014 Religious Landscape study conducted by the Pew Research Center, 70.6 percent of Americans still claimed a Christian label,[6] and even those who did not adhere to a faith system still grappled with questions like "what is the *meaning* of life?" and "why are we here?" Spirituality does not mean religion; rather it refers to deep feelings and beliefs about the values, purposes, and meaning of human existence. Spirituality is not synonymous with religion, but rather religion is one form of expression of spirituality. As individuals, regardless of our faiths, we use communication to satisfy our longing for answers regarding these profound questions that cannot be directly answered. Some use prayer, while others employ meditation or read philosophy.

For those who use prayer, there is an even deeper question related to the spiritual needs fulfilled by communication. Communication scholar Quentin Schultz refers to this question as the "God Problem,"[7] wherein some people may use prayer to communicate to God, but how do we know we are being answered? How does God actually speak? These are profound questions about communication rooted in its ability to help us seek answers to and fulfill our spiritual needs. Intrapersonal communication, or communication with oneself, is also a vital part of other forms of spiritual communication that employ meditation and self-reflective practices.

UNDERSTANDING HOW WE COMMUNICATE

Communication takes many different forms. In this section of the chapter, we will dissect communication to better understand how messages are constructed and how they are delivered. We will first discuss the nature of symbols and their relationship to our thoughts, and then we will discuss three models of communication that explain how messages travel (and sometimes don't) between people in virtually any situation. As we will explain, communication does not function in one way, as there are several paths through which messages can travel.

The Building Blocks of Communication

Many disciplines break down their subject matter into things called **units of analysis**—what the researcher is trying to understand or study. Biologists use cells, chemists use molecules,

UNIT OF ANALYSIS
the item that the researcher is trying to understand or study

mathematicians use numbers, and communication scholars use symbols. Symbols are not just words; they can take many forms. One of the simplest ways to understand the study of symbols in all their forms is provided by C. K. Ogden and I. A. Richards in their book, *The Meaning of Meaning.*[8]

Ogden and Richards proposed that meaning is in people, not words. This proposal can also be extended to the use of other symbols. People give words and other symbols meaning through interpretation, because words and symbols mean nothing until we give them their essence. Ogden and Richards illustrated how the process of interpretation works. There are three parts of a semantic triangle: the referent, the symbol, and the thought. The symbol is a representation, such as a word or image. A referent is an actual object that you are trying to communicate to another person. We use thought to connect the symbol to the referent. It is in our minds, through thought, that we connect the symbol and the referent. Once this relationship has been established, we can use the symbol (such as the word "table") to represent the thing (an actual table) when we are communicating with others who share our same symbol system (our language: English, Latin, Spanish, Arabic, etc.). This allows us to share meaning with other people, even if the things that we are communicating about are not actually present. See Figure 1.2 for an illustration.

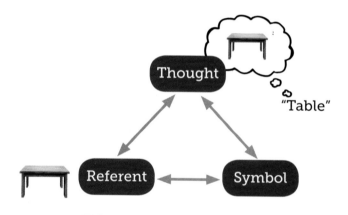

FIGURE 1.2 Semantic Triangle

As you can see, Ogden and Richards provided a clear way to analyze communication by treating symbols as the units of analysis. We do not, however, communicate using just a symbol, but rather by using symbol systems. Language is a type of symbol system, as are traffic signs, and even the Periodic Table of Elements. These systems allow people to communicate with each other, but the processes by which we send messages using symbol systems is more complex than this.

Models of the Communication Process

There are three primary models used to explain the communication process, and each contains the same basic elements. The process begins with a sender **encoding**, or creating, a message. The sender then sends the message through a **channel**, or pathway through which the symbols travel to a receiver or receivers. Some examples of channels are text

ENCODING
the process of creating a message using symbols

CHANNEL
pathway through which the symbols travel

messages, television, radio, phone, email, and even your own voice. When travelling through the channel, the message invariably encounters noise, or anything that interferes with the receiver's ability to properly receive the message. For some examples of types of noise our messages typically encounter, see Table 1.1. On the other end of the channel is the receiver, who decodes, or interprets, the symbols within the message, thus giving them meaning.

NOISE

anything that interferes with the receiver's ability to properly receive the message

DECODING

the process of interpreting the symbols within a message

Physical Noise	Psychological Noise
• Other sounds (people talking, air conditioner, shuffling papers, etc.) • Visual barriers • Poor volume and projection • Distractions in the room • Hunger, tiredness, and other bodily limitations	• Preoccupation with other thoughts • Emotional reaction to the topic • Prejudice or ill will toward the speaker • Unwillingness to listen • Resistance to the message

TABLE 1.1   Types of Noise

These basic components serve as the foundation for each of the three models of the communication process we will now explore in further detail.

Action model of communication. The action model of communication goes by two other names: the Shannon-Weaver model, and the linear model. The first of these alternate names represents the scholars responsible for the model's development, and the latter name reflects how the model works, as you will see. In the action model, communication is understood as a one-way process, in which the sender sends a message to a receiver, who decodes it. According to this model, the process stops there, as represented in Figure 1.3, but over time communication scholars recognized the process of creating and communicating meaning is not so linear.

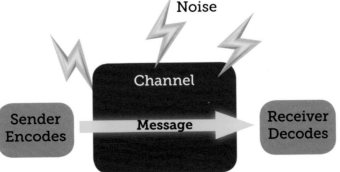

FIGURE 1.3   Action Model of Communication

FEEDBACK

the various verbal and
nonverbal responses
to the message by the
receiver

CONTEXT

the physical,
emotional, and
psychological
environment in which
the communication
event takes place

Interaction model of communication. The interaction model expands the action model, using all the same elements, but adding two more in order to show communication as a two-way process instead of a linear one-way process as shown in Figure 1.3. The first of the added elements to the model is feedback, or the various verbal and nonverbal responses to the message by the receiver. In the interaction model, feedback takes place after the receiver decodes the sender's message. The second added component is context, or the physical, emotional, and psychological environment in which the communication event takes place. When we communicate, we take the context into consideration when it comes to the words we use, the way we act, dress, and respond, and so the interaction model, Figure 1.4 on the following page, acknowledges this aspect of the communication process. Despite these additions, the two-way nature of the interaction model still does not completely capture the nature of the communication process, and so scholars developed a third, more complete model.

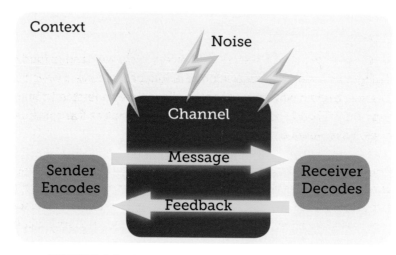

FIGURE 1.4   Interaction Model of Communication

Transactional model of communication. The transactional model updates both the action and interaction models of communication in one key way. The model does not differentiate between the sender and the receiver, seeing both parties as sender and receiver, as illustrated in Figure 1.5. This feature of the model shows the simultaneous nature of communication, where we are sending messages to the other person even while we are decoding the message the other person is sending. In this model, communication flows both ways at the same time, which is a much more realistic characterization of the communication process.

Now that we have explored both what communication can do for us, and how it works, we need to dispel some misconceptions about communication that many people hold.

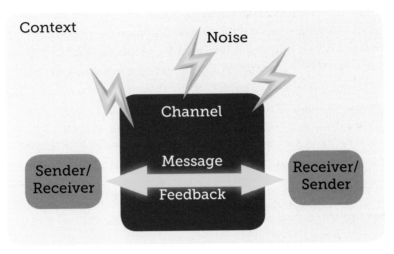

FIGURE 1.5   **Transactional Model of Communication**

Communication Myths

Starting from birth, when we cried to let our caregivers know we needed food or a new dia-
per and continuing on through our acquisition of language, we have always communicated
with others. This may explain why many people believe they understand communication so
well, even though they likely do not. In this section, we will explore five common misconceptions many people have about communication.

Myth #1: Everyone is an adept communicator. As noted in the previous section, we all have
extensive experience with communicating, but just because we do something often does
not make us experts in it. For example, a person may keep track of her personal finances,
but this does not make her an expert at finance. Many people also cook, but that does not

Protests and Controversial Speakers

Recently college and university cam-
puses have rescinded or cancelled
invitations to controversial speakers
to deliver remarks at their campus. In
some instances, the decision to cancel
occurred after protests or threats of violent protest if the speaker was allowed
to speak. Former President Obama
has remarked that colleges should not
do this sort of thing, and allow the free
exchange of ideas—especially those
with which you disagree. Consider
whether the protests, themselves a form
of communication, are ethical points of
entrance for people into a debate about
a controversial figure. When else might
they express their disagreement? What
makes a protest "right" or "wrong"?

make them all chefs. What does make someone an expert in something is extensive training in his or her field, and most people do not have extensive training in communication. This is not to say that your experiences are bad or that you are impolite or even a bad communicator, but rather that there is a host of information on communication with which you are unfamiliar. This book will provide you with some of that information in a practical way so you can improve your communication skills.

Myth #2: Communication can solve any problem. Although communication can help to repair relationships and solve problems in many different circumstances, there are times when communication can actually make things worse. As social as people are, they also need their space, and it can be frustrating when we fill that space with constant communication. Additionally, not everything needs to be discussed or even addressed, and so leaving some topics alone is better than confronting them. More communication in these cases is not better; it can make things worse. In certain cases, communication can also let people know it may be

DIALING DIVERSITY

The Culture of Business Cards

When two professionals meet, it is common practice to exchange business cards. The business cards often contain a company name, the individual's name and job title, contact information, and sometimes even a picture. In the United States, it is common to see people take a business card, not look at it, and simply place it in a pocket or even fold it up. They also may take the card and write some notes on it during the meeting. Americans do not find this practice offensive; however, other cultures do. For instance, in Japan professionals expect a person to whom they give their business card to read it and then put it in a place that will keep it from being crinkled. They see this as a sign of respect, because the business card for them is a shorthand for who they are and what they have accomplished, a resume of sorts. To write on it, fold it, or ignore it tells them that not just the card, but who the card represents, is not of any value to the receiver. In the Middle East, when presenting your card do so with your right hand and not your left. In India that protocol is the same, but also make sure you include academic achievements, degrees and certifications on your card as that is expected. When interacting with people from different backgrounds, it is important to take their expectations into account. If you do not, you risk damaging or even destroying the relationship. Ignore business cards at your own risk!

time to move on, even when the intent is to bring two people back together. We will return to this myth in more detail when we cover interpersonal conflict in a later chapter.

Myth #3: There is only one type of communication. Communication is a very broad field, and it covers a lot of activities, but there is no one way to communicate properly. The type of communication we choose to engage in is dependent on the situation in which we find ourselves. Debate and argumentation work in some cases, but dialogue can be more effective in others. Sometimes, listening is the best thing we can do. Our choice depends on the purpose of the interaction and with whom we are speaking. If a person does not adjust the way in which they communicate based on the context in which they find themselves, they increase the probability of misunderstandings and potential problems.

Myth #4: Any communication is good communication. Not all communication is positive, and sometimes we need to exercise restraint and not share certain comments or thoughts with others. Just because you want to say something, or even have the right to say something, does not mean it is good to say it. Just like any tool, communication can be used in a negative way, and, therefore, it is not always good. As an example, think about interruptions. Just because you feel the need to contribute at that moment does not mean it is a good idea to do so. Interrupting others, though communication, is not going to create a positive experience.

Myth #5: More communication will ultimately make people agree with you. Many people believe that the reason others disagree with them is that they have not been clearly understood. As a result, they continue pushing their ideas in an effort to help the other person understand, and thus agree. It can often be the case, however, that the other person does understand what is being said, and yet still does not agree with it. More communication does not produce agreement in these instances, but may instead invite the opposite. It is important to recognize when a point is made and the other person just does not agree, because the more you talk in these cases, the more entrenched the other person is likely to become in the disagreement.

So far we have illustrated the complex nature of communication, how it works, and some common misunderstandings about the process people hold. In the final section of this chapter, we will define what it means to be a competent communicator.

THE COMPETENT COMMUNICATOR

Just as there are several misconceptions regarding communication, there are things communication scholars know make up good communication between people. When we think of good communicators we have encountered, we often think of those people as being able to effectively and appropriately interact in any situation. This is also how scholars define communication competence. The effectiveness of communication refers to how well it achieves its purpose, and embedded within this definition is the idea that the strategic

COMMUNICATION COMPETENCE
the ability to effectively and appropriately interact in any given situation

choices we make about how we communicate with others in a given situation directly influence the degree to which our message can be successful. The appropriateness of communication refers to our ability to pay attention to the rules and expectations of a given situation, something made very difficult when it comes to interacting with people from different cultural backgrounds. In this section of the chapter, we will detail five characteristics exhibited by competent communicators.

Self-awareness

SELF-MONITORING
the process of being attuned to how your actions and messages impact others

A competent communicator pays attention to his or her behaviors and comments, and how those influence or affect other people. The process of being attuned to how our actions and messages impact others is called self-monitoring. People who are high self-monitors pay close attention to how they look, sound, and react, as well as what they say when in situations with other people. By contrast, low self-monitors pay minimal attention to these things, and are thus not aware that they may be making a negative impression on others. Being a high self-monitor allows people to adjust to different responses and situations.

Responsiveness and Adaptability

Good communicators must not only be cognizant of their own actions and reactions, but also must be able to act upon those observations in a way that is appropriate to the situation. Responding to others and adapting your messages and behaviors in different social situations is an important skill exhibited by competent communicators. Remember that communication is not a one-size-fits-all tool, and thus competent communicators know how to adapt their communication to the responses of others and the various situations in which they find themselves.

GENERALIZED OTHER
a composite mental image we use to practice our potential statements or behaviors before we actually enact them

Person-centered Messages

Too often we get lost in ourselves and forget to consider other people. Good communicators consistently take other people's thoughts, ideas, and feelings into account and create what researcher Jesse Delia calls "person-centered messages."[9] Noted scholar, George Herbert Mead, proposed a concept called the generalized other, which is a composite

The fundamental problem of communication is that of reproducing at one point either exactly or approximately a message selected at another point. Frequently the messages have meaning; that is they refer to or are correlated according to some system with certain physical or conceptual entities.[10]

—C. E. Shannon

mental image upon which we practice our potential statements or behaviors before we actually enact them.[11] This allows us to anticipate how we think other people might react, and thus adapt accordingly. It also helps us experience empathy, or the ability to understand and feel the emotions that another person is experiencing. People who are other-oriented have strong generalized others, while those who are more focused on themselves skip the step of anticipating reactions through the generalized other altogether.

Cognitive Complexity

In most cases, there is more than one potential explanation for a behavior or message, and cognitive complexity is the ability to recognize multiple ways in which a situation or message could be understood or interpreted. This skill involves being attuned to the dimensions of the context in which people find themselves, and their ability to appreciate the different variables that could influence what, why, and how another person acts and speaks the way they do in a given circumstance. Increasing cognitive complexity involves patience and a willingness to have an open mind.

Ethics and Civility

Competent communicators understand and act upon what they believe is the right way to interact in a given situation. They communicate honestly, use good manners, are polite, and also are assertive. All but the last of these qualities may be something you readily understand, but it is important to note that assertiveness does not mean aggressiveness. Competent communicators know how to respectfully state a position in a way that does not offend others or make them defensive, and that is what we mean by being assertive. Competent communicators also know when to exercise self-restraint and to not share something with another party. Communicating in a civil and ethical fashion involves knowing the right and wrong way to communicate, acting on the former, and doing so in a manner that respects both yourself and those around you.

Being a competent communicator is much more involved than many people realize. In this book, we use the best research by experts in the field to provide you with a detailed understanding of how to improve your communication skills.

EMPATHY

the ability to understand and feel the same way as another person

COGNITIVE COMPLEXITY

the ability to recognize multiple potential ways in which a situation or message could be understood or interpreted

S U M M A R Y

In this chapter, we defined communication and provided insight into the benefits good communication produces for people. We also explained the various components of the communication process, and dispelled some widely held myths regarding communication. Finally, we introduced some qualities and characteristics of competent communicators that will be further explored throughout the remainder of this book. Communication is a complex process that works differently in different situations, and as we go further, we will delve into different communication contexts and share the tools that will help you improve your interactional skills in those situations.

CHAPTER 1 KEY IDEAS

- We communicate because communication fulfills physical, instrumental, relational, identity, and spiritual needs.

- We communicate using symbol systems that include referents (actual things), thoughts (mental constructs or ideas about those things), and symbols (words or images that represent both the referent and thought).

- There are three models of communication: the action model, the interaction model, and the transactional model.

- There are five common misconceptions or myths about communication: (1) everyone is an adept communicator, (2) communication can solve any problem, (3) there is only one type of communication, (4) any communication is good communication, and (5) more communication will ultimately make people agree with you.

- The five characteristics exhibited by competent communicators include (1) self-awareness, (2) responsiveness and adaptability, (3) person-centered messages, (4) cognitive complexity, and (5) ethics and civility.

CHAPTER 1 KEY TERMS

Unit of analysis	Context
Encoding	Communication competence
Channel	Self-monitoring
Noise	Generalized other
Decoding	Empathy
Feedback	Cognitive complexity

ACTIVITIES AND DISCUSSION QUESTIONS

1. Watch the TEDEd video, "How Miscommunication Happens (and How to Avoid It)" created by Katherine Hampsten, which is available online at https://ed.ted.com/lessons/how-to-avoid-miscommunication-katherine-hampsten. How does this video help to clarify the models of communication? Which part of the communication model is represented by the lump of clay?

2. Consider the three models of communication. For each model, draw an image or think about a metaphor that will help you remember the key features of each model. What is a situation that exemplifies communication happening in each of these models?

3. Think about a recent conversation that you had with another person. What types of noise distracted you and your conversation partner during that conversation? How might you reduce or overcome some of those types of noise during your next conversation?

4. Are you a competent communicator? Create a list of each of the characteristics of a competent communicator. Reflect back on your communication for the past month and add notes about evidence about how well you did or didn't exhibit each characteristic of competent communication. Rate yourself (or ask several people who know you well to rate you) on a scale of 1-10 for each characteristic to begin to identify your strengths and weaknesses.

5. Which of the five aspects of the competent communicator do you think that you need to work to improve the most this semester? How will this aspect of competent communication help you in your relationships and later career?

COMMUNICATION, CULTURE, AND **DIVERSITY**

Our ability to instantaneously communicate with people over great distances has had numerous effects on our lives, not the least of which is exposure to myriad different people, cultures, languages, and beliefs. We encounter these diverse audiences in classrooms, on social media, as business clients, medical patients, and even as family members. Such richness and diversity is both exciting and challenging. It makes appreciating the backgrounds and the experiences of others an essential part of becoming an effective communicator. More than ever, we must ensure that we are sensitive and respectful toward others when we speak, which makes it more likely they will listen to what we have to say.

In this chapter, we explain how culture and diversity impact our communication with others. First, we will define culture and investigate its different dimensions. We will then provide some detail on specific categories that constitute and influence the diverse audiences we encounter when we communicate in any context. Finally, we will offer some concrete suggestions for enhancing your ability to interact successfully with diverse groups of people in a variety of situations.

UNDERSTANDING CULTURE

CULTURE
the distinctive ideas, customs, social behavior, products, or way of life of a particular nation, society, people, or period

According to the Oxford English Dictionary, culture is defined as "the distinctive ideas, customs, social behavior, products, or way of life of a particular nation, society, people, or period."[1] Geert Hofstede, one of the first social psychologists to study culture, offers another take, defining culture as "the collective programming of the mind distinguishing the members of one group or category of people from another. The 'category' can refer to nations, regions within or across nations, ethnicities, religions, occupations, organizations, or the genders."[2] No matter which definition you prefer, culture is a complicated, powerful component of human development and life. It influences self-images, priorities, personalities, and how we communicate with one another.

CO-CULTURES
smaller specific cultures that intersect in our lives

We are not part of only one overarching culture. Instead, we belong to, and are impacted by, a variety of smaller, more specific cultures. These smaller groups, called co-cultures, exist within and alongside larger cultural groups, allowing individuals to simultaneously belong to several cultures and co-cultures. Sometimes we even feel conflicted between the different cultures to which we belong.

Let's look at an example to illustrate how cultures work and collide in our lives. Darius grew up in a Russian American family and is a practicing Roman Catholic. Darius happens to be quite proud of his ethnic heritage, and also makes sure he attends mass every Sunday. He does not speak Russian, however, nor does he agree with all the church's teachings. Nevertheless, many of the customs and beliefs of both groups inform Darius's perspective on the world around him. Many of his friends in his neighborhood are Russian, and he belongs to the Knights of Columbus, a Catholic charity dedicated to helping the sick, disabled and needy in their communities, but none of his Russian neighborhood friends are affiliated with that organization. Darius belongs to both cultures, which constitute co-cultures within the larger American or Western culture, and this causes a degree of conflict for him when the cultures collide.

One type of culture that is particularly influential is national culture. The specific traditions of a national culture vary greatly among countries, but according to Hofstede, national cultures can all be understood through six consistent dimensions.

For effectively cooperating with people who are from other nations, there are two basic conditions that have to be fulfilled. The first is speaking or having learned a shared language, and the second is acting according to shared rules and standards.

—Geert Hofstede

High vs. Low Power Distance Culture

Cultures with high power distance have high levels of inequality in power distribution in organizations, families, and other institutions, whereas cultures with low power distance have less inequality. Democratic countries typically have low power distance, for instance, because everyone has an equal share in decisions, while high power distance is more likely in monarchies and dictatorships where only a few have access to power and others are removed from decision making. In terms of families, those with high power distance tend to adhere to parents' decisions and seek the permission of elders for certain actions. Those families with low power distance embrace a more inclusive approach, where major decisions, like moving or choice of school for children, is arrived at through a group discussion and decision, not the edict of a parent or elder. Power distance, or more aptly put, distance from power, plays a large role in how individuals and groups behave and helps identify things they value. For instance, low power distance cultures seem to value freedom of expression and dissent more, while high power distance cultures value stability, tradition, and experience.

High vs. Low Uncertainty Avoidance Culture

Cultures with high uncertainty avoidance have a low tolerance for ambiguity and minimize the possibility of uncomfortable, unstructured situations by enforcing strict rules, safety measures, and a belief in absolute truth. Cultures with low uncertainty avoidance have fewer rules, take risks, and are tolerant of change. This cultural characteristic can also be seen in interpersonal relationships, as we will discuss later. For example, individuals who hail from cultures with high uncertainty avoidance will ask questions to reduce their uncertainty over the status of a relationship, while those who are more comfortable with uncertainty will allow things to move along naturally and not inquire about the status of a relationship to reduce their own stress. Again, this characteristic of cultures provides a view as to what a particular group may value. High uncertainty avoidance cultures may value things like planning and stability, while low uncertainty avoidance cultures tend to be more flexible and open to spontaneity and change.

Individualist vs. Collectivist Culture

Individualistic societies have loose ties between individuals and expect each person to look out for himself or herself and his or her immediate family. Collectivist cultures have strong ties between individuals, strong communal bonds, and often live in extended families that are deeply loyal to the group. Individualistic cultures value things like personal achievement and personal opinions, while collectivistic cultures tend to value things like group harmony over any one person in the group. This cultural characteristic manifests in some unique ways. For example, in individualistic cultures, such as the United States, people tend to pride themselves on speaking their minds and saying what they mean, regardless of the impact it might have on another person. Conversely, in collectivistic cultures, people will tend to "talk around" an issue until the other side realizes what is being said. This maintains group harmony while still getting a point across, but it takes much more time and effort than the direct nature embraced by individualistic cultures.

Masculine vs. Feminine Culture

Masculinity and femininity refer to the distribution of emotional roles between the genders and the difference in the values of men and women. In masculine cultures, men are typically highly assertive and competitive, and women are somewhat assertive and competitive. In feminine cultures, men and women are both much more modest and caring. Masculine cultures tend to emphasize competition, whereas feminine cultures emphasize cooperation and consensus. These masculine and feminine cultural behaviors have been identified through extensive research on gender and communication. Linguistics scholar Deborah Tannen coined the term "genderlect" to more clearly illustrate that gender is a cultural difference and that men and women simply communicate differently, thus creating their own cultures through their different styles of interaction. One fundamental difference she found was in the purpose of communication, as a masculine style of communication is one seeking to establish or defend status and express competition, while a feminine style of communication is one where the purpose is establishing connections and creating cooperation.[3]

Long-term vs. Short-term Orientation Culture

Cultures with long-term orientation are pragmatic and focus on future rewards, with an emphasis on saving, persistence, and adaptation. Cultures with short-term orientation focus on the present and past and emphasize national pride, tradition, social obligations, and saving "face" in the here and now. What is interesting about this cultural characteristic is that "long" and "short" mean different things in different places and to different people. To some, a long-term orientation means thinking about next week, next month, or perhaps next year. It might even pertain to thinking about long-term career goals and where one wants to be in five years. To others, that type of thinking is still short-term. Keep in mind some cultures have existed for thousands of years, and as such they have a very different conception of long-term. They may plan in terms of decades or even generations—a very different way of thinking about time than looking at the next few days, months, or even years. Like other cultural characteristics, long-term versus short-term orientation should be viewed on a linear scale, and not as a "one or the other" form of existence. Some cultures are more long-term in their thinking than others.

Indulgent vs. Restrained Culture

Indulgent cultures freely allow gratification of desires that allow individuals to enjoy life and have fun. Additionally, indulgent cultures value things like individual happiness, vacation, and leisure time, and the expression of emotions and thoughts. Restrained cultures have strict social norms and discourage acting simply out of want. In fact, in restrained cultures, many of the indulgent behaviors are curbed and governed through strict social and familial norms and rules, because they are seen as potentially rude. Leisure and vacation are not seen as that important in more restrained cultures. Although this is the newest of the cultural dimensions to be identified and studied, there have been some thoughts on its impact in a globalized workplace. For instance, those who come from more restrained cultures may not freely express dissent or unhappiness, and this could be detrimental to a working environment; conversely, those from more indulgent cultures may be more likely to speak out of turn or to say something inappropriate that can also have a detrimental impact on work productivity and group cohesion.[4]

It is easy to see how different nations and countries can differ along these spectrums. It is important to note, though, that Hofstede believed these dimensions fall along a continuum, and do not exist as simply "either-or." For example, a culture is not either collectivistic or individualistic, but falls somewhere in between each on a line.

In addition to the six dimensions of culture identified by Hofstede, Edward T. Hall[5] explains that most national cultures can also be identified by how much importance is placed on nonverbal cues. In low-context cultures, such as the United States and Germany, meaning is derived mostly from the language used in an interaction, and less emphasis is placed on the nonverbal communication, environment, and situation. In high-context cultures, such as Korea and Saudi Arabia, a great deal of meaning is derived from the nonverbal expressions, environment, and situation in which the communication is taking place, and less emphasis is placed on the words.

EXPLORING CULTURAL DEMOGRAPHICS

Hofstede's original six dimensions of culture, along with the one proposed by Hall, allow us to begin to understand the complexity of different cultures. This understanding can enhance our ability to interact with people by helping us see how they might differ from us in terms of values along these continuums. Next, we will explore some different cultural categories in addition to nationality, beginning with race and ethnicity.

Race and Ethnicity in Culture

Race is a common cultural marker as well as a demographic category we find on college and job applications, census data, and other types of reports. Race refers to a set of physical characteristics shared by a group of people, such as skin color, body type, facial structure, and hair color. These physical characteristics are genetically inherited and reflect adaptations to the geographic region in which someone's ancestors previously lived. However, there is no biological difference between races in other characteristics, such as intelligence, athleticism, or other abilities. The common physical characteristics help individuals identify with each other and eventually form communities.

Another cultural marker that developed due to the close proximity of people is ethnicity, but ethnicity should not be confused with race. Ethnicity refers to a group of people who identify with each other based on a common experience, which might include geographic or national origin, ancestry, history, cultural and social norms, religion, race, language, ideology, food, dress,

LOW-CONTEXT CULTURES

meaning is derived mostly from the language used in an interaction, and less emphasis is placed on the nonverbal communication, environment, and situation

HIGH-CONTEXT CULTURES

a great deal of meaning is derived from the nonverbal expressions, environment, and situation in which the communication is taking place, and less emphasis is placed on the words

RACE

a set of physical characteristics shared by a group of people, such as skin color, body type, facial structure, and hair color

ETHNICITY

a group of people who identify with each other based on a common experience, which might include geographic or national origin, ancestry, history, cultural and social norms, religion, race, language, ideology, food, dress, or other factors or other factors. Ethnicity is sometimes (but not always) related to national heritage. At times, violent conflicts and disputes evolve out of differences in ethnic heritage and values between two or more groups. At other times, several ethnic groups might coexist peacefully in the same nation. In fact, Tufts Professor Colin Woodard argues that the United States is really made up of eleven nations, each of which has a different history, ancestry, and set of deep-seated attitudes.[6]

A recent example of ethnic tension can be seen in the Crimea region of the Ukraine. In 2014, Russian-speaking citizens of Ukraine sought support from the Russian Federation when the political situation in the country became unstable, and ultimately voted to secede from Ukraine and join the Russian Federation. Ukrainian nationals in Crimea disagreed with this approach, and an international crisis ensued that still dominates much of the eastern border of the Ukraine shared with Russia.

Ethnic heritage can also be a source of reinforcement for individual identity through cultural celebrations. In major American cities, Italian Americans celebrate the Feast of San Gennaro, a food festival central to their culture. A number of cities also have areas designated Little Italy, Little China, and so on, where people who share that ethnic heritage settled. These areas offer a great opportunity to explore some of the ethnic differences between people in fun, interesting, and, if you like food, tasty ways.

Sex, Gender, and Sexual Orientation

Another set of significant cultural categories refers to a person's physical, psychological, and romantic definitions of their identity. To properly appreciate how these aspects of a person's self-concept relate to culture, we must first differentiate between the various ways we define ourselves. According to the American Psychological Society[7], sex refers to a person's biological classification as male, female, or intersex (a general term that stands for a range of situations that do not fit the typical binary groups of male or female) based on their reproductive organs and chromosomes. Sex is a relatively objective way of identifying the group to which a person belongs based on biology. Often, job applications and college applications ask for this information but are prohibited from using it to make decisions. Males, females, and intersex individuals are also often depicted with symbols as shown in Figure 2.1 on the following page.

Sex is also often incorrectly used as a synonym for gender, which is quite different. Gender is a social construction that includes all of the beliefs, attitudes, actions, and roles associated with being masculine, feminine, androgynous, and so on. A person's biological sex informs their gender identity, but gender is more than simply the expression of self through physical characteristics. Gender identity includes a person's sense of self as being along a range of possibilities that include identifying as a woman, non-binary, genderqueer, agender, or a man. Gender roles include the societal expectations for individuals who identify with a particular gender. It is important to note that these expectations vary across cultures and that gender expression (i.e., the ways people communicate their gender identity though their clothing, hairstyle, etc.) can be quite different across as well as within them.

SEX
one's biological classification based on reproductive function

GENDER
a social construction that includes all of the beliefs, attitudes, actions, and roles associated with being masculine, feminine, androgynous, etc.

GENDER IDENTITY
a person's sense of self as being along a range of possibilities that include identifying as a woman, non-binary, genderqueer, agender, or a man

GENDER ROLES
societal expectations for individuals who identify with a particular gender

GENDER EXPRESSION
ways people communicate their gender identity

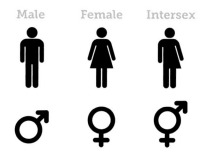

Male   Female   Intersex

FIGURE 2.1   Male, Female, and Intersex Images and Corresponding Symbols

In addition to sex and gender, there is an emotional and romantic dimension. A person's sexual orientation refers to the sex and gender identities to which a person is romantically and sexually attracted. Sexual orientation includes many categories, but the three most common categories include whether a person is attracted to those of a different sex (heterosexual), of the same sex (gay or lesbian), or both men and women (bisexual). A person's sexual orientation is both intensely personal and, for some people, a public declaration of belonging to a group (i.e., coming out).

SEXUAL ORIENTATION
the sex and gender to whom a person is romantically and sexually attracted

Gender: Law vs. Lived Experience

In many cases, laws are written using categories of sex-assigned at birth, and not the more fluid concept of gender. In June 2014, this conflict of terminology and practice resulted in a controversy in the state of South Carolina. Chase Culpepper, a 16-year-old who previously identified as male but now identifies as female, went to the Department of Motor Vehicles to have her driver's license photo wearing makeup. When she arrived at the DMV, they required her to take off her makeup, stating she did not look like a boy and that the makeup constituted a disguise (their reasoning being that it is illegal to wear a disguise for a driver's license photo). Although she ultimately wiped off the makeup for the photo and received her license, she, along with her family and the Transgender Legal Defense and Education Fund, complained that this requirement violated her right to gender expression protected by the First Amendment. Chase's story serves as a clear example of the difference between sex and gender, and how the definitions of gender and sex under the law may differ from the lived experience of an individual. Furthermore, the episode shows how certain labels carry certain expectations for society and cultural groups.

In 2018 professional golfer Tadd Fujikawa revealed himself as gay on his Instagram account, and his coming out as a part of the gay community stands as a recent example of how sexual orientation is not only personal, but can also be considered cultural. Many cities across the globe hold Pride Fests and Parades that are public celebrations of lesbian, gay, bisexual, transgender, and queer (LGBTQ) culture and history. These events serve to create and reinforce ties between individuals who identify in similar ways and to help educate the public as well as promote understanding and acceptance in local communities of sex, gender, and sexual orientation diversity.

Age

We do not often think of age as a cultural marker, but it definitely operates as one in any society. While none of us will be the same age for the rest of our lives, a person's age tells others something about his or her life experiences as well as some possible attitudes, and beliefs they might hold. Let's look at a few examples of different generational cultures in the United States.[8]

- The GI Generation is sometimes referred to as the Greatest Generation. This is the generation that fought during World War II.

- The Silent Generation is too young to fight in World War II but came into adulthood during the rise of the middle class and relatively prosperous time that followed.

- The Baby Boomers are the children of the GI generation, grew up with Woodstock and the Vietnam War, and tended to focus on careers and set high expectations for their children.

- Generation X graduated from high school in the '80s and '90s and tend to be independent, resilient, and adaptable.

- The Millennials graduated from high school after 2000, and they tended to be very protected by their parents and had high expectations set for them.

The generation that each person lives in shapes his or her experiences, expectations, and attitudes toward others. Not everyone from a specific generation acts and believes the same way, but people always identify with the times in which they grew up. As these different generational groupings illustrate, age as a cultural group is not as simple as "old" and "young" or "elderly" and "middle-aged." Those labels are defined purely by a number and fail to recognize the importance of each person's experiences and how those inform a person's generational culture. In fact, we will all be labeled "old" or "middle-aged" at some point, but the generation to which we belong will not change.

PHYSICAL AND COGNITIVE DIVERSITY

Age, ethnicity, race, sex, gender, and sexuality are not the only ways in which we are differ-ent. In fact, unless you have an identical twin, you are probably the only person who looks exactly like you, acts like you, and thinks like you. Considering there are now more than seven billion people on Earth, there is a great deal of physical diversity among humans. However, our differences go beyond appearances and also include abilities. Some people have especially high levels of specific physical abilities (for instance, Usain Bolt holds world records in both the 100- and 200-meter dashes due to his ability as a sprinter), while others have lower levels of specific physical abilities (for example, Helen Keller could not see or hear). These differences make us no better or worse than someone else, but rather add to the richness of human experience.

At some point, most, if not all, of us will experience some type of physical or cognitive impairment. Some of these are permanent, while others are temporary; some are due to genetics, others the result of an illness or accident. Some people are born blind, for example, while others may develop blindness due to macular degeneration later in life. Some others may lose their sight temporarily, such as after surgery. This variety of causes is important to note because not all people with the same impairment are the same; instead, they may share a similar limitation or level of ability. These differences also do not define the person, but rather are a part of us, just as age, ethnicity, and race are a part of us.

Likewise, there is great diversity in our cognitive abilities and preferences. There is a broad range in IQ, learning styles and preferences, interests, memory, and experience among people. Many cognitive challenges are not immediately apparent when we meet someone, such as dyslexia, Attention Deficit Hyperactivity Disorder (ADHD), Alzheimer's disease, or memory loss. Like physical impairments, some people live with these challenges for their entire lives, while others might experience them for a shorter period of time. Medication, for example, can impact a person's short-term memory, as can a concussion.

Additionally, there is a wide degree of variability in how people cognitively process information and learn about the world around them. Some people understand con-cepts by reading about them, while others prefer to see a picture, and others still may prefer to examine a model. The idea of different modalities for human learning has been explored extensively by psychologist Howard Gardner, and formalized under his theory of multiple intelligences as shown in Figure 2.2 on the following page. **Multiple intelligence theory** proposes that although all individuals can access and learn about the world through each of the nine intelligences he identified, people differ in the strength of their aptitude or preference for those various intelligences. Although controversial, Gardner's theory illustrates how all people develop differently and experience the world in different ways.[9]

MULTIPLE INTELLIGENCE THEORY

although all individuals can access and learn about the world through each of the nine intelligences, people differ in the strength of their aptitude or preference for those various intelligences

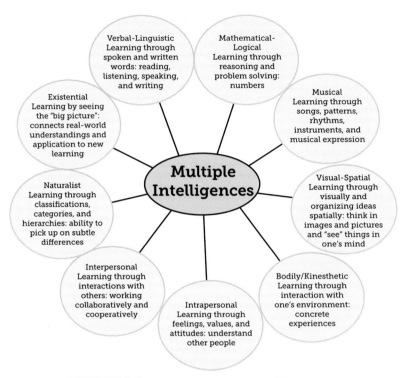

FIGURE 2.2 Multiple Intelligence Theory

Ideological Diversity

We have thus far focused on largely physical differences between people, but diversity of thought is just as important. This type of diversity often emerges in politics, where people hold different ideas on policy and effective governance. These views are the result of a commitment to an **ideology**, or set of ideas, beliefs, and ideals that form one's worldview and provide a basis for action. Ideology is the basis for political beliefs and is heavily influenced by the family and society in which we grow up. As Colin Woodard showed when defining the Eleven Nations in the U.S.[10], there is a great deal of ideological diversity even within the United States, and that ideological diversity expands even more when we consider the entire globe. Not every country has, or even wants, a democracy. Let's focus a bit on ideological diversity in the United States specifically.

We often think of the United States as practicing a two-party system, and for all practical purposes this is true, but to believe the two parties contain individuals that completely agree or share worldviews would be foolish. The Democratic Party, for example, consists of people who place different priorities on various issues, and this sometimes manifests in intraparty squabbles. Some Democrats care about limiting government spending (they are called Blue Dog Democrats), while others are more concerned with civil rights and social issues. They do not agree on every issue. The same can be said for Republicans, who contain some Libertarians who believe in very small government, others who care about advancing social issues from a religious perspective, and others still who want to lower taxes and promote business. The fact of the matter is the two parties merely cloud the vast political and ideological diversity that exists in the United States. To use "liberal vs. conservative" dichotomies to describe people and groups does not come close to acknowledging the variety of thought on public issues that exists in the United States.

Religious Diversity

One final area of difference that both creates its own cultural norms and enhances diversity is religion. There are numerous different faiths practiced in the United States, and despite the prevalence of the Abrahamic faiths (Judaism, Christianity, and Islam) each contributes to the fabric of our culture in its own way. In 2009, the U.S. Census Bureau issued a statistical breakdown of the religious affiliations of people in the United States. In it they found a tremendous amount of diversity, including within Christian faiths, where they identified 30 different denominations. Each of these faiths has different religious perspectives, practices, and beliefs. The report also included a note regarding the growing number of Muslim, Wiccan, Buddhist, and non-religious people in the US.[11] In fact, the more recent 2014 Pew Religious Landscape Study reported a sharp decline in the number of people who identify as Christians in the United States between 2007 and 2014 from 78.4 to 70.6 percent. There was also a 6.7 percent spike in unaffiliated individuals during the same period, also called "nones," who do not identify with any particular faith tradition.

The growth of non-religious, "unaffiliated but spiritual," and "nones" requires some discussion. It is a mistake to assume knowledge of someone's beliefs based on his or her specific affiliation, just as it is unwise to assume someone has no faith or belief in morality/spirituality because they are unaffiliated with a religious group. Many people still hold beliefs privately, and should not be discounted or counted simply based on the religious groups with whom they identify. Understanding and appreciating these differences, while not necessarily agreeing with them, is essential for developing a respectful community.

Religious groups also play important roles in local, state, and national communities. They often do good work on behalf of the community in which their members live and help to promote charitable endeavors across the world. Churches, synagogues, mosques, and temples

Political Parties and Voting

During elections people tend to believe you must vote for either a Democrat or Republican. In fact, some go so far as to tell those who would vote for someone else that they are "throwing away" or "wasting" their vote because that person cannot possibly win. Consider both the accuracy and the ethical nature of such an argument. What are its implications?

all also practice their own culture by providing members opportunities to connect with each other and share stories and experiences. These efforts build their religious culture, but also contribute to the larger community's culture.

COMMUNICATING IN A CULTURALLY DIVERSE WORLD

To be a competent communicator in any situation you need to understand, acknowledge, and appreciate the diversity that cultural differences provide our society. The differences in language, experiences, values, beliefs, and perspectives can enrich our lives in many ways, but require communication grounded in the purpose of understanding others rather than trying to convince them of anything. It requires us to be perceptive of the context in which we find ourselves, as well as the ways that context might be different for someone else. In this final section, we provide three tips to help enhance your ability to use communication to understand and respect differences between people.

Dreamer, *Supergirl*, and Representations of Sexuality

Every year the non-profit advocacy organization called the Gay and Lesbian Alliance Against Defamation (GLAAD) issues their media awards to honor and acknowledge various platforms and networks for their accurate, fair, and inclusive representations of various forms of sexual orientation. One network that has received significant praise in recent years is the CW, as they have numerous main characters on primetime shows who are lesbian, gay, bisexual, and transgender. The network is also famous for their adaptations of superheroes from the DC Comics label. In the fourth season of *Supergirl* the show introduced the character Dreamer, drawn from the pages of DC Comics, but did so by casting transgender actress Nicole Maines. Not only was the character portrayed by a transgender actress, it also was written as a transgender superhero, the first on television. Increased fair and inclusive representations of individuals from the LGBTQ community on television is an important way of communicating acceptance for the vast amount of diversity in society. It is yet another example of how communication through media can help perpetuate positive perceptions of diverse populations.

Make the Message Accessible

As a speaker, it is important to consider the range of abilities in your audience and to adapt your presentation where possible to help the entire audience understand what you are saying. For instance, you might need to add captions to film clips, avoid combining red and green on slides so that those with colorblindness can read your text, and include signposts and transitions that make it easy for your audience to follow along if their attention wavers for a few moments. Using microphones, handouts, and other assistive methods may help people better follow your message, regardless of any limitations or challenges they may have. Another way to make information more accessible is to create stories that use references with which the audience might be familiar so they can understand how the concepts relate to their lives.

Focus on Similarities, Not Differences

Though you might think that acknowledging the different abilities or backgrounds of others may make you seem like you understand them or are trying to help them, they may take issue with this. It calls them out in front of others and specifically heightens the differences they may not want others to know. So, act no differently, and whenever possible if you need to make an accommodation of sorts, do so in a way that everyone shares in it so as not to segregate your audience. If at all possible, it is far better to focus on the ties that bind an audience together than the things that make people feel different.

Avoid "ist" Language

This is the type of language that demeans, ignores, inappropriately calls attention to, or disrespects members of a separate culture or group. This includes ageist, racist, and sexist language that does not respect the humanity of other people. This type of language depicts the other group as a passive object and not an active subject, thus making them seem less than the group of the person making the statement. Remember, the more ways you can emphasize commonalities between people, the more positively received your appeal will be.

Following these three simple tips will enable you to become more effective when developing, sending, and receiving messages in a variety of contexts. They ask that you be a respectful, observant, and thoughtful communicator.

SUMMARY

In this chapter, we discussed the relationship between culture, communication, and diversity. We first explained the theoretical underpinnings of culture and explored the various dimensions all national cultures share to some extent. We then discussed several different categories of difference that both are their own cultural groups and contribute to a diverse society. We also offered some suggestions for how to effectively appreciate differences through communication.

CHAPTER 2 KEY IDEAS

- Each of us belongs to and is influenced by several cultures and co-cultures.

- Hofstede identified six dimensions of national cultures: (1) high vs. low power distance, (2) high vs. low uncertainty avoidance, (3) individualism vs. collectivism, (4) masculinity vs. femininity, (5) long-term vs. short-term orientation, and (6) indulgence vs. restraint.

- Low-context cultures derive meaning primarily from language, while high-context cultures derive a great deal of meaning from nonverbal expressions, the environment, and the situation in which the interaction is taking place.

- Race refers to a set of physical characteristics shared by a group of people, whereas ethnicity refers to a group of people who identify with each other based on a common experience.

- Sex is one's biological classification as male, female, or intersex, whereas gender is the social construction associated with being, for example, masculine, feminine, or androgynous. Sexual orientation refers to the sex and gender to whom a person is romantically attracted.

- Humans have diverse experiences related to their generational differences, physical and cognitive ability, ideology, and religion.

CHAPTER 2 KEY TERMS

Culture	Gender
Co-cultures	Gender identity
Low-context cultures	Gender roles
High-context cultures	Gender expression
Race	Sexual orientation
Ethnicity	Multiple intelligence theory
Sex	Ideology

ACTIVITIES AND DISCUSSION QUESTIONS

1. Watch Yassmin Abdel-Magied's TEDx talk, "What Does My Headscarf Mean to You," available online at https://www.ted.com/talks/yassmin_abdel_magied_what_does_my_headscarf_mean_to_you. Which cultures and co-cultures does she identify as ones to which she belongs? How can we be more aware of the assumptions that we make about others and work to seek to eliminate these unconscious biases?

2. Watch Julien's Bourrelle's TED talk, "How Culture Drives Behavior," available online at https://www.youtube.com/watch?v=l-Yy6poJ2zs. How does he help us understand the impact of culture on the way that we see the world?

3. What are some of the cultures and co-cultures to which you belong? Make a list of as many cultures and co-cultures you can think of that you identify with. (This response can be a simple list instead of a paragraph.) How has your experience as part of these cultures and co-cultures shaped your experience?

4. Sex, gender, and sexual orientation are concepts that are often misunderstood, and there are often new terms introduced to help describe nuances that are not fully conveyed by terminology that is officially recognized by the American Psychological Association and other organizations that help to establish formal terminology. How should you respond when you are not sure what someone uses or if you encounter terminology with which you are not familiar? What is communicated when you do or do not use someone's preferred terminology and pronouns?

5. Watch this video on privilege: https://youtu.be/hD5f8GuNuGQ. How would you define privilege? In what ways have you experienced privilege (or the lack thereof) in your life? How does this help us understand visible and invisible types of diversity? Why is it important to be aware of the diverse backgrounds and experiences of others?

3

PERCEPTION AND THE SELF

Even though we all live in the same world, we do not experience, define, or describe it the same way. A group of people can watch a movie or listen to a song and walk away with different ideas about its worth, quality, and value. How is it we can all experience the same thing, yet walk away with different ideas regarding what happened? How can people have two different ways of describing the same emotions, attitudes, events, and actions? The fact is we each pick and choose the things we pay attention to, and then we give them meaning through communication. So, when you watch a movie with a friend, you may focus on the outstanding performance by the lead actress and walk away with a positive impression of the film, while your friend might form a more negative view because they focused on the poorly constructed special effects. Neither person is objectively wrong; each emphasizes different aspects of the same thing and reaches a different conclusion. This phenomenon is human perception at work.

In this chapter, we explore the concept of perception, specifically how it relates to the way we understand and present ourselves to others. We will first identify the stages of the perception process, and then discuss how we attribute meaning to our surroundings and ourselves. We will then explore the idea of the self-concept, or self-image, and from there explain how we manage our public image. Although it may not seem so at first, perception is a key component to understanding how communication influences our identity and the world around us.

HOW PERCEPTION WORKS

PERCEPTION
the process of giving meaning to the things we notice in the world around us

We don't often think about how we choose what to pay attention to in our surroundings; we just do it. To fully understand the unconscious and conscious choices we make about such things, it is important to define and discuss how perception works. Perception is how we establish meaning for our experience of the world around us and the people in it. The process unfolds in three distinct stages, each of which we will examine in this section. We will also discuss the various things that can influence our perceptual abilities, including cultural variables and personal biases.

Three Stages of the Perception Process

There are three stages of the perception process, and they follow a specific order that should make intuitive sense. In many ways, the perception process is a lot like constructing a speech in that you first pick a topic and collect information about that topic, then create a structure so the information makes sense, and finally you offer your assessment of what the information means. As you will see, this is what we do all day as we pay attention to the things that occur around us.

SELECTION
the act of choosing to attend to, consciously or subconsciously, specific stimuli in the environment

Stage #1: selection. We learn at a very early age that our five senses enable us to know the world around us. We feel, smell, hear, taste, and see things and then make determinations about those experiences by evaluating our sense experience. Either consciously or subconsciously selecting what to experience is the first stage of perception. When you choose certain stimuli in your environment to experience, you are involved in selection. We typically choose things out of the vastness of the world around us for a few different reasons. First, we tend to pay attention to things that are unusual, unexpected, or unique, like a loud sound in a place you normally would not expect to hear it, such as in a library. Second, we pay attention to mundane things that we see repeatedly, like a person who wears the same tie three or four days in a row, or an announcer who uses the same opening line every broadcast. Finally, intense experiences also heighten our attention, such as when we smell something really intense or see something shocking in a picture or video. We select different things because the uniqueness, commonality, and even intensity of things differ for each of us. What is unique for one person might be common for another.

ORGANIZATION
the categorization of stimuli we select to pay attention to

SCHEMAS
mental frameworks for organizing information about experiences

Stage #2: organization. Once we choose an experience to attend to, we classify it by determining which things we already know that are and are not similar to it. This categorization of stimuli is called organization. Just like the selection part of the process, when we organize stimuli we use our unique frames for understanding. When doing this, we employ mental frameworks, called schemas, and use them to connect the new stimuli or ideas to others that are already stored in our brain. As a metaphor, you might think about your brain as being like a computer with numerous folders. Each folder is filled with files about related concepts, memories, experiences, individuals, and thoughts. When you encounter a new concept, experience, or thought, you compare it to the files in each folder and store it in a folder with related concepts. For example, if you were to eat a starfruit for the first time, you would access your mental folder with memories of other types of fruit to compare the taste and texture, and then store a memory of eating the starfruit with the memories of other fruits.

Researcher Peter Andersen suggests that our schemas about other people typically take four forms (Table 3.1): physical constructs that emphasize things like appearance, role constructs that focus on a person's position or job, interactive constructs that hone in on the way people behave, and psychological constructs that stress a person's mood, emotions, and feelings.[1] Schemas apply to certain situations and environments, as well as people, so that we have a general construct for what our rooms look like and how stores, such as grocery stores, are laid out. This allows us to take new information and determine what it is like to better appreciate what the experience or person may share with someone else and thus develop appropriate responses.

Physical	Is the person a man or woman? Is the person tall, short, or medium height? Is the person old, middle-aged, or young?
Role constructs	Is the person my friend? A coworker? A family member? A neighbor? A police officer? A doctor?
Interactive constructs	Is this person acting appropriately? Is this person acting insensitively? Do I think the person is friendly?
Psychological constructs	Is the person in a good mood? Is this person happy? Sad? Does this person seem to care about what we are discussing? Are they bored with our conversation?

TABLE 3.1   Four Schemas about Other People

Stage #3: interpretation. Noticing something and even categorizing the experience does not complete the perception process; you still must provide it with its meaning. Interpretation, the final step of the perception process, occurs when we assign meaning to an experience or person. It is here, where we interpret stimuli, that we likely see the most differences across people, as they assign different significance and even meaning than another person to the same experience.

During this stage, we make an important determination that affects how we will respond to stimuli, which is we decide if a stimulus, such as a person's communicative behavior, is in line with what we expect and/or desire. According to expectancy violations theory,[2] we hold expectancies for what is appropriate and/or typical for a type of person (a grocery store clerk) or a specific relationship partner (our brother).[3] More often than not our expectancies are upheld during conversations, but when our expectancies are violated, a process of evaluation is activated that determines how we will respond to the violation. In this process, we assess the valence of the violation. Sometimes a violation is negative (e.g., someone talks too loudly when you don't expect or want them to, such as in a library) and other times positive (e.g., a romantic interest texts you out of the blue). We also assess the communicator reward value, which is how positive or negative we feel about a person who

EXPECTANCY VIOLATIONS THEORY

theory that we hold expectancies for what is appropriate and/or typical for a type of person

VALENCE OF THE VIOLATION

process of evaluation that determines how we will respond to the violation

COMMUNICATOR REWARD VALUE

how positive or negative we feel about a person who commits a violation commits a violation. This assessment kicks in especially when a violation is not clearly negative or positive or can have multiple interpretations, so then our feelings about the person figure more into our interpretation of their behavior. When a person we perceive as positive violates an expectancy, we are more likely to forgive the violation or even see it as a good thing. When a person who we don't view favorably violates an expectancy, we are more likely to view the behaviors as negative. As we will discuss in the chapters on relationship development and relationship maintenance, we have expectations and desires for certain behaviors and benchmarks in our relationships. When these are violated it is important to consider the valence of the violation and the reward value of the person before reacting to the violation.

Overall, our interpretations are always influenced by many different variables. For instance, our interpretations can be affected by what we know about the other person or the experience. We can read an email from a close friend and know when she is joking, but if the same thing is written by someone we don't know very well, we may not see the joke—and it may not even be intended as a joke at all! Our own personal experiences also color how we interpret different events. Someone who has had to go without food at some point in his or her life may see donating money to a food pantry as the most important act of charity a person could do, while someone else who went homeless for a time may see the most important charity as one providing shelter, such as Habitat for Humanity. Our own experiences affect how we interpret different situations, experiences, or even the actions of others. Finally, our level of agreement or degree to which we identify with a person may influence how we see that person's positions, statements, or behaviors. Ultimately, each of us brings different sets of internal lenses to the same occurrences, and therefore interpret them differently despite seemingly experiencing the same exact thing.

Perception and Attribution

When we observe others engaging in various activities, we often make assumptions about why the other person is engaging in that particular activity. These assumptions about motive, or attributions, generally fall into one of two categories: situational and internal.[4] When we make a **situational**, or external, attribution, we assume that another person is doing something because of factors in his or her environment or the situation. For example, if someone is late to a meeting with us, we could assume they had trouble finding parking or would otherwise be on time for our scheduled conversation. When we make an **interpersonal**, or internal, attribution, however, we assume that the person did something because of their character or disposition. For example, we might assume that the person who was late for our meeting is bad at time management, and that if they cared about our conversation, they would not be late. It's important to note that when we are trying to explain others' behavior, we have a tendency to overestimate the influence of internal characteristics and underestimate the influence of situational factors. This is known as the **Fundamental Attribution Error**.[5] For example, when someone does not call us back, we are more likely to think the person forgot or doesn't care about the relationship, both internal attributions for the behavior,

SITUATIONAL ATTRIBUTION
the assumption that another person is doing something because of factors in the environment or the situation they are in

INTERPERSONAL ATTRIBUTION
the assumption that another person is doing something because of her or his character or disposition

FUNDAMENTAL ATTRIBUTION ERROR
the tendency to overestimate the influence of internal characteristics and underestimate the influence of situational factors when evaluating someone else's behavior

rather than thinking their professor kept the class late or that someone else called them before they could call us.

Influencing the Perception Process

Just as many different forms of noise can interfere with the communication process, there are a multitude of different things that can interrupt, influence, and affect our perceptions of the world around us. It is important to remember that how we perceive things and people is constantly impacted by who we are and what experiences we have had.

Physical influences. Our own bodies affect what we choose to attend to in our environments, as well as how we interpret them. In any given moment we experience a physiological state of being, or temporary condition of the body. All of us know what it feels like to be tired, hungry, or sick, and each condition results in a different response. We might be quick to anger when we are tired, focused only on food when we are hungry, or unable to focus on anything when we are sick. Even for adults, these conditions impede our ability to interact successfully with other people, because they change our perceptions of the actions and statements of others, as well as the environments in which we find ourselves.

We also have more permanent conditions that affect us throughout or lives. These physiological traits rely on our senses and manifest in a variety of different ways. For example, different people are more productive at different times of day. Researcher John Medina breaks down this trait into three types, aptly named after different birds. Larks are people who are most productive in the morning, and their attention and abilities trail off

PHYSIOLOGICAL STATE
temporary condition of the body

PHYSIOLOGICAL TRAITS
permanent enduring physical conditions that impact us throughout our lives

LARKS
ten percent of the population who function best early in the day

Symbols: Perception Becomes Reality

Symbols are all around us, and we each can interpret different things from them. For a case in point, simply look at the critically acclaimed book and television series *Game of Thrones*, created by George R. R. Martin. At the beginning of the second book and second season of the television series, a red comet streaks across the sky. Some characters perceive this as an omen for war and blood and others as a symbol of the family's rise to power. Others still see it simply as a red comet. The same experience was observed by several different characters, who organized it according to their knowledge and beliefs, and then interpreted it to mean something very different. In each case, the interpretations led to choices the characters would make in subsequent chapters and episodes. Our perception becomes our reality, and we all experience different realities in the same world, a fact that George R. R. Martin used to set the stage for a part of his award-winning stories.

OWLS
twenty percent of
the population who
function best at later
times of the day

HUMMINGBIRDS
seventy percent
of the population
who function well
throughout the day

in the afternoon and evening. Larks constitute 10 percent of the population. Owls are 20 percent of the population, and they fittingly operate best at later times in the day and often are found working well past midnight. The remaining 70 percent of us are hummingbirds, who are ready for action at any time—though some of us will be a little more larkish or owlish than others.[6] The point here is that this trait is both physical, as it has to do with your body's rhythms, and enduring, meaning it is a characteristic that you exhibit throughout your life. You can easily see how, depending on which category you are in, your perception of events and people can be influenced by time of day.

Cultural influences. Culture plays a significant role in how we perceive things, more so than what we recognize. In the previous chapter, we discussed different dimensions of culture, and to illustrate how those dimensions influence perception, let's look at a few examples. Recall that collectivist cultures place more of an emphasis on the family or community than individual achievement. Certain Asian cultures tend to be more collectivistic than Western cultures, so it may come as no surprise that it is sometimes much more acceptable to copy someone else's work in those cultures than it is in Western societies.[7] This is because copying is perceived as sharing to help the larger community and not as stealing from another individual.

As an example of gender differences, women in the United States have been socialized to speak more to express emotions and seek emotional support, whereas men have been brought up to talk for more functional problem-solving purposes. So, when a wife comes home from work and starts to share some of the difficulties she had that day with her colleagues, her husband might immediately launch into a list of suggestions for how she can do something different to fix those problems. The wife gets upset and an argument ensues. Why? Because the wife just wanted to express her feelings without receiving advice in return, and the husband thought he was helping with her workplace relationships. The potential communicative differences between the genders are evident here.

The power distance dimension of culture also influences perception. Recall that high power distance cultures exist where the population is far removed from authority, and low power distance cultures share power among individuals. With that in mind, think about someone who works for a company with very clear lines of authority, where individual creativity is not necessary or encouraged. Now think of this person leaving that job after years of experiencing that culture and going to work for Google, where there is almost the complete opposite corporate structure. At Google, people are encouraged to explore ideas, and the company's headquarters looks like a combination of a playground and a corporate office building. This person may have certain challenges adjusting to the different corporate culture.

Occupational influences. What we do for a living also influences what we see and how we see it. Professions come with particular sets of training that allow people to be attuned to specific things in certain situations. Physicians see more than most people about how the body functions, and even within that profession, there are subspecialties where doctors are more adept at seeing things in particular areas of the body. Attorneys notice nuances in the law, farmers pay attention to different nutrients in soil, and mechanics are attuned to various cars' sounds and what they might mean. Content knowledge and specific training allow people to pay attention to certain things others may not notice.

Additionally, individuals might have a different view of how things fit together, depending on their level of responsibility within an organization. For example, in higher education, individual instructors know very well what is going on in their classrooms and what resources they need. The chairs of departments know the needs of the entire unit as a whole, and are best able to make decisions about where to allocate resources within the department. The same is the case for deans when it comes to overseeing resource requests and needs for all the different departments in a college. The higher up the administrative ladder, the broader the view and understanding of how the needs of different departments can and need to be addressed. Higher-level administrators are aware of more issues across the university, so they notice more things that individual faculty and staff may not see.

Psychological influences and biases. There are a variety of other psychological influences that play a role in our perceptions. The first, and perhaps most familiar, of these is stereotyping. Stereotyping occurs when we create generalizations about groups of people and apply them to individuals that we believe are members of that group. Stereotyping itself is not a bad thing; in fact, it allows us to function when we initially meet someone. The problem occurs when we hold tight to these rigid expectations and act as if they are true, and not just conceptual schemas that need to adapt once we understand individuals and how they might differ from their group. We also need to understand stereotypes as malleable, knowing we must adjust our assumptions when we encounter someone who is a part of the group for which we have a stereotype but who does not conform to all parts of the stereotype. Stereotypes can lead us to perceive what we expect but also to notice things we don't necessarily expect.

STEREOTYPING
generalizations about groups of people that are applied to individuals we believe are members of that group

Downsizing in the University Setting

ENGAGING
ETHICS

In Spring 2018, the University of Wisconsin Stevens Point became the latest university to announce the elimination of academic departments and layoffs due to budget challenges. However, there has been some controversy over how the university selected which departments would be impacted, with some faculty claiming they were never consulted. What are the ethical expectations for decisions like this by management? Does it differ between industries? What does it say about the culture of an organization?

PRIMACY EFFECT

people are prone to emphasizing the first impression of something over any subsequent impressions when forming their perception of an event or person

RECENCY EFFECT

people are prone to using their most recent experience with someone as their overriding impression of the person

POSITIVITY BIAS

the tendency to highlight and overemphasize positive information and characteristics when creating an impression

NEGATIVITY BIAS

the tendency to focus our efforts on picking out negative information or qualities in a person or situation

EGOCENTRIC

people who are completely focused on themselves and ignorant of the needs of others

Primacy and recency effects. Two other factors that influence perception relate to the order in which we experience things. One of the most critical moments is the first, whether it is in a speech, an interview, a date, or a sales meeting. The principle known as the primacy effect explains that people are prone to emphasizing the first impression of something over any subsequent impressions when forming their perception of an event or person. Psychologist Solomon Asch, one of the early pioneers in exploring the primacy effect in interpersonal interactions, found that when people are evaluated favorably at first, they are more likely to be seen in a good light going forward, with the impact of later negative information about that person diminishing.[8] The same can be said for things like actors and authors, whose initial work we tend to emphasize more than their later ones, even if the follow-ups are disappointing. On the other hand, if someone sets a negative first impression, positive information that is shared later is likely to be weighed less heavily or discounted altogether.

In addition to what occurs first, the recency effect also helps explain our perceptual abilities. It refers to when we allow our most recent impressions to hold more sway than earlier ones. This is important when we consider how we leave interactions. Consider job interviews, where your first impression is no doubt very important, but so is how you end the interview. A firm handshake, leaving a business card or resume, and following up with a quick thank-you note are all ways to leave a lasting recent impression on your prospective employer. Just getting up and leaving when the questions are concluded is not likely to leave a good recent impression.

Positivity and negativity biases. Timing of impressions is one thing, but so is the type of information we choose to focus on when creating impressions of people and events. In some cases, such as during the initial stages of a romantic relationship, people tend to highlight and overemphasize positive information and characteristics when creating an impression. This is called positivity bias. In other cases, we can be overly critical and focus our efforts on picking out negative information or qualities in a person or situation, and this is called negativity bias. People who are unhappy or otherwise disinterested in a situation are more likely to use the negativity bias when evaluating information about experiences than people who are either happy or even ambivalent.

Egocentrism. The final influence on perception we will cover is our own capacity to focus on how things affect ourselves. For most of us, we are our favorite topic to talk about, but we are not everyone else's favorite topic. This creates a need for us to manage our own desire to talk about ourselves with the desires of other people to tell stories of their own. People who are not able to do this are considered egocentric, or completely focused on themselves and ignorant of the needs of others. This focus on the self is something everyone experiences as a child, but most grow out of by adolescence and young adulthood. When we allow our own egocentrism to impact our perceptions, two things happen. First, we tend to believe the people around us do, see, and experience things in the same manner we do. Second, we tend to see things happening as directly related to ourselves, thus we see people acting in particular ways toward us because we think they either really like us, or perhaps they are out to get us.

PERCEPTION AND THE SELF

It should come as no surprise that perception affects how we define ourselves, and also influences how we define our environment and the people in it. Communicating about what we perceive begins with how we see ourselves. In this section of the chapter, we turn our attention to the idea of the self-concept, or the set of perceptions you have about yourself that define who you are, also known as your identity. We will first examine the four characteristics shared by all self-concepts before moving to a discussion of how we manage our self-concepts. In doing so, we will discuss the notion of "faces" and the process of negotiating our understanding of our various faces in different situations.

Defining the Self-Concept

Our **self-concept** is the image that we have about who we believe we are. Our identities are quite complex. We may think we are simple people, and that we might be an "open book" to others, but our self-concept involves more than we realize. We cannot keep track of or remember everything that has happened to us, but those experiences all influence the way we see ourselves. So, in short, despite being unable to remember everything, it all leaves its mark on how we understand ourselves. Additionally, even though we all have different self-concepts, our identities all share four characteristics.

SELF-CONCEPT

the image we have of who we believe we are

Self-concepts are shaped by others. How each of us perceives our self is due in large part to how others respond to us and what others say about us. George Herbert Mead explains that we experience the "self" indirectly from the standpoint of others, so we could think of other people as being the mirror that shows us who we are.[9] Part of this influence is through direct communication; when others repeatedly tell us that we are smart, funny, athletic, kind, or outgoing, we begin to believe those things about ourselves and behave in ways that reflect those beliefs. Part of this influence is through indirect communication or reactions that we see from others; your self-concept will be impacted in different ways if others listen to you with respect when you speak, versus whether others ignore you or look at you with disdain. We are also influenced by what we *think* other people are thinking about us. We imagine how we appear to others and consider how others might be evaluating or judging us based on that appearance, and that imagined perception influences our self-concept. As is shown on the next page in Figure 3.1, John Kinch summarized this process by explaining that our self-concept influences our behavior, and others respond to our behavior.[10] How we perceive the responses of others then influences our self-concept, which in turn influences our behavior, making this an ongoing cycle.

Self-concepts are multifaceted. People often think they are the same person no matter what situation they are in, but that is just not true. In fact, we define ourselves differently depending on the situation and the people we are with. Sometimes we focus on our religion, at other times our gender, still other times our age or profession, or even our own estimation of our values and behaviors. We do not have one self, but rather we are the sum of many different smaller selves, each representing a part of our overall self-concept. To assume that one part is the sum total of who you are is to essentialize yourself by one demographic or characteristic and to deny the other parts that make you, you.

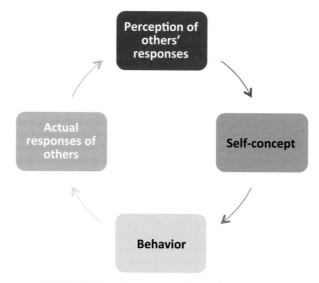

FIGURE 3.1   Process of Self-Concept

The Evolving Self-Concept: Bob Ross

© Getty Images.

The idea that a person's self-concept is both enduring and changeable can best be seen through any of the hundreds of success stories in America.[11] For instance, take a look at surprise Internet sensation Bob Ross. Ross, who passed away in 1995 is arguably more famous now as a YouTube celebrity, than he was when he hosted *The Joy of Painting* on PBS from 1983-1994.[12] Interestingly, Ross was not always a painter, and in fact his love of the craft and his calm demeanor are a direct result of his 20-year career in the Air Force. Ross, a high school dropout, enlisted in the military at age 18 and rose to the rank of master sergeant. During his time in the military he saw snow and mountains for the first time, having grown up in Florida; scenes that he would love to paint later in his life. The military role also required him to be "tough" and "mean" as he put it, but when he finally finished his military service he vowed never to yell or raise his voice again—resulting in the dulcet tone he is now famous for from his show. Ross's self-concept evolved over the years as he incorporated both new experiences and reflected on his own behaviors and attitudes. Truly, he represents how one's self-concept can and does evolve over time.

Perhaps the best way to understand the multifaceted nature of our self-concept is to differentiate between the parts we know with the parts others know about us. Psychologists Joseph Luft and Harrington Ingham proposed a simple image that represents the various dimensions of the self. Creatively called the **Johari Window**, after grafting their two names together, the model—Figure 3.2—breaks down what we and others know about ourselves into four distinct areas.[13] The first of these is the open area, which contains those things that both we and others know about ourselves. The second area, the hidden area, contains things you know about yourself but do not share with others. The blind area includes the reverse of the hidden area; it includes things we do not know about ourselves that others know about us. The final quadrant, the unknown area, involves parts of ourselves that neither we nor others know about, such as how we might respond to certain situations in the future. In the Johari Window, not all quadrants are of equal emphasis or importance for each person, and the importance of each area can increase or decrease in different circumstances, but they all influence how we see ourselves and how others see us, as well.

JOHARI WINDOW
a four-quadrant model describing the different aspects of our self-concept based on what we and others know about ourselves

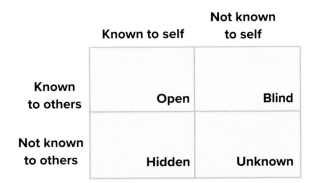

FIGURE 3.2 Johari Window

Self-concepts are somewhat subjective. What we know about ourselves can be broken down into two types of information: subjective and objective. Objective facts include things like height, weight, age, hair color, or even shoe size. When we interpret a fact such as a person weighing 115 lbs, we do so by examining the objective fact through the lens of the person's age, sex, or even occupation. For example, we come to different conclusions about a teenage boy who weighs 115 lbs (underweight) than we would about a twenty-something young woman (more appropriate weight). Most of our self-concept is driven by subjective interpretations and opinions. What this means is that people cannot be counted on to evaluate themselves objectively or accurately.

Sometimes, people overestimate their positive attributes. For example, many recent graduates of college rate themselves as better than average or excellent communicators, and yet employers have repeatedly told colleges that graduates need to improve their communication skills. Clearly there is a disconnect between these two groups; perhaps the individuals responding to the survey have a much higher estimation of their communication skills than their employers and colleagues.[14] Sometimes, the opposite is true, and people negatively evaluate their own abilities and attributes. This is particularly prevalent with people who suffer low self-esteem and depression. In either case, there is a subjective assessment of a person's self-concept that is more powerful than any objective element of her or his identity when it comes to defining how the person sees himself or herself.

Self-concepts endure and change. We develop our self-concepts over a long period of time as we accumulate experiences with our surroundings and the people we encounter. It is a slow process, and one that does not change on a whim, which makes a self-concept relatively enduring. These characteristics are further enhanced by the fact that as we get older, we tend to associate with people who confirm our understanding of ourselves.[15] This simply serves to reinforce our constructed self-concept, but just because it is built and reinforced does not mean it cannot change.

Like a house, the foundation may remain but we can change the structure from time to time. As our brains develop, it can impact our self-concept, and as John Medina notes in his book *Brain Rules*, the two most active developmental times for our brains are when we are around two years old and in our teenage years. Once we reach adulthood, major changes to our self-concepts are much less common.[16] Significant life events such as marriage, a death of a loved one, a serious illness, or moving to a new area can also change our self-concepts. Strong self-concepts adjust and adapt to the changing circumstances brought about by life. Even though there are aspects foundational to our self-concepts, our definitions of who we are can change over time and with new experiences.

UNDERSTANDING OUR MANY FACES

Now that the complicated nature of our self-concept is becoming increasingly clear, we might start wondering how different situations interact with aspects of our identity. After all, our friends know us in ways our parents do not, and our instructors know us in ways both of those groups do not. It is a good question, so we will now investigate the mental work we do to manage the perception of ourselves in different contexts.

Facework

FACEWORK

the behaviors we exhibit to create and maintain the positive perception of ourselves

Regardless of the situation, we always want people to have a positive impression of us. No one wants to portray himself or herself in a negative light. The behaviors we exhibit to create and maintain the positive perception of ourselves is called facework.[17] We conduct facework within three different contexts, and we are also always looking out for and responding to things that might damage our own self-concept.

One of the primary contexts in which we work to create a positive image of ourselves is in social situations. These include efforts to create friendships, romantic relationships, and other social interactions with people. This desire to have others like and respect us is called our fellowship face.[18] We want others to perceive us as friendly, so we do our best to come across that way with others when we meet them. This type of behavior plays a very important role when you take the primacy effect into account.

The second face we seek to create concerns respect more than friendliness and likeability. The competence face refers to efforts to promote our expertise to others, and it manifests in professional settings or places where you want people to believe you are knowledgeable on a topic. When we want people—whether they are friends, family, or colleagues—to respect us for what we do and know, we are concerned with our competence face. When people do not get respect from others, it hurts their competence face and can negatively impact their own self-esteem.

The third, and final, face we seek to maintain with others is related to our desire to be seen as independent. We all want to be seen as capable of doing things on our own, something that comes into play when students transition from high school to college. This, and other times when we want to be seen as responsible and capable in our own right, represents the expression of our autonomy face, which refers to when we seek to avoid others making decisions and doing things for us by being seen as capable. In individualistic cultures, the autonomy face is a much larger part of a person's self-concept and thus must be managed more carefully in different situations.

Sometimes we encounter things that threaten to damage the image we work to present to others, and these are referred to as face threats. For instance, college students sometimes grapple with the idea that they are autonomous adults living on their own during the school year, but they are still dependent upon their parents for some forms of aid. That dependence is a threat to the autonomy face element of their self-concept. We may also experience threats to our fellowship face when a first date does not go well and someone does not want to see us again romantically. This type of face threat can be very disheartening, but it illustrates that how we manage threats to our face is just as important as the face itself, because we could hole up and never go out again, or reevaluate the situation in a way that does not cause us stress or anxiety.

FELLOWSHIP FACE
an effort to fulfill the need to have others like and respect us

COMPETENCE FACE
the effort to promote our expertise on subjects to others so they respect us

AUTONOMY FACE
the perception that we can do things on our own and our desire to avoid others making decisions for us

FACE THREATS
things that threaten to damage the image we work to present to others

When our social poise is attacked or teased, we feel the need to restore or save face. When we are being complimented or given credit for a job well done in front of others (i.e., in an individualistic culture), we feel our social self-worth is enhanced and stroked.[19]

—S. Ting-Toomey & A. Kurogi

Managing Our Many Faces

IMAGE MANAGEMENT

the process of coordinating the presentation of our self-concept with various groups in different situations

Despite the fact that we define ourselves differently in different situations to different people, we also try to maintain consistency with the images each group has of us. Image management is the process of coordinating the presentation of our self-concept with various groups in different situations. Managing multiple images across various groups is collaborative and complex, but essential for successful relationships in any context. Image management is collaborative in that our self-concept is constantly influenced by the interaction between ourselves and others. We seek to present ourselves in a specific manner, and when people accept that image, we continue to behave in ways that are consistent with the image they reinforce. If, however, our image does not seem to be accepted by others, we adjust it until it is accepted, or we simply move on from the potential relationship with that individual.

Image management is also complex because of the multiple audiences we encounter and the need to monitor all the different parts of ourselves we show to others, both intentionally and inadvertently. One skill we can develop to make this management easier is self-monitoring, which, as we learned as we addressed the basics of communication, is the ability to be aware of our own behaviors and statements and how they affect other people. Low self-monitors will speak without thinking about how another person might respond, while high self-monitors tend to consider how their statements might be received. Low self-monitors can often create the image of a selfish person, because they say and do things without attention to their surroundings. Sometimes we say that these people have no "internal filter." It is important to work on monitoring your statements and actions so you can cultivate the best possible perception of you by others.

Additionally, it is important for us to help others manage their image, or face, while also allowing others to help us manage our own face. Each of us occasionally does something embarrassing, makes mistakes, and engages in conflict with others at various times in our lives. In these types of situations, there are many things we can do to help one another prevent losing face before the situation, support the face of others during the interaction, or to repair face afterward. For example, we can pre-apologize, consult with others during the interaction, and even justify our statements and actions after the fact. All of these can help mitigate any damage to face that might occur.

SUMMARY

In this chapter, we defined perception and how it impacts the way we see ourselves as well as how others see us. We first detailed the three stages of the perception process before explaining the various situational influences and personal biases that can impact how we perceive the world around us. We then spent time exploring the notion of the self-concept and how it manifests in various ways through our desire to be seen in specific ways by other people. Finally, we explored how we can manage our self-concepts and images in our dealings with others through the process of self-monitoring.

CHAPTER 3 KEY IDEAS

- The three stages of the perception process are selection, organization, and interpretation.

- We have a tendency to overestimate situational factors when making attributions about our own behaviors, and overestimate the role of interpersonal factors when making attributions about others' behaviors, which is known as the Fundamental Attribution Error.

- Perception is influenced by physiological states and traits, culture, occupation, and psychological biases.

- Our self-concept is the image we have about who we believe we are. Our self-concept is shaped through our interactions with others, is multifaceted, is subjective, and will both endure and change over time.

- The Johari Window breaks what we and others know about ourselves into four distinct areas: open, blind, hidden, and unknown.

- We engage in facework to create and maintain a positive perception of ourselves. There are three primary types of faces that we seek to maintain: fellowship face, competence face, and autonomy face.

CHAPTER 3 KEY TERMS

Perception	Stereotyping
Selection	Primacy effect
Organization	Recency effect
Schemas	Positivity bias
Expectancy violations theory	Negativity bias
Valence of the violation	Egocentric
Communicator reward value	Self-concept
Situational attribution	Johari Window
Interpersonal attribution	Facework
Fundamental attribution error	Fellowship face
Physiological state	Competence face
Physiological traits	Autonomy face
Larks	Face threats
Owls	Image management
Hummingbirds	

ACTIVITIES AND DISCUSSION QUESTIONS

1. Watch Trevor Maber's TED-Ed animation, "Rethinking Thinking," available online at https://ed.ted.com/lessons/rethinking-thinking-trevor-maber. How does this help us understand the perception process? What type of situational and interpersonal attributions were made in this scenario? Was a Fundamental Attribution Error made?

2. Describe a time that you made some attributions, or assumptions, about the reasons that another person did something in which you later found out that you were wrong. What type of attributions did you make, and what were those assumptions? What were some of the other factors that you later discovered were influencing the situation? Why do you think you made a Fundamental Attribution Error in this situation?

3. Meet with a friend or find a partner in class. Each person should draw two Johari Windows (one for you, one for your partner) and fill in the four quadrants on each. After you have filled in as many characteristics as possible for both windows, compare windows with your partner and see what differences each of you noticed in each other. Which characteristics that each of you identified were most surprising to each of you?

4. Are you a low or high self-monitor? Are you a good judge of your own behavior? Ask several key people in your life to "get real" with you. Do they notice you doing things that are annoying, distracting, disrespectful, kind, or thoughtful of which you are unaware? Do they think you are too conscious of your behavior? What did you learn about yourself, and how might you become more aware of your communication behaviors coming forward?

5. Describe a time that you had to engage in image management. What type of face did you seek to create in this situation? Was it effective?

DIALOGIC
COMMUNICATION

We need only scan the cable news networks and assorted newspaper columns to notice that American society is frequently shaped as aggressive, polarized, and uncivil. Popular news and entertainment shows model communication as combative, not as a means to understand each other or critically examine statements and evidence. The same can be said for expressions on Facebook, Twitter, and other social media tools, where it is not uncommon to find people making disparaging, hateful, and even violent statements about others. Mass media tools can enhance our communication with each other, but sometimes they seem to encourage us to treat others poorly.

As we have already discussed, to be a competent communicator means you are able to understand and respect other people in a variety of contexts. In this chapter, we discuss how to communicate effectively and respectfully in any situation. In subsequent chapters, we will explain how this method of interaction works in specific contexts. The method is called dialogue, which, simply put, is communicating in a way that both respects others and encourages them to want to listen, while also listening in a way that encourages others to want to speak.[1] Scholar John Poulakos expounds upon this definition by identifying three components necessary for dialogue to take place: the self, the other, and the in between. For Poulakos, the focus is on the "actual happenings between" people where they "stand

DIALOGUE
a style of communication that respectfully encourages others to want to listen, while also listening in a way that encourages others to want to speak

before each other prepared to meet the uniqueness of their situation and follow it wherever it may lead."[2] Dialogue thus requires an openness to change and appreciation for the other person's perspective.

In this chapter, we will first explore the concept and discuss the various components of good dialogic communication identified by communication scholars. In the second part of the chapter, we will examine various attitudes of dialogue to illustrate not just what dialogue is, but also what it looks like. Finally, we will offer some suggestions for developing dialogic communication in any context.

DEFINING DIALOGUE

Like many things in this book, dialogue may sound simple on the surface, but it is more complicated than meets the eye—and challenging to put into practice! Perhaps you associate the term dialogue with conversations in movies or plays, or maybe you regard any exchange between people as a dialogue. As we will illustrate, dialogue is much more nuanced. In this section, we will investigate the four key elements of dialogue, paying particular attention to the notion of civility. This will then allow us to see how each of these components serves as the foundation for the dialogue characteristics we will discuss later in the chapter.

Civility

CIVILITY

the ability to treat others with respect so that we can have a lasting, peaceful, and positive interaction

The first, and perhaps most essential, component of dialogue is civility. We always want people to treat us with respect, and so it stands to reason we should do the same in our dealings with others. Civility is the ability to treat others with respect, so we can have a lasting, peaceful, and positive interaction. Many people associate being civil with being passive, fake, or weak, but as we will see, that is not the case.[3] There are three fundamental parts of civil behavior, and as we explore each, keep in mind that just because people may be familiar with some of these concepts does not mean they always know how to consistently put them into practice.

POLITENESS

the act of showing consideration for others in accordance with societal expectations

Politeness. Parents always remind their children to be polite to others, but how is it that when people become adults they sometimes model aggressive and hostile behavior toward others? Politeness is a simple concept, simply meaning to show consideration for others in accordance with societal expectations. The difficulty is not with showing consideration for others, but rather with navigating the societal expectations in given contexts. We have different social norms and rules for different places, people, events, and cultures. More succinctly, politeness is the use of tact when speaking to others.

Politeness often gets confused with "being nice," or as a tactic for manipulating others. Some people view politeness in others as an attempt to hide something, making them skeptical of the motives of others. We propose a definition of politeness in contrast to rudeness, rather than as a veil for some ulterior motive that may not be there. Rudeness consists of behaviors that make others uncomfortable, violate social decency, and are inappropriate or demeaning, while politeness consists of none of those things. Civil communicators exercise a degree of self-monitoring, assessing the contexts in which they find themselves to determine the best way to be considerate toward other people and thus avoid being seen as rude. Politeness often manifests itself through the exhibition of good manners. Good manners refer to those polite behaviors that encourage positive relationships with others. Good manners are sometimes legislated, like putting electronics in "airplane mode" while in flight, but most are social expectations people have of others. Here are a few good manners that apply to most communication settings.

GOOD MANNERS
those polite behaviors that encourage positive relationships with others

- Be on time for meetings and appointments.

- Patiently wait in line.

- Don't talk with your mouth full.

- Say "please" and "thank you."

- Respect other people's property.

- Don't look at, or answer, your mobile phone while in the middle of a conversation.

As you can probably imagine, engaging in each of these behaviors can help create a positive perception of a person by others. Just think about what we tend to think of people who do the opposite.

Respect for others. Respect is acknowledging the inherent dignity of the other person as a human being, regardless of what we may think about him or her. Respect does not mean subservience or deference, but rather an effort to understand another person and an acknowledgement of his or her ideas and presence. Scholar Richard Johannesen refers to this as a spirit of mutual equality, and describes it this way: "although society may rank participants of dialogue as of unequal status or accomplishment, the participants themselves view each other as persons, not as objects to be manipulated or exploited. The exercise of power and superiority is to be avoided. Participants do not impose their opinion, cause or will."[4] In other words, everyone has an equal stake in the discussion, and no one person is privileged over another. Communication with a spirit of mutual equality entails not forcing one's perspective on someone else but instead remaining open to receiving the perspective of another as equally significant as one's own position or ideas. No one likes to be ignored or to go unnoticed, and so providing that minimum level of recognition is a good baseline for treating people with respect. When we do this to others, we encourage them to reciprocate, and this creates a positive relationship in which we can have honest and frank discussions, even when we disagree.

RESPECT
the practice of acknowledging the inherent dignity of other people as human beings

ASSERTIVENESS
the practice of clearly, calmly, and confidently making positions and ideas known to others

Respect for self. Civility is not only about how we treat others, but it is also about how we treat ourselves. We must respect our own opinions, ideas, and humanity in interactions just as much as we need to do that for other people. To do this is an important, if generally unacknowledged, component of civility whereby we are assertive. To be **assertive** means to clearly, calmly, and confidently make our positions and ideas known to others. It is important that we feel comfortable expressing our opinions and hearing those of other people. It is disrespectful to ourselves and devalues what we have to say if we sit quietly and never share our own ideas, thus eliminating a chance for other people to understand our perspective and perception of the situation.[5]

Assertiveness is not to be confused with aggressiveness. Aggressiveness implies a desire to win, compete, or otherwise move the other side to silence. Aggressiveness is rude and creates a very uncomfortable situation for everyone and can come across in the words we use, the volume and tone of voice we use, and the facial expressions and hand gestures we make. When we are assertive, we are comfortable knowing we have made our contribution, regardless of whether the idea is adopted by others. On the contrary, when we are aggressive, we seek to win and dominate the conversation. Knowing how to be assertive, but not aggressive, is a key component of being civil.

Seeds of Peace: The Maine Experience[6]

In the early 1990s, journalist John Wallach began a program called Seeds of Peace designed to bring young people from geographic locations rife with conflict together, so that individuals on both sides of the conflict interact with their perceived "enemies." The youths range in age from 13 to 18, and spend parts of their summer with each other at a camp in Maine where they live and interact together. The goal is that through meeting and talking with each other for an extended period of time that these "seeds" of peaceful interaction will return home and build a founda- tion for peace as they grow older and become more active in their communities. To ensure that the impact is not restricted to the summer, the participants in this very selective camp receive continual support after they leave in the form of dialogue sessions, cross-cultural visits, and development workshops. As of 2014, there have been participants in the Seeds of Peace program from the Middle East, Afghanistan, South Asia, and India. It is an astounding example of how dialogue can help improve relations between parties who are seemingly in perpetual conflict.

Presentness

Being civil does not in and of itself create dialogue; there are other important components to this form of communication we must note. One of the biggest challenges to engaging in dialogue with another person or group of people is giving them your undivided attention. When we give our full attention to someone and avoid mental distractions, or noise, we are then practicing presentness. Presentness involves a commitment to the moment, and more specifically, the other person in the moment with us. As communication scholar Ron Arnett puts it, "relationship centered communication that is sensitive to what happens to both self and other approaches dialogic communication."[7] This is harder than it sounds; just think about a time where you received particularly good or bad news and then had to pay attention in class. You were likely not able to give undivided attention to the class because of the distraction the news became.

It is important to note that the human attention span is finite, which means we only can maintain attention for a certain period of time because doing so requires a great deal of mental effort. Our ability to focus is a skill we can build with practice.[8] Many people erroneously believe they can multitask and pay attention to someone while doing something else. For any cognitive function that requires you to focus, such as driving, reading, or paying attention to a speaker, it is actually physically impossible to multitask. As molecular biologist John Medina notes, "We are biologically incapable of processing attention-rich inputs simultaneously."[9] So, as you can probably see, it is impossible to do something else that requires cognitive effort while participating in a dialogue, because you simply would not be paying attention to what the other person is saying. It also should be noted that doing something else while someone is talking to you is considered rude in almost any social setting.

Unconditional Positive Regard

So far we have explored how dialogue involves civility and presentness, but those are only parts of the equation. The third element of dialogue is what psychologist Carl Rogers referred to as unconditional positive regard, or accepting others with a positive attitude. Although he applied it specifically to therapists, it works in any interactions we might have with people. Keeping an open mind and seeing the potential good in others creates an environment where people feel comfortable expressing ideas and speaking about potentially controversial topics. Unconditional positive regard does not mean you agree with the other person, only that you believe the other person wants the best for you and you want the best for her or him.

Operating with unconditional positive regard is not easy, and it involves taking some risks, but the rewards outweigh potential costs. Of course, if a person repeatedly shows you they are deceitful or cannot be trusted, then your positive regard will diminish. Without the presence of deceit, however, you should believe in the best of others. Most interactions are not competitive, and so we should not operate within them as if the other person is "playing us." The idea of unconditional positive regard illustrates the importance of character in any communication situation.

PRESENTNESS

a commitment to the moment and the other person in the moment with us; giving your undivided attention

UNCONDITIONAL POSITIVE REGARD

a component of dialogue originated by Carl Rogers; accepting others with a positive attitude

Mutual Equality

In any social, familial, or professional setting there is a power distribution. Parents have power over children, supervisors have power over employees, and so on. This can, and often does, influence the communication patterns and styles people use when interacting with each other, and in many cases, the simple presence of positional authority can diminish the chance of a true dialogue between people. In a dialogue, the expressions and ideas of every party are valued at the same level; no one person is valued less or seen as unable to provide a positive contribution. The premise that each person can make an equal contribution to the interaction is the principle of mutual equality, and it is the fourth and final component of a good dialogue.

A dialogue depends on the free exchange of ideas between parties, even when those ideas might be at odds. As Ron Arnett puts it, dialogue conducted with a spirit of mutual equality seeks the "unity of contraries," or a way to bridge positions that seem at odds. These tensions occur when authority is present, but also when interests seem mutually exclusive, such as a concern for self versus the community or power and responsibility. For mutual equality to happen in a system or environment where one has authority or power over another requires setting aside the power dimensions and communicating in a way that values the contributions made by everyone. Here are some actions that create mutual equality.

- Collaborating on a solution
- Sharing your goals with all involved
- Paraphrasing what others say to ensure understanding

Now look at these behaviors that stress the power dimensions between participants and see how they might discourage dialogue.

- Responding to every statement others make
- Keeping information from other participants
- Beginning the discussion with your desired decision

Dialogue is public engagement with difference and offers no assurances for correctness or resolution. The absence of dialogue propelled by tenacious hope to meet ideas contrary to one's own assures societal demise.[10]

—Ronald Arnett, Duquesne University

Engaging in communication with others in a civil manner and setting aside any existing power dimensions creates a dialogic environment where people are comfortable expressing ideas, even when they conflict. Creating this type of environment, though, is much harder than explaining what it looks like. Now that we have defined what dialogue is, let's briefly take a moment and illustrate what dialogue is not.

WHAT IS NOT DIALOGUE

People commonly misconstrue two other forms of communication as dialogue, when, in fact, they are not. True dialogic communication contains a deep respect and recognition for the other parties in the interaction, and it is also not about winning anything but rather about understanding peoples' unique positions and perspectives. This is not to say these other forms of communication do not have their place; they do. In most interactions with others, dialogue works far better.

Just because we are talking with someone else does not mean we are in a dialogue with him or her. In fact, sometimes we are actually conducting a monologue. A monologue is a style of communication where only one voice is respected. This does not mean it is the only voice that is heard, but it does mean that only one voice matters in the discussion. In certain

MONOLOGUE
a style of communication where only one voice is respected

Science vs. Faith: Bill Nye vs. Ken Ham

One of the most popular PBS television programs to run in the 1990s was *Bill Nye the Science Guy*, hosted by scientist and former Boeing mechanical engineer Bill Nye. Since his show finished airing, Nye has made numerous appearances promoting science education to people across the United States. Ken Ham is CEO of Answers in Genesis, and founder of the Creation Museum in Petersburg, Kentucky. Ham established the Creation Museum to make the case to the public that the Christian Bible's book of Genesis explains creation literally. In February 2014, the two men, one a proponent of evolution, and the other an adamant evangelical creationist, met to debate their positions. The central goal for both parties was to prove the other wrong. They did not attempt to understand each other or explore the positions the other articulated, but rather sought to demonstrate how the opponent's evidence was erroneous. This is an example of a debate, not a dialogue. It is also one of the more common approaches to communicating ideas in the public forum, whether in a formal setting like this, or in a two-minute clip on a cable news show. The idea is to push one's position at the expense of the other.

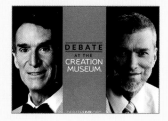

contexts, monologues work well, such as in the military where commanding officers need their troops to follow a directive. Without such a structure, the military loses discipline and is far less effective. Monologues are also sometimes helpful in crises when time is of the essence, such as when emergency personnel are coordinating search and rescue efforts after a tornado or other natural disaster. Monologues, though, are not helpful in situations where group participation and commitment are necessary for success.

DEBATE

a competitive form of communication where parties critically listen to each other with the goal of defeating the opponent's argument, not understanding the other's perspective or finding common ground

In addition to monologues, some people also confuse dialogue with a more competitive form of communication, debate. In debates, parties critically listen to each other with the goal of defeating the opponent's argument rather than understanding a perspective or finding common ground. This is, unfortunately, the type of communication modeled for most people through television news programs. Two people with opposing views are asked to speak in short periods of time and argue his or her side against the other person's side. There is no attempt to build common ground but rather to "win points" by undermining the ideas and evidence of the other person. This type of communication does not promote collaboration, and although it is necessary and even appropriate in some situations, it often can get in the way of true understanding.

ATTITUDES NECESSARY FOR DIALOGUE

Now that we have uncovered the philosophy behind dialogue, we can better understand the different attitudes one needs to effectively participate in dialogue. These attitudes help illustrate what the proper context is for dialogue to take place. Without the right attitude, true dialogue and understanding are difficult to come by. In this section, we will examine four different attitudes that contribute to a strong positive dialogic experience between people.

Open-mindedness

Central to dialogue is the belief that no one has a monopoly on good ideas, and that the ideas of others might be better than our own. When we enter into a dialogue, we must be ready to critique our own ideas as well as those of other people. Often, someone else may see something in our ideas that could be improved or notice something we missed, and we must be ready to accept this feedback. Dialogue is a matter of identifying the best idea possible through an understanding of multiple perspectives. Being open-minded calls us to withhold judgment while we completely listen to our conversational partners; in doing that, we can gather all the information possible about an issue. This attitude flows from the central premise of dialogue related to respecting other people.

GENUINENESS

the act of being direct, honest, and straightforward regarding what we believe and think

Genuineness

Recall that in a dialogue we must respect ourselves as well as the other party, and in order to do so, according to Richard Johannesen, we must enter into an interaction with an attitude that is genuine.[11] Genuineness means being direct, honest, and straightforward regarding what we believe and think. This allows us to be true to ourselves as well as the other person by not hiding our thoughts or denying ourselves the right to contribute to the dialogue. People who try to communicate strategically or tactically are more likely engaging in debate, and, in trying to manipulate the course of the discussion, prohibit true dialogue from taking place. This is self-centered rather than other-centered communication, which carries great risk for the relationship if uncovered.

Being genuine can carry its own risk, as you might be operating in a genuine manner while the other person is not, thus creating a situation where you might be taken advantage of by the other party. We must be genuine to create trust, but being genuine also makes us vulnerable in interactions with people who are not trustworthy. In these situations, you might want to reveal truths in a gradual manner as you get to know the other person. This will minimize, but not eliminate, the risk; as long as your contribution is true and honest, you are still being genuine.

Sensitivity

While being genuine (direct, honest, and straightforward) is important for furthering dialogic communication, you should also be **sensitive** to how others might receive and be affected by your "honest" verbal and nonverbal messages. As we discussed in the chapter on communication, culture, and diversity, understanding and respecting diversity is key for engaging in competent communication. We need to remember that the people we communicate with are not always the same as us. They might come from different religious backgrounds or have different ideological points of view. Additionally, in the chapter on perception and the self, we explored how perception is integral to the communication process. How we communicate with others inevitably affects how others see us, how they see themselves, and how they view our relationship with them. Therefore, it is critical that you are sensitive to what others might perceive as insensitive communication, from everyday exchanges where offenses might be "smaller" but are still intentional and insulting to the other person (e.g., interrupting a colleague during a meeting), to those that are not necessarily intentionally insulting but can come across as such (e.g., a white person assuming someone with dark skin is "from somewhere else" and asking them where they are from, even though they are both English speakers living in the same city), to intentional mean-spirited statements and actions, including "ist" language that is meant to denigrate and cause distress to the other person.

SENSITIVE
understanding and respecting diversity

Activating sensitivity as you interact with others will help you engage in good dialogue as it shows others that you care how your messages affect others. Receivers should also display sensitivity in how they interpret and react to insensitive messages, although senders bear the most burden with regard to sensitivity. It really is true to advise yourself and others to think before you speak!

Agreeableness

One of the key characteristics of a good dialogue is being agreeable. Being agreeable means remaining open to the idea that you might agree with the other person. We often focus on the overall argument or position and not its parts. If we enter into a discussion with an attempt to be agreeable, we allow ourselves to recognize points we might agree with as opposed to a totalizing statement of agreeing or disagreeing with a person. We might disagree with her or his conclusion but find places of agreement in the evidence the person uses to get there. When we stress areas of agreement rather than the things on which we disagree, we create a much more comfortable climate for communication and generate a positive impression of ourselves for other people.

Agreeable communicators not only seek to find the things on which they agree with another person, but they recognize the person is not the argument. They do not equate a person's character or identity simply with a position they might take on an issue.

Ethical Integrity

As you might imagine, an attitude derived from a sense of morality and desire for fairness is important for anyone engaging in dialogic communication. Morality is our inner sense of right and wrong. Our desire for fairness is shaped by that understanding in specific contexts. Holding true to our sense of right and wrong and consistently applying it in any situation we might encounter is a hallmark of integrity, or the maintenance of a consistent application of our values in every situation. There are a whole host of different ethical approaches, some derived from philosophy and others from theology. Regardless, they each inform our sense of what is right and good in a particular situation. Strong ethical character has long been a hallmark of communication, going all the way back to the Roman philosopher and teacher Quintilian, who required his students to demonstrate that they were "a good man speaking well."[12]

No matter the philosophy or theology that informs one's moral center, a good person always seeks what is good for his or her community, not necessarily what is best for himself or herself, and is clear about that motive when explaining a position to others. Law professor Steven Carter describes this type of moral integrity as having three main components: "(1) discerning what is right and what is wrong, (2) acting on what you have discerned, even at personal cost, and (3) saying openly that you are acting on your understanding of right from wrong."[13] In dialogue, we must be willing to examine ideas—even our own—for how they reflect our values and then act according to those values.

In fact, in 1999 the National Communication Association created, and since promotes, a Credo for Ethical Communication. The Credo contains nine principles for ethical communication. Take a look at what professionals who study communication believe are the tenets of ethical communication:

NCA Credo for Ethical Communication
(approved by the NCA Legislative Council, November 1999)

Questions of right and wrong arise whenever people communicate. Ethical communication is fundamental to responsible thinking, decision making, and the development of relationships and communities within and across contexts, cultures, channels, and media. Moreover, ethical communication enhances human worth and dignity by fostering truthfulness, fairness, responsibility, personal integrity, and respect for self and others. We believe that unethical communication threatens the quality of all communication and consequently the well-being of individuals and the society in which we live. Therefore we, the members of the National Communication Association, endorse and are committed to practicing the following principles of ethical communication:

We advocate truthfulness, accuracy, honesty, and reason as essential to the integrity of communication.

We endorse freedom of expression, diversity of perspective, and tolerance of dissent to achieve the informed and responsible decision making fundamental to a civil society.

We strive to understand and respect other communicators before evaluating and responding to their messages.

We promote access to communication resources and opportunities as necessary to fulfill human potential and contribute to the well-being of families, communities, and society.

We promote communication climates of caring and mutual understanding that respect the unique needs and characteristics of individual communicators.

We condemn communication that degrades individuals and humanity through distortion, intimidation, coercion, and violence, and through the expression of intolerance and hatred.

We are committed to the courageous expression of personal convictions in pursuit of fairness and justice.

We advocate sharing information, opinions, and feelings when facing significant choices while also respecting privacy and confidentiality.

We accept responsibility for the short- and long-term consequences for our own communication and expect the same of others.[14]

Each of the attitudes we have discussed—open-mindedness, genuineness, agreeableness, and ethical integrity—all serve as the foundation to actual communicative behaviors that create a dialogue born from the definition of dialogue we explored earlier in the chapter. In the next, and final section of this chapter, we will explore some of those behaviors.

DIALOGIC BEHAVIORS

Knowing what dialogue is and even approaching it with the right attitude does not guarantee a successful interaction using this style of communication. What we can control, however, is our attempt to create what group communication scholar Jack Gibb calls a supportive communication climate. Gibb contrasts a supportive climate, where people are comfortable exchanging ideas and differing opinions with each other, with a defensive communication climate. A defensive climate is one where people feel attacked and threatened by the other party. Gibb identified six contrasting behavior types that could create either supportive or defensive communication climates. In Table 4.1, you can see his communication behavioral typology.[15]

Supportive Behaviors		Defensive Behaviors	
Description	Nonjudgmental statement or account	**Evaluation**	Statement that passes judgment in some way
Problem orientation	Seeks to find a good solution to a problem	**Control**	Seeks to impose a specific solution
Spontaneity	Thought up at the moment	**Strategy**	Preplanned approach designed to manipulate a person or situation
Empathy	Cares about the other person's feelings	**Neutrality**	Doesn't care about others' feelings
Equality	Two people are equal as humans	**Superiority**	One person is greater than the other in some characteristic (e.g., power, wealth, intellect)
Provisionalism	An idea seems promising, pending further consideration	**Certainty**	An answer is final and requires no further consideration

TABLE 4.1 **Supportive and Defensive Behavior Types**

In this section, we will build upon Gibb's categories and offer six specific behaviors you can employ to conduct a successful dialogue by creating a supportive communication climate. Be forewarned, however, that these behaviors are easier explained than implemented; they take a lot of patience and practice.

Separate Facts from Interpretation

In the chapter on perception and the self, we covered the perception process, and the final stage in that process is interpretation. As you recall, interpretations take symbols, events, and experiences and give them meaning, but we all do not give the same meaning to the same things. These interpretations are not facts, and to have a good dialogue we must avoid treating them as such. When people offer interpretations or judgments that are different from ours, they do not necessarily have the facts wrong; they just have a different way of seeing something. Rather than suggesting others are incorrect, interpretive differences illustrate a perceptual gap between ourselves and the other person that we need to bridge through dialogue.

We often deny the opportunity for dialogue by issuing opinions as though they should be accepted as facts. For instance, saying, "The cost for car insurance is $750 a year," is a statement of a fact. If you instead said, "The car insurance here is expensive," you would be offering an interpretation, not a fact. You could adjust this second statement to make it more dialogic by adding the qualifier, "I believe that" to the beginning of the interpretation, making it clear that your statement is an interpretation and not a fact. The more specific and factual we can be in a dialogue, the easier it will be to understand why someone believes the way she or he does.

Ask Clarifying Questions

As you can probably imagine, in many situations it can be difficult to either keep up with a conversational partner or differentiate between fact and interpretation. The most effective dialogic tool for managing these challenges is asking clarifying questions. These questions must be handled in a manner consistent with the principles and attitudes inherent in dialogic communication, meaning they are nonjudgmental and they do not implicitly state a position in the form of a question. Nondialogic questions might look like the following examples in the left column of Table 4.2.

Nondialogic Questions	Dialogic Questions
"So, you are telling me you did not take out the garbage last night despite what our neighbors said?"	"What time did you take out the garbage last night?"
"Don't you think that spending money on that dress is a waste of your hard-earned cash?"	"How much money will you have left after buying that dress?"
"Can't you see how that job is beneath you?"	"What new responsibilities will you have in this position?"

TABLE 4.2   Nondialogic and Dialogic Questions

Each of these questions is not designed to achieve understanding but is rather a tool to forward a position disguised as a question. These are examples of leading or loaded questions. These questions do not encourage dialogue, as they do not demonstrate open-minded communication.

Clarifying questions, on the other hand, are focused on furthering understanding through the solicitation of information from another party. These questions do not attack or express judgment, but rather invite further explanation on a topic or issue. Look to the right column of Table 4.2 on the previous page for some examples of clarifying questions that encourage dialogue.

Each of these seeks information and does not imply judgments. By asking questions this way, communicators invite discussion without putting a person on the defensive.

Allow Other People to Speak Fully

We all can think of a time when we got excited and wanted to either add to the conversation or respond to what someone was saying. In order to create a climate that encourages dialogue, however, we must allow the other person to finish their thoughts before we jump in. This is one of the most common conversational miscues people make: believing they know where someone is going with a statement and so, in their excitement, jumping in and finishing the statement for the other person. Although it may be done with a desire to show support for the other person, this interruption can be construed as rude and may actually end up hurting more than helping to facilitate dialogue. Interruptions often hurt the listener as well as the speaker by denying them the opportunity to hear everything.

To allow other people to speak fully and thus avoid interruptions, it is essential to put your desire to speak to the side so you can focus on your role as a listener. This role is just as important as speaking in a dialogue, and demonstrating the ability and desire to pay attention to the speaker throughout his or her statement helps create an environment in which you listen in a way that encourages others to speak. Additionally, when you listen carefully to the speaker throughout his or her statement, you are modeling that behavior and communicating to others that they should also listen in a way that encourages you to speak.

Take Notes

One thing you can do to keep yourself from interrupting someone and keep pace with what is being said is to take notes. Students do this in most all classes, mainly to create organized study materials for upcoming exams. Little do they realize that note taking would benefit their ability to have constructive and successful interactions with other people. We simply cannot recall everything another person says. The more time that passes between the action and the time we try to remember it, the more we forget. This cognitive loss makes it even more important to keep a written record of important points in conversations so that later, when we need to revisit what was covered, we can return to our notes.

Taking notes also assists us during conversations or presentations in that rather than interrupting a person in the moment they say something, we can write down our questions or comments and wait until it is our turn to speak. This keeps us from forgetting the comment or question and allows us to contextualize it with the statement to which our question or comment is responding. Note taking also demonstrates to the other people in the conversation that you are paying attention, which creates a comfortable communication climate where people feel as if you value their contributions. This is a way of physically demonstrating respect for the other person by giving her or him your attention.

Give Complete Attention

Earlier in the chapter we pointed out how multitasking interferes with effective dialogue. Many professors have policies regarding the use of computers and cell phones in their classes, likely because they have witnessed students using computers to do things other than follow along in class. The same thing happens in business meetings, where colleagues often will text or look at their phone during meetings. These activities are disrespectful to the other people in the conversation because they show that person is not paying complete attention. Not only do distractions increase the risk of important information being missed, but relationships and personal credibility could be damaged as well.

Whether it is in class or in a meeting, it is important to give someone your complete attention. You would want the same when you speak, and so giving others your attention is equally important. Keep in mind that attention does not mean simply staring at the other person; it rather involves being fully present and expressing interest in what is being said.

Social Media Dialogue

Social media has changed the way people communicate. We can instantaneously send messages that are private or public about any topic we choose. Politicians, sports teams, and corporations all now use social media platforms to inform, convince and galvanize people. Social media, however, is fraught with challenges, from lying to cyberbullying. How can we use social media dialogically to create a digital public square? What are the challenges to doing so? What might dialogue on a social media platform look like?

Own Your Own Statements

The final behavior we will discuss that encourages a dialogic climate for communication is owning your own statements. This involves using "I" language instead of "you" language. "You" language puts people on the defensive because it can come across as accusatory. We often do this when we have negative feelings and begin blaming other people or events for the way we feel, thus abdicating our ability to control our own emotions. This diminishes respect for ourselves and comes across as though others can control us. See Table 4.3.

"You" Language	"I" Language
"You are a liar."	"I think I need more convincing."
"You never let me finish."	"I have not fully explained myself."
"You are driving me crazy!"	"Please give me a moment."

TABLE 4.3   *"You" and "I" Language*

Each of the "I" statements focuses on the speaker and illustrates his or her ability to both be in touch with emotions and feelings and express them in a way that does not attack the other party. "You" language shows that the communicator is not able to express emotions well and relies on attack or blame to express how they feel. It is easy to see how such language choices could destroy opportunities for dialogue.

SUMMARY

Dialogue can be a truly effective tool when interacting with other people. Its goal is mutual understanding, not necessarily agreement. It is a style of communication that encourages people to want to listen and speak. We first examined what dialogue is, breaking it down into four key parts. We then discussed the four attitudes necessary for engaging in dialogue with another person, before ending the chapter with a discussion of six behaviors that encourage dialogue in any situation.

CHAPTER 4 KEY IDEAS

- The four key characteristics of dialogue are civility, presentness, unconditional positive regard, and mutual equality.

- Civility requires politeness, respect for others, and respect for self; without a willingness to assert one's feelings and thoughts, true dialogue cannot take place. Civility is more than just "being nice."

- Dialogues differ from monologues in that monologues respect only one voice; they differ from debates because in a dialogue the goal is understanding, not necessarily agreement.

- The five attitudes one must have to enter in to a true dialogue are open-mindedness, genuineness, sensitivity, agreeableness, and ethical integrity.

- When engaging in a dialogue, it is important not to confuse interpretations with facts, ask clarifying questions when you do not understand something, do not interrupt others, give full attention, take notes, and own your own statements.

CHAPTER 4 KEY TERMS

Dialogue	Principle of mutual equality
Civility	Monologue
Politeness	Debate
Good manners	Genuineness
Respect	Sensitive
Assertiveness	Agreeable
Presentness	Morality
Unconditional positive regard	Integrity

ACTIVITIES AND DISCUSSION QUESTIONS

1. Watch Celeste Headlee's TEDx talk, "10 Ways to Have a Better Conversation," available online at https://www.ted.com/talks/celeste_headlee_10_ways_to_have_a_better_conversation. How do her ten tips relate to each of the components of and attitudes necessary for dialogue?

2. Watch Adam Galinsky's TEDx talk, "How to Speak up for Yourself," available online at https://www.ted.com/talks/adam_galinsky_how_to_speak_up_for_yourself. Why is assertiveness such an important element of dialogic communication? How does perspective-taking allow us to be more dialogic?

3. Watch Dr. Sarah Steimel's TEDx Talk, "Invitational Rhetoric," which is available online at https://www.youtube.com/watch?v=easT0tsPXiE. What is invitational rhetoric? What are the similarities and differences between dialogic communication and invitational rhetoric?

4. In order to be more present when you are with others, silence and put away your phone and other technological devices. Try putting your phone away for an entire day. What do you notice in your interactions with others and in your observations of the world around you that you might have otherwise missed? How do you see phones and other devices interfering with others' interactions?

5 LANGUAGE

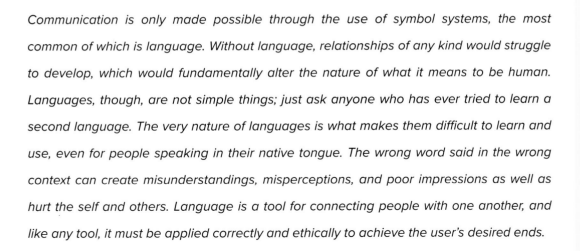

Communication is only made possible through the use of symbol systems, the most common of which is language. Without language, relationships of any kind would struggle to develop, which would fundamentally alter the nature of what it means to be human. Languages, though, are not simple things; just ask anyone who has ever tried to learn a second language. The very nature of languages is what makes them difficult to learn and use, even for people speaking in their native tongue. The wrong word said in the wrong context can create misunderstandings, misperceptions, and poor impressions as well as hurt the self and others. Language is a tool for connecting people with one another, and like any tool, it must be applied correctly and ethically to achieve the user's desired ends.

In this chapter, we explore the nature of language in an effort to illustrate its complexities and help you improve your ability to use it appropriately and effectively in your lives. We will first examine the four basic characteristics all languages share. We will then explore different ways language can be used to create meaning and enhance understanding between people. Next, we will discuss some challenges to understanding cross-cultural language and metaphor, and how to overcome them. Finally, we will present some suggestions for how to employ language in a way that encourages dialogue.

LANGUAGE CHARACTERISTICS

Symbols are the building blocks of language, and a fundamental component of a symbol is that it has meaning. A sound, image, or utterance by itself does not mean anything unless we give it meaning. For example, when someone clears his or her throat, we may not pay it any heed and thus afford it no meaning; we also might take it to indicate the individual wants to say something—thus providing the sound its own meaning. In short, words only have meaning insofar as we give it to them. When we give signs and symbols meaning, like we do with words in a language, they are composed of four characteristics: they are arbitrary, they are ambiguous, they are abstract, and they are negative.

Arbitrary

ARBITRARY

term that describes symbols themselves as having no direct connection with the things they represent

The first characteristic of language is that it is arbitrary, meaning the symbols themselves have no direct connection with the things they represent. For example, the word "selfie" has no real relationship with a picture of yourself; it only has a connection through the thought the symbol creates in our minds. The term "selfie" could have been something else entirely, but as a community of people using the same language, we essentially agreed that the symbol "selfie" represents a picture you take of yourself using a mobile device. The term is merely a label that has been coordinated by people to mean roughly the same thing to everyone in that group. We say "roughly," because when someone says "selfie," we all get a different image of a selfie in our minds; some of us picture one that we took of ourselves, others perhaps a photo posted to social media, and still others might envision someone actually taking a selfie. The fact that the labels we choose to represent things are arbitrary in nature explains how different languages can have different words for the same thing.

SEMIOTICS

the study of the social production of meaning from sign systems like language

Semiologist and linguist Ferdinand De Saussure helped illustrate how we make sense out of arbitrary signs.[1] He was very interested in how signs functioned and became known as one of the fathers of semiotics, or the study of the social production of meaning from sign systems like language. De Saussure breaks down the system into three parts. The first is the signifier, which is the physical thing as we perceive it in the world around us. For example, as we see in the diagram below, an example of a signifier might be an actual table. The second is the signified, which is the idea or mental construct of that thing. This is the meaning associated with the signifier. Even though there are a lot of different ways particular tables might look or feel, the signified is the general idea we carry around in our minds of what a table is like. The third part of this system is the sign, or the arbitrary symbol that represents both the signifier and the signified.

SIGNIFIER

the physical thing as we perceive it in the world around us

SIGNIFIED

the meaning associated with the signifier; the idea or mental construct of the signifier

SIGN

an arbitrary symbol that represents the signifier and the signified

In this case, the word "table" is the sign that represents both a specific, physical table, and the idea of what a table is. There is no necessary relationship between the word "table" and the actual object and idea of what a table is, but over time those who speak the English language have come to an agreement to use the word "table" as the sign that represents the thing and the idea, while those who speak Spanish use the word "mesa" as the sign that represents this same signifier and signified; refer to Figure 5.1 for a visualization of this relationship. Due to the arbitrariness of language and signs, there are many different signs for the same signifier, which can create confusion. Nevertheless, that there can be many signs for the same signifier illustrates the fundamental characteristic of language, where the words are not the things, but rather representations of those things that we interpret.

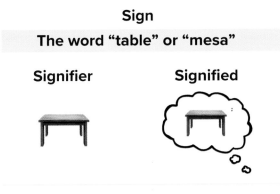

FIGURE 5.1 **A Visual Explanation of Sign, Signifier, and Signified Using the Word, "Table."**

Ambiguous

A second fundamental attribute of language is that it is ambiguous. By that, we mean that words do not have absolute meanings and can be used for a variety of different contexts and purposes. The ambiguity of language allows terms and symbols to mean different things in different contexts. For instance, the "peace sign" of holding up two fingers has also meant "victory," and in some cultures it is actually a profane expression. The word "wicked" can also be interpreted in several different ways; it is the name of a musical, it can mean something that is evil, and it can also mean something that is very enjoyable or interesting.

The ambiguity of language comes from its connection to a history of usage and understanding. As Roland Barthes explains, symbols (especially words) have two different types of meaning attached to a sign without understanding its history of usage and application.[2] The first type of meaning, its denotative meaning, is, for all intents and purposes, a sign's dictionary definition. But words are not always used according to their literal definitions, as most of the time we use words for their connotative, not denotative meanings. Connotative meaning is that which comes from a set of associations a word brings to mind in a person. Individuals and groups can have different connotative meanings for the same word, because of the emotions and experiences tied to that term.

Both denotative and connotative definitions reflect correct meanings of words, but we usually interpret words based on their connotative meanings. To illustrate the difference, look at the nature of synonyms, or words that have the same literal meaning. For example, synonyms for the word "car" include "carriage," "wagon," "motor vehicle," and "truck," but when

AMBIGUOUS

term that describes words as being without absolute meanings

DENOTATIVE MEANING

the meaning prescribed to a sign without understanding its history of usage and application; its dictionary, or literal, definition

CONNOTATIVE MEANING

meaning that comes from a set of associations a word brings to mind in a person we use each of these terms, we create a different image in someone's mind as to what we are speaking about. We depend on those associations to reduce the ambiguity of the terms we use, and it is evident that the ambiguity of language can easily lead to misunderstandings and misperceptions.

Abstract

ABSTRACT

the idea that language is not tangible or concrete

The third characteristic of language is that it is abstract—not tangible or concrete. It cannot be held, moved, or physically experienced. The mind must understand and interpret language, and words cannot be processed any other way. The abstract nature of language allows human beings to think about and talk about things that could be or might have been. Language does not need to refer to something specific or physical, but rather it can refer to things like ideas, values, and beliefs.

Abstract language can also refer to a set of terms that refer to things that are intangible or not specific. To this end, some terms are more specific than others, and can generate more concrete images in a receiver's mind. The more precise the language, the less abstract the ideas, and the closer two parties can come to sharing meaning. Figure 5.2 is an example of how this works in a visual representation often called the ladder of abstraction.

FIGURE 5.2 Ladder of Abstraction

Negative

NEGATIVE

the idea that language separates things from their natural state, thus telling us not only what something is, but what it is not

Language is also inherently negative—not negative in the sense that language is bad, but rather that it creates a void or separation. Scholar Kenneth Burke, who contributed a great deal to our understanding of language, noted that through the process of labeling something, we are both saying what the thing is as well as what it is not. He proposed that this gives language a negative quality because the label divides things between what is and what is not. In communication, sometimes the best way to help people understand what you are saying is to explain the negative, or what you don't mean, with a statement.

TERMS AND STRUCTURES OF LANGUAGE

The flexibility of language allows it to take several forms when we use it. The different words and structures allow us to create interesting messages that encourage other people to listen and can also help people understand our meaning in a variety of ways when we try to explain something complicated. The varied word choices and structures of language make speeches, conversations, and ideas memorable to an audience or conversational partner. In this section of the chapter, we will examine several different language structures that can make what we say more appealing to others.

Metaphoric Language

Since all language represents something else, all language is metaphoric. A metaphor is a linguistic device that highlights qualities of two objects in an explicit comparison. There are six different types of metaphors we will discuss in this section, and each does different things.

Simile. One of the more common language structures we use when speaking to others is a simile. Similes are language devices that compare two things through the use of "like" or "as." Similes allow the comparison to focus on a specific attribute shared by two different things rather than saying those two things are exactly the same. Similes also contain both of the compared items in the statement, which is to say the comparison is explicit. Let's look at an example: "You are like a kid at Christmas." The qualities shared by the two items (the person and a child at Christmas) relate to their excitement, while it is clear that the person is not being called a child. It is a distinction with a difference, as both the person and the child that person is compared to retain their core qualities, but share in their degree of excitement. It is important to remember that all similes are metaphors, but not all metaphors are similes.

SIMILES

metaphoric language devices that compare two things through the use of "like" or "as"

Synecdoche. Similes are a type of metaphoric language that is identified through the explicit statement of "like" or "as," but synecdoche, the second type of metaphor we will discuss, does not have such an easy marker. Instead, synecdoche is a metaphor that uses one part of something to refer to the whole thing. Look at the following example of synecdoche: "She is learning her ABCs." In this statement, ABCs refers to the entire alphabet, not just the first three letters, but that part of the alphabet is being used to refer to the whole alphabet. In fact, just about any acronym is a synecdoche. There are others as well, like the navy saying, "All hands on deck," where "hands" refers to all personnel.

SYNECDOCHE

a metaphor that uses one part of something to refer to the whole thing

Metonym. A third form of metaphor is identified by its use of tangible objects to refer to intangible things. Metonyms create a much more vivid, colorful, and concrete vision for things that people have a hard time understanding. Such tools can help explain concepts, theories, ideas, and values in ways most people can understand by taking these abstract items and tying them to an experience or thing people have seen, touched, smelled, or otherwise experienced through their senses. One of the most common examples of a metonym is the use of "blood, sweat, and tears" to imply hard work; another is using "heart" to refer to passion or love. Not every task results in someone leaking blood, sweat, and tears upon

METONYM

a metaphor that is identified by its use of tangible objects to refer to intangible things completion, but the image conveys hard work in any context. Nor do people actually "wear their heart on their sleeves" when they display emotions, but the metonym here helps paint a vivid, interesting picture.

Archetypal. Most metaphors are culturally specific and rely on knowledge of a specific community and their experiences to work. For example, saying that a salesperson needs to "get across the goal line" with a sale is a metaphor that is unique to Americans, because it is drawn from the version of football only played there, so people from another culture likely will not understand its meaning. That being said, there are metaphors drawn from the human experience that use things every person can relate to because the comparison uses something we all experience or know to shed light on something else. Metaphors that use common human experiences to help describe another object are referred to as archetypal. Things like "light" and "dark," as well as "sickness" and "health," are common human experiences that can be used to give meaning to other things. For instance, when we say there is a "light at the end of the tunnel" with a class, we mean the class is almost over. Since light and tunnels are part of the human experience nearly everywhere, this archetypal metaphor is not bound to a specific culture.

Mixed. In everyday conversations we often use metaphors to compare two things that have no inherent connection with each other, creating incongruous comparisons. Some of these mixed metaphors make use of two different metaphors that do not logically fit but mean the same thing, like saying "We need to hit the bull's-eye or we will have to punt this decision to later." Here, an archery metaphor is mixed with a football metaphor, but the meaning is fairly easy to discern. The fact that bull's-eyes and punting have nothing to do with each other does not detract from the meaning, but when read literally, the metaphors do not really work and create a pretty funny statement.

Dead. Metaphors are such a common part of our language that often when we use them we forget their origins and the characteristics of the object used for the comparison. These metaphors have lost the creative element from which they initially drew their power and now are just accepted as everyday phrases rather than the metaphors they are. Such commonplace phrases have become dead metaphors. Just think about the following and see if you can resurrect the original source of the comparison for the metaphor: "eye of the

---

ARCHETYPAL
metaphors that use common human experiences to help describe another object

MIXED METAPHORS
phrases that make use of two different metaphors that do not logically fit; compare two things that have no inherent connection with each other, creating incongruous comparisons

DEAD METAPHORS
metaphors that have lost the creative element from which they initially drew their power and now are just accepted as true terms, rather than the metaphors they are

---

Many people who disagree on one or many issues are said by some to have a "communication problem." I, however, would argue that these people don't have "communication problems" but rather problems of substance which in turn cause them to have difficulties in communicating with each other.

—Richard Vatz, Towson University

needle," "body of an essay," "flowerbed," "seeds of doubt," and "branches of government." Each of these words and phrases contains a metaphoric element that implicitly compares it to something else, but we don't actually make the comparison in our minds. Thus, we have killed the original metaphor used for the comparison.

Language Structures

Metaphoric terms are not the only way we can create interesting and appealing messages. We can also play with the structure of the terms we use and organize our messages into forms that invite people to listen. In this section of the chapter, we will detail five ways to structure language that can increase the appeal of a message for its audience, regardless of whether it is one person, a small group, or a large gathering.

Repetition. One of the old maxims of communication is that if you want people to remember something important, tell it to them, tell it to them again, and tell it to them a third time. This approach can also be applied for effect with words and not just information, and when we repeat words and phrases either immediately following the initial statement or in the same location in a message we are using repetition. By "the same location" we mean at the beginning of consecutive sentences or paragraphs. So, when Martin Luther King Jr. used the phrase "I have a dream" in consecutive sentences, he used repetition to make his phrase memorable for his audience.

REPETITION
the practice of repeating words and phrases either immediately following the initial statement or in the same location in a message

Alliteration. There are only so many sounds we can make, and speakers can add aural interest when using the same sound in consecutive words. When we use the same vowel or consonant sound at the beginning of consecutive words, we are using alliteration. This makes particular content much more noticeable to an audience and increases the likelihood an audience will retain what was said. Just think of childhood tongue twisters like, "Sally sells sea shells by the sea shore," and you will see the power of alliteration. The key to making alliteration work is that each of the words must relate to each other and the topic at hand, because if you just use words that start with the same sound but do not have anything to do with each other, it will create a message no one understands. Just look at the previous example of Sally, who was selling sea shells on the sea shore—something you might actually believe was happening because the content tells a story that makes sense. Conversely, the alliterative effect would be lost if the sentence was "Sally smites smiles on the septic state."

ALLITERATION
the practice of using the same vowel or consonant sound at the beginning of consecutive words

Parallelism. A third strategy for using terms to create maximum appeal involves placing related words or phrases in a pattern that highlights what they have in common. When we similarly structure words, phrases, or clauses in this way we are using parallelism. Here are a few examples of parallelism in sentences.

PARALLELISM
the practice of placing related words or phrases in a pattern that highlights what they have in common

> "She is an actor, writer, director, and producer."
> "Water, food, shelter, and love are all necessary for a happy life."
> "He is a passionate, dedicated, and enthusiastic advocate for his cause."
> "Peace leads to progress and prosperity."

Each of these statements uses similar properties to describe something. In the first statement, all of the jobs described are related to the production of theater or television shows. The second statement contains four things humans need to survive. The next statement uses adjectives rather than nouns to create the parallel structure. The final example is even more interesting because it uses alliteration in the parallel structuring, which illustrates these linguistic devices are not mutually exclusive, but can, when appropriate, be combined to create an even more memorable and effective message.

Parallelism is especially important when you have a single subject accompanied by a series of verbs or a series of nouns accompanied by a single verb. For example, you might say, "My puppy Einstein likes to run, to play, and to sleep," or "My puppy Einstein likes running, playing, and sleeping." However, you would be violating principles of parallelism if you were to say, "My puppy Einstein likes to run, playing, and to sleep."

ANTITHESIS

the practice of placing two contrasting ideas side by side in a parallel structure

Antithesis. The fourth way to structure language is a specific application of parallelism, but because of its unique qualities, we treat it separately. Antithesis occurs when two contrasting ideas are placed side by side in a parallel structure. John F. Kennedy gave perhaps the most famous example of antithesis in his inaugural address when he declared, "Ask not what your country can do for you, but what you can do for your country."[3] John Milton also made use of antithesis in his book *Paradise Lost*, when he wrote about the devil, "Better to reign in Hell, than serve in Heaven."[4] One final example comes from the popular adage, "You can please some of the people some of the time, and even some of the people all of the time, but you can never please all of the people all of the time." In each of these statements, contradictory phrases are used to play off each other to make a point. Antithesis is a creative tool that forces the audience to think about what was said to discern the meaning, but it also generates a very memorable phrase or sentence in the message, increasing the likelihood it will stick with the audience.

NARRATIVE

a story that's told when trying to explain or argue something with an audience

Narrative. Metaphoric language and creative turns of phrase like those we have discussed so far are effective tools, but their appeal can be made even stronger when included within larger stories. Not all stories, though, are equal, so it is important to consider what we know about good stories when constructing messages for others. Narrative theory proposes that all humans are story-telling animals, and that everything we say, no matter how short or long, is a story. Most of the time the characters are implied and the action is all that is stated, like when we explain to a partner or friend how our day went. Other times, characters need to be more explicitly stated, such as when we recount something we witnessed or heard about. Regardless, stories are a powerful tool when trying to explain or argue something with an audience, because we always control how the story unfolds through how we tell it.

According to Walter Fisher, the theorist responsible for developing the narrative paradigm, there are two important qualities for judging stories you should use when both crafting your own messages and examining the messages of others.[5] Does the story ring true within its own world and does the content of the story makes sense? This is the concept of **narrative coherence**. It asks questions such as: Do the responses of characters to events seem rational? Are the characters consistent? Do events seem plausible and believable in the world of the story? Do things happen in an appropriate order that makes logical sense? In addition to narrative coherence, we must also consider **narrative fidelity**, or whether the story rings true to the audience. Narrative fidelity tests how well the story reflects the values and beliefs of the audience. If stories do not reflect the values of an audience, then they are not very appealing or effective devices.

NARRATIVE COHERENCE

feature exhibited by a story with content that hangs together and makes sense

NARRATIVE FIDELITY

term for describing how well a story reflects the values and beliefs of its audience

GUIDELINES FOR USING DIALOGIC LANGUAGE

Engaging in a dialogue necessarily involves language, but how we employ that language and what we say makes the difference between a successful encounter and one that is uncomfortable and potentially hostile. When you wish to achieve understanding between two or more people, it is important to take great care with the language choices you make when describing how you feel and what you think. The linguistic choices we make often make the difference between establishing an atmosphere conducive to dialogue or creating a more combative environment that makes genuineness and understanding difficult to achieve. In this section, we will explore some guidelines for using language that is ethical and encourages dialogue.

Use Inclusive Language

One of the key components to generating support and creating a dialogic environment is letting the other party know you identify with his or her needs. One way of doing this is by using the pronoun "we" instead of "I," "me," or "you." When speaking with "I" and "me," you set yourself apart from the other party and create division, whereas if you use "we" language you create the perception you are on their side and one of them. Inclusive language goes even further than pronouns, though.

Whenever possible, use gender neutral language. If you use gender specific terminology like "he," "she," or "man," you make assumptions about the makeup of that particular subject that might not be true. For example, you should say "member of Congress" instead of "congressman," "service member" instead of "airman," "flight attendant" instead of "stewardess," and "businessperson" instead of "businessman." The gendered versions of these terms tend to exclude people who you may not want to exclude, and create a negative perception of you and your perspective. It is a matter of courtesy and politeness to use the nongendered terms, and it will go a long way toward creating a comfortable communication environment with others, particularly people who do not know you.

Avoid Profanity

PROFANITY

vulgar and irreverent language

There is hardly a place in American society where profanity, or vulgar and irreverent language, is not used. Television programs, both cable and network, depict characters who use it; books and magazines now even place it on their covers; and people use it throughout their daily lives in conversations, memos, and emails. Profanity, however, often does not gain you anything, and comes with the risk of insulting, offending, or otherwise irritating people. It also creates the impression that you are not well-spoken and that you are rude. Limiting profanity and knowing the risks to your image that come with its use are important.

Avoid Hate Speech

Profanity is not the only form of language that people find offensive; phrases and terms that attack a person or group of people based upon their gender, ethnicity, religion, sexual orientation, social actions, or any other category that indicates applications of a negative unwarranted stereotype can also destroy the potential for dialogue. Some people use these types of terms in an attempt at humor, but they fail to see how others might receive the message and thus take an unnecessary risk of offending someone else. Remember that being sensitive to the audience's perspective is essential for dialogue.

Use Culturally Appropriate Metaphors

IDIOMS

metaphoric expressions whose meanings are not predictable from their usual use, but must be inferred from cultural markers

As enticing as metaphors can be when writing a speech or telling a friend a story, it is important to recognize not every metaphor works for every audience. Often, metaphors are tied to experiences within a specific culture and do not translate to those who come from outside of that group. This creates one of two problems in translation that can make understanding more difficult to achieve.

The first problem is called idiomatic equivalence. Some metaphors we use are included in expressions called idioms. Idioms are metaphoric expressions whose meanings are not

ENGAGING ETHICS

Profanity in the Workplace

For a long time, profanity has been used to shock people. It is considered disrespectful, uncivilized, and impolite. It is also frowned upon at work as it comes across as unprofessional. In fact, Anthony Scaramucci, former Director of Communications at the White House, was fired for referring to colleagues in a newspaper article using profane language. Consider under what parameters swearing at work might be tolerated or acceptable. Are there any potential benefits? What are the dangers of allowing oft-inappropriate language at work?

predictable from their usual use but must be inferred from cultural markers. An example of a culturally specific idiom is the phrase "to stop on a dime." Clearly, to understand this phrase one needs to be familiar with American currency, both in terms of its name and its size. Using this phrase with someone who is not familiar with dimes can cause them to feel embarrassed and even defensive that they do not know what it means, thus hindering the ability to engage in dialogue.

The second problem is related to the fact that different people in different cultures potentially do not share the same experiences or cultural values. Thus, using language that depends on shared experiences or values creates problems with what we call experiential-cultural translation. Basically, if someone has not seen or experienced something, then using that object as a metaphor for something else will only serve to further confuse the situation. Being other-centered and dialogic requires us to pay attention to our language choices and use phrases we believe our audience will understand.

Use Familiar Language

Being dialogic requires a person to be honest with herself or himself as well as others, and nothing damages credibility like trying to use words with which you are not familiar.

The Cultural Limits of Metaphor

In the 2014 Marvel superhero action hit, *Guardians of the Galaxy*, and its 2017 sequel, a team of interstellar misfits comes together to save the universe. Among this group is the brusque and violent Drax the Destroyer, played by Miguel Batista. One of the characteristics of Drax that makes him both frustrating to his teammates and hysterical for the audience is his inability to understand metaphors. Drax takes everything literally, including in a scene where the character Rocket Raccoon complains that some things just go over Drax's head. Drax immediately responds, "It would not go over my head. I would catch it." Drax also fails to appreciate the synecdoche metaphor offered by Chris Pratt's Star-Lord when he tries to convince Drax not to harm a teammate. Star-Lord mimes the action "cut her throat," meaning to kill, and Drax replies he did not plan to cut her throat, but kill her in a different way. These interactions create comedic confusion, but also illustrate the power of metaphoric language and the necessity to understand that not everyone understands metaphors the same way—especially if they come from another (intergalactic) culture.

Picture/courtesy Everett Collection. Copyright © 2014 Walt Disney Studios Motion Pictures.

Mispronouncing words or using them inappropriately only creates a negative impression of you by others. Additionally, if others believe you are trying to portray yourself as more knowledgeable or experienced than you are, then they will see you as insincere, which will damage your ability to engage in a dialogue. It is important that you acknowledge what you do and do not know and that you use words, metaphors, and phrases with which you are comfortable. This is not to say you should not develop a better vocabulary, but you should make sure that you understand the meaning of terms to ensure you are using new words and phrases correctly. At the very least, acknowledge you may not be using them correctly.

Be Specific and Concrete

One of the common errors people make in conversations is "dancing around the issue," or not being clear. In a dialogic environment, it is essential that you try to be as specific and concrete as possible to facilitate understanding between yourself and your audience or conversational partner. The vaguer or more abstract the description you provide, the less likely the other party will be able to accurately interpret your meaning. Concrete language, which may include the use of vivid examples, helps an audience see things how you intend those things to be seen. Specific details also help remove emotion from controversial situations and allow people to focus on a clear issue and topic without the trappings of the emotions the topic may carry on an abstract level.

The Power of Video Communication

In 2010, columnist Dan Savage created a YouTube video with his partner Terry Miller to help stem the tide of youth suicides by teenagers bullied for their sexual preference. Their goal was to serve as an illustration of the thousands of gay adults who survived the challenges and difficulties of growing up gay in a heteronormative world. Their video inspired others to do the same and led to the creation of the It Gets Better Project. According to www.itgetsbetter.org, more than 50,000 videos have been created that have been viewed over 50 million times. Submissions have come from politicians, actors and actresses, social activists, and everyday people. Each of these videos, however, serves as a synecdoche for a larger community and goal.

Use Descriptive, Not Evaluative, Language

Related to the idea of specificity is the practice of using descriptive rather than evaluative language, which you may recall from Gibb's categorization of supportive and defensive language types from the chapter on dialogic communication. Descriptive language simply lays out objective facts or observations without any form of judgment, whereas evaluative language either expressly or implicitly provides an evaluation of those facts or observations. We often issue judgments and evaluations as though they are facts and not interpretations, but this does not contribute to a dialogic environment. In situations where controversial ideas or topics are being engaged, it helps create a supportive dialogic communication environment when we simply describe things rather than render judgments.

Take the following example: a person is late for work and his boss calls him in and says, "You must not care about your job because you seem to want to show up whenever you feel like it." This takes the behavior, supplies an evaluation, presents it as a fact, and destroys any opportunity for dialogue. Instead, imagine if the manager said, "I noticed you were twenty-five minutes late today. It's the third time this has happened this week. What is going on?" This is a description of the behavior and an opportunity for the employee to explain himself. Perhaps he has a sick child or had to take mass transit to work. By phrasing the observation as a description, the manager does not put the employee on the defensive and instead invites him to a dialogue in which the behavior can be explained. In the first example, where the boss issued an evaluation, the employee is far less likely to engage, and if he does so, it will likely not be in a productive manner.

SUMMARY

In this chapter, we worked to unravel several of the mysteries of language. We provided the four characteristics that all languages share before exploring the terms and structures that make language interesting and evocative. In that discussion, we covered metaphors, detailing several different types and providing examples of each. We also examined some strategies for structuring language to both enhance its appeal and its ability to be remembered by a receiver. Finally, we provided seven practical guidelines for using language in a way that encourages dialogue and understanding between two parties.

CHAPTER 5 KEY IDEAS

- Language is arbitrary, ambiguous, abstract, and negative.

- Language systems have three parts: the signifier, the signified, and the sign. The sign (symbol) is composed of both the signifier (the object) and the signified (the mental picture that we have of the object).

- There are six types of metaphors: simile, synecdoche, metonym, archetypal, mixed, and dead.

- Five of the language structures that can help increase the appeal of a message for its audience include repetition, alliteration, parallelism, antithesis, and narrative.

CHAPTER 5 KEY TERMS

Arbitrary	Archetypal
Semiotics	Mixed metaphors
Signifier	Dead metaphors
Signified	Repetition
Sign	Alliteration
Ambiguous	Parallelism
Denotative meaning	Antithesis
Connotative meaning	Narrative
Abstract	Narrative coherence
Negative	Narrative fidelity
Similes	Profanity
Synedoche	Idioms
Metonym	

ACTIVITIES AND DISCUSSION QUESTIONS

1. Watch Dr. Anne Curzan's TED talk, "What Makes a Word 'Real'?" available online at https://www.ted.com/talks/anne_curzan_what_makes_a_word_real. What does this teach us about language?

2. Watch the TED-Ed video, "Where Do New Words Come From?" created by Marcel Danesi, which is available online at https://ed.ted.com/lessons/where-do-new-words-come-from-marcel-danesi. How can these different types of word origins be explained by the characteristics of language that you learned about in this chapter?

3. Watch Win Chesson's Stanford Graduate School of Business presentation, "Why Gender-Inclusive Language Matters," available online at https://www.youtube.com/watch?v=I2YNrEgKHZY. Why is it so important to use inclusive language?

4. Watch this video produced by the psychology department at the University of North Texas about microaggressions: https://www.youtube.com/watch?v=ZahtlxW2CIQ. In your own words, what is this concept? Have you ever been the subject of any of the forms of microaggressions discussed in the video? Have you ever witnessed someone else as a target of one of these microaggressions? Have you been the person to com-

mit any of these microaggressions against others? How did you feel in these situations? How can microaggressive messages be avoided or altered so they did not produce such effects?

5. Choose one of the commencement speeches that is available online at http://apps. npr.org/commencement/, a historic speech available at http://www.historyplace.com/ speeches/previous.htm, or choose a speech that you think has been especially impact-ful. Print a copy of the transcript. Go through the transcript and identify as many uses of metaphoric language or language structures as you can in that speech.

NONVERBAL COMMUNICATION

Words are not the only way people communicate with one another. In fact, we interpret more meaning from nonverbal communication than we do from the content of what is said. *Nonverbal communication* refers to the elements of communication that do not involve words but nevertheless transmit messages. Whereas words have meanings that people can look up, there is no such dictionary for nonverbal communication, making it dependent on the receiver's interpretation. We can change our speaking style and either avoid or use particular words and phrases in different situations, but nonverbal communication is much more difficult—yet incredibly important—to control.

To put the importance of nonverbal communication into context, just imagine different speaking situations. In job interviews, employers examine not just what you say, but how you say it, the manner in which you are dressed, the posture you keep in your chair, and even the strength and quality of your handshake. When out on a date, we pay attention to how other people respond to our stories, how they sit, how their voice sounds, and how much eye contact they make. We also employ appropriate nonverbal behaviors when speaking to teachers or supervisors, such as standing until they ask us to take a seat. The list goes on and on, but the theme is the same: appropriate nonverbal communication is essential in any interaction.

NONVERBAL COMMUNICATION
the elements of communication that do not involve words but nevertheless transmit messages

In this chapter, we explore the various dimensions of nonverbal communication. First, we will briefly outline the three basic principles of nonverbal communication. Then, we will discuss the numerous functions it plays in communication, before examining the different types of nonverbal communication people exhibit in their interactions with others. We will conclude with some guidelines for using nonverbal communication in a way that encourages dialogue and a supportive communication climate.

PRINCIPLES OF NONVERBAL COMMUNICATION

Like any concept, nonverbal communication has its foundation in certain principles. These principles help guide our understanding of how nonverbal communication works and why it functions the way it does. There are three basic principles we will explain, and each is equally important. The first relates how nonverbal messages convey information regarding emotions and relationships. The second principle refers to how nonverbal communication works in tandem with verbal messages to help maintain relationships. Finally, and perhaps most importantly, is the principle that explains how nonverbal messages are context-based, where the same nonverbal display can mean something different to various groups in different situations.

Conveys Emotional and Relationship Information

Verbal messages contain information about both the logical coherence of what is being stated as well as information that could potentially influence the emotional disposition of an audience toward that topic. Since it lacks the ability to be structured and argued, nonverbal communication does not contain any information regarding the logical dimensions of a message. Instead, it helps people understand the emotional aspects of a message and the relationship between the speaker and his or her audience or conversational partner. Although words can carry emotional meaning, nonverbal expression carries the emotional weight.

Think about trying to understand if someone is happy without seeing a smile or hearing a laugh, or consider whether you can determine if someone is upset or distraught without some sort of nonverbal cue from her or his facial expressions or body language. It's very difficult to be certain about the emotional content of messages that are not accompanied by nonverbal cues, particularly in written forms, because our actions convey the emotions that underlie our words. For example, consider all of the possible emotional meanings that could accompany the verbal message, "That's great." Depending on the nonverbal messages accompanying the words, along with the tone of voice, that statement could convey excitement, anger, frustration, disappointment, happiness, or so many other emotions. In fact, according to some communication research, vocal cues like tone of voice, volume, and rate of speech are more accurate tools for decoding emotions than even gestures and facial expressions![1]

In addition to emotional information, nonverbal behaviors also tell us what the relationship is between two parties. Consider watching a person enter an office. How do you know whose office it is, or who the boss is in this situation? You can tell by looking at who sits, who stands, and even who invites the other person to sit. Additionally, the structure of an office can tell you things about the types of relationships people wish to have with those that enter. Head nods, hugs, and handshakes (particularly who extends his or her hands first) also serve as indicators of the relationship between people.

Maintains a Relationship with Verbal Messages

Nonverbal communication helps us interpret verbal messages, and verbal messages also can help us understand nonverbal behaviors. The two forms of communication are related and have a sort of symbiotic relationship. Neither one alone can accurately convey all the information we want to send, but together they have that potential. Communication scholar Judee Burgoon estimates that between 65 to 70 percent of meaning in a message comes from nonverbal communication, with the rest coming from language.[2] As we will see later in this chapter, nonverbal behaviors can function in accordance with our verbal messages, and sometimes they can present information that is opposite of what we are saying. For effective communication, we must strive to keep a degree of consistency between what we say and what we do while we say it.

Relies on Context for Its Meaning

No dictionary for translating nonverbal communication exists, making it a challenge to accurately interpret nonverbal messages. What we do have available to help us understand the meaning behind nonverbal behaviors is context, but we do not read the situation correctly all the time. In interpreting what we perceive as relevant nonverbal messages, we look at things like the situation, events that may influence the person sending the message, what we know about the person sending the message, and even what is said while delivering the nonverbal communication. What goes on around the nonverbal communication essentially feeds the meaning we assign it.

Additionally, the meaning of nonverbal communication is directly tied to culture. Although emotions are universally human in nature, how we express them varies from group to group. In certain Arab cultures, for instance, grief is expressed openly, while in certain Asian cultures it is seen as inappropriate to express emotions in such a way. In Europe, a sign of friendship between people, even of the same sex, is to embrace and kiss, while in the United States this is not a common practice. Different behaviors are used in various cultures to express the same emotions and appreciating these differences in context is important for becoming a skilled and effective communicator. Even so, certain basic emotions have been found to be interpreted similarly across cultures. Psychologist Paul Ekman shared photographs of behaviors that indicated happiness, fear, disgust, anger, sadness, and surprise to participants from five non-European countries and found they were all equally accurate in identifying the emotional display in the photographs.[3] Cultures have different norms for expressing certain emotions and messages, but there are certain behaviors that seem to be universally attached to particular emotions.

Even the behaviors themselves can contain multiple possible meanings, and identifying the correct one largely depends on how you read the context in which the nonverbal message is conveyed. This underscores the ambiguity of symbols and gestures, in that a smile in one situation can mean happiness, while in another it could be an indicator of someone hiding something. A head nod could also mean a great many things, such as agreement or a sign of respect and deference to the speaker. Context is key in reducing this ambiguity and interpreting nonverbal communication, and so appreciating the contextual dimension of nonverbal message interpretation is a foundational principle of nonverbal communication.

FUNCTIONS OF NONVERBAL COMMUNICATION

Nonverbal communication can serve any one of six different functions in our delivery of messages to others. Most often it works hand in hand with verbal communication; however, that is not always the case. At one time or another everyone experiences a situation where they misinterpret a nonverbal display, or they create confusion through their own nonverbal messages. Additionally, we have all been in situations where if the nonverbal elements of the interaction are stripped away it loses its charm, uniqueness, and enjoyable nature. In this part of the chapter, we will define the six functions of nonverbal communication, and show how they can help, and in some cases hinder, the effectiveness of your communication.

Kneeling During the National Anthem

Source: Keith Allison from https://flickr.com/photos/27003603@N00/37721041581

In Fall 2017, large numbers of NFL players engaged in a protest whereby they kneeled during the national anthem. This was the same form of protest former NFL quarterback Colin Kaepernick conducted alone the year before. To some, this was a free expression of First Amendment rights, protesting policies and positions of the government specifically regarding race. To others, including President Trump, who weighed in calling for the protesting players to be punished, it was a sign of disrespect to the flag and the military. Understanding the meaning of the protest required an appreciation for context. Despite being allowable under the First Amendment, why was or why wasn't this protest the "best" way to get the players' message across? Was President Trump's response appropriate? What could have promoted more dialogue, if anything?

Repeating

Although there is no dictionary that helps us discern the meaning of nonverbal actions and messages, we can often infer what they mean through their immediate context, or how they are used. One aspect of that context can be when a nonverbal message follows a verbal statement. This can occur when we say hello and then extend our hand for a handshake. We may also refer to a person and then point at them, or state a location and then motion in the direction that we referenced. When our physical actions that follow verbal messages reinforce what is said, we are using the repeating function of nonverbal communication. Nonverbal messages that repeat verbal messages can serve a wide array of purposes for us, and often we do not think about them as repeating when we use them.

REPEATING

the function of nonverbal communication whereby the physical actions that follow verbal messages reinforce what is said

Accenting

One of the most powerful aspects of nonverbal communication is that we do not have to always wait until we finish speaking to take advantage of it. Often, we can use nonverbal behaviors while we are speaking to help get a point across, underscore the importance of a statement, or express an emotional dimension of a message. When we use nonverbal behaviors to augment a message while we deliver it, we are using them to accent the verbal meaning we sent. Public speakers sometimes pound a podium when making an important point, for example. Accenting verbal messages with nonverbal behaviors helps highlight parts of the message as important for the receiver and is a useful function in a host of situations.

ACCENTING

the function of nonverbal communication whereby nonverbal behaviors augment a message while it is delivered

Complementing

A third function of nonverbal communication that shares some qualities with accenting, but is different in that it is more subdued, is complementing. When the nonverbal behavior occurs at the same time as the message and displays the same content, then the nonverbal behavior complements the message. This is similar to accenting, in that the behavior and spoken message are consistent with each other; however, in accenting, the behavior is meant to increase the intensity of the message, whereas with complementing, there is no such amplification. We find nonverbal behaviors that complement messages in cases where people smile while saying hello, laugh while telling a funny story or joke, and cry when delivering sad or disappointing news. These behaviors do not increase the intensity of the message or repeat the message after it is spoken, but rather simultaneously display the same message as the verbal statement itself, thus complementing the content.

COMPLEMENTING

the function of nonverbal communication whereby nonverbal behavior occurring at the same time as the message displays the same content

Substituting

In some circumstances, we may not either want, or even be able to say, anything right away. In those situations, it does not mean we are restricted from communicating, because we can still send messages through our nonverbal behaviors. The function of nonverbal communication whereby our physical actions take the place of our verbal messages is called substituting. People substitute nonverbal behaviors for verbal messages quite

SUBSTITUTING

the function of nonverbal communication whereby physical actions take the place of verbal messages often. During conversations we issue head nods rather than saying, "I understand;" we smile to indicate we like someone, rather than saying it outright; and we shrug our shoulders when we don't know something. Even the University of Texas Longhorns have a hand gesture that symbolizes an affiliation with the school!

Regulating

Perhaps the most essential function performed by nonverbal communication relates to its ability to help order our interactions with others. We rely on nonverbal behaviors more than verbal ones to know when it is our turn to speak, ask questions, or when a conversation is over or beginning with someone else. The actions that govern the course of an interaction with another person perform the **regulating** function of nonverbal communication. These types of behaviors include things like raising your hand to speak, putting up a hand to stop someone from interrupting while you finish a statement, or pausing in a conversation after asking a question to indicate a response is desired. These nonverbal actions, and others, allow us to conduct conversations and dialogues with other people in a relatively orderly manner.

REGULATING

the actions that govern the course of an interaction with another person

Conflicting

Nonverbal communication is not an exact science, and ensuring our actions correspond to our words the way we intend them to is not an easy task. As a result, we sometimes issue verbal messages that say one thing, while employing nonverbal communication that indicates another. When this happens, our nonverbal communication serves a **conflicting** function, and it can create, at minimum, confusion between the sender and receiver. In interpersonal relationships, we can smile and laugh with a date, and even say to her or him that we would like to get together again—except our nonverbal behaviors can indicate the opposite is true. In less awkward moments, we might say to turn right but point to the left. These conflicting messages present barriers to effective communication and underscore both the important role our nonverbal communication plays in creating meaning and sending messages, and how difficult they are to control.

CONFLICTING

when a verbal message says one thing while corresponding nonverbal communication indicates something different

TYPES OF NONVERBAL COMMUNICATION

Many people believe that nonverbal communication is simply about hand gestures and facial expressions, but those are only two small aspects of the larger realm of nonverbal communication. Recall the definition from the beginning of the chapter: elements of communication that do not involve words, but nevertheless transmit messages. This encompasses more than just how we use our hands or express emotions through our face. It actually involves things like how we treat time, decorate our personal space, and even the clothes we choose to wear. All in all, there are eight different types of nonverbal communication and in this part of the chapter we will describe each of them in turn.

Kinesics

The first type of nonverbal communication we will discuss is the one with which most people are typically familiar. Kinesics refers to nonverbal behaviors related to the movement of the body. These include everything from gestures, which are physical movements used to convey a message, to how we frame and orient our body to another person or audience, or our posture. See Table 6.1 for a brief list of gestures commonly used to express emotions. We'll talk more specifically about gestures in the chapter on delivery.

Gesture	Emotion Conveyed
Smile	Joy, happiness
Frown	Sadness, disappointment
Grimace	Pain, displeasure
Open arms	Friendliness, fondness
Furrowed brow	Confusion, anger
Tapping fingers	Nervousness, boredom

TABLE 6.1 Gestures Used to Express Emotions

Our posture also sends messages to the other party. If we have an open posture, or have the majority of our body facing the audience or other person, we indicate interest and attention. On the other hand, if we have a closed posture in which we shield our body from the other person, it can indicate not only lack of interest, but also possibly fear. Additionally, people have a tendency to mirror, or replicate, the posture of the other person when they are interested in them and believe they are interested as well. Whether it is through gestures, posture, or eye contact, kinesics can serve a variety of purposes for the messages we convey, and they come in several different forms: emblems, illustrators, affect displays, regulators, and adaptors. We'll reference posture in the chapter on delivery as well and how it can be used effectively.

- Emblems are the relatively small number of nonverbal behaviors that can usually be correctly translated into words. Examples of emblems include shaking hands, pumping a fist, or holding up one's hand.

KINESICS
nonverbal behaviors related to the movement of the body

OPEN POSTURE
the posture achieved when the majority of one's body faces the audience or other person

CLOSED POSTURE
the posture achieved when one shields his or her body from the other person

MIRROR
the practice of replicating the posture of the other person to indicate mutual interest

Nonverbal behaviors not only provide essential context for making sense of verbal statements, they convey messages in their own right. Communicators ignore the nonverbal signals at their own peril.

—Judee Burgoon, University of Arizona

- Illustrators serve to emphasize a spoken message, and include things like pounding a fist on a table, nodding your head while saying something you wish to stress, or furrowing your brow when asking a question.

- Affect displays are displays of emotions through the use of our bodies, and manifest in a variety of different ways. We might jump up and down when excited, laugh when happy, cry when sad, or change our position toward the other person when we are upset.

- Kinesics often serve the regulating function of nonverbal communication. We indicate turn taking in conversations by raising our eyebrows or holding out our hands. This defines a regulator. We also use it to order classroom participation by raising hands and pointing to who might speak.

- Adaptors are nonverbal behaviors that work to satisfy bodily needs, but may create confusion in others when used. Think about shifting your position in a chair when it is uncomfortable, something that another person might interpret as your desire to end the conversation. Using adaptors frequently can lead to the perception that you are nervous or even being dishonest.[4]

Oculesics

OCULESICS
the use of eye contact to send messages

Related to kinesics is the use of eye contact to send messages, something researchers also refer to as oculesics. We use eye contact to convey interest or lack of interest in another person, respect or disdain for the person or her or his message, and a host of other emotions, attitudes, and thoughts. In Western cultures like the United States, maintaining eye contact is seen as a sign of respect and attention, while in other cultures it is interpreted as aggressive and negative. When dating, we show our interest in the other person through how we look at them. The eyes are, as the saying goes, truly "the windows to the soul."

Proxemics

PROXEMICS
how we use space to convey information

Whereas kinesics and oculesics involve the use of our bodies to send a message, proxemics involves how we use space to convey information. A person's use of space can say a lot about her or his identity, interest in another person, personality, and power. Edward T. Hall, the researcher responsible for coining the term "proxemics," also identified four *distance zones* that are typically used by Western cultures. Each zone invites a particular interpretation of how a person views and is viewed by others.

Intimate distance. This zone stretches from touching to about a foot and a half apart. This is what most people consider their own space. Encroachment on this space by those who are not invited to do so can create a high degree of defensiveness, discomfort, and even aggression. It is a space typically reserved for those with whom a person is intimate.

Personal distance. This space extends from a foot and a half to about four feet apart and generally indicates friendship or collegiality. For instance, when you walk with your friends to lunch, you do not walk hand in hand, but you are generally within a few feet of each other.

Social distance. This zone stretches from about four feet to twelve feet apart and is an area that people with whom we have little to no connection might pass through. We might conduct business transactions in this zone, but it is not the place where we keep our intimate or personal friends.

Public distance. From twelve feet on, the distance conveys a formal situation. Teachers and presenters speak to audiences at this distance, and it conveys a very professional and formal atmosphere with little personal association. At this distance, some might feel the speaker could be cold and uninterested, which is a risk, particularly for those in the teaching profession.[5]

Haptics

One of the behaviors that occurs within intimate space is touching, and the study of how touch expresses meaning to others is called haptics. Different types of touch can serve to amplify a verbal message, reinforce it, and even at times contradict it, but the one constant is that touch is key for sending emotional dimensions of a message to another person—perhaps more so than any other form of nonverbal communication. It may come as no surprise that touch is closely related to a baby's attachment to a caregiver, particularly a mother. We also use touch to exert control, convey emotion, and express an affiliation with another person, and the meaning and values placed on expressing messages through touch are culturally driven. Perhaps the most obvious way touch conveys messages occurs when partners or parents hold hands, kiss, or hug to display their love for one another.[6]

Chronemics

Not all nonverbal communication relates to tangible objects like the body and space. One abstract way in which we send nonverbal communication involves time. Chronemics is the branch of nonverbal communication that involves how people treat, value, react to, and structure time. In terms of their use of time, people typically fall into one of two chronemic categories: monochronic and polychronic. Monochronic people like to do things one at a time, break their time up into small manageable units in a schedule, and value promptness. Polychronic people, on the other hand, tend to try and do several tasks at the same time, tend to keep much more fluid schedules, and are not particularly concerned about whether someone is "on time." Whether someone is monochromic or polychromic is influenced heavily by culture. For a list of differences between monochronic and polychronic people, see Table 6.2 on the following page.

HAPTICS
the study of how touch expresses meaning

CHRONEMICS
the branch of nonverbal communication that involves how people treat, value, react to, and structure time

MONOCHRONIC
the category of chronemics marked by liking to do things one at a time, breaking time up into small, manageable units

POLYCHRONIC
the category of chronemics marked by trying to do several tasks at the same time and having a more fluid approach to scheduling time

Monochronic People	Polychronic People
Do one thing at a time	Do many things at once
Concentrate on the job	Are highly distractible and subject to interruptions
Take time commitments (deadlines, schedules) seriously	Consider an objective to be achieved, if possible
Are low-context and need information	Are high-context and already have information
Committed to the job	Are committed to people and human relationships
Adhere religiously to plans	Change plans often and easily
Are concerned about not disturbing others; follow rules of privacy and consideration	Are more concerned with those who are closely related than with privacy
Show great respect for private property; seldom borrow or lend	Borrow and lend things often and easily
Emphasize promptness	Base promptness on the relationship
Are accustomed to short-term relationships	Have a strong tendency to build lifetime relationships

TABLE 6.2 Differences Between Monochronic and Polychronic People

The use of time conveys emotions and indicates what a person values. For instance, who you choose to spend your time with shows how you feel about people and how you prioritize them in your life. The treatment of time also functions as a regulatory expression of nonverbal communication through the allowance of turntaking in conversations. Respecting another person's desire to respond and not "hogging the air" illustrates an understanding of time in a conversation and the right all people have to a share of that time. Noted communication scholar Dr. Dawna Ballard has done some interesting work on the concept of work/life balance and found that although time management may make us feel more comfortable, it does not necessarily make us more productive—managing our attention, however, does influence productivity![7]

Olfactics

OLFACTICS

the dimension of nonverbal communication related to smell

Another nonverbal aspect of communication that does not involve the body or space is olfactics, the dimension of nonverbal communication related to smell. As with all nonverbal messages, the meanings attached to smells differ by culture. For example, some cultures do not cover up the odors their body produces because it is understood as a natural phenomenon, while other cultures go to great effort to cover up scents. A person's sense of smell is directly tied to his or her memory, and certain aromas can create an inviting and relaxing atmosphere because they remind someone of home or the beach, while other smells create a negative reaction in a person based on bad experiences or memories. These memories, in turn, influence the perception a person has regarding another individual or situation. Smells are most often unintentional messages, but they help people create meaning nonetheless.

Vocalics

The final type of nonverbal communication we will discuss is often confused with verbal communication because it emanates from people's vocal chords and mouths, but it is not verbal because it does not involve words. **Vocalics** are those things that contribute to the maintenance or creation of sound in your voice that help to convey meaning. These are not language, but rather a nonverbal element closely tied to how we send verbal messages to others. Our vocalics can help to express emotions, attitudes, and interest in subjects or people. There are several different types of vocalics: volume, tone, rate, vocalized pauses, and gasps and sighs.

VOCALICS
those things that contribute to the maintenance or creation of sound in your voice that help to convey meaning

Volume. Volume refers to how loud or soft a person's voice is. When someone is quiet, we might infer they are shy or perhaps not interested in the subject. When they are loud, we might see it as an expression of excitement or perhaps anger.

Understanding Dialogic Nonverbal Communication

Understanding and respecting how others use time and space is a key component to creating and sustaining positive relationships with them. Even when people do not have the same understanding of time or keep their living spaces the same way we do, it does not mean that their approach is necessarily wrong. In an episode of the hit television sitcom *The Big Bang Theory*, Sheldon Cooper, played by Jim Parsons, makes the mistake of inferring that his neighbor Penny is crying out for someone to help her clean her apartment when he notices it is in tremendous disarray. Unable to allow this to continue, and unable to accept that his neighbor has a dirty apartment, Sheldon ultimately sneaks into her apartment in the middle of the night and cleans it for her. This enrages Penny, who was obviously not seeking the assistance Sheldon believed she needed. Here we see the ambiguity of meaning inherent in Penny's use of space, as well as the imposition of Sheldon's own way of interpreting events. If he saw her apartment as dirty, he assumed that she must be dirty as well. The results caused a serious confrontation between Sheldon and Penny.

s_bukley / Shutterstock.com

Tone. Tone is the emphasis we place on syllables, sounds, words, and phrases that results in the overall sense of "warmth" and interest in our voice. Monotone delivery of a message that has little or no variation might both convey and create disinterest in a subject. In fact, research on tone indicates people find those who speak in a monotone voice unattractive.[8] Tonal variation can enhance our audience's interest, convey our own interest in the subject, and add an emotional quality to what we are saying.

Rate. Rate refers to how fast you deliver a message. When people speak too fast we might infer they are trying to deceive us, but there are also cultural components that impact the rate at which we speak. For instance, people in the Northeast speak much more quickly than those who live in the southern part of the United States. The average rate of speech is around 150 words per minute, but certain circumstances influence whether we speak slower or faster than that.[9,10]

Vocalized pauses. There are two types of pauses: silent and vocalized. Silent pauses occur when there is a momentary cessation of any sound, while vocalized pauses occur when people use sounds and words like "uh," "um," and "y'know" to fill the void. Excessive use of vocalized pauses might create a perception in the audience that you do not know what you are talking about or are an incompetent speaker, while the strategic use of silent pauses can enhance your credibility and give the audience time to catch up to you.

Gasps and sighs. One final type of vocalic is the use of breath to convey a message. We do this through gasps and sighs. Gasps usually indicate surprise or fear, while sighs demonstrate frustration or even that a person is tired and uncomfortable.

We employ vocalics whenever we speak, but how and to what end people use different levels of volume, tone, rate, or pausing is, as with all of nonverbal communication, tied to cultural expectations.

Artifacts

ARTIFACTS
objects used to communicate information about yourself to those around you

The eighth type of nonverbal communication takes place through artifacts. Artifacts are objects used to communicate information about yourself to those around you. They express your attitudes, feelings, mood, beliefs, interests, hobbies and even ideology. For example, how people dress gives clues to the other person or audience about what they value, how they interpret the situation, and what type of personality they have. Consider the meaning people place on tattoos or the concept of the "power tie." How you look conveys a great deal of information for others to interpret. Artifacts are also prominent in dorm rooms, living spaces, and offices. People who keep a desk between them and the visitor's chair might be seen as rigid and authoritative, while those with a more open setup typically are seen as warmer. What we surround ourselves with, what we wear, and even the colors with which we choose to decorate ourselves and our environment reveals a great deal about us without saying a word.

GUIDELINES FOR DIALOGIC NONVERBAL COMMUNICATION

A dialogic environment is not simply built on verbal messages, but nonverbal ones as well. Recall that genuineness is a component of dialogue, and we are neither genuine nor civil with others when our nonverbal messages contradict what we say. We perceive others as being deceptive when we see inconsistencies in a person's verbal message and nonverbal behaviors. Nonverbal communication can also be a source of confusion for people because its meaning is so ambiguous. To help you navigate the complexities and vagaries of nonverbal communication, we will now provide five guidelines for creating and maintaining a dialogic environment through nonverbal communication.

Ask Clarifying Questions

Nonverbal behaviors can vary in their meaning, and we all might interpret the same action differently. We can remove ambiguity from our interpretations by asking a person what a specific action meant to her or him. If someone furrows her brow while you explain a topic, you might want to ask her if she is following along. She may be confused, and you will not be able to adapt appropriately unless you ask. Asking what people mean by their facial expressions, use of touch, or even how they have their office structured can help to gain clarity

---

International Culture of Decorum

One of the most significant challenges for American professionals travelling abroad is adjusting to the different treatment accorded to time in other cultures. In most parts of the United States, there is a high value placed on punctuality and timeliness. It is generally expected that meetings will begin at the time they are scheduled, and that everyone will be there at the agreed upon time. Additionally, meetings in American culture typically are task oriented, hence the phrase "Let's get down to business." In some Latin American and European cultures, however, the value is placed less on time and more on relationship building. People can typically run late to meetings without any negative connotation to their tardiness, and the initial meetings typically contain less "business" and more socializing. This is because these cultures value interpersonal connections and getting to know those with whom they do business. So, when trying to expand or develop business interests with people from these cultures, it is also just as important to build personal interests.

about the meaning inherent in those nonverbal expressions. Clarity is essential for creating understanding and a comfortable communication climate between two parties.

Don't Assume Others Understand

Just as we may need to ask clarifying questions of others regarding their nonverbal expressions, we must be ready to answer those same questions from others. Additionally, we must understand the ambiguity of nonverbal behaviors and appreciate that others may infer something other than we intend in what we do. Finally, this guideline should serve as a caution not to use excessive nonverbal communication with people you don't know well, as they lack the experience to accurately infer your meaning in those expressions. Do not expect others to understand what your nonverbal expressions mean.

Control Your Nonverbal Reactions

Practicing self-restraint and self-monitoring are key elements of establishing a dialogue that must be practiced with nonverbal and verbal communication. We may insult someone by grimacing or laughing at the wrong time during an interaction, and we may also express interest when none exists if we do not monitor and restrain our nonverbal reactions. This is not to say you should not have any nonverbal reactions, for that is impossible, but you should monitor your physical reactions so they do not reveal what you might be feeling or thinking at times when it is inappropriate to share that information.

Use Situationally Appropriate Nonverbal Expressions

Not every situation allows you to express your thoughts or feelings as directly as others might, so you must stay tuned into the context of the interaction to know what is appropriate and what is not. For instance, if you interview for a position with a company and know the person who is conducting the interview, should you greet them with a hug or handshake? If you arrive at the office of a professor for an unannounced visit, do you walk right in and sit down, or do you knock and wait to be invited in? Do you end a first date with a kiss, hug, or high five? The situation dictates the nonverbal expression that is most appropriate, and so it is important to be aware of what would be expected in a given circumstance and act accordingly.

Learn Cultural Differences in Meaning

As we have noted throughout the chapter, different cultures give different meanings to various nonverbal expressions. Learning those meanings and what might be expected is essential for successful communication in intercultural interactions. Do not behave in an ethnocentric manner and expect the other party to understand your nonverbal expressions and values, and don't hold others to behaving the same way you do. Understand the cultural expectations and behaviors as best as you can before entering into the situation. In some international businesses, this can mean the difference between closing a deal and closing off an opportunity.

SUMMARY

In this chapter, we explored the complex nature of nonverbal communication and discussed the various forms through which we send messages without words. We provided three foundational principles of nonverbal expression and detailed the six functions nonverbal messages perform in our lives. Then we explained the eight different types of nonverbal communication before concluding with five guidelines for effectively using nonverbal communication to create a dialogic environment.

CHAPTER 6 KEY IDEAS

* Nonverbal communication conveys emotional and relationship information, maintains a relationship with verbal messages, and has meaning that is based on the context.

* Nonverbal communication can serve six different functions: repeating, accenting, complementing, substituting, regulating, and conflicting.

* There are eight different types of nonverbal communication: kinesics, oculesics, proxemics, haptics, chronemics, olfactics, vocalics, and artifacts.

CHAPTER 6 KEY TERMS

Nonverbal communication	Kinesics	Chronemics
Repeating	Open posture	Monochronic
Accenting	Closed posture	Polychronic
Complementing	Mirror	Olfactics
Substituting	Oculesics	Vocalics
Regulating	Proxemics	Artifacts
Conflicting	Haptics	

ACTIVITIES AND DISCUSSION QUESTIONS

1. Watch Allan Pease's TEDx talk, "Body Language, the Power Is in the Palm of Your Hands," which is available online at https://www.youtube.com/watch?v=ZZZ7k8cMA-4. How can you be more conscious about the messages that you are sending and the impression that you are creating with your body language?

2. Watch Lin-Manuel Miranda's sonnet that he delivered as his acceptance speech after winning a Tony Award for the best original score for "Hamilton," available online https://www.washingtonpost.com/video/national/love-is-love-lin-manuel-miranda-delivers-sonnet-to-orlando-victims/2016/06/13/868c2974-3186-11e6-ab9d-1da2b0f24f93_video.html?utm_term=.818bd00dfd93. Which function of nonverbal communication is most utilized in his performance?

3. What nonverbal messages do the physical artifacts that you wear and carry with you communicate to others. Consider your clothes, bag, jewelry, makeup, hat, the things that you carry with you, etc. What messages are you trying to share with these artifacts? How might others interpret these artifacts?

4. In a group, ask one student to start silently acting out a role while everyone else watches closely. As others begin to figure out the situation being portrayed, they should join in playing other roles and responding to each other the way that they would in that situation. For example, the first person might begin by playing a saxophone, and others might join in playing other instruments in the band. In another scenario, someone might begin pitching a ball, and others might join in to portray a baseball game. To successfully create a scenario, all group members will need to carefully observe and respond to one another using only nonverbal cues.

7
LISTENING

Mark Twain once quipped, "If we were supposed to talk more than we listen we would have two tongues and one ear." Twain could not have hit the mark better if he tried, and the numbers bear this out. Just think, there is one of you, while there are numerous other people you interact with throughout your life. With that many different voices, you will naturally listen more than you speak. Still not sure? Studies have consistently found that people listen approximately 45 percent of the time, compared to speaking 30 percent of the time, reading 16 percent of the time, and writing a mere 9 percent of the time.[1] Clearly, listening is an essential part of being an effective communicator.

Listening is more complicated than people realize. Often, we confuse it with hearing, which is the physiological process of capturing sound conducted by the ears to the brain. Listening, however, as defined by the International Listening Association, is "an information processing task carried out in a social, interactive, or communicative environment."[2] More succinctly, listening is the process of receiving and interpreting spoken or nonverbal messages. Listening, therefore, is communicative, while hearing is physiological. Hearing is something our bodies do, while listening is a skill we can develop and improve. Moreover, listening is often reported as one of, if not the most, important skills people need in society today. In this chapter, we will first determine what listening is by dispelling some common

HEARING
the physiological process of capturing sound conducted by ears to the brain

LISTENING
the process of receiving and interpreting spoken and/or nonverbal messages

misconceptions people have about it as well as present a model for the listening process. We will then explain the different purposes listening serves for us, and the primary types of listening we use to achieve those ends. Third, we will cover the challenges we face to using effective and accurate listening in a variety of communication situations. Finally, we will provide tips for how to engage in listening that encourages others to speak, which you will recall is one of the core components of dialogue.

LISTENING MYTHS

Listening is perhaps the most misunderstood element of the communication process. People often feel that since they have been listening most of their life then they know how to do it. The fact of the matter is that in the traditional education system we do very little to train students how to listen properly, and yet it is one of the most fundamental skills for being a good communicator. Listening is more than just receiving sounds; it is an important and complex cognitive process that is difficult to master. In this section, we will examine six common misconceptions people typically have about listening.

The Importance of Dialogic Listening

According to the National Institute of Deafness and Other Communication Disorders (NIDCD), roughly 17 percent of Americans report some form of hearing loss. Additionally, roughly 15 percent of Americans between the ages of 20-69 experience hearing loss due to exposure to loud sounds at work or during leisure time.[3] Those who are born deaf enter into a very specific subculture in society, one with several different languages (in the U.S. it is often American Sign Language) and its own university (Gallaudet University in Washington, DC). Among this group is an even more special subset. The Hearing Health Foundation reports that roughly 60 percent of combat veterans who return from Iraq and Afghanistan return home with hearing loss, making it the number one war wound.[4] Hearing loss can significantly impact a person's ability to acquire language skills and socialize because they can feel as if others are not listening to them. However impaired their hearing, a person with hearing loss can still listen and be listened to because listening is a communicative process, not simply a physiological activity.

Listening Is the Same as Hearing

People often mistakenly treat listening and hearing as synonymous. People who are hearing impaired have some form of physical obstruction or structural difference in their ear that impedes the reception of sound. This can be mitigated in some cases with hearing aids, cochlear implants, or even surgery. On the other hand, when people are not good listeners, it has nothing to do with a physical challenge and more to do with difficulties in concentrating. Listening is, therefore, a skill that can be developed and improved through practice and effort.

"I'm a Good Listener"

Just because you listen more than you perform any other communicative behavior does not mean you are good at it. In fact, people tend to overestimate how good they are at listening, and underestimate how good others are at listening. This basically means everyone thinks they are better listeners than everyone else—something that cannot be true. When we believe we are good at something, we tend not to work at it, and so when we overestimate our own listening abilities, we don't work to improve our listening skills. This is a cycle that creates poor listeners. The only way to break the cycle is to work at being a better listener.

Effective Listening Is Hard to Learn

The skills needed to be a good listener are not that hard to learn or understand, but the challenge is putting them into consistent practice. There are a lot of distractions that keep us from implementing good listening behaviors consistently. To that end, the most important ability to develop for good listening is concentration and attention. When we can train ourselves to focus and not be easily distracted, good listening comes quite easily. Later in this chapter, we will provide you with some guidelines for behaviors that will help you improve your listening ability, and you will see they are not difficult, but making them a habit is the real test.

Intelligent People Are Better Listeners

There are several problems with this notion, not the least of which is the poor definition of intelligence. Psychologist Howard Gardner has levied some fairly groundbreaking criticisms of IQ tests and how they privilege only two types of knowledge acquisition over the many other ways people learn,[5] while using things like college or advanced degrees to determine intelligence are obviously problematic as a measurement of intelligence. Additionally, the more people believe they know, the more they typically want to speak—not listen.

There is, however, a correlation between people who are emotionally intelligent and their listening ability. **Emotional intelligence** is defined as the ability a person has to assess, identify, and manage his or her own emotions, while also appreciating and responding to the emotions of others in a civil manner. Those with high emotional intelligence are other-centered and consequently better listeners than those who cannot pay attention and respect

EMOTIONAL INTELLIGENCE
the ability a person has to assess, identify, and manage his or her own emotions, while also appreciating and responding to the emotions of others in a civil manner

the feelings and emotions of their audiences or conversational partners.[6] So, emotional intelligence is related to listening ability, while intellect is not.

Older People Are Better Listeners

Although we increasingly encounter situations where we need to exercise our listening skills as we get older, age does not automatically improve our ability to listen. With age comes habits, and these can be either good or bad. If we practice good listening skills earlier in life and incorporate them into our communicative repertoire, then we will be better listeners as we get older. If, however, we practice poor listening skills, those habits will be difficult to break as we get older. Put simply, age has little to do with our listening skills.

Women Are Better Listeners than Men

RAPPORT TALK

language meant to develop relationships and exchange emotional information

REPORT TALK

the exchange of information, solutions, and problem-solving strategies

Our listening capacities do not depend on gender or sex. Instead, research tells us that women and men at least perceive themselves to communicate differently, and one approach is not necessarily better than the other. According to scholar Deborah Tannen, women tend to communicate through **rapport talk**, or language meant to develop relationships and exchange emotional information. Women have reported that they listen more in a people-oriented way than men, meaning they listen with the intention of making a connection with the other person. Men, on the other hand, tend to engage in **report talk**, or the exchange of information, solutions, and problem-solving strategies. Men have reported that when they listen to messages, they are more content-oriented instead of people-oriented, which leads them to listen to more of the substance of a message versus the emotions or relationship elements. So, while men and women might listen with different orientations, neither approach is necessarily objectively better than the other.[7]

As you can see, there are many erroneous perceptions regarding listening. Listening is also not a one-size-fits-all concept, as there are different purposes for which we listen and different types of listening in which we engage. In the next part of the chapter, we will explain the process of listening as well as explore these purposes for and types of listening.

THE PROCESS OF LISTENING

HURIER MODEL

the six steps of listening

Listening is a process rather than a single act, meaning it involves several steps, or what Judi Brownell represented through the **HURIER model**[8] (See Figure 7.1 on the next page). The first step in listening is taking in cues, or hearing (H). This is where the sounds or words are first experienced by the listener. We hear or take in a lot of cues throughout our day, but that does not constitute listening. We must move on to the next step, understanding (U), in order to listen.

Understanding involves making sense of the cues we take in through our ears, eyes, or even fingers (when reading in braille). If you've ever heard someone speak a different language that you didn't know, then you realize the importance of this part of the listening process. We can't truly be listening unless we can understand the words a person is using, but we can try to by asking them questions and/or learning to speak their language.

FIGURE 7.1   HURIER Model

The third step is remembering (R). You must be able to store information you gain through interaction as well as retrieve it later. Just think of an example of when a supervisor is giving feedback to an employee. The employee has to be able to take in their supervisor's comments and recall them later if they want to ask follow-up questions. If they aren't really listening, then that will not happen. Remembering is a key point in the listening process, and most people don't do it very well. In fact, most people recall very little of the specifics of what they hear, which is why we sometimes use "hacks" to help us in the future, like associating someone's name with an image (e.g., Drew with someone drawing a picture) or creating an acronym (e.g., the HURIER model is one!).

The next stage is interpreting (I). Here you take in all the cues (verbal and nonverbal) and make meaning out of them. Given the unique combination of cues in a situation, you will come to your interpretation of a person's message. For example, your mother says, "Take out the trash." Depending on her tone of voice and eye contact, you might interpret her message as either forceful and directive or as tentative and questioning. It is important to consider at this stage if you automatically assume the meaning of someone's message or if you are carefully considering the specific cues in the conversation as well as cultural and contextual factors.

The second to last stage of the listening process is evaluating (E). This is where you make a judgment about the truth-value of a message. Here you make a distinction between opinion and fact, for example. An important step in society today, evaluating a message can mean the difference between being "duped" and being a critical thinker.

The last stage in the process is responding (R). At this point, the listener signals to the other person that they have received the message, or what is commonly called giving feedback. Responding can take many forms, both nonverbal and verbal, and can range from more passive responses (e.g., silence, nodding your head) to more active responses, such as giving advice or criticism. It is important to consider your responses to a given situation and try to "match" them to the other person's messages. Giving advice, for example, can be seen as face-threatening and the other person might become defensive. Asking questions about and/ or paraphrasing what you think they are saying can go a long way to making the best choice in your listening response.

WHY AND HOW WE LISTEN

Listening allows us to tune in to the world around us, and the information we gather through listening helps form our perceptions of people, places, objects, and ideas. There are four primary purposes listening serves in this respect. These range from listening for enjoyment, to listening to glean information. In this part of the chapter, we will discuss each in turn. We will also explain the difference between the two ways we process information when we listen.

Listening Purposes

We do not always engage in listening for the same reasons. Just as we have several purposes for speech, we also have multiple purposes for listening. There are four primary purposes for which we use listening, and each can manifest in any type of communication situation, whether it is an interpersonal environment, a speech, or in a small group context. It all depends on what you want to focus on and what you hope to retain or achieve in that moment. To that end, it is important to know why you are listening and what you hope to get out of the event, because that will help you identify your listening purpose.

LISTENING FOR APPRECIATION
listening for enjoyment; it is not high in cognitive commitment

Listening for appreciation. The first reason we engage in listening is for appreciation. When we **listen for appreciation**, our goal is to enjoy something on which we focus our attention. The most common examples of this type of listening are listening to music while driving or working out, listening to dialogue in a movie or television show, listening to a comedian on the radio, and listening to a story told by a friend. There is not a high degree of cognitive effort when we listen for appreciation. The goal here is to have fun with what you are listening to, and not necessarily to understand the motives behind what is said or to disagree with what the other party may be proposing.

LISTENING FOR COMPREHENSION
listening to understand and learn something new; requires a significant degree of mental effort

Listening for comprehension. The second reason we listen is to comprehend or understand something. When we **listen for comprehension**, we want to understand something we do not know so that we can learn something new. We engage in comprehension listening when we take a class and listen to a lecture, go through orientation with a new employer, and even when we meet someone new and they share information about themselves. This type of listening requires more mental effort than appreciative listening, and the goal is not necessarily enjoyment, but rather understanding.

LISTENING TO SHOW SUPPORT
listening to a speaker to make him or her feel valued and to show the person we care about what he or she has to say

Listening to show support. The third reason we listen is to **show support** in a relationship. When we listen to show support, we are listening to someone else because we want the other person to feel like they are valued and that we care about what this person has to say.

The goal in this type of listening is to develop or maintain a relationship and to demonstrate how much we care about the other person. When we listen as someone tells us about her day, share in a friend's good news, or lend a sympathetic ear to someone who needs to vent about a tough situation, we are listening to show support for that relationship.

Critical listening. The fourth and final purpose listening serves is criticism, but not in the form of negative attacks on someone else. Critical listening is when we evaluate a message and assess whether or not we agree with what is said. When we listen critically, we also are open to disagreeing with a part or even all of a message, yet we take in everything offered by the other side before making our judgment. To do this requires the largest degree of cognitive effort of any listening purpose. We may listen critically to a political speech, a proposal for weekend plans by friends, and sometimes lectures on controversial topics or materials.

CRITICAL LISTENING
listening to evaluate a message and assess whether or not we agree with what is said; requires the most cognitive effort of any listening purpose

Two Ways We Listen

Regardless of what our goal is with listening, we use listening in one of two different ways. The first is active listening, which occurs when we pay a high degree of attention to a message. We process, store, and potentially evaluate the content of the message to reach conclusions or an understanding about what was said. We usually show that we are actively listening by using eye contact and facial expressions to respond to the message, and perhaps also by leaning in or nodding. We use active listening at times for each of the four purposes we just explained.

ACTIVE LISTENING
listening with a high degree of attention to a message; we process, store, and potentially evaluate the content of the message to come to conclusions or an understanding about what was said

We might be watching a murder mystery or someone may be telling us a very engaging story about a trip they just took, and we pay those messages a great deal of attention because we want to understand or evaluate what is being relayed to us. That would constitute active listening for appreciation. Active listening for comprehension or criticism would involve paying attention so you completely understand what is said and can either integrate it into your own body of knowledge (comprehension) or determine whether you agree with what was proposed or not (criticism). For example, you might be transitioning into a new position and thus you need to listen to the details of your new job so you understand what you need to do. On the other hand, when we listen to political speeches, we might try and focus on the proposal and how it might impact our own life so we can make a judgment regarding whether or not we support the candidate's ideas.

The second way we might listen is passively. Passive listening occurs when we do not engage the topic in any noticeable way and just try to absorb what is said. When we listen passively, we do not engage in much evaluation, nor do we question our own understanding of what is said. Most listening for appreciation is passive listening, but you can also see examples of passively listening for comprehension or criticism when you look around a classroom and see people who do not participate, take notes or ask questions about the content. Passive listening can be risky, because you elevate the chances of daydreaming and losing your ability to follow the speaker.

PASSIVE LISTENING
listening without engaging the topic in any noticeable way, trying only to absorb what is said

Regardless of which listening purpose we try to achieve and whether we do so actively or passively, we do not always listen the way we want to, and sometimes we fail to listen at all. In the next part of this chapter, we will unpack several different behaviors people may mistakenly think are listening.

NONLISTENING

NONLISTENING

providing the appearance of listening without actually paying attention to the message

Due to the high degree of cognitive effort involved in effective listening, we cannot maintain it for long periods of time. Just like exercise, we tire out after a while. We often try to hide the fact we lost focus on the message by maintaining an appearance of attention without the actual attention. We sometimes spot others engaging in these behaviors , but it is very hard to prevent ourselves from falling into the trap—especially if a conversation is lengthy. When we do this, we are engaging in nonlistening. Nonlistening typically takes six different forms, which we will now examine.

Pseudolistening

PSEUDOLISTENING

the practice of hiding our inattention by appearing to actually listen through nonverbal and verbal responses that make it appear as though we understand what is being said

One of the most common forms of nonlistening occurs when we hide our inattention by appearing to actually listen, a process called pseudolistening. We all have either done this or noticed someone doing this in a conversation when they nod or offer some other simple response like "yeah" to appear as though they are processing what is said, but then are unable to repeat what was said. This form of deceptive interaction looks like listening, and even sounds like listening, but it is not listening. This also negatively impacts the ability to have a dialogue because without someone's full attention, true understanding cannot be achieved—although the speaker may believe it has occurred because of the "yeah" statements by the pseudolistener.

Much of the exciting research in listening studies how the senses affect how well we listen and how we can make use of the powers of our brains to listen, use, and remember things. You can save yourselves a great deal of time, effort, and even money, if you work harder to listen throughout your life. The failure to listen results in lost friendships and lost resources.

—Melissa Beall, University of Northern Iowa

Glazing Over

Often called daydreaming, glazing over is when a person loses complete attention with what is going on around them and thinks about something else entirely. We notice people who glaze over when they stare blankly at us when we are speaking, or when they focus on something outside or in a different direction than where the message comes from. Glazing over might not initially appear as a negative behavior, but it can create feelings of frustration and even depression in the speaker because the speaker feels they are boring their conversational partner or audience. This can often come about when the message or story may not be very interesting to the person listening, or perhaps the listener has other more pressing concerns on his or her mind at the moment. Nevertheless, glazing over is not listening, and barely pretends to be.

A significant contributing factor to both glazing over and pseudolistening is the fact that we all have spare brain time. This is the gap between the roughly 150 words a minute we can speak, and the 650 words per minute we can mentally process. The gap creates openings for our brains to do something else, thus leading to opportunities for glazing over or turning our internal attention to something else.

Ambushing

Often times when we listen critically to a message, we focus only on the weaknesses of what the other person is saying and ignore the strengths of her or his position, thus we only hear what confirms our opinion. When we listen with a goal to attack the weak points of the other person, then we are not truly listening; we are ambushing the person. We are not processing and evaluating the other person's message in its totality and are simply seeking to argue. Sometimes we confuse ambushing with constructive criticism, but they are not the same because constructive criticism is offered in a way that takes the positive

GLAZING OVER
losing complete attention with what is going on and thinking about something else entirely, often staring in a different direction than the speaker

SPARE BRAIN TIME
the gap between the roughly 150 words a minute we can speak, and the 650 words per minute we can mentally process

AMBUSHING
the practice of focusing only on the weaknesses of what the other person is saying and ignoring the strengths of his or her position

---

Listening to Controversial Speakers

Imagine your university or college invites a controversial speaker to campus. You do not agree with the person's message but find that plenty of people on campus plan to attend. Now, consider why these individuals might want to attend and listen to the speaker. Could it be possible there are multiple purposes behind their attendance? How might you respond or engage these people in expressing your disagreement without assuming they all are attending for the same purpose or reason? Also, consider how often you decide not to listen to someone because you disagree with them.

and negative dimensions of a position into account and does not focus solely on the weak points. Ambushing does not promote collaboration or dialogue and often exacerbates interpersonal tension.

Prejudging

PREJUDGING

the practice of entering an interaction with a judgment about what we believe will be said before the person has a chance to present it

With today's technology, we can easily find out the background of a speaker with who we may not be familiar; we also know our friends and family members well, and so we tend to have an idea of what they will say when we get into discussions with them. This information can be useful, but when we use it to evaluate speakers and their message before they even have a chance to deliver it, then we prevent ourselves from listening. Even if we sit through the entire presentation or statement and do not interrupt or challenge what was said, we are not truly listening to our conversational partner if we simply hold to what we thought our partner was going to argue or say before they even spoke. When we enter an interaction with a judgment about what we believe will be said before the person has a chance to present it, we engage in prejudging, not listening. This eliminates any potential for dialogue, understanding, or relationship building.

Selective Listening

SELECTIVE
LISTENING

the practice of choosing what the main points are in a message regardless of what the speaker says

We do not always enter interactions with a closed mind and prejudgments rendered about the speaker and his or her message. Sometimes we stop listening in the middle of a statement because we believe we have heard the main points. When we do this, we stop listening to the entire message and filter out things we deem unimportant, regardless of whether or not the speaker believes those details are essential or interesting. This process of selective listening, where we choose what the main points are in a message regardless of what the speaker says, creates the potential for miscommunication, disagreement, and confusion. Listening is hard work, and using this shorthand that privileges your own listening abilities in a way that likely overestimates them tries to get around this cognitive effort. Remember that one of the fundamental misconceptions of listening is that we all believe we are better listeners than other people.

Advising

ADVISING

the practice of interrupting a person to offer suggestions and opinions in an effort to be helpful even when they were not sought

There are times when we want to support and help other people when they talk about problems or challenges they face, and this is only natural. But we must only offer advice in these situations when the person actually seeks it, and to make that determination we must listen attentively and fully. When we interrupt the person or offer suggestions and opinions when they were not sought, then we make the mistake of advising. We may believe this is being supportive, but it actually represents a form of nonlistening through which we did not pay attention to what other people were saying or what they were looking for from us. Offering advice in this situation ignores their message and illustrates ineffective listening in the guise of offering support.

It might seem like there are more ways not to listen effectively than there are to listen well, which might be true. Nevertheless, there are some good practices that will improve your listening skills and create a communication environment in which you can interact with others.

GUIDELINES FOR DIALOGIC LISTENING

Creating a dialogic environment necessarily involves treating listening as an important behavior. Not only must we focus on being good listeners, but we must also encourage and help others to do the same. As we have mentioned in this chapter, there are numerous challenges to effective listening, thus making it sound easier than it actually is. Knowing how to work on your listening skills and how to spot nonlistening in others will help you engage in dialogic communication and increase the chances that you and the person you converse with truly understand what is being discussed. In this last part of the chapter, we will provide you with six guidelines for improving your listening. These are in addition to the suggestions offered in the dialogue chapter, which as you recall, also focuses on listening behaviors.

We Hear What We Want to Hear

Copyright © 1997 Miramax/courtesy Everett Collection

In the Oscar-winning film *Good Will Hunting*, a judge sentences the title character to counseling after getting into a fight. Dr. Gerald Lambeau, Will's reluctant benefactor, sets Will up with a series of different counselors, and at each meeting Will interacts in a rude manner in order to not undergo therapy anymore. Finally, he meets Dr. Sean Maguire, played by Robin Williams, and again he enters with a preconceived notion of how the therapist will act, behave, and what he will care about. He proceeds to engage in a series of behaviors designed to have the same effect, but Maguire continues to see Will, played by Matt Damon. In one scene, Maguire tells Will a story about his late wife and how he met her by giving up tickets to the 1975 World Series. Initially, Will is focused more on the fact Maguire did not go to the game than the relationship that Maguire developed with his wife as a result of the decision. Will heard what he wanted to hear, and not what Maguire meant with his story. This scene thus serves as an example of selective listening exhibited by Will.

Stop Talking

This sounds trite and crude, but it is true. You cannot listen to the other person if you are talking. This includes when we talk over people, interrupt them, and even finish sentences for them. These all involve you talking, and therefore not listening, to the other party. When we speak, we are not listening to the other person, and when we speak a lot, we are both not giving the impression we care about the perspective of the other and also not providing them with the opportunity to share their thoughts. Being aware of the amount of time you spend talking and making a conscious effort to allow others to speak and finish their thoughts is a cornerstone of dialogue. So, the first, most basic guideline for listening effectively is to stop talking.

Make Listening a Goal

There are many different ways in which people can appear to be listening but actually aren't, so simply being quiet and not talking does not mean you are listening. Listening to the other person's message must be a conscious goal, and so we need to enter into interactions with a goal of listening to the other party. If we choose to spend time with another person, we should want to hear what the other person has to say, so we must work to be attentive and set a goal to listen well. This can be accomplished by making sure there are minimal distractions around when you are spending time with the person. Think about things like putting your phone away, stepping away from your computer, and even closing the door.

Remove Distractions

Given that so many things can interfere with our ability to listen, from noise, to other types of distractions, we must try to minimize these obstacles as best we can to create an opportunity for dialogue. Environmental obstacles can usually be resolved by moving to a quieter space or a room that keeps such distractions to a minimum. If you are not feeling well, this can also impede your ability to listen. If possible, changing the time of the meeting to one where you will be feeling better is a good course of action. Your own beliefs and attitudes can also prove to be significant impediments to listening effectively and accurately, so make sure you are in a positive frame of mind and willing to set aside personal biases to openly hear another person's message. None of these options are easy, nor are they always viable, but knowing what might distract you from listening and trying to mitigate its impact is a great step toward creating a comfortable, dialogic communication environment.

Listen for Ideas

There is no way you will be able to remember everything a person says. In fact, two concepts we covered earlier in the book tell us what we are most likely to remember from a message or interaction. Recall from the chapter on perception and the self that the recency effect suggests we will remember the most recent thing we hear, and the primacy effect suggests we will remember the first thing someone says. Rather than focusing on the first and last things a person says, we should try and listen for the ideas being presented and not the minute details surrounding those ideas. If you understand the ideas being presented, then you can understand the message even if you would use different words to express the same ideas.

Listen to the Nonverbals and Content

Content often gets the bulk of our attention, but content alone does not encompass the message someone sends—a point made clear in high context cultures. How someone says something can be just as important as what they say or do not say, so listening for tone, rate, and pitch and staying attuned to eye contact and other physical mannerisms can help you listen more closely to what the person is actually saying. If you get caught up trying to follow just the content of a speaker's message, you may miss out on nonverbal indicators they use to tell you what is truly important, whether they believe the message to be true or not.[9]

Focus on Agreement and Not Disagreement

When we listen to people make a case for something, we often listen for the things with which we disagree. This is a defensive position and a behavior that is hard to change. Instead of looking for what is different or that which you oppose in someone's statement, look for places of agreement. You might not agree with every point, but if you can find some common ground, it is possible to build from there and perhaps eventually find a compromise. Listening for agreement also lets the other person know you are listening with an open mind and not simply seeking to shut down the person or make the person appear as though they are wrong. This creates a relaxed environment where people become more open to expressing their ideas and thoughts with each other. When we just look for disagreement, that is all we will find, and we will not be able to change minds or move to common ground. This tactic requires you to be patient, open, genuine, and critical all at the same time.

SUMMARY

In this chapter, we delved into the concept of listening, a fundamental aspect of communication. We first dispelled six different misconceptions about listening and how it works. We then defined the four main purposes for listening and the two ways in which we listen. Next, we outlined the six different ways in which people appear to listen, but are not actually processing messages in their entirety, if at all. Finally, we provided six guidelines for developing good listening skills that encourage dialogue and effective communication.

CHAPTER 7 KEY IDEAS

- There are four purposes of listening: listening for appreciation, listening for comprehension, listening to show support, and critical listening.

- We engage in active listening when we pay a high degree of attention to the message, but we engage in passive listening when we just try to absorb what is being said without significant mental or conversational involvement.

- There are six types of nonlistening behaviors: pseudolistening, glazing over, ambushing, prejudging, selective listening, and advising.

CHAPTER 7 KEY TERMS

Hearing	Active listening
Listening	Passive listening
Emotional intelligence	Nonlistening
Rapport talk	Pseudolistening
Report talk	Glazing over
HURIER model	Spare brain time
Listening for appreciation	Ambushing
Listening for comprehension	Prejudging
Listening to show support	Selective listening
Critical listening	Advising

ACTIVITIES AND DISCUSSION QUESTIONS

1. Watch William Ury's TEDx talk, "The Power of Listening," which is available online at https://www.williamury.com/tedx-san-diego/. What are the reasons that he gives for why it is important to listen?

2. Watch Julian Treasure's TEDGlobal talk, "5 Ways to Listen Better," available online at https://www.ted.com/talks/julian_treasure_5_ways_to_listen_better?language=en. Try practicing each of the strategies that he recommends.

3. Which of the six nonlistening behaviors are you most often guilty of engaging in? How has that behavior impacted a recent conversation? How will you work to avoid this nonlistening behavior in a future conversation?

4. As a class, start with four volunteers. Ask two of the volunteers to leave the classroom. The first person should tell the second person a detailed story, and then sit down. Bring the third volunteer into the room. The second volunteer should tell the same story in the same way to the third volunteer, and the process should be

repeated with the fourth volunteer, who should re-tell the story for the entire class. Afterward, debrief what happened with each subsequent storytelling with the entire class. What type of listening did the volunteers engage in? Were they successful at listening and retelling the story? Which details were retained, and which were lost over the course of the storytelling exercise? What made some details more memorable than others?

RELATIONSHIP
DEVELOPMENT

Thus far, we have focused on the different dimensions of the communication process, a process that takes place in a variety of different contexts. Over several chapters, we turn our attention to one of those contexts: interpersonal relationships. Interpersonal relationships are close associations or acquaintances between two or more people. These relationships might be based on love, community or business interactions, friendship, family, or some other social commitment. In this chapter, we will first discuss what interpersonal relationships are and why they are an important part of our lives. Next, we will explain four theories about how relationships develop. Finally, we will suggest some guidelines for using dialogue to build and maintain strong interpersonal relationships.

CHARACTERISTICS OF INTERPERSONAL RELATIONSHIPS

Interpersonal relationships include relationships with friends, family, coworkers, neighbors, and others with whom we interact and feel a personal connection. Interpersonal relationships can include social relationships, which are informal, voluntary relationships such as acquaintances, coworkers, and casual friendships. We also have intimate relationships, which include relationships with romantic partners, family, and our closest friends. Interpersonal relationships are the foundation of communities and help fulfill some of our deepest needs, which we'll talk about in more detail in the chapter on communication in intimate relationships. In addition, because of their voluntary and sometimes fleeting nature,

INTERPERSONAL RELATIONSHIPS
close associations or acquaintances between two or more people; relationships might be based on love, community or business interactions, friendship, family, or some other social commitment

SOCIAL RELATIONSHIPS
informal, voluntary relationships such as acquaintances, coworkers, and casual friendships

we are more likely to treat social relationships like commodities that have costs and benefits. In this section of the chapter, we will highlight four characteristics of interpersonal relationships and illustrate how they serve fundamental and important purposes in our lives.

Create and Maintain Identity

IDENTITY

how we understand our own qualities, beliefs, values, and characteristics as unique or different from others

As we discussed earlier in the book, communication through language allows us to label ideas, concepts, objects, and just about anything else, thus giving it meaning. Language functions similarly when we decide to describe ourselves in a particular way and therefore give ourselves particular meaning. That meaning becomes a part of one's **identity**, or how we understand our own qualities, beliefs, values, and characteristics as unique or different from others. Our identities come from both how we see ourselves and how others see us, and both come from the communication within the social relationships we form with others. Put simply, we define ourselves through our associations with others.

Fulfill the Need to Belong

Psychologist Abraham Maslow proposed a hierarchy of human needs, and just above the base needs of shelter, safety, and food was what he identified as the need to belong.[1] We all have a deep need to be accepted by others, and this is accomplished by connecting with people through communication. We seek people who accept us for who we are, and we do the same for them. These social relationships become a source of self-esteem and stability in our lives. The need to be accepted and belong to a larger group is a core part of the human psyche, and communication allows us to create those bonds with other people in our daily lives. Sometimes we seek to belong to groups with similar interests, and sometimes we look for people who share certain experiences. The former of these is part of identifying with whom we wish to become friends, while the latter can have health benefits, as seen through organizations like Alcoholics Anonymous and Narcotics Anonymous.

Allow for the Creation of Communities

COMMUNITY

refers to both a specific place where people share certain characteristics or a feeling of fellowship with others who share attitudes, interests, and beliefs

It is no surprise that community and communication share the same Latin root word, *communis*,[2] because without the connections provided by communication we would not be able to create and live in communities. **Community** can refer to both a specific place where people share certain characteristics and communicate with one another, as well as a feeling of fellowship with others who share language, attitudes, interests, and beliefs. The formation of communities occurs when groups of people fulfill their needs to belong by finding in each other common characteristics and talking about them. Before the advent of media, communities were based mostly on the locations where people lived in close proximity to each other. Now we refer to communities in a variety of ways, some using demographic categories (e.g., The African American community, the LGBT community), while others use interests to bind groups, such as when people play video games together (e.g., Gaming community). One type of interest-community that has become quite popular is the CosPlay community. CosPlay refers to the practice of dressing up in the costume of your favorite gaming, comic book, or movie character. People go to elaborate lengths to create attire and makeup for these costumes, and often they can be seen attending massive conventions like the San Diego Comic-Con, or attending movie premieres for films like *Star Wars* or specific Marvel or DC characters (e.g., *Thor, Guardians of the Galaxy, Wonder Woman*).

Communities are also bound by rules that govern the interactions of their members. These rules often refer to communication behaviors that are either expected or required by members. When people violate these rules, they are reprimanded by the community, and if the offense is great enough, the person may be expelled from the group. The process of being expelled from a community is called **excommunication**, because the person is no longer allowed to live among or even speak to those in the group to which they once belonged. This shunning is, in some cases, meant to teach the person a lesson before allowing them re-entry into the group, but the exile can be permanent in other instances.

EXCOMMUNICATION
an exile from a community one belonged to whereby one is shunned into reconciliation or completely exiled; it requires no communication between the individual and the community

Involve Rewards and Costs

Interpersonal relationships reward us with more than helping us create identities for ourselves or establishing a community; they also bring physical and material benefits as well. Friends help us move, listen when we need to vent regarding some emotionally distressing situation, and even might loan us money when we need it on occasion. Friends also provide us with a sense of belonging and connection that, as you may recall from Maslow's hierarchy of needs, is one of the key things all people require for a well-balanced life.

Interpersonal relationships also involve certain costs, and these costs are the mirror image of the rewards we receive. After all, we invest time, emotional energy, and even money into people that we care about deeply, while we probably do not do that with others. Every time you are there when a friend needs you for emotional support, to lend a few dollars, or even to give her or him a ride home, it is a cost of the friendship. As we will learn shortly, there is only so much we are willing to invest in friendships, as these costs can add up to a point where you will no longer work to sustain the relationship.

THEORIES OF RELATIONSHIP DEVELOPMENT

Now that we have discussed the characteristics of interpersonal relationships, we will investigate four theories about how relationships are formed: Attraction Theory, Uncertainty Reduction Theory, Social Penetration Theory, and the Stage Model of Relationship Development.

Attraction Theory

The process of choosing and selecting our friends and romantic partners is rooted in perception. We observe a characteristic about a person, organize it into a category with which we are familiar, and ultimately interpret it in either a good or bad light. When it comes to

INTERPERSONAL ATTRACTION
a force that draws us to someone else

PHYSICAL ATTRACTION
we are drawn to someone's physical appearance because we like the way the person looks

SOCIAL ATTRACTION
we see the other person as someone with whom we would like to engage in social interaction and be friends

TASK ATTRACTION
we like to work with them and can count on them to get a job done

determining whether we wish to initiate a relationship, we refer to interpersonal attraction, or observing a force that draws us to someone else. There are three types of interpersonal attraction: social attraction, physical attraction, and task attraction.[3] When we have social attraction with someone, we see the person as someone with whom we would like to be friends or get to know. When we are physically attracted to someone, we are drawn to someone's physical appearance because we like the way the person looks. When we have task attraction with someone, we like to work with the person and can count on her or him to get a job done.

Considering these three types of attraction, it should be no surprise that attraction is not restricted to physical attraction for romantic purposes, or that there are different characteristics that attract us to different individuals for a variety of reasons. Sometimes physical qualities intrigue and attract us, while other times we are interested in someone's knowledge, expertise, personality, or dependability. Regardless of the reason we are drawn to someone to form a relationship, there are certain things that serve to enhance someone's attractiveness to us.

Appearance. The first thing we notice about most people we meet is their appearance, and so attraction often begins when someone looks physically appealing to us. What is physically appealing to one person, however, may not be to another, and the standards of beauty have changed over time and differ by culture. For instance, if you look closely at some famous portraits from the Middle Ages, you will see men and women who would not be what society considers attractive today—but in their time they were the height of beauty. Appearance is a fundamental force in interpersonal attraction, but we differ in how we judge it.

Proximity. Typically, people seek out friends and romantic relationships with those people who are around them. Now, however, thanks to the internet, cell phones, and the increased availability and affordability of travel, the definition of proximity has changed and its importance in terms of attraction has lessened. That reduction in influence comes with risk. Some people have friends they have never met in person with whom they have had extensive relationships online. Sometimes the people they believe they are talking to are not who they claim to be. Regardless, proximity still retains influence over attraction within small communities and neighborhoods where people gather together, because they share a common area of residence.

Similarity. This may not be very surprising, but research shows that we are more likely to establish relationships with people with whom we share interests, values, beliefs, and other characteristics. People who share our experiences and worldviews reinforce our own identities and thus are a more welcome presences in our lives. On a practical level, they also make it easier to find things to do together and to talk about. For example, if you are signed up for a dance class, you might strike up conversations with people there because you know they share that interest with you. We are thus more likely to be attracted to those who are like us. Keep in mind, however, that similarity does not mean that all people interested in the same things as you are will become friends—there are always areas of difference we have with one another.

Complementary difference. The world would be a boring place indeed if we all were the same and only sought out relationships with those who were like us. This is not to say we seek out people who are completely opposite to ourselves, but rather that we do form relationships with people who are different in ways that we see as adding something to ourselves or our communities. The differences in these relationships are understood as positive elements, not negative ones that create friction. Forming friendships based on complementary differences is challenging, because it necessarily involves being open to changing our views on the world based on the other person's different perspective—and this is very hard to do if we are convinced our way of seeing things is the one true way.

Uncertainty Reduction Theory

Deciding to strike up a conversation with someone in the hopes of gaining a new friend can be a somewhat scary proposition, because you do not know how the other person will react or what they might feel. Sharing deep information about yourself with someone is even more of a daunting task because it involves taking a leap of faith and investing trust in the other person. Communication professors Charles Berger and Richard Calabrese understood this reluctance and trepidation we all feel about interacting with other people because of our inability to always accurately predict the outcome of the meeting. Berger and Calabrese developed the **Uncertainty Reduction Theory**, which focuses on "the assumption that when strangers meet, their primary concern is one of uncertainty reduction or increasing predictability about the behavior of both themselves and others in the interaction."[4]

Types and stages of uncertainty. There are two kinds of uncertainty that we face when we meet someone for the first time. **Cognitive uncertainty** occurs when we do not know what the beliefs and attitudes of the other person are, and **behavioral uncertainty** occurs when we do not know how the other person will behave in a particular situation. Most people are uncomfortable with uncertainty, so we interact with others to reduce the uncertainty we feel about the possible reactions of others, and the more we communicate with the other person, the less uncertain—or more confident in our ability to predict the response of the other person—we become.

When we meet another person for the first time, we usually go through three stages as we work to reduce uncertainty. The first stage is the **entry stage**, during which we follow culturally accepted rules for interactions and politeness, including greeting one another, making small talk, and laughing at jokes. The second stage is the personal stage. In the **personal stage**, we begin to explore the other person's attitudes and beliefs while also disclosing some of that same information about ourselves. The third and final stage is the **exit stage**, when both individuals decide whether or not to continue the relationship.

UNCERTAINTY REDUCTION THEORY
the idea that increased knowledge of another person improves our ability to predict future behaviors and thus reduces our own uncertainty

COGNITIVE UNCERTAINTY
occurs when we do not know what the beliefs and attitudes of the other person are

BEHAVIORAL UNCERTAINTY
occurs when we do not know how the other person will behave in a particular situation

ENTRY STAGE
first stage of Uncertainty Reduction Theory during which we follow culturally accepted rules for interactions and politeness, including greeting one another, making small talk, and laughing at jokes

PERSONAL STAGE
second stage of Uncertainty Reduction Theory during which we begin to explore the other person's attitudes and beliefs, while also disclosing some of that same information about ourselves

EXIT STAGE
final stage of Uncertainty Reduction Theory during which both individuals decide whether to continue the relationship or not to pursue the relationship

We do not always have the desire to reduce uncertainty about another person, and there are three variables that can influence whether we wish to do so.[5] The first of these is whether we anticipate future interactions with the other person. If we believe we will see the person again, we will want to reduce our uncertainty as much as possible so we can better gauge the possible behaviors and reactions they might exhibit. If, on the other hand, we do not think we will see the person again, we are not as concerned with reducing uncertainty about them. The second variable is whether or not the person has something we want or need. If the other person does, we want to be able to better predict future behaviors so we can maximize our chances of receiving what we want from her or him; however, if the person doesn't have anything important to offer us, we don't feel the urge to reduce uncertainty, because predicting her or his future behaviors will not gain us anything. Finally, we like to reduce uncertainty when the other person acts in some odd way that seems abnormal or inconsistent with our expectations. These weird behaviors can throw us off, and thus call for us to reduce uncertainty so that we can adjust and know what to expect in the future.

Strategies to reduce uncertainty. There are three different strategies we can use when trying to reduce uncertainty when meeting someone for the first time.[6] The first way to reduce uncertainty is by using a passive strategy, which involves unobtrusively observing the other person. For example, you might watch as the other person interacts with others, listen in on conversations that are easy to overhear, or observe her or him completing other tasks. The second way to reduce uncertainty is by using active strategies, which involve engaging in activities to learn more about the other person while avoiding direct contact with them. For example, you might ask a mutual friend about the person or search for the person using Google or Facebook. The final way to reduce uncertainty about another person is by using interactive strategies, which involve engaging in direct contact or face-to-face conversation with them. For example, you might ask the other person questions or start a conversation.

All in all, Berger and Calabrese's Uncertainty Reduction Theory helps us understand relationships by explaining that we are motivated to reduce that uncertainty by engaging in and reciprocating information sharing because we are uncomfortable with uncertainty about others when we first meet them. As we reduce our uncertainty, we are also likely to increase the intimacy level of our disclosures and like the other person more. We like to be around those whom we can generally accurately predict their responses and behaviors. We typically don't like feeling uncertain about friends, loved ones, or acquaintances.

Social Penetration Theory

Developing and maintaining strong relationships does not solely depend on attraction or reducing uncertainty in those initial interactions with others; it also involves getting to know more about the other person after the initial attraction draws you together. In an effort to understand this development, social psychologists Irwin Altman and Dalmas Taylor devised a theory to explain how we form these close connections with others. Their theory, Social Penetration Theory, proposes that the process of creating and maintaining deeper intimacy with another person takes place through gradual and mutual self-disclosure.[7]

PASSIVE STRATEGY

unobtrusively observing the other person

ACTIVE STRATEGY

engaging in activities to learn more about the other person while avoiding direct contact with him or her

INTERACTIVE STRATEGY

engaging in direct contact or face-to-face conversation with the other person

SOCIAL PENETRATION THEORY

the process of creating and maintaining deeper intimacy with another person takes place through gradual and mutual self-disclosure

Self-disclosure occurs when one person voluntarily shares personal history and information regarding attitudes, feelings, values, and experiences with another individual. Altman and Taylor explained that the self-disclosures we make to others have two qualities, and both are important in developing friendships.

Qualities of self-disclosure. The first of these qualities is the depth of the penetration, or how much we share on a specific topic or subject with another person. The other is breadth of self-disclosure, which refers to how many topics we share with other people. We can develop friends with whom we share a lot of information about only one or two subjects because that is where our interests collide, and we can have friendships where we share deeply about a broad number of subjects. There are also relationships where we share only superficial information about a lot of subjects, because we are either guarded or not quite sure about the strength of the bond between ourselves and the other person.

Stages of mutual self-disclosure. It is important to know that when we develop relationships, the deep sharing of information on a subject takes place over time and is thus a gradual process. To best understand Social Penetration Theory, think about peeling away the layers of an onion. When we first meet someone, we only know the person's superficial

SELF-DISCLOSURE when one person voluntarily shares personal history and information regarding attitudes, feelings, values, and experiences with another individual

---

Doctor Who Illustrates Social Penetration Theory

MEDIATED MOMENTS

The longest running television show of all time is the British program *Doctor Who*. The show originally aired from 1963-1989, before taking a 16-year hiatus and returning in 2005 for a run that is still ongoing. The show focuses on a humanoid alien known as "The Doctor," who travels through time and space combating evil. One of the Doctor's abilities is to regenerate into a new body when close to death, and this has allowed thirteen actors actors—most recently, female—to play the role throughout the show's history. The current doctor is female. Each "new" Doctor has all the memories of the previous one but a very different personality. The Doctor also takes on a human travelling companion who becomes one of his closest confidants. Each time the Doctor enlists a new companion, that person works to get to know the Doctor, initially focusing simply on their quirks and ability to travel through time and eventually understanding their internal conflict about identity and roles in history. The process by which these companions get to know the Doctor is a perfect illustration of social penetration theory, as they begin by knowing only surface level characteristics of the Doctor before learning deeper core elements about the Doctor, thus creating a strong bond of fellowship between them.

AL Robinson / Shutterstock.com

layers, but as we peel away more and more, we eventually know her or him in a much deeper and more meaningful way. This process of getting to know someone through mutual self-disclosure involves five potential stages: orientation, exploratory affective exchange, affective exchange, stable exchange, and depenetration.

- **Orientation stage:** In this stage, individuals engage in small talk and follow social norms for appropriateness and social desirability. You might use simple clichés, but you are mostly engaging in surface-level conversation and are not revealing much information about yourselves. Think about this as the casual, polite conversation that you might have when you meet someone on the first day of class, while walking your dog, or waiting in the checkout line at the grocery store.

- **Exploratory affective exchange stage:** In this stage, individuals begin to reveal themselves by sharing personal attitudes and opinions about some moderately personal topics like government, education, and current events. You are not yet talking about private or personal matters or sharing vulnerable information with others, but individuals in this stage are casual friends or acquaintances and are still feeling out the relationship.

- **Affective exchange stage:** In this stage, individuals begin talking about private and personal matters, and they might begin using personal idioms that are unique to that relationship or even begin engaging in criticisms and arguments from time to time. At this stage, you are becoming close friends, and in romantic relationships, this stage might involve more intimate touching or kissing.

- **Stable exchange stage:** In this stage, individuals have a deep level of trust and are sharing their deepest personal thoughts, beliefs, and values with one another. Both partners can predict the emotional reactions of the other person, and they are closely connected to the other person in an intimate (though not necessarily romantic) relationship.

- **Depenetration:** In this stage, individuals begin to withdraw from the relationship and stop disclosing information to one another. Often, individuals feel that the costs of the relationship exceed the benefits, and the relationship is terminated.

 ENGAGING ETHICS

Greetings and Self-disclosure

It is common to most people that when they are asked, "How are you?" or, "How are you doing?" that they reply with a general one-word answer like "fine" or "good." These answers offer no real details and aren't really answers to the question being asked, but rather serve to, among other things, circumvent self-disclosure for any number of reasons. Is it right to answer the question this way? Why would you avoid telling more to someone? What would make you reveal more?

It is important to note that relationships do not have to go through all of these stages. Most of our everyday interactions and acquaintances never go beyond the orientation or exploratory affective stages. Some of our most intimate friendships, family relationships, and romantic relationships are enduring relationships that might remain at a stable stage through decades of our lives, while others go through depenetration and lead to the end of the relationship.

STAGE MODEL OF RELATIONAL DEVELOPMENT

So far, we have learned about three theories that help us understand the beginning of a relationship, and one theory that explains how relationships grow closer over time and perhaps eventually end the relationship. However, none of the theories we have discussed so far tells us much about how a relationship de-escalates over time. Communication scholar Mark Knapp expands the theories that we have learned about so far and more thoroughly addresses how relationships develop as well as how relationships devolve in his Stage Model of Relational Development (Figure 8.1), which identifies five stages through which individuals come together in a relationship and five stages through which individuals come apart.

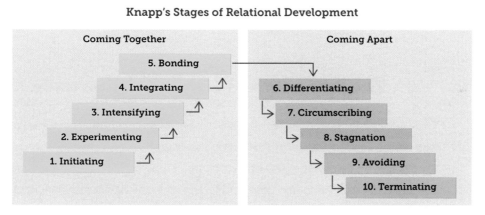

FIGURE 8.1 **Stage Model of Relational Development**

Changes in relationships take place for many reasons: partners' feelings and experiences with one another, health, economics, the presence or absence of children, relationships with other family members, work, and professions. In short, change is an intrinsic and inseparable aspect of close relationships.[8]

—Altman & Ginat

"Coming Together"

INITIATING STAGE

when you take the first step to interact with someone you are interested in

EXPERIMENTING STAGE

where you engage in conversation about surface-level interests and topics with the other person to see if your interest is expanded or not

INTENSIFYING STAGE

you invest more time in each other and learn more about a person's history, interests, and goals

Stage #1: initiating. There needs to always be a beginning to any relationship, and so the initiating stage occurs when you take the first step to interact with and try to make an impression on someone you are interested in. This includes both verbal initiation, like a greeting or casual conversation, or nonverbal initiation, such as making eye contact and smiling. Thanks to the advent of the Internet and the proliferation of dating sites such as eHarmony, Match.com, and Itsjustlunch.com, the initiating stage is no longer restricted to in-person communication. People can initiate relationships digitally by examining a person's profile and determining if they want to strike up a conversation.

Stage #2: experimenting. Contrary to what the name may make you envision, this stage does not involve a lab. The experimenting stage is where you engage in conversation about surface-level interests and topics with the other person to see if your interest is expanded or not. This helps us determine how much we have in common with the other person, and whether or not we wish to continue relationship development with that person.

Stage #3: intensifying. In the intensifying stage, you move from surface-level conversation and activity, to deeper, more meaningful interactions. During the intensifying stage, you invest more time in each other, begin to share private information, and learn more about a

The Symbols and Sanctity of Marriage

SECTION 3 OF DOMA IS OVERTURNED

The Defense of Marriage Act (DOMA) was signed into federal law by President Bill Clinton on September 21, 1996. At the time, DOMA had two important provisions: 1) marriage was defined as a union between one man and one woman, and 2) that states did not have to recognize marriages performed in other states. The first provision was repealed in 2013, which meant at the federal level a marriage could occur between two men, two women, or one man and one woman. This was a significant moment in the history of marriage within the United States, as it created a space for same-sex couples to be formally recognized as couples, for example, on their tax returns. On June 26, 2015, in the case of Obergefell v. Hodges, the US Supreme Court overturned all state bans on same-sex marriages and required them to recognize marriage licenses from other states, which made same-sex marriage permitted across the country. This decision made it possible for all same-sex couples to achieve this particular form of bonding in their relational development. The piece of paper, and all that comes along with it, is a symbol of the couple's commitment to each other and their relationship.

person's history, interests, and goals. During this stage, partners commonly develop nicknames for each other and express their desire for deeper commitment.

Stage #4: integrating. During the integrating stage, the two individuals begin to develop a sense of an identity for their relationship with each other. In the case of a romantic partnership, the individuals think of themselves as a couple and do more things together. There is a high level of investment of time and resources into the relationship and activities the two do together. During this stage of the courtship, friends expect to see the two together, and their connection is largely public knowledge. They socialize with other couples, sign cards together, and perhaps even move in together to more completely integrate the social, financial, and emotional aspects of their lives.

Stage #5: bonding. Relational partners in the bonding stage make their deep commitment formal and public through an engagement, marriage, or commitment ceremony. These pronouncements of the long-term deep commitment the couple has for each other display to others the significance of the relationship between the partners. For some couples, the bonding stage lasts a lifetime, though for others the relationship will eventually begin to dissolve despite the couple's best intentions when they made a bonding commitment.

"Coming Apart"

Stage #6: differentiating. As work, family, friends, and other interests begin to exert pressure on the couple, the two people in the bonded relationship might begin to think of each other more as separate individuals than as a partner in a couple. At this point, each person might begin developing her or his own hobbies or begin doing more things separately from the partner—in other words, they are differentiating themselves from each other or (re)constructing their identities as more separated than together.

Stage #7: circumscribing. When a couple reaches the circumscribing stage, the individuals begin to live mostly separate lives. Each person has his or her own friends, activities, possessions, and space, and there are now boundaries for what the couple will and will not talk about together. Some topics are avoided entirely in order to avoid arguments, but the disagreements about those issues persist.

Stage #8: stagnation. At this stage, the relationship has become stagnant. The couple is still together, but the individuals are living separate lives and rarely talk with one another because they see little point in communicating. The couple might be staying together for their children or out of apathy because a formal separation or divorce might be inconvenient or impossible for other reasons.

Stage #9: avoidance. By the time a couple reaches the avoidance stage, both individuals deliberately avoid contact with the other person. Both people avoid eye contact, do not speak to the other person, are physically detached, and might even try to leave and return at different times so that they won't see each other, even if they are still living in the same

INTEGRATING STAGE
partners begin to develop a sense of an identity for their relationship with each other

BONDING STAGE
partners make their deep commitment formal and public through an engagement, marriage, or civil union

DIFFERENTIATING STAGE
occurs when the partners begin to separate themselves from each other

CIRCUMSCRIBING STAGE
happens when the partners are primarily living different lives and their conversations are increasingly limited in scope and depth

STAGNATION STAGE
when couples move into the stagnation stage, they are still a couple, but primarily in name; they are neither moving forward or backward in the relationship but have hit a point when they are not relating on an intimate level

AVOIDANCE STAGE
the couple actively avoids interacting with each other so they will not have to face each other

home. In some cases, this manifests as married partners sleeping in separate bedrooms to avoid the other person.

TERMINATING STAGE

the final phase of relationship deterioration; couples end their current relationships and move into a post-relationship phase where they may or may not continue to have contact as separated individuals

Stage #10: terminating. At this stage, the relationship completely ends. In the case of a married couple, the terminating stage might include moving out, filing for divorce, dividing belongings, and making decisions about the custody of pets and children.

Most relationships will not go through all 10 of these stages, but as current divorce rates show, this does happen for some relationships. It is also important to note that relationships can go forward and backward through these stages, so a couple that begins to differentiate can go backward toward being a bonded couple again and are not necessarily doomed to a failing relationship.

DIALOGIC COMMUNICATION IN DEVELOPING RELATIONSHIPS

While many of the people we meet will pass through our lives without another encounter, others will become friends, colleagues, neighbors, casual acquaintances, romantic partners, or family members. As the saying goes, first impressions count, and establishing a first impression that demonstrates you care about hearing from the other person will go a long way toward building relationships. Not to mention, approaching new relationships with dialogue allows you to understand and learn about different people, their experiences and their beliefs—even if you won't see them again. Below are a few suggestions for maintaining dialogic communication as relationships begin.

Balance How You Express Your Feelings

You don't want to reveal everything you are thinking and feeling all the time, especially when you are meeting someone for the first time, nor should you keep everything to yourself. Neither approach in the long term will help you if you continue to develop the relationship. In your earliest interactions, observe the rules for politeness in your particular cultural context. As the conversation progresses and you begin to disclose more, communicate honestly about yourself, but also pay attention to what and how much the other person is disclosing so you can reciprocate those disclosures without overwhelming the person with private information that should typically only be shared in a more developed relationship.

Give the Benefit of the Doubt

If the other person you are interacting with says or does something that could be interpreted negatively, consider that you might be making a Fundamental Attribution Error. There might be situational factors impacting the other person's behavior. The person might appear upset or tense because they haven't been sleeping well. He or she might appear distant because of a recent tragedy; they might even be sick. The point is, we never know what might be influencing the mood or disposition of another person, and so we owe it to others to give them the benefit of the doubt that some things that may come across as rude or negative were not intended that way. This means we should seek to learn more rather than rushing to judgment.

Exercise Empathy

Be attuned to the emotional state of your partner and try to recognize when they need support and when they might need space. Listen to your partner and try to put yourself in their emotional shoes. Sometimes all a person needs is someone to listen, so be careful not to interrupt or offer unsolicited advice. Empathy is different from sympathy and involves listening more than anything. Often, our first reaction is to share a common experience we have had with the person who is having a tough time, but remember they need to express themselves more than they need to hear about your experiences. That is not to say those experiences aren't helpful, but that relaying them at the proper time and place is a must for practicing effective empathy.

Invest Time in Your Relationships

Perhaps the biggest sign that a relationship may be in decline is the reduction in time spent with each other. When you are in a social or intimate relationship with someone, spend time on the relationship through e-mail, phone calls, text messaging, or even letters. Nothing lets others know they are valued and important like spending time with them, or letting them know you spent time thinking about them. But remember: this is not about quantity of time, but rather spending quality time with people. In some of the strongest friendships, people can go long periods of time without speaking, but when friends finally reconnect, it is like there was never a gap. That's because the quality of the time investment is so strong that people know they count and matter to the other party.

SUMMARY

In this chapter, we began by discussing the characteristics of interpersonal relation-ships—specifically how they develop. We first explored the four characteristics of both intimate and social interpersonal relationships. We then discussed three theories that help to explain why we begin relationships with other people. We then explored Knapp's 10 stages of relational development, before providing some practical ways to encourage dialogue in interpersonal relationships.

CHAPTER 8 KEY IDEAS

- Interpersonal relationships help us create and maintain our identity, fulfill the need to belong, allow for the creation of communities, and come with rewards and costs.

- There are three types of interpersonal attraction: social attraction, physical attraction, and task attraction. Some of the factors that enhance attractiveness include appear-ance, proximity, similarity, and complementary difference.

- Uncertainty Reduction Theory states we are uncomfortable with uncertainty in inter-personal relationships, so we use passive, active, and interactive strategies to reduce uncertainty. There are three stages that we go through as we reduce uncertainty: (1) the Entry Stage, (2) the Personal Stage, and (3) the Exit Stage.

- Social Penetration Theory proposes that we create and maintain deeper intimacy with another person through mutual self-disclosure. The five stages of Social Penetration Theory are (1) Orientation, (2) Exploratory Affective Exchange, (3) Affective Exchange, (4) Stable Exchange, and (5) Depenetration.

- Knapp's Stage Model of Relational Development identifies five stages through which individuals come together and five stages through which individuals come apart.

CHAPTER 8 KEY TERMS

Interpersonal relationships	Passive strategy
Social relationships	Active strategy
Identity	Interactive strategy
Community	Social Penetration Theory
Excommunication	Self-disclosure
Interpersonal attraction	Initiating stage
Physical attraction	Experimenting stage
Social attraction	Intensifying stage
Task attraction	Integrating stage
Uncertainty Reduction Theory	Bonding stage
Cognitive uncertainty	Differentiating stage
Behavioral uncertainty	Circumscribing stage
Entry stage	Stagnation stage
Personal stage	Avoidance stage
Exit stage	Terminating stage

ACTIVITIES AND DISCUSSION QUESTIONS

1. Describe a situation in which you tried to reduce uncertainty when you met someone for the first time. What strategies did you use to reduce uncertainty? What happened in each of the three stages, and what was the outcome?

2. Find a video clip that shows two individuals in one of the five stages of Social Penetration Theory from a favorite movie or TV show. Describe the scene or share the clip. Identify and define the stage that you believe is illustrated by this clip and justify why you believe this clip is a good example of that particular stage.

3. Identify a romantic couple in a TV series or movie that goes through several of Knapp's Stages of Relational Development. Describe how they went through each stage and what events or behaviors made it clear that the characters were in each of these stages. At what stage were the characters when the TV series or movie ended?

4. A lot of people use communication technologies to get to know others. Look at your social media patterns. How often do you use passive strategies to reduce uncertainty about other people? How often do you use active and interactive strategies? Do you reduce uncertainty with others differently online than when interacting face to face?

RELATIONSHIP MAINTENANCE

In the last chapter, we talked about how relationships develop, particularly during their early stages. Once we have developed a relationship, we need to find ways to sustain and maintain the interpersonal bonds that are important to us. **Relationship maintenance** refers to the work we do to keep a relationship going in a condition with which both partners are happy. Just as a car will begin to have problems and eventually break down entirely if we do not perform regular maintenance such as adding fuel, changing the oil, and adding air to the tires, our relationships will also deteriorate and eventually die if we do not give them the attention and work that are required to keep them strong.

In this chapter, we explore the complex task of maintaining an interpersonal relationship. First, we will briefly outline the various behaviors that communication scholars identify as being key elements to sustaining strong relationships. We will then discuss several theories of relationship maintenance: Social Exchange Theory, Communication Privacy Management, Everyday Talk, and Relational Dialectics. We will conclude by discussing some guidelines for using dialogic communication in our relationship maintenance practices.

RELATIONSHIP MAINTENANCE
the work we do to keep a relationship going and in a condition with which both partners are happy

RELATIONSHIP MAINTENANCE BEHAVIORS

Communication researchers have come up with a list of relational maintenance behaviors that partners use in their relationship: positivity, assurances, sharing tasks, acceptance, self-disclosure, social networks, and relationship talks.[1] Positivity includes communication that is optimistic and upbeat, such as complimenting one's partner or being cheerful during conversations. Assurances are used when partners communicate their commitment to each other and the relationship, like when a husband tells his wife that he would marry her all over again, or when friends talk about what their relationship will be like in their old age.

When partners share tasks by doing things, such as sharing the chores around the house or helping one another get ready for work in the morning, they communicate that they respect one another. Acceptance occurs when we make our partners feel like we will care for them no matter what, which makes us feel safe and validated in our relationships. You will recall self-disclosure from the chapter on listening how it involves revealing things about ourselves such as our feelings, experiences, and goals to our partners. When we self-disclose to another person, we are entrusting the person with a piece of ourselves, which in turn helps to maintain our bond with them.

Relationship Maintenance Within Families

Maintaining a relationship takes work, but it seems to especially take work in stigmatized relationships such as a same-sex relationship, where friends and family may not be as supportive of the lifestyle or bond between the partners. In the chapter on relationship development, we discussed the Defense of Marriage Act (DOMA) and how its partial repeal has brought public recognition to thousands, if not millions, of couples in the United States. With this official recognition sometimes comes the more interpersonal recognition, and hence support, for these relationships. If a couple is seen as valid in the eyes of the partners' families and friendship networks, then they are likely to spend time with the couple, getting to know them individually and as a unit. They also might offer various forms of support when the partners or the relationship needs it (e.g., grandparents offering to babysit the grandchildren for the parents when they need time alone). When couples do not have the support of their networks, it can be very challenging to stay together when things get rough. While we have a relationship with one other person, we need the support of friends and family to maintain it over the long haul.

Relationship talks happen when we discuss our relationship with our partners, a process that is meta-communicative, or, simply, communication about communication. Taking time to talk frankly about the relationship, how we feel about it, and where we want it to go, shows the other person we care about the relationship and we want to maintain it. Finally, we can do a lot to maintain our relationships through our social networks. We do this by spending time with and getting to know one another's "circles" and families, who will likely serve as sources of support for the relationship in times of need. We also maintain our relationships through our social networks by supporting our partners in spending time with their friends and family.

META-COMMUNICATIVE
communication about communication

THEORIES OF RELATIONSHIP MAINTENANCE

As the advertisement goes, there is no one way to eat a Reese's, just as there is no one way to maintain a relationship. Every relationship is unique, and so it is impossible to craft a one-size-fits-all explanation of how to effectively maintain strong positive interpersonal connections with others. One thing that is certain, however, is that doing so requires work by both parties. Relationships change over time, and so if we want the relationship to continue then we must always work to maintain them in the event they undergo some wear and tear. In this section of the chapter, we introduce four communication theories that begin to explain the complicated nature of relationship maintenance.

Social Exchange Theory

A common perspective on relationships of all types is to view them through an economic prism, where we evaluate their costs and benefits in order to decide if they are worth maintaining. Psychologists John Thibault and Harry Kelley formalized this economic evaluation into Social Exchange Theory, which proposes that relationship behavior is regulated by the evaluation of the perceived rewards and costs of the interaction by both sides.[2] This evaluation is a simple mathematical equation that looks at the benefits gained from a relationship, subtracts the costs, and determines the outcome. If the outcome is positive, then we continue the relationship; if it is not, we let it dissipate, so we try to maximize the benefits and minimize the costs. This is known as the minimax principle.

Relationship Worth = Rewards − Costs

FIGURE 9.1 Minimax Principle

Of course, some of the benefits and costs of our relationships are not easily calculated, and the perceived level of benefits and costs of particular interactions will vary from person to person. For example, some of the perceived benefits of relationships might include companionship, emotional support, social support, instrumental support, and feelings of love and belonging. Some of the perceived costs of a relationship might include time doing things you do not enjoy with the other person, emotional distress, or being asked to do things for

SOCIAL EXCHANGE THEORY
a theory suggesting that relationship behavior is regulated by the evaluation of perceived rewards and costs of the interaction by both sides

MINIMAX PRINCIPLE
principle describing the tendency to maximize the benefits and minimize the costs in relationships

the other person. If we are happy with the overall perceived balance of costs and rewards, then we are generally satisfied with the relationship.

Our satisfaction with and decision to continue a particular relationship is also impacted by our expectations and prior experiences. According to Social Exchange Theory, there are two different ways in which we make the determinations regarding which relationships we keep and which we replace. The first is the **comparison level**, "CL," which refers to our general expectations for a certain type of relationship, such as a friendship or romantic relationship. We have ideas about what each type of relationship should be like based on our previous interactions with others, our family interactions, cultural expectations, and the ways that each type of relationship is portrayed in the media. If our current relationship meets or exceeds our comparison level, then we are satisfied with the relationship; if it falls short of our comparison level, then we are dissatisfied.

Second, we often compare our current relationship to the other relationship options we believe are possible. Sometimes we try to determine if the outcomes would be better with another person, or what the threshold would be for changing relationships. As we perceive other people as more attractive alternatives, our existing relationships become less stable. When we compare existing relationships to other possible relationships, we use the **comparison level of alternatives**, "CLalt." Ultimately, the best situation is when we believe our relationship is better than our comparison level and our comparison level of alternatives, which means we are satisfied and want to maintain the relationship.

The comparison level of alternatives also explains why some people stay in unsatisfactory relationships. It is common for people to stay in abusive relationships because their abusive partner has convinced them they are worthless, that nobody else would want to be with them, or because they have never been in a healthy relationship and do not believe such a relationship is possible. If a person does not think there is a better alternative, sometimes a bad relationship is perceived as better than not having one at all.

Communication Privacy Management

As the theories in the relationship development chapter demonstrate, relationships necessarily involve the sharing of personal information with another person. Sometimes we share information with others we do not wish to be shared any further. Communication scholar Sandra Petronio found the management of this process of sharing secrets and private information with other people fascinating, and so she developed a theory to explain how it works. **Communication privacy management** offers a map of sorts to navigate the way people manage private matters that are shared with others.[3]

All of us have **private information**, which is information we believe we have the right to own. When we consider information to be private, we do not believe that information should be shared widely with other people unless we have made an intentional decision to share that information with them. Private information can be information that we see as positive or

COMPARISON LEVEL
our general expectations for a certain type of relationship, such as a friendship or romantic relationship

COMPARISON LEVEL OF ALTERNATIVES
expectations arising from comparing existing relationships to other possible relationships

COMMUNICATION PRIVACY MANAGEMENT
a theory that offers a map of the way people manage private matters that are shared with others

PRIVATE INFORMATION
information we believe we have the right to own

negative, and as permanently or temporarily secret from other people. Examples of information that someone might consider to be private include medical conditions, new relationships, GPA, immigration status, income, or sexual orientation.

Any time we share information with others, we create co-owners of that information. These co-owners are often deliberately chosen, or **deliberate confidants**, meaning we make a conscious decision to disclose the information to them, but they are also sometimes accidental, such as when others overhear our private conversations. Petronio was primarily concerned with deliberate confidants, because people often establish rules regarding how the information they purposely share with someone should be handled. When you share private information with someone else, you create a **boundary linkage** with that person. The rights and responsibilities we ascribe to the person with whom we share the information are elements of **boundary ownership**, because they establish the boundaries, or rules, for the spread of the information. When we establish with whom the other person can share the information, we establish the degree to which the information has **boundary permeability**. Sometimes we do not want the information to be shared with anybody else, which establishes a thick boundary. Sometimes there are a few particular individuals with whom we give the person permission to share our private information. Yet other times, we are comfortable having the private information shared fairly widely, which is a thin boundary. When we share private information, we must tell the other person whether the private information should be kept in confidence.

DELIBERATE CONFIDANT

a person with whom we intentionally share information meant to be kept in confidence

BOUNDARY LINKAGE

the practice of sharing private information with another individual

BOUNDARY OWNERSHIP

the rights and responsibilities we ascribe to the person with whom we share private information

BOUNDARY PERMEABILITY

the degree to which a confidant can share private information with others

Boundary Turbulence in Personal Relationships

In the television show *Nashville*, guitar player Deacon Claybourne is diagnosed with liver cancer after years of alcoholism. His niece, Scarlett, is with him when he receives his diagnosis, and, at first, Deacon is adamant that he does not want anybody else to know he has cancer. Scarlett finds that keeping Deacon's medical condition a secret is a huge burden, because she cannot talk with anybody else about the distress she feels about his diagnosis and the fact that she might lose the family member she has been closest to through her entire life. Keeping this secret for him affects her work and her relationships. Eventually, Deacon shares his diagnosis with a small group of people, including his ongoing romantic interest, Rayna, and their daughter Maddie, both of whom are initially hurt that he kept this information secret from them for so long. While Scarlett was able to maintain a thick boundary around the information about Deacon's medical condition and avoid boundary turbulence, her distress also showed that sometimes it is challenging to be a co-owner of private information about another person.

BOUNDARY TURBULENCE

occurs when information we believe is private and shared in confidence is broadcast to other parties

Problems in relationships occur, however, when information we believe is private and shared in confidence is shared with others. This form of boundary turbulence can occur for a variety of reasons, but the two most common are a direct violation of established boundaries or the failure of both parties to explicitly state the boundaries for the information. Sometimes our friends or partners deliberately share our private information with others, even though they know we do not want them to, while at other times they accidentally share the information, such as when they are talking with us about the information in a public place. At other times, our partners share the information because they do not realize that you considered that information to be private.

Social relationships with any degree of depth necessarily involve sharing confidential information, but when that trust is broken, we must make a determination of how to proceed with the relationship. In some cases it constitutes an end to the relationship altogether, but in other situations we still retain the relationship because of the rewards it provides us. Ultimately, what communication privacy management shows us is that relationships are complicated phenomena that involve a degree of trust and a leap of faith.

Everyday Talk

You might assume that it is easy to determine whether a relationship does or does not exist and exactly what type or stage your relationship is in based on the amount of intimate or private information being shared. In reality, though, relationships are much more complex. Once you have engaged in interpersonal interactions with another person, you have begun to develop a relationship history with that other individual. While the nature of your relationship will likely change over time, you can never go back to having never had a relationship. Even if you fall in love, marry, and then divorce someone, the relationship is not actually over; instead, you now have a relationship history together that will influence future interactions (or perhaps the avoidance of future interactions) with that partner. Our feelings about a particular relationship also fluctuate from day to day, and some days we have doubts or anxieties about a relationship that we do not feel on other days.

Steve Duck explains that our relationships are "unfinished business," and that relationships are always in the process of becoming, rather than in a static state.[4] Relationships are a

The potential for production, not just reproduction, is present in every new encounter between relationship partners; parties continue to construct the meaning of their relationship, and through their adaptations in meaning, they construct new relationship identities.[5]

—L. A. Baxter

process that happens over time, and a great deal of a relationship takes place in the context of our joint activities and mundane, ordinary conversations. In fact, Daena Goldsmith and Leslie Baxter found that, even in our most intimate relationships, most of our conversations are composed of everyday talk as we experience and enact our relationships.[6] Goldsmith and Baxter developed a list of 29 different kinds of "everyday talk" that fit into six separate categories. Even in our most intimate relationships, many studies have shown that most of our conversations involve superficial and informal talk (small talk, catching up, gossiping, joking around, etc.), not deep or relational talk (love talk, making up, talking about problems, conflict, etc.).

These findings show us that our everyday interactions and conversations are just as, if not more, important than the big, memorable events in our relationships. While we might keep pictures of birthday celebrations, graduations, weddings, vacations, or other events that mark important milestones in our lives and relationships with friends, romantic partners, or family members, it is the boring, everyday conversations and interactions that do the most to help us to develop and maintain our relationships. Even simple things like watching television shows and movies or playing video games together can help to strengthen our relationships because we are investing time in the other person.

Relational Dialectics

The final theory about how relationships function that we will discuss is Relational Dialectics Theory. Relational Dialectics is not so much about how relationships form, but rather, how we negotiate our relationships over time. While Social Exchange Theory and Communication Privacy Management Theory help us understand how we decide whether to stay in a relationship and manage information in that relationship, and Everyday Talk helps us understand the importance of our mundane conversations and interactions, these theories do not give us a complete picture of how we understand and manage competing desires and the ebb and flow of relationships over time.

Leslie Baxter and Barbara Montgomery argue that our relationships are the products and the producers of dialectical tensions. These tensions occur because we simultaneously have several essential, yet oppositional, needs or desires within our relationships.[7] For example, as we saw in Uncertainty Reduction Theory, most people want certainty about the other person in their relationships and attempt to gain it through mutual self-disclosure. However, too much certainty might leave us feeling bored when we feel like we know our partner too well, and we might soon be craving a bit of spontaneity and mystery. We want both of these needs to be fulfilled simultaneously, though at times we might fluctuate back and forth about which need is more important. These dialectical tensions are internal struggles both parties experience throughout the relationship and must constantly manage while working to maintain it. Baxter and Montgomery identified three primary dialectical tensions that are experienced in all relationships and found that each manifests itself in different ways within a relationship between the partners themselves, as well as between the relational couple and the outside world.

EVERYDAY TALK

interaction that includes mundane, ordinary conversations across our daily experience, making up our relationships in addition to the more noticeable, "bigger" moments, such as our first big fight or a marriage ceremony

DIALECTICAL TENSIONS

tensions that occur because we simultaneously have several essential yet oppositional needs or desires within our relationships

CONNECTION AND AUTONOMY

the internal dialectical tension of integration and separation; spending time with a partner and spending time alone

INCLUSION AND SECLUSION

the external dialectical tension of integration and separation; spending time alone as a couple and spending time as a couple with others

CERTAINTY AND UNCERTAINTY

the internal form of the stability and change dialectic; the desire to count on things to occur and the desire to have novelty in the relationship

Integration and separation. The first is the dynamic between being a couple and being individuals separate from one another. Within a romantic relationship, this is labeled as the connection and autonomy dialectical tension, and it manifests, for example, when it comes to how much time you want to spend with a partner and how much time you wish to spend on your own. While you want to feel close to your partner and do things together (i.e., feel connected), you also want to maintain a sense of yourself as an individual with your own separate interests and activities (i.e., have your autonomy). What makes this even more of a challenge is that we need to participate in relationships in order to learn who we are and who we want to be; we also need to do things as individuals and bring those experiences back into our relationships in order for them to grow. The external form of the integration and separation dialectical category is labeled inclusion and seclusion, and it involves having a desire to spend time as a couple with friends and family, while also wanting to spend time alone together as a couple.

Stability and change. The second dialectical tension involves having a desire for the comforts of a stable, consistent relationship, while also having a desire for spontaneity. Relationships without spontaneity can be dull and deteriorate over time, while those that are wildly unpredictable might be too exhausting to maintain. The internal form of this tension is certainty and uncertainty and includes the desire to count on some things to occur regularly in a relationship, while also having some novelty in the relationship. For example, a couple might have a tradition of going out for dinner for every birthday (certainty), but one time a partner surprises the other with a homemade meal or a surprise birthday party with friends (uncertainty). The external form of this tension is conventionality and uniqueness.

Lifespan of Relationships

Relationships have a lifespan, and sometimes no matter how close we might have been, we grow apart from others. This happens in romantic relationships and well as in social relationships and family relationships, particularly when we are experiencing life changes (such as beginning college or becoming a parent) or when geographic distance becomes a barrier. When we sense a romantic relationship is coming to an end, we usually have a conversation in which we "break up" the relationship, but often with friendships and family relationships, we often simply let things fall away. Is it possible to also notify individuals of the end of a friendship? Under what circumstances? When it comes to communicating with partners about the end of a romantic relationship, what communication method might be best? Email, in person, text message, or over the phone? Why?

Couples may, for example, always go out with the same group of friends, or they may do something with a different group they have never met. Healthy relationships require that couples balance the ordinary with the unexpected.

Expression and nonexpression. More so than the other dialectics, this one explicitly refers to communication. The internal form, openness and closedness, refers to the degree of disclosure partners have with each other. Some topics are freely shared, while others are not and are kept close to the vest. The external manifestation of this tension is revelation and concealment, and it covers what the couple shares with others in the community. This includes the decision whether to publicly announce that two people are in a relationship, or to keep their relationship secret for a while.

Effectively managing dialectical tensions. Although the presence of these tensions is inevitable and may seem challenging, you can and do manage them in your relationships every day. Also, while you might often choose to value one part of the dialectic over another (e.g., you and your partner decide it's time to take some time apart, so you privilege autonomy for a while), you can manage these tensions in a variety of ways. There are six productive ways that couples can manage these tensions.[8]

- **Spiraling inversion** takes place when we alternate back and forth between attending to our needs. For example, a couple might decide to spend time together on the weekends, but not spend time together during the week so they also have time for their individual work, interests, and friends. They cycle back and forth between autonomy and connection over time.

- **Segmentation** takes place when we choose to privilege the parts of the dialectical pair based on different contexts. For example, you and your partner might decide that you are willing to talk openly about your families and friendships, but you do not want to talk at all about past romantic partners. So, for certain topics you are open with each other while other topics are kept private.

- **Balance** takes place when we try to find a compromise that allows us to partly fill each need while also sacrificing some of each need. For example, you and your partner might decide to give up some of your alone time to be with friends, but also sacrifice some important times with friends to be together.

- **Integration** takes place when we are able to completely fulfill both opposing forces at the same time without sacrificing part of either one. For example, a family dinner might allow you to enjoy time together while also talking about individual experiences and accomplishments that happened during your days.

- **Recalibration** involves reframing contradictions so we do not see the two opposing forces as being in contradiction with one another. For example, you might decide that spending time alone exercising or relaxing to take care of yourself is also helping take care of your relationship, because you will be more relaxed and able to enjoy the time you do spend together.

OPENNESS AND CLOSEDNESS
the internal form of the expression and nonexpression dialectic; refers to the degree of disclosure partners have with one another

REVELATION AND CONCEALMENT
the external form of the expression and nonexpression dialectic; refers to what couples share with the community and what they do not

SPIRALING INVERSION
method of managing tensions that takes place when we alternate back and forth between attending to our needs

SEGMENTATION
method of managing tensions that takes place when we choose to privilege the parts of the dialectical pair based on different contexts

BALANCE
method of managing tensions that takes place when we try to find a compromise that allows us to partly fill each need while also sacrificing some of each need

INTEGRATION
method of managing tensions that takes place when you are able to completely fulfill both opposing forces at the same time without sacrificing part of either one

RECALIBRATION
method of managing tensions that involves reframing the contradiction so you do not see the two opposing forces as being in contradiction with one another

REAFFIRMATION

method of managing tensions that involves accepting that you cannot reconcile the contradiction and celebrate what the dialectical tension means for the couple's unity

* **Reaffirmation** involves accepting that contradictions cannot be reconciled, instead celebrating what the dialectical tension means for a couple's unity. For example, you might discuss how the tension between wanting to spend time together and alone shows that you have a healthy, strong, normal relationship.

All four of these theories of relationship maintenance offer us something unique for understanding our relationships and how they are maintained; each gives us specific concepts that help us make sense of our relational worlds. Theories are sense-making devices, and each one makes arguments about the world we can choose to accept and use or not.

DIALOGIC COMMUNICATION IN ONGOING RELATIONSHIPS

While our relationships should be enjoyable and fun, they require time, attention, and work to maintain. We must consciously work to maintain them in positive ways, or they will eventually fade. Below is a list of suggestions for keeping social relationships alive while privileging dialogue.

Embrace New Experiences

Relationships gain greater depth and strength when the two people share more interest and experiences with one another. When a partner asks you to try something new that they enjoy, be open to the experience and try it. Such a leap of faith and spirit of exploration will only deepen your bond, whereas shooting it down will blunt the development of a relationship. But, do remember that maintaining some sense of stability, predictability, and routine in your relationships is also important.

Privilege Quality and "Quantity" Time

Quantity of time matters just as much as quality of time with our relationship partners, whether they're friends, romantic partners, family members, or other social acquaintances. Even simple conversations recounting what happened during our day, talking about current events, and joking around show that we value the other person and enjoy his or her company. Those everyday activities and conversations are what make up our relationship, and when we make plans to do even mundane things together, we are demonstrating an ongoing commitment to our relationship.

Demonstrate Fidelity to the Relationship

Make sure your partner knows you value the relationship through verbal and nonverbal communication. Spend time with them, help when they ask for it, and inquire about his or her interests, activities, and feelings. These actions reinforce for the other person that you are committed to and value the friendship. We enter into relationships because we value the other person and feel valued by her or him; if you do not consistently express that value to the person, you risk damaging and even ending the relationship. Time is the most precious commodity we have, and so how we spend it and whom we spend it with speaks a lot about what relationships we value.

Avoid Judging or Controlling Your Partner

Social relationships are built on mutuality, and when one person begins to judge the actions, beliefs, or attitudes of another or attempts to control their choices and behaviors, then the relationship will greatly suffer. Remember, people choose to be in relationships; when they feel they can no longer be themselves because another person is domineering or judgmental, they might seek better alternatives to those relationships.

Celebrate Commonalities and Appreciate Differences

Relational partners share a range of different attitudes, interests, and beliefs. These overlapping activities and perceptions should be celebrated, and that's the easy part of relationships. The hard part is accepting that your partners will not always share your values, beliefs, and ideas. When these differences occur, you should work to understand why the other person sees things the way they do, but do not try and change them. The differences between partners can, as we mentioned earlier in the chapter, be complementary and thus enhance relationships—so long as we understand and accept those differences.

Give Your Partner Space

Even in the closest of relationships, we still need to have a sense of individuality. Plan activities with your partner, but also continue to explore some interests and activities on your own. Having some separate activities and friendships will help each of you continue to develop as individuals, give you something to talk about to help enrich your conversations together, and help you keep a sense of your own identity as an individual as well as part of a partnership.

SUMMARY

In this chapter, we continued our exploration of interpersonal communication by examining how we maintain relationships with others. We briefly covered key relationship maintenance behaviors identified by communications scholars as key elements of successful interpersonal associations. We then delved into four prominent theories that begin to explain how the maintenance of relationships takes place. Finally, we provided some key tips for using dialogue to maintain healthy relationships with other people.

CHAPTER 9 KEY IDEAS

- Relationship maintenance refers to the work we do to keep a relationship going and in a condition with which both partners are happy.

- Social Exchange Theory suggests that we evaluate our relationships based on the perceived rewards and costs in order to decide whether to stay in a relationship. Relationship satisfaction is based on comparison level, which is our set of general expectations for a certain type of relationship, and comparison level of alternatives, which is our comparison of our current relationship to other possible alternatives.

- Communication Privacy Management Theory helps us understand how people manage private information that is shared with others and how we establish rules for the spread of that information.

- Even in our most intimate relationships, most of our conversations consist of mundane, everyday talk. Those ordinary, everyday interactions help us to maintain our relationships and can be just as or even more important than deep relational conversations.

- In our relationships, we experience a set of dialectical tensions, which are oppositional needs or desires within our relationship. The three primary types of dialectical tension include integration and separation, stability and change, and expression and nonexpression.

CHAPTER 9 KEY TERMS

Relationship maintenance	Everyday talk
Meta-communicative	Dialectical tensions
Social Exchange Theory	Connection and autonomy
Minimax principle	Inclusion and seclusion
Comparison level	Certainty and uncertainty
Comparison level of alternatives	Openness and closedness
Communication privacy management	Revelation and concealment
Private information	Spiraling inversion
Deliberate confidant	Segmentation
Boundary linkage	Balance
Boundary ownership	Integration
Boundary permeability	Recalibration
Boundary turbulence	Reaffirmation

ACTIVITIES AND DISCUSSION QUESTIONS

1. Think about a fictional character (in a book, movie, or TV show) who stayed in a romantic relationship, even though it was not a good relationship for them. Briefly explain the scenario and then use social exchange theory to analyze why that person might have stayed in the relationship.

2. Think about a time that you disclosed private information with another person. Use Communication Privacy Management Theory to explain how you shared this information, how the boundaries were negotiated, and whether boundary turbulence occurred.

3. Explain a situation in which you and a relationship partner (romantic partner or friend) experienced a dialectical tension in your relationship. What was the situation, and what characteristics made it that particular type of dialectical tension? What strategy did you use to manage that dialectical tension?

4. Watch this TEDx Talk presented at La Sierra University by Shasta Nelson, available here https://www.youtube.com/watch?v=hmJyWreER7A. She coins a term called "frientimacy" in her discussion about three elements of healthy friendships. What is her assessment of how "friendtimacy" works? Now, reflect on her discussion of loneliness and your own experiences of "frientimacy."

COMMUNICATION IN
INTIMATE
RELATIONSHIPS

In this chapter, we turn our attention from general relationship development and maintenance to some of the most important relationships in our lives: intimate relationships. Intimate relationships are deeply personal bonds we have with other individuals that are accompanied by affective communication and a sense of belongingness. Perhaps more than any other type of relationship, the intimate associations we form with others significantly impact both the development and quality of our lives.

The first relationship we ever form is the intimate bond with our parents or caregivers when we are born, and this bond later grows to include the relationship with our entire family. Beginning in childhood we develop close friendships, and, for some, these friendships are among the most important connections. Later in life we also create intimate bonds with partners, wives, husbands, and perhaps children of our own. These relationships are complicated in nature and impacted by culture, but they are all held together through communication.

In this chapter, we explore the basic tenets of intimate relationships by first explaining the fundamental characteristics these types of associations contain. We will begin by turning our attention to the characteristics of romantic relationships and discuss how these bonds are formed, developed, and potentially dissolved through communication. We will

INTIMATE RELATIONSHIPS
deeply personal bonds that we have with other individuals that are accompanied by affective communication and a sense of belongingness

then examine families and how communication turns these connections into cherished relationships in our lives. Next, we will turn our attention to the unique nature of friendships. Finally, we will discuss how you can use dialogue to create and maintain constructive and rewarding intimate relationships with other people.

COMPONENTS OF INTIMATE RELATIONSHIPS

Not every relationship we form is intimate and, in fact, most are not. Think about how many different people you come into contact with every day. Now try to remember how many of them whose name you recall. It's probably not that many, and you can probably not remember details about even more. That's because those people, the people we know and recall a great deal about, are those with whom we formed intimate relationships. The reasons why we choose to form an intimate relationship with one person and not another are myriad, but the characteristics of the communication we use in those close associations is consistent. In this section we will explain five basic qualities shared by communication in intimate relationships.

Involve Deep Commitment

When we buy a cup of coffee or have a conversation with the cashier while buying groceries, we typically do so without thinking about the future of the relationship and accept we may not talk to the person again. There are other individuals that we interact with often at school, work, the gym, or in our communities we might talk to on a regular basis, and even socialize with from time to time, but with whom we have a casual social relationship rather than a deep personal connection. Everyday interactions with acquaintances and even casual friends are important in that they often help us to accomplish tasks and provide companionship and a sense of community as we live our lives, but those social relationships are fleeting and usually end if one of the parties moves to a new geographic location or if the activities that brought you together end.

When we have an intimate relationship with someone, however, we want to positively connect with the person over and over again in the future, hope to have that desire reciprocated, and work toward facilitating future conversations and activities with that person, even if geographic distance or schedule changes become obstacles to doing so. This is the quality of commitment, or the desire to do whatever we can to stay in the relationship regardless of what happens. The commitment is a promise we make to ourselves and the other person that the relationship will not only continue, but will continue to be strong.

COMMITMENT
the desire to make efforts to stay in the relationship regardless of what happens

Commitments in intimate relationships take many forms, and can even be codified legally through marriage contracts, birth certificates, or adoption certificates. We might make financial commitments to a partner or family. Ultimately, though, the deep commitment of intimate relationships is an emotional and chronemic commitment whereby we value the feelings of the other person and seek to spend a great deal of time with them. This emotional connection is deep and comes with a sense of responsibility for the other person's well-being and the well-being of the relationship. Regardless of the difficulties, arguments, challenges, or problems in a relationship, there is an ongoing promise to work through it and preserve the connection.

Promote Interdependence

One quality that makes intimate relationships so unique and powerful is that the depth of the commitment and connection to the other person creates a high level of interdependence between the relational partners. This means that what affects one person in the relationship affects the others. This can sometimes be said of casual acquaintances as well, but the level at which the interdependence exists in intimate relationships is what distinguishes it from casual acquaintances. Think of it as prioritizing, since we would likely put the needs and desires of our partners or family above those of coworkers.

In one sense, the intimate relationships we form with others make the other person an extension of oneself. Intimate others become part of how we identify ourselves; for instance, in some situations, you might begin to introduce yourself as the partner, spouse, daughter, brother, parent, or close friend of someone with whom you have an intimate relationship. Our intimate relationship partners are the first people with whom we share important parts of our lives, just as they share important parts of their lives with us first. Both parties become part of the other, joined in one category of family, siblings, partners, couples, spouses, or even close friends.

Require Constant Maintenance

Recall the concept of Social Exchange Theory from the chapter on relationship maintenance. Just like when we manage elements of our daily lives, we choose to invest different quantities of time, effort, emotion, and attention to different relationships. What we expect to get in return is based on what we believe we put into the relationship. In intimate relationships, we invest a significant portion of our resources and hope that it is returned by the other party. The degree of investment is also ongoing. Investment is not a matter of spending one day a week or month with the other person, but instead choosing every day to tend to the relationship. Intimate relationships have a consistent quality to the investment we put in them, and we expect the other party to be similarly invested.

Tend to Be Fluid Rather Than Static

All relationships have beginnings, middles, and ends, and they fluctuate in intensity during different periods. For this reason, it is important to understand that relationships are not simply static things, but rather processes you undergo or travel through. As we discussed a moment ago, what happens to one person affects the other, and we all experience different things that affect our moods, attentions, emotional states, and perceptions of our surroundings all the time. Sometimes the effect is barely noticeable; at other times it is dramatic and results in a fundamental change in the way we see the world around us. Since we are constantly influenced by our surroundings, so too is the relationship between ourselves and our partners or families influenced and adjusted based on those events. As a result, intimate relationships are fluid and ever changing.

Require Management of Tensions

The external experiences that influence relationships and leave them in a constant state of flux also can create tensions that the parties must manage in order to maintain their relationship over time. As we learned in the chapter on relationship maintenance, relationships are filled with dialectical tensions, or challenges that come from having several sets of essential, but at times oppositional, needs or desires.[1] For example, there are times when we want and need our family's communication to change. Children get older and their relationships with their parents must be revised. The move into adolescence can be the most challenging to negotiate for children and parents. The children are becoming more independent and want to be spoken to in increasingly more mature ways. Parents sometimes struggle with these changes, because they don't want to see their children grow up. The changes are necessary, however, to reach a "new normal," though that new normal will change again in later years.

DIALING DIVERSITY

Cultural Diversity of Marriage Traditions

In the United States, voluntary marriages are the norm; however that is not the case across the globe. In fact, in India there are a variety of different approaches to marriage. In a tradition rooted in the historic Vedic religion of India, parents of a girl would announce the intention of their daughter to marry and invite interested suitors to come forth at a specific time and place in a wedding hall. The daughter would then choose her husband from the men gathered there. The Gandharva marriage tradition relies simply on mutual consent between a man and woman with no rituals or even witnesses. Other marriage practices in India include traditional arranged weddings by parents and, recently, voluntary nuptials based on mutual love and affection. The idea of love as the primary reason for a wedding is actually a cultural development rooted in the West.[2]

ROMANTIC RELATIONSHIPS AS INTIMATE RELATIONSHIPS

When we think of intimate relationships, many of us think first about romantic relationships. Romantic partnerships come in many different forms, just like families, but one common characteristic they share is that there are no genetic ties between participants. Romantic relationships evolve, and sometimes even dissolve, over time, and romantic relationships come with their own communication challenges and issues. In this part of the chapter, we will first briefly define the characteristics and types of romantic partnerships that exist in society before explaining the development process these relationships go through.

Characteristics of Romantic Relationships

Not all romantic relationships are the same, as each couple creates, negotiates, and sometimes violates the rules that govern the association. For this reason, it is quite difficult to pin down the characteristics all romantic couples share; rather, we can identify some typical attributes that many, but not all, romantic partnerships contain.

Open vs. closed romantic relationships. The traditional way of defining a romantic partnership is through the exclusive nature of the relationship, meaning that both parties do not have romantic bonds with anyone other than each other. This is a closed relationship. There are, however, some romantic relationships that are open, and both parties are free to see other people while still holding a deep commitment to each other. In fact, polygamy is the practice of marrying more than one partner, and there are cultures that continue this practice of open relationships even today.

Voluntary vs. arranged marriages. In Western cultures, marriages and romantic pairings are typically voluntary. Each person enters into the relationship freely and has the right to end the relationship. In some cultures, however, marriages are arranged for children by parents to maximize family social standings, financial status, or for other reasons. The parties who are contracted to marry sometimes have no say in the matter, and in some cases, they do not even meet until their marriage. In other cases, family members introduce potential partners that the family has approved and give the couple some time to get to know each other before letting the couple decide whether they are compatible and willing to marry. Some cultures have different practices for arranged marriages that might give individuals more or less ability to decide whether they want to marry. In arranged marriages, the individuals might not feel deep love before deciding to marry, something that typically does not happen with truly voluntary romantic relationships.

Opposite-sex vs. same-sex couples. Traditionally, marriages and romantic relationships have been defined as existing between opposite sex partners, but recent history has changed that. Following the 2015 Supreme Court decision in *Obergefell v. Hodges* in the United States the federal government recognizes same-sex couples for tax and benefits purposes. This was not the case at the turn of the century. American culture is becoming more accepting of same-sex couples and supportive of equal rights, as can be evidenced through the changes in legislation and their growing presence in television shows like the popular *Modern Family* and *Glee* sitcoms and reality shows like *Extreme Guide to Parenting*.

Married for life vs. divorced. When couples marry, they typically believe it is a lifetime commitment. Unfortunately, divorce statistics illustrate that many marriages are not lifetime commitments. Marriage commitments wane and dissipate for a variety of reasons; however, there are a host of other reasons, such as social, familial, and community support that help preserve marriages even through difficult and trying times. One of the most influential factors in the success or failure of a marriage is communication, both before and during married life. For instance, marriage expert and scholar John Gottman found that communication is key to predicting the success or failure of relationships based on how people interact with each other.[3]

Types of Romantic Relationships

INTERDEPENDENCE

the quality of intimate relationships whereby one person's actions influence the other and vice versa; refers to the degree of connectedness between the two individuals, including how the couple shares time and space within their home

Just as there are many different types of romantic relationships, there are also several different types of relationship patterns that can be seen in romantic relationships and marriages. Mary Anne Fitzpatrick and her colleagues[4] have found that there are three dimensions important for classifying marital relationships: interdependence, ideology, and conflict. Interdependence refers to the degree of connectedness between the two individuals, including how the couple shares time and space within their home. Recall from the chapter on communication, culture, and diversity that ideology refers to the beliefs and values the individuals have about what marriage and family life should be like, and can include placing a value on stability and predictability or on spontaneity and relational uncertainty. Conflict refers to whether the partners try to resolve differences through open conflict or whether they avoid conflict. We will talk more about this in the chapter on interpersonal conflict.

Traditional. Couples who have traditional relationships have a high level of interdependence, share conventional ideologies about marriage, and avoid marital conflict. In these marriages, both individuals take on conventional sex roles; the wife usually takes her husband's last name, the couple spends a lot of time together, and the individuals disclose a lot of information to one another. Traditional couples are also likely to keep regular schedules and share the same spaces in their home. While traditional couples do not avoid talking about problematic issues, they try to do so in a neutral way and avoid engaging in open conflict.

Separate. Separate couples tend to have low levels of interdependence, share conventional ideologies, and avoid conflict. Similar to traditional couples, separates have conventional views about marriage, family, and sex roles and are likely to avoid conflict. However, separates spend far less time together, talk less, disclose less information to one another, maintain a psychological distance, and spend time in separate spaces.

Independent. Independent couples tend to have a high level of interdependence, share unconventional ideologies, and openly engage in conflict. Like traditional couples, independent couples disclose a lot to their partner, spend a lot of time together, and often have long conversations. However, independent couples do not think that relationships should constrain individual freedom and are likely to have less conventional sex roles, are likely to maintain separate spaces (e.g., separate home offices), and do not always keep regular schedules. Independent couples are also more likely to engage in open conflict when a problematic issue arises.

Mixed. Mixed couples include spouses who have different definitions for their relationship. For example, one partner might define the marriage as traditional while the other partner might define the marriage as separate based on the dimensions of interdependence, ideology, and conflict. Mixed couples could see themselves as having any two of the three marriage types described above, and approximately 40 percent of all couples fall into this category.

FAMILIES AS INTIMATE RELATIONSHIPS

Now that we have talked about romantic relationships and the marriages that result in some of those romantic relationships, it only seems natural to move on to talking about families. Families are unique and complex forms of intimate relationships. In some ways we have no control over our family, but in others we do. For example, we have no control over the family into which we are born, but we do choose our mates and can build our own families. In this part of the chapter, we will describe the common ways families are defined or created, explain how families function as systems, describe the types of families, and finally explore some of the significant communication issues families confront.

Creating a Family

There are three ways in which families form in society, and many families form in more than one way. The first of these is the most obvious: through genetics. The second way families can be created in a society is through the law, whereby the government recognizes a family unit. The third, and final, way is through role enactment.[5]

Most, but definitely not all, families share genetic information and are biologically related. Keep in mind, though, this relates to parents and children, not the parents themselves, as marriage partners come from different families. The children share half their genetic information with each biological parent, thus connecting the family through genetics. This shared DNA often results in close connections between individuals, especially as they grow up in that particular family structure. It is important to note, though, that there are several different methods through which families form intimate bonds with children who do not share any biological information—for instance, through adoption, foster care, and surrogacy.

Families are such an important element of a stable society that governments and communities care about how they are constituted and managed. It is for this reason there is a legal dimension to, and option for, establishing a family. When a couple marries, they must get a civil license for the marriage through their local or state government office to certify the union. Legal protections for couples often includes things like tax filing status, custody of children, the right to make medical decisions for a family member when they are unable to do so for themselves, and the ability to share employer-provided healthcare benefits.

Families also always contain roles and typical behaviors for members. It is these roles and behaviors that create the perception of a family unit. These include things like living together, caring for each other, identifying as a family to the community, and showing a genuine interest in the development of each other's lives and interests. These roles can manifest in genetic families as well as adoptive or surrogate ones. The existence of familial roles contributes to the use of "family" as a metaphor for teams, companies, and other typically social groups that do not have the legal designation as a family or genetic ties to one another.

The Family System

SYSTEM

interdependent parts that interact with and affect one another

OPEN SYSTEM

a system in which parts both affect and are affected by events within and outside the system

The tight bonds that give families their intimate quality also create a system of operation within them, meaning they are composed of interdependent parts that interact with and affect one another. Researcher Paul Watzlawick defined families as complex self-regulating arrangements of feedback loops between the people involved that are governed by rules established by its members.[6] In other words, families each have their own unique rules and ways of operating. Families also adapt as things happen and as members interact with one another. These family systems are referred to as open systems, or those systems where parts both affect and are affected by events within and outside the system, and they exhibit certain qualities.

Families are influenced by context. As an open system, families and their members are constantly adapting to the things that happen at home and outside. People change, and family systems change with them.

Families foster interdependence. All systems experience the pull and push of individual parts, and families are no different. Resources are shared by all in the system, and conflicts can arise when these are in short supply. Additionally, happiness is shared; when one member has something positive happen, the entire family reacts and responds to that event.

A family is greater than the sum of its members. A family is more than just an individual, creating its own identity that manifests when all or a few members are together. The shared identity influences individual identities, just as the individuals in the system contribute to the overall family dynamic.

Families contain multiple systems. Each family contains certain groups within it that have their own dynamics. Parents and children interact in specific ways, as do siblings with each other. Those siblings also have different relationships with individual parents than they do when the parents are together. These different permutations of members have their own unique system within the larger family system.

Families establish change-resistant systems. It is incredibly difficult to change the ways families communicate once patterns are established within the unit. It is not impossible, but it is challenging. Just think how difficult it is for parents to adjust to the changing dynamic of their relationship with children when they go off to college.

Family Types

Just as marriages can be described as fitting into different categories based on several communication dimensions, families can also be described as fitting into different categories or types depending on how family members interact with one another. **Conversational orientation** is the degree to which family members are encouraged to participate in unrestrained conversation about a range of topics, and **conformity orientation** is the degree to which the family emphasizes homogeneity of attitudes, values, and beliefs. Mary Anne Fitzpatrick and her colleagues argue that families can be divided into four different types based on their conversation orientation and their conflict orientation as represented in Table 10.1.[7,8] Families typically fall into one of four types: consensual, pluralistic, protective, and laissez-faire.

	High Conversation Orientation	Low Conversation Orientation
High Conformity Orientation	Consensual	Protective
Low Conformity Orientation	Pluralistic	Laissez-faire

TABLE 10.1 **Types of Families**

CONVERSATIONAL ORIENTATION
the degree to which family members are encouraged to participate in unrestrained conversation about a range of topics

CONFORMITY ORIENTATION
the degree to which the family emphasizes homogeneity of attitudes, values, and beliefs

Drug Abuse and the Family

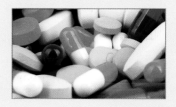
ENGAGING ETHICS

Drug abuse is the leading cause of accidental death in the United States. In recent years an epidemic of opioid abuse has impacted the nation. Each of these victims (or addicts) has a family, and the impact of their affliction spreads to the family. The instinct of families is to help; however, providing money or food and supplies to opioid addicts is often counter-productive as it simply gets repurposed for the purchase of more drugs. Families can fall apart over this as they are unable to see how the people they love cannot be helped in the traditional way. Significant damage is done to trust within the family. Consider this impact on the family system and how, as Watzlawick notes, family systems are change-resistant. How does a parent or sibling maintain love and support for the addicted family member in light of these challenges? What communicative behaviors might help the family change and truly assist the afflicted person?

Consensual families. These families are high in conversation orientation and high in conformity orientation. These families encourage open conversation and the exploration of ideas, but there is also a high amount of pressure to agree in order to preserve the existing hierarchy. While children are encouraged to speak, the parents ultimately make the decisions for the family and take time to explain those decisions to the family. Decision-making is often distributed among the adults, so that one makes some types of decisions while the other makes other types of decisions.

Pluralistic families. These families are high in conversation orientation but low in conformity orientation. These families encourage open, unrestrained communication and evaluate all family members' contributions on their own merit. Parents and children participate equally in family decision-making, and children usually become independent and autonomous. Pluralistic families spend time together and share a great deal, but they also value autonomy and spend time apart engaging in individual activities.

Protective families. These families are low in conversation orientation and high in conformity orientation. These families emphasize obedience to authority, and parents make decisions for their children and rarely explain the reasoning for their decisions.

Laissez-faire families. These families are low in conversation orientation and low in conformity orientation. Family members are uninvolved, have very limited conversations, believe that all family members should be allowed to make their own decisions, and have little interest in those decisions.

Communication Issues in the Family System

Communication issues within families can take two primary forms. The first are the communicative actions that help to strengthen the family identity, while the second are those communicative patterns that negatively influence the family and its members. To be clear, communication issues refer to the *ways* in which families communicate rather than the *topics* about which they communicate.

RITUALS

repetitive behaviors that contain a unique meaning for members, and each family develops their own traditions

Positive communicative actions within a family include those things that create a sense of history and identity for members. These might include certain family rituals and traditions, like eating certain foods on holidays, modes of celebrating birthdays, and even how and when everyone gets together for meals. Rituals are repetitive behaviors that contain a unique meaning for members, and each family develops their own traditions. In many cases, these traditions trace back many generations, while other families begin rituals in the hopes of making it a "new" family tradition to uniquely shape family identity. Research has also shown that importing traditions from one's family past into a new family is especially important in building a sense of cohesion in blended and adopted families.[9]

A second positive communication action that enhances the family identity is that of telling stories. Every family has its own stories about generations past, current members, and important events in the history of the family. Telling and retelling these stories to each successive generation connects a new member not just with those present but also with family members from the past. Families also take comfort in the fact that their stories may be added to this long narrative of the family in future generations.

On the opposite end of the spectrum, there are communicative patterns that can negatively impact those in the family system. These patterns are driven by the power, status, and control dimensions inherent to human organizations, including families. In a **complementary interchange**, the interaction between members of the system is based on acknowledged differences in power, such as what exists between parents and children. In a **symmetrical interchange**, communication between members seeks to neutralize the power difference and treat each other equally. When family members seek to exert dominance over one another or exhibit control over another member, they engage in complementary interchanges, and when they do so, they risk creating stress in the entire system despite the fact such behaviors may be necessary at times. Symmetrical interchanges are

COMPLEMENTARY INTERCHANGE
interaction between members of a system that is based on acknowledged differences in power

SYMMETRICAL INTERCHANGE
communication between members that seeks to neutralize the power difference and treat each person equally

The Big Bang Theory and Arranged Marriages

One of the most successful sitcoms in recent years is *The Big Bang Theory*, about a group of eccentric university professor friends. Finishing its twelfth and final season in spring 2019, it is the longest multi-camera television series in 79 episodes. The story initially focuses on roommates and California Institute of Technology physicists Leonard and oddball Sheldon, their close friends, MIT educated engineer Howard and Indian astrophysicist Rajesh who hails from a wealthy family in India. Together, with Leonard's love interest, Penny; Howard's wife, Bernadette; and Sheldon's equally eccentric partner, Amy Farrah-Fowler, the show often pokes fun at Rajesh's inability to find and hold girlfriend. In the twelfth

season a storyline emerged where Rajesh finally acceded to his father's marriage with an Indian professional woman living in the same area as Rajesh. The two are set up on a date, begin to get to know each other all while simultaneously planning their wedding. At one point they both acknowledge they don't know each other as well as they thought, and call off the wedding to slow down their relationship development. It's a comedic representation of relationship development and arranged marriages that manages to illustrate the cultural differences of the approaches to matchmaking while also respecting the inherent differences between this approach and traditional notions of romance in the West.

much healthier approaches to communication where no one seeks to exert dominance over another and everyone is able to communicate and do things based on their own merits. However, these patterns also come with the risk of **enabling communication** that is not assertive, and thus may allow members to continue abusive, addictive, and otherwise negative behaviors.[10] Enabling communication helps create an environment where negative behaviors are not stopped, and thus end up being encouraged to continue.

ENABLING COMMUNICATION
interaction that is not assertive and thus allows members to continue abusive, addictive, and otherwise negative behaviors

FRIENDSHIPS AS INTIMATE RELATIONSHIPS

Now that we understand the ways in which romantic and family relationships are important intimate relationships, we will turn our attention to one of the most unique relationships in our lives: friendships. While some friendships are acquaintances that would best be categorized as casual social relationships, some of our friendships can be the closest, most intimate, and sometimes even the longest relationships in our lives. First, we will cover the five qualities that constitute friendships, before discussing some of the dialectic tensions inherent in these forms of relationships. Anytime we are close to someone, and the person feels close to us, tensions can and do arise.

The Qualities of Friendships

Friendships are characterized by five different common elements. We don't necessarily think about these things when we form friendships, but they exist nonetheless. In this section of the chapter, we will discuss these five different characteristics that constitute the friendships in our lives.[11]

Friendships are voluntary. Part of what makes friendships so powerful is that they are one of the few relationships we freely choose to make or unmake. While you can't choose your neighbors, classmates, coworkers, or family members, you do get to choose your friends. If you want to end a friendship, all you have to do is make that decision, whereas ending a marriage or family relationship requires a long legal process, and deciding not to be neighbors or coworkers with someone requires that you find a new place to live or acquire a new job. Knowing that you have chosen, and continue to choose, each other as friends can create a very powerful bond between two people.

Because of the conscientious choices and beneficial consequences of friendship, communicating as friends has important ethical and political potentials.

—**William Rawlins, Ohio University**

Friendships are personal relationships. While we sometimes see other individuals with whom we have interpersonal relationships as part of a certain group or class (sister, parent, child, teacher, etc.), we see each of our friends as unique individuals. We privately negotiate our friendship with our friends, and each of our friendships is a distinctive relationship.

Friendships are pervaded by a spirit of equality. Even though we might have different levels of education, socioeconomic status, ability, age, or other characteristics than our friends in other contexts, we view our friends as equals within the context of our friendship and deliberately choose ways of interacting that emphasize that sense of equality.

Friendships are characterized by mutual involvement. As communication scholar William K. Rawlins explains, "The bonds of friendship result from the collaboration of two individuals in constructing a shared social reality. This interpersonal reality evolves out of and furthers mutual acceptance and support, trust and confidence, dependability and assistance, and discussion of thoughts and feelings."[12] Both parties must be actively engaged in a friendship for the friendship to continue to exist.

Friendship implies affective ties. We care about, are concerned for, have positive feelings toward, and often have a deep love for our friends.

Dialectical Tensions in Friendships

Our friendships sometimes serve different purposes depending on the stage of our lives, ranging from childhood playmates, to college friends, to later-life companions. Just as we feel strains from dialectical tensions in our romantic relationships, Rawlins argues that we face a slightly different set of dialectical tensions in our friendships. The first two dialectical pairs are tensions that arise from our cultural conceptions of friendship. The final four dialectical pairs are tensions that emanate from the relationship itself and are referred to as interactional dialectics. Just as we must work to manage dialectical tensions in our other relationships, we must constantly negotiate the dialectics within our friendships.

Private and public. We often feel pressure to interact publicly with our friends in ways that are deemed socially acceptable and expected, while at the same time having our own personal expectations and ways of interacting in that particular friendship. For instance, cross-sex friends might feel like they have to partially disguise their friendship in public out of concern that others might think there is a romantic or sexual relationship, while they might be able to talk and express their friendship much more openly when in private.

Ideal and real. We have cultural expectations for what friendships should look like and how we should interact with our friends, and this is often sometimes very different from how individuals interact with specific friends in everyday life.

Freedom to be independent and freedom to be dependent. Just as we have a desire for both autonomy and connection in our romantic relationships, we want to be able to pursue our individual interests without interference from our friends, but we also want to be able to depend on our friends when we need help.

Affection and instrumentality. We want to be friends with others because we care about them as people and have affection for them, but we also want to be friends because friendships are utilitarian or instrumental in that they help us achieve other things.

Judgment and acceptance. We want our friends to accept and support us in our actions, but at times we also want our friends to give us honest evaluations or criticisms, and vice versa.

Expressiveness and protectiveness. We want to be able to be open and share vulnerable information with our close friends, which shows a great deal of trust, but at the same time, there is often information we do not want to share with our friends because we consider it private.

DIALOGIC COMMUNICATION IN INTIMATE RELATIONSHIPS

One of the primary reasons intimate relationships reach the end is a lack of good communication between partners, either at the beginning stages of the relationship regarding expectations and values, or during the period of bonding. Using dialogue with a partner helps to mitigate these problems before they happen, in many cases because it is based on achieving understanding. Understanding your partner, family member, or friend and what his or her beliefs, values, goals, and desires are is a key element to any successful intimate relationship. In this final part of the chapter, we will provide you with some guidelines for successfully enacting dialogue in your intimate relationships.

Be Honest About Your Feelings

This may seem obvious, but it is also quite hard to do in the moment. Many people do not want to hurt or offend their partner, and they feel disagreement can hurt them so they resist the urge to express this disconnect. Asserting your own opinions and helping your partner or family understand your perspective on an issue, however controversial, leads to positive outcomes, not negative ones, for the relationship. Being honest and open about how something makes you feel, how you perceive something, or what you would like to do is part of the foundation of any intimate relationship. Additionally, you must be prepared to accept openness and honesty from your partner and family as well.

Own Your Own Statements

In being open and honest, we also must own our own feelings. This means acknowledging your feeling, instead of placing blame or attributing the feeling to someone or something else. For example, when we say, "You make me so mad," we are issuing an accusatory statement that also relinquishes our ability to control our own emotions by saying some-one else can dictate how we feel through how she or he acts. Instead, point to the specific behavior and say, "I get upset when you don't clean the dishes after you eat." Here you own your own feeling, and are specific about what incites that emotion, so the other party knows what to address.

Focus on the Other Person

Perhaps what makes relationships intimate is not the depth of yourself you share, but the focus, care, and attention you place on the other person. Maintaining that interest and appreciation for his or her beliefs, attitudes, emotions, interests, goals, and activities is what keeps partnerships together. A genuine affection is borne not only out of a sense of sharing oneself, but also in caring enough to let the other person share himself or herself with you.

Approach Conflict Constructively

Later in this book we will address interpersonal conflict in greater detail, but handling it in a constructive and not destructive way is essential for intimate relationships. When you care about the other person and have a deep commitment to her or his well-being, then conflict can be a constructive platform from which relationships can evolve and grow. Do not attack people or assume motives, but rather engage to understand the roots of the disagreement and work to bridge any gaps that may exist.

Welcome Different Experiences

The richness and diversity of experiences people have and are interested in having are what make being in a relationship such a rewarding experience. In initiating a relationship or main-taining a family connection, you must be open to the different opinions and interests of the other person and not approach them as opportunities to dominate and control. Respect a person's background, goals, and experiences, and they will likely reciprocate. Also, be open to trying things that might make you uncomfortable, but be sure to share your perception of the experience with your family member or friend.

Discuss the Status of the Relationship

It is important to be on the same page with others with whom you have intimate relationships, and to do this you should periodically check in about the state in which you see the relation-ship. You might discover the other person disagrees, but you also might get an opportunity to have your perception reinforced. Knowing the relational status allows you to determine the best labels to use or behaviors to exhibit. These types of moments can come about after long periods of noncommunication with family members, but also more commonly happen in romantic relationships at that awkward moment when one person in the couple sees the relationship in one way, but the other person might not. Talking about this issue adds to the intimate nature of the relationship, but does come with risk—and reward.

SUMMARY

In this chapter, we explored different types of intimate relationships. We discussed three primary forms of intimate relationships: those that exist in romantic partnerships, those that occur in families, and those that are our closest friendships. We detailed the characteristics of all three relationship forms, how they develop and change, and what issues are typically confronted in these relationships. Finally, we provided some guidelines for creating dialogue within intimate relationships with family members and romantic partners.

CHAPTER 10 KEY IDEAS

- Intimate relationships share five basic qualities: (1) they are marked by individuals deeply committed to one another, (2) they entail interdependence, (3) they require constant investment to maintain, (4) they are fluid, not static, and (5) they require the management of tension.

- Three of the most important types of intimate relationships in most people's lives are romantic relationships, family relationships, and friendships.

- Marriages can be classified based on the level of interdependence, ideology, and approach to conflict within the couple. The four types of marriages are traditional, separate, independent, and mixed.

- Families can be created through genetics, law, or role enactment. Families are systems with their own self-regulating arrangements of feedback loops. Families can be categorized based on their conversation orientation and conformity orientation into four distinct types: consensual, pluralistic, protective, and laissez-faire.

- Friendships are voluntary personal relationships that are pervaded by a spirit of equality, characterized by mutual involvement, and imply affective ties. We experience a slightly different set of dialectical tensions in our friendships than in our romantic relationships.

CHAPTER 10 KEY TERMS

Intimate relationships	Conformity orientation
Commitment	Rituals
Interdependence	Complementary interchange
System	Symmetrical interchange
Open system	Enabling communication
Conversational orientation	

ACTIVITIES AND DISCUSSION QUESTIONS

1. Choose a married couple from a TV show or movie that you have watched recently and find a video clip of an interaction that is typical of that couple. What type of marriage do you think that they have? Why do you think they have that particular type of marriage?

2. Aziz Ansari's book, *Modern Romance*, was written based on the work of a team of leading social scientists. The book begins with a chapter that traces the history of how couples typically met and decided to marry in the United States, and the research shows that expectations for our relationships with our partners, how we meet, and why we do (or don't) decide to marry are very different than they were even a couple of generations ago. How are your expectations for whether, when, and how you might find a partner and decide to marry different from the expectations of your parents, grandparents, and great-grandparents?

3. Does your family or culture typically expect individuals to choose their own partner or to have family members help to arrange a partnership? What are the norms and expectations for family involvement in dating and marriage in your culture?

4. Consider the qualities/characteristics of family systems. How do you see each of these qualities play out in your own family system? What type of family were you raised in? Provide some examples from your own experience that illustrate this family type. How have those experiences impacted the type of family that you might eventually want to create?

5. Choose two of the dialectical tensions experienced in friendships and explain how you have experienced these tensions with one of your close friends. Give examples of situations in which you struggled with each of these tensions and explain how you and your friend managed that dialectical tension.

MEDIATED
RELATIONSHIPS

As technology has advanced, the media we use to interact with others has changed a great deal. Prior to the invention of the telegraph in 1832, individuals had to rely on either face-to-face communication or written letters. Letters had to be physically carried across geographic space from the writer to the recipient, which could take a great deal of time if the recipient was far away. The invention of the telegraph allowed messages to be sent long distances almost instantly, though messages still had to be transmitted back and forth one at a time, which allowed for a greater control of message construction.[1] Later, the invention of the telephone finally allowed synchronous communication and interactive conversations across long distances. If we fast forward to today, our options for mediated communication have expanded tremendously, leaving us with more options for communicating and maintaining relationships with others across time and space than any generation before (Figure 11.1).

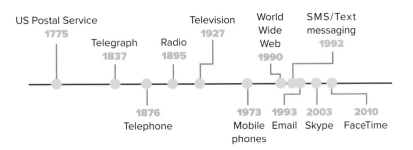

FIGURE 11.1   **Major Innovations for Mediated Communication**

In this chapter, we will first discuss the types of social media that are now available and then explain how the use of mediated communication impacts the relationships between—and perceptions of—self and others. Finally, we will provide a few tips for engaging in social media with a dialogic spirit.

MEDIATED COMMUNICATION

Earlier in the book, we discussed various models of the communication process. You may recall the linear and transactional models of communication, with the former providing no explanation for feedback, and the latter allowing for constant and continuous messaging by both parties. Communication through media, especially electronic media, which we will focus on in this chapter, can work in either the linear or transactional format. Sometimes, however, there may be a slight or significant time lag between communication by both parties through their electronic platforms. In this section of the chapter, we explain how this time lag helps us further categorize communication before explaining some specific types of mediated communication.

Modes of Mediated Communication

All mediated communication, including social media, can be categorized in several different ways. The first way considers whether communication occurs simultaneously or in a back and forth exchange over time. Synchronous communication is communication that occurs simultaneously. In synchronous communication, both parties of the conversation are able to respond to one another in the moment. Examples of synchronous communication include a face-to-face conversation, a phone conversation, a Skype or FaceTime video call, and even an instant messaging or text message conversation in which both parties are online and engaging in the conversation at the same time.

SYNCHRONOUS COMMUNICATION
communication that occurs simultaneously

ASYNCHRONOUS COMMUNICATION
communication that occurs when the communicators are sending and receiving messages at different times

Asynchronous communication, on the other hand, is communication that occurs when the communicators are sending and receiving messages at different times. Examples of asynchronous communication might include mailed letters, emails, online message boards or review sites, Facebook messages, or even text message conversations in which there is a gap in time between responses. Each of these modes of interaction allow people to take their time to respond to the initial message.

Types of Mediated Communication

In the early years of the Internet, most users consumed information from a relatively small number of content producers and information that was posted online was fairly static, meaning that once something was posted on a website, it was likely to stay there and remain unchanged for a while. Around the beginning of the twenty-first century, though, we began to see a transition to Web 2.0, in which almost all internet users generated online content and frequently updated or added to the information posted online, largely as a result of the development of social media sites. Social media include forms of electronic communication through which users create online communities to share information, ideas, personal messages, and other content. A few examples of social media platforms include Facebook, Twitter, Pinterest, Spotify, Yelp, Instagram, Snapchat, Blogger, YouTube, Groupon, and numerous other sites that have likely been developed and become popular since this chapter was written. Now, almost anyone with Internet access and a little bit of experience using applications can easily add and edit online content.

The second way to categorize types of mediated communication is on a continuum from impersonal to hyperpersonal communication. Impersonal communication is communication that occurs in order to facilitate some type of transaction and is based primarily on social roles in the particular situation. Examples of impersonal communication might include a phone conversation with a receptionist to schedule a dental appointment, a brief interaction at a fast food restaurant to order and pay for a meal, an email reminding you of a deadline, or a review of a product posted on Amazon that shares information about the product with other potential buyers. Researchers used to believe that computer-mediated communication was more impersonal than face-to-face interpersonal conversations, but now some types of computer-mediated communication can actually exceed face-to-face conversation in users' ability to create an impression, present information about oneself to another person, and achieve relational goals.[2]

Hyperpersonal communication occurs when computer-mediated communication has a higher level of affection, emotion, liking, solidarity, and intimacy than face-to-face conversations. Online communication allows communicators to focus more on their message because they do not have to monitor behavioral cues. Online technologies also give communicators the ability to craft the image they convey by emphasizing some characteristics and downplaying others. Such hyperpersonal online communication can allow individuals to find support from others with similar experiences online, but it also makes it possible for individuals to create fake identities and deceive others in what sometimes become painful situations.

SOCIAL MEDIA
forms of electronic communication through which users create online communities to share information, ideas, personal messages, and other content

IMPERSONAL COMMUNICATION
communication that occurs in order to facilitate some type of transaction; based primarily on social roles

HYPERPERSONAL COMMUNICATION
computer-mediated communication that has a higher level of affection, emotion, liking, solidarity, and intimacy than face-to-face conversations

Social Media and Privacy

ENGAGING ETHICS

The anonymous nature of the web allows for a variety of different activities that enhance our lives, but also the opportunity for people to behave in ways that are inappropriate and, in some cases, dangerous and illegal. The line between the two is often blurry. For example, employers often will look at social media posts of applicants for positions to see what their "real" personalities and beliefs are. Is this ethical or acceptable? Why or why not? In other instances old emails, tweets, and posts have been unearthed about individuals who are then punished for those actions. How do these actions comport with ethical behaviors?

Yet another way that we can categorize types of social media is by the type of information shared or the function served by the social media. Some social media sites allow members to connect with others that they know offline or who share similar interests, such as Facebook, GooglePlus, and LinkedIn. Some sites, such as YouTube, Flickr, and Vimeo, allow users to post and watch online photo or video content, while others such as Spotify or Netflix allow you to stream commercially produced media, while also sharing recommendations with friends in social networks. Blogging sites, such as Blogger and Wordpress, allow users to post entries with text, photos, video, and even music for followers, while a microblogging site, such as Twitter, allows users to post messages that are no more than 280 characters in length.

MEDIATED SELF AND MEDIATED OTHERS

Think about your own Facebook friends list, the people that follow you on Twitter, and the people with whom you have exchanged emails or text messages in the past week. How many of them are people that you have met in person? Chances are, you have met most of the people you communicate with online in face-to-face interactions and probably even see some of them on a fairly regular basis. While mediated communication opens up the possibility of connecting with other people online that you have never met and would be unlikely to encounter in day-to-day life, the reality is that most people connect with people they already know in their "offline" lives when communicating online.[3] Mediated communication often serves as a way to grow, enhance, and maintain relationships with people we already know, such as keeping in touch with old friends when moving to a new place or beginning college, and maintaining and intensifying relationships with people we interact with often.

Interpersonal Relationships and Media Impact

There are three primary ways that media impact messages in interpersonal relationships.[4] First, the medium can modify the message, which means that the medium we choose to communicate certain messages can change how others receive those messages. For example, choosing to use a text message instead of face-to-face communication to break up with a romantic partner might result in a bitter response from your partner and others who perceive your actions as cold; however, using that same technique in another relationship might give your partner a sense of relief that they didn't have to have an awkward break-up conversation with you. Choosing to tell someone that a loved one passed away via a Facebook post instead of a phone call might leave some friends or relatives feeling hurt that you communicated such sensitive information in such an uncaring way, while others might view it as your way of getting the information out quickly and simultaneously while saving your emotional energy from having to call so many different people with the same news. In some cases, it is difficult to predict how your choice of medium will affect your interactions with others, but typically you can refer to the richness of the message and match it to the richness of the mode of the communication.[5]

Media Richness Theory states that "lean" messages, such as clarification questions (e.g., "Are we meeting for dinner at 6 or 7 o'clock?"), are best suited for "lean" media, such as email or text messaging, because these types of messages are considered straightforward. "Rich" messages (e.g., telling your spouse that there are problems in your marriage) that include complex and potentially emotional content are expressed best using "rich" media (e.g., face to face or over the telephone); however, these are merely guidelines, and sometimes very "rich" interpersonal interactions (e.g., seeking and receiving social support from others) can occur online.[6] Online interactions can be a lot like face-to-face interactions now, given the advances in technology, which allows us to feel a high level of social presence while relating with others when using these communication media.

CATFISHING

the practice of pretending to have a different identity via social media in order to initiate and maintain a relationship with another person

Hyperpersonal Communication, Fabricated Identities, and Fake Relationships

MEDIATED MOMENTS

AP Photo/ESPN Images, Ryan Jones

In 2018 Twitter and Facebook escalated the removal of fake accounts and "bots," as part of a response to findings that Russia had used these tools to spread disinformation during the 2016 presidential election. In total, by July 2018, Twitter was removing an average of upwards of one million accounts a day, and Facebook had announced the removal of 32 accounts which had posted material consistent with Russian election interference. In 2012, University of Notre Dame football player Manti Te'o thought his girlfriend had died. He and the woman had only communicated online, but later he found out that her existence had been entirely faked. An acquaintance, Ronaiah Tuiasosopo, had apparently orchestrated the entire relationship by making up the woman via social media and pretending to be her in phone calls to Te'o. Tuiasosopo has admitted to using another woman's photos to create the made-up girlfriend, Lennay Kekua, who he said was a Stanford University undergraduate student. This is an example of what has been termed catfishing, which is when a person pretends to have a different identity via social media in order to initiate and maintain a relationship with another person. Catfishing uses the ability of social media to maintain a distance between communicators to create a false sense of intimacy between correspondents, representing a unique danger to the online environment.

Online interaction might also provide certain benefits over face-to-face communication. For example, online support groups can offer you the opportunity to talk to and/or learn from many other people who have faced a similar situation (e.g., your child has a serious illness) but who might have different perspectives.[7] You can also share and discuss these sensitive topics at your convenience and without the challenge of talking in front of others in a face-to-face setting where you might feel apprehensive to talk about such things with strangers.[8] These are some of the benefits of online communication over offline interactions; choosing which is appropriate and functional in a given situation is important and should not be taken lightly.

The second way media impact messages in interpersonal relationships is understood by viewing the medium as part of a causal chain, meaning that the use of one media type might lead to the use of another media type. For example, someone might send a friend a cryptic text message to spark curiosity and get that friend to initiate a phone call. A particularly difficult face-to-face conversation might lead to an apology text or email, or vice versa. A set of Facebook posts about how you are feeling might cause a coworker to stop by your desk and ask you how you are doing and if you need any help at work. If you think about it, probably many of your everyday interactions span across several different communication media. This is not necessarily a bad thing, but you should be mindful when shifting from one form to another to make sure you are not unintentionally violating any norms of communication and/or of the relationship(s) with the other person or people who are a part of the interaction.

Third, the types of media used in a relationship communicate something about that relationship, regardless of the messages that are sent using those media. For example, most people communicate with those they are closest to via several media. For instance, you might communicate with your closest friends or romantic partner face to face, via phone calls, with text messages, through written notes and emails, and through social media such as Facebook, Instagram, or Snapchat on a regular basis. However, you might choose to only communicate with more distant others, such as coworkers with whom you are not particularly close, via face-to-face and email communication. As we become closer to or more distant from particular individuals, the number of channels or types of media through which we communicate might also increase or decrease. Additionally, we might choose to talk with others via specific media to conform to social expectations for that particular type of relationship. For instance, one study found that people tend to engage in everyday talk less often with cross-sex friends than same-sex friends when face to face and on the phone, but these differences are not seen when communicating with same-sex and cross-sex friends online.[9] A female student might be less likely to engage in a lot of everyday talk face to face with a male friend because other friends might begin asking whether they are a romantic couple; instead, those two friends will probably engage in more everyday talk online or through text messages, which allows for less public communication.

As stated earlier, it is important to mindfully choose when to use mediated communication, and the particular form, in order to match it to the message you wish to convey; it is equally important to consider the relationship you have with the person (or want to have with the person). For example, it is likely better to talk to your boss about a salary increase in person instead of sending her an email asking for a raise. This particular message is typically considered a "rich" one, so you should choose a "richer" medium. Also, you want to convey to her that you are assertive, and so talking to her in a face-to-face meeting is the better context for communicating that quality. Emailing her is certainly the less face-threatening choice, but if you want to earn the raise, then showing you are assertive and professional will likely help your case.

Tips for Effective Email Communication

1. Determine whether email is the best medium for your message or interaction. For sensitive topics, you might want to consider having a face-to-face conversation or making a phone call instead.

2. If emailing in a professional relationship, format the email (e.g., use a salutation; include an opening, body, and concluding paragraph; and sign your name) and construct the message accordingly (e.g., use titles when appropriate, such Dr. or Mrs., and use formal language, such as Good Morning or Hello instead of Hey). Always use the person's name versus a generic "Hi" when you are emailing someone in particular. This shows respect as well as attention to detail.

3. Use a meaningful subject line that summarizes your message so the recipient knows what your message is about before they begin to read it. If you are emailing a professor about a class, it is also a good idea to include the course number or name in the subject line.

4. Always review your message for typos and other technical errors. This is your message, and it will say something about you and the relationship you have with the person. Don't let the person potentially think you are lazy or don't care about them by sending a sloppy message.

5. Consider at what time you send the message. Emails always have a time and date stamp, and these potentially could add meaning to your message in ways you might not immediately recognize. So, think about it before hitting send!

6. Allow adequate time for a reply, if a reply is needed. Once you have received a reply, acknowledge that you received the reply, even if no further information needs to be shared.

7. Remember that email is a written record. Even if you delete an email, the other person may not and it is possible that deleted emails will remain on a server for years after you thought you deleted the message. In some states, all emails on state-owned servers (such as at public universities) are considered public record and can be requested by anyone as part of open records regulations, which are sometimes referred to as "sunshine laws." If you are unsure of whether you want your words kept "on file" or made public, then consider using the telephone or talking to the person face to face instead.

8. Note that ALL CAPS can be interpreted as screaming, so use it and other formatting possibilities with care.

Benefits and Challenges to Mediated Communication

Most of us will initiate, develop, maintain, and/or negotiate our relationships using mediated communication at some point, whether it is in a work relationship, family relationship, friendship, or romantic relationship. There are many benefits as well as challenges to communicating using mediated forms, and it is important to take these into consideration as you choose how to communicate in your various relationships.

One-way mediated communication benefits the workplace is when workers use it while telecommuting. Workplaces are increasingly allowing workers to telecommute, which allows employees to spend less time commuting and perhaps have more flexible work arrangements, while simultaneously decreasing the cost of office space for companies. Many large national and international companies frequently need to have teams work together from multiple distant locations. While email and phone communication have been possible in such work situations for years, newer computer-mediated communication has increased productivity and made it easier to navigate time zone differences.[10] The downside to this is that there might also be reduced interpersonal affect and group solidarity, which then can decrease overall team effectiveness over time.[11] However, new technologies that allow for richer communication and increased visual cues during conversations, such as video conferencing, offer the promise of even more effective interpersonal communication in long-distance workplace relationships. At the same time, being online can also have negative effects in the workplace if you become a "cyberslacker" and are too distracted by your technological outlets. A recent Forbes article[12] reported that 64 percent of workers visit non-work related websites daily and waste anywhere between an hour to ten or more hours of their workday spending time on the web. There is some evidence, however, that a little bit of "cyberslacking" might increase your productivity if the break in work rejuvenates you for taking on your next task.

You have probably already experienced long-distance family relationships, friendships, and perhaps even romantic relationships, especially if you or some of your friends attended college away from home. It is probably no surprise that the benefits and challenges people face in these types of long-distance interpersonal relationships are different than the challenges they face in workplace relationships.

Although humans have maintained mediated relationships for millennia, computer technologies create new opportunities for us to maintain relationships. In the coming decades, mediated communication will probably become even more central in our personal and professional lives.

—Andrew Ledbetter, Texas Christian University

Military families often experience long-distance relationships (e.g., deployments), and career and educational opportunities often result in people living in separate, physically distant places from their partners or spouses and other family members.[13] Partners and families often use communication technologies because such technologies are cost effective, save time, and allow a sense of connectedness across space. Family members are just a click away, and families may now communicate using Skype or FaceTime, which helps to increase their sense of connection and satisfaction in these relationships. The use of communication technologies can also pose challenges to long-distance family members. The availability of communication via Facebook, for example, can cause some family members to feel too connected and increase their need for clearer boundaries around their relationships.

You likely have friends with whom you communicate using online technologies, and many of them are probably friends who live in different cities, states, and even countries. The advances in communication technologies, such as email and social media sites, have certainly helped people form more friendships and maintain them for longer periods of time. And these relationships are not just with our closest friends; we often create and keep "weak ties" with others, since it is so easy to do so with social media sites such as Facebook. Unfortunately, one potential negative outcome of spending time "catching up" with all of our Facebook "friends" is that it can make us depressed. Recent research has shown that time spent on Facebook is negatively related to one's mood.[14] So, why do we continue to spend time on Facebook? The same research speculated that we make an "affective forecasting error," where we expect the time we spend on Facebook will actually make us feel better, when in reality it can make us feel worse. It's important to remember to spend time talking to your friends on the phone or in person in addition to using these technologies. A careful balance of face-to-face and mediated communication should help maintain these relationships for years to come.

Long-distance romantic relationships also can benefit as well as be challenged by reliance on communication technologies such as texting, email, and social media sites. Of course, the available technologies allow romantic partners to communicate while they are apart, and their regular use has been shown to positively affect these relationships.[15] However, long-distance romantic partners typically limit their conversations to topics that won't provoke conflict. Most couples want to keep the conversations they do have positive.[16] The distance can place pressure on couples to make the limited time they have together extra special. But these patterns of interaction translate into partners creating an idealization of their relationship, which means they hold a false sense of the relationship that highlights the positive.[17] The planning and pressure for intensive togetherness time can take a toll on the couple and limit the amount of time they have available to spend with friends and family, which adds even more stress to the relationship.[18]

Fortunately, the availability of numerous forms of mediated communication, including many channels that allow partners to hear changes in vocal tone and see facial expressions, have made it easier for relational partners to initiate, develop, and maintain frequent and meaningful communication across distances. But, as discussed above, we must also be aware of the potential challenges these communication technologies pose for our relationships. In the last section of this chapter, we provide some advice for using these media so you maximize their potential benefits.

DIALOGIC COMMUNICATION IN MEDIATED RELATIONSHIPS

While the opportunities for communication via different technologies are numerous, the possibilities for deceiving, offending, and even hurting someone while using them are equally as great. Newspapers are filled with stories every day of someone using Twitter to insult someone else, people losing their jobs for Facebook posts, or even individuals pretending to be someone they are not for nefarious reasons. Despite these potential pitfalls, mediated communication provides many opportunities for dialogue and positive interactions that enhance our quality of life. Below we offer some suggestions for fostering and maintaining dialogue when communicating using technology.

DIALING DIVERSITY

Supplementing Communication with the Internet

Everyone seems to be online these days. This is increasingly true for people in the United States age 50 and older. Recent estimates report upwards of 77 percent of people aged 50 to 64 and 53 percent of people 65 and older are online, and one in three are using social media.[19] This picture is quite different from even 10 years ago, when, for example, the number of people 65 or older online was less than half what it is today. Social media, such as Facebook and Instagram, are great places for keeping up to date on immediate and extended family members, and more than 70 percent of senior citizens typically use the Internet daily. It seems that when given the training necessary to navigate the online world, seniors will transform into enthusiastic users. Moreover, the majority of seniors (seven out of ten) own mobile phones. So, if you want to speak with your grandparents and they are not answering their landline, try texting them or messaging them on Facebook—they are likely online!

Be Honest

As we've discussed in previous chapters, it is important to be honest in order to facilitate dialogue in your communication with others. This couldn't be more important than when talking via technology. Whether you are talking to a client or coworker, or communicating with a family member, friend, or romantic partner, being sincere will pay off in the long run.

Consider if the Medium Fits the Message

Always choose the technology to fit the message. For example, don't manage conflict with your partner through wall posts on your Facebook page. This not only allows all of your friends to see your conflict, it also creates distrust in the relationship. In other words, think before you post.

Take Care with What You Share

Always remember that what you post on the Internet has the potential to come back and haunt you later on. This is particularly important today, since employers often check the social media sites of job candidates. You also never know who might be seeing your texts; even if you delete a text message from your phone, it is possible for the person to whom you sent the message to share the message with others, and it is sometimes possible for phone companies to retrieve past messages. So, make sure you can live with the consequences if your messages get into the wrong hands!

Avoid Using Media to Maintain Relationships

While technology has added so many opportunities to manage our relationships, we must be cautious that we don't rely too heavily on them. If you want to have healthy, long-lasting ties, you are best served by using a mixture of face-to-face and online communication with your partners. In order for your relational partners to want to continue their ties with you, they must see that you not only want them on your list of friends but also that you care enough to visit them in person or call them on the phone on a regular basis.

Interact Online as if Face to Face

There are numerous examples of people who take to online blogs, comment forums, websites, and even text messages to use the advantage of distance from the recipient to send hostile, rude, or aggressive statements. In 2013, San Francisco 49ers placekicker David Akers was on the receiving end of death threats by fans for his performance, prompting him to quit Twitter. Doubtless, those fans would not have said these things if they were right in front of David Akers. Treat your mediated messages as if the person is standing in front of you, and convey the respect and dignity every person deserves.

SUMMARY

In this chapter, we explored the influence media and technology have had on developing and maintaining relationships. We defined the various types of media and social media available for use today, and then examined the impact these tools have on how we define ourselves and others. We also discussed some of the benefits and challenges that media and social media bring to relationship maintenance. Finally, we provided some tips for engaging in social media and mediated communication in a way that facilitates dialogue and minimizes the potential pitfalls that can occur without your conversational partner in front of you.

CHAPTER 11 KEY IDEAS

- Some forms of mediated communication are synchronous, which means that the partners communicate simultaneously, while others are asynchronous, which means that messages are sent and received at different times.

- Mediated communication can be impersonal, or based primarily on facilitating a transaction, or hyperpersonal, which is when mediated communication has higher levels of affection, emotion, liking, solidarity, and intimacy than face-to-face conversation.

- The medium through which we choose to communicate can impact our interpersonal relationships, lead to the use of other media, and communicate something about the relationships.

- Mediated communication can have both rewards and challenges when it is used to maintain local or long-distance relationships.

CHAPTER 11 KEY TERMS

Synchronous communication	Impersonal communication
Asynchronous communication	Hyperpersonal communication
Social media	Catfishing

ACTIVITIES AND DISCUSSION QUESTIONS

1. Watch Amber Case's TED talk, "We Are All Cyborgs Now," available online at https://www.ted.com/talks/amber_case_we_are_all_cyborgs_now. What are the challenges and benefits that she believes technology brings to our relationships? Do you agree or disagree? Why?

2. Watch Dr. Sherry Turkle's TED talk, "Connected, but Alone," available online at https://www.ted.com/talks/sherry_turkle_alone_together. What are the benefits and drawbacks that she believes technology brings to our relationships? Do you agree or disagree? Why?

3. What are some of the modes of synchronous and asynchronous communication that you use every day? When do you think that it might be advantageous to use each? Why?

4. For one day, keep track of how often you interact with others via mediated communication. Who do you interact with most using mediated communication, and are the same or different people than you interact with in person? Which channels do you use to communicate most often? Are there patterns in what you communicate about in each channel?

5. Pick a long-distance relationship that you have had in your life (friend, family member, romantic partner, etc.). Has mediated communication allowed you to maintain that relationship? Why or why not?

INTERPERSONAL
CONFLICT

One of the most misunderstood elements of human life is the friction that can develop among people over values, ideas, material objects, respect, and attitudes. These conflicts can be small in scale, like those that occur between romantic partners or colleagues, or larger in scale, such as those that lead to aggressive, and sometimes even violent, altercations between communities. Regardless of the scope or scale, conflict often encourages an uncomfortable feeling in people and the closer proximity of the individuals, the more uncomfortable the conflict feels.

Perhaps if we understood conflict a bit more we might manage it so these situations would become beneficial rather than potentially destructive. Conflict, after all, is natural, and not always a bad thing. If managed appropriately, conflict can result in relationship growth between people. On the other hand, if managed poorly, it can lead to the dissolution of the bond between individuals. Make no mistake, however, we are not proposing communication can always resolve conflicts. It can, however, help avoid some conflicts and work through others. Communication is, after all, both a source of conflict and the way in which we resolve the tensions created by conflict.

In this chapter, we explore the concept of interpersonal conflict by first defining it and examining some reasons why we perceive conflict as negatively as we typically do. We will

CONFLICT

an expressed struggle between at least two interdependent parties who perceive incompatible goals, scarce resources, and interference from the other party in achieving those goals *then identify and explain the primary reasons conflict exists in interpersonal relationships before discussing good and bad ways we manage conflicts. Finally, we will offer some concrete advice for how we can use the principles of dialogue to ensure we maximize our ability to turn conflict into a positive and not a negative.*

DEFINING CONFLICT

The most widely accepted scholarly definition of interpersonal conflict was offered by William Wilmot and Joyce Hocker: "an expressed struggle between at least two interdependent parties who perceive incompatible goals, scarce resources, and interference from the other party in achieving those goals."[1] In this part of the chapter, we will break down this definition, clarifying what actually constitutes conflict and what does not. We will also explore some of the metaphors we use to describe conflict and how they, as powerful language devices, influence our approaches toward conflict.

Expressed Struggle

The key word in this part of the definition of conflict is not struggle, but rather "expressed," because you cannot actually be in an interpersonal conflict with someone unless both of you are aware there is a difference between you. The expression of the conflict is fundamental for conflict, but it does not need to be expressed through verbal statements alone. In fact, romantic partners often realize they are in a disagreement simply by the looks on each other's faces. Nonverbal expression can express a dispute with someone sometimes even more effectively than the content of what is or might be spoken! Think about saying you agree with someone or that you are "OK," when your nonverbal reaction communicates the opposite. Such a behavior may contribute to the expression of a struggle between two people.

The second half of the phrase, "struggle," can mean a variety of things. It can simply mean a disagreement with someone or something stronger than merely disagreeing. Struggle may sound physical in nature, but often it is more a "tug-of-war" over ideas, values, or decisions. Whenever two or more sides present arguments in favor of differing positions on the same topic, then there is a struggle.

Two Interdependent Parties

Not all expressed disagreement constitutes a conflict, as the parties must also depend upon each other for something. For instance, you may disagree with a political leader over their position on something. Even if you make that dissent loud and clear, this is not actually a conflict because you do not depend on the leader for anything. Romantic partners and families, on the other hand, often engage in interpersonal conflicts because they depend upon each other. Romantic partners depend upon each other for a host of things, and thus conflict becomes a natural part of their lives. Children in families require the food, housing, and love that parents provide, while parents also want the joy and company of their children.

It is important to note, however, that interdependency does not require a familial or romantic connection. When we dine at a restaurant and interact with a server or cook, there is a small degree of interdependency. The restaurant employee depends on us having a good experience so we pay our bill and tip well, while we depend on them for providing a pleasurable experience and delivering delicious food. There is, then, an interdependent relationship that can create conflict. If you have a problem with the food or the service or, on the other hand, if you are rude to the staff of the restaurant, then a conflict can ensue because it will quickly become an expressed struggle between two interdependent parties.

Perceived Incompatible Goals and Scarce Resources

Perception is key to conflict. Recall our discussion in the chapter on perception and the self, and remember that perception is different for everyone. That is, we can experience the same event as someone else but perceive it differently. The potential for perceptual differences to create conflict then becomes readily apparent. Often, conflicts emerge when two people seek to achieve different goals, and this results in some rather significant disputes.

People who are interdependent by definition work together, but doing so with different ideas about the aim of their joint efforts invites conflict. In some instances, we do not see that we are working together to achieve different goals until we get to the end, but there are also times when a person might have a **hidden agenda**. A hidden agenda is a goal we keep secret from other parties while working with them. It is both disheartening and upsetting when we discover

HIDDEN AGENDA

goals people keep secret from other parties while working with them

---

Cultural Differences in Conflict Management

In the chapter on communication, culture, and diversity, we discussed cultural influences on communication, and nowhere is this made more apparent than in the strategies people from different cultural backgrounds typically rely on for conflict management. For example, individualistic cultures such as the United States tend to emphasize the competing or avoiding approaches to conflict. This is driven by the individual nature of the culture; people feel like if something is important to them, they must win it. Also, if something is uncomfortable, people in individualistic cultures often believe they should not put themselves in such a situation if they can avoid it. On the flip side, collectivist cultures like China emphasize compromise and accommodation because they seek to reduce discord and discomfort for everyone. Just as there are myriad diverse groups in the world, so too are there myriad reasons behind why we choose one conflict management style over another.

that someone working with us had a hidden agenda, and expressing those feelings to the other person creates conflict.

Different perceived goals are not the only thing that may result in a dispute, as perceived scarce resources also create opportunities for disagreements. We often deal with finite resources, such as time, money, and material objects, and sometimes we cannot equitably share these resources with others. For instance, you and a friend may interview for the same job, but there is only one position to be had. This can create an uncomfortable situation between you. Within romantic relationships, spending time with each other is very important, but if one partner does not feel they are being attended to adequately, the person may express this concern and create a conflict regarding time management for the relationship. Money can also come between people, as there is only a finite amount that someone can spend or use. It can prove distressing when choices need to be made about spending funds.

Interference from the Other Party

In addition to perceiving incompatible goals and scarce resources, the parties might believe the other is, or will be, interfering with achieving the goal or acquiring the resources necessary to achieve the goal. Interference can come in many forms, such as physical obstruction, political maneuvering, or even an unwillingness to express or provide support for the effort. Although it may just seem like you are remaining neutral when you fail to provide support or encouragement, the other person might understand it as interference. Perceived interference creates a defensive climate between two parties, and a defensive climate suggests there is some assault to defend against.

HOW WE TALK ABOUT CONFLICT

In the chapter on language, we discussed language and explained how some of the ornamental linguistic devices like metaphors are powerful tools in describing how we see the world. Conflict is a prime example of how the metaphors we use to describe this abstract concept reveal our perceptions and feelings about engaging in disputes with other people.

One of the most common sets of metaphoric expressions people use to describe conflict reveals an interpretation of it as aggressive, nasty, and something to avoid. Look at the following ways we describe conflict: "conflict as war," "conflict as a fight," "conflict as trial and tribulation," and "conflict as explosive." Each of these invites aggressive tactics aimed at completely dominating the other party. There is no good will, emphasis on collaboration or compromise, and certainly no respect for the other person. When we describe conflict this way, we encourage "surrender" by the other person, and it is no surprise that when we encounter people who see conflict in this manner, we often just want to avoid it.

Another set of metaphors people use to describe conflict illustrates a more strategic and less aggressive construction of it. Think about these metaphoric descriptions of conflict:

"conflict is a game," "conflict is a bargaining exercise," "conflict is a dance." Games, bargains, and dances all require some type of strategy or movement to counter the other side. Those who use these metaphors often enjoy conflict as a mental exercise to achieve their own ends while outmaneuvering the other person. These metaphors still see conflict as something to win and not work through, but to these people, winning the conflict involves subtler and less aggressive approaches to making that happen.

The way we describe conflict can influence how we approach disputes when they arise. If we think of conflict as "an opportunity" and "a journey," we might then see the positive prospects it can provide. These types of metaphors encourage a more optimistic and less dreary approach to these challenging situations that allow us to grow as partners, friends, and colleagues.

REASONS THAT CONFLICT EXISTS

When we unraveled the definition of conflict, we identified its primary sources as perceived incompatible goals and scarce resources. As you might recall from the chapter on perception and the self, perception can be impacted by many different factors and plays an important role in our self-concept, how we perceive others, and the reasons to which we attribute others' behaviors. These differences in perception mean that we all see the world a little bit differently, which is why most conflicts arise in the first place. Douglas Stone, Bruce Patton, and Sheila Heen, who are part of the Harvard Negotiation Project, explain that there are three primary reasons why we have different stories about our experiences, which are ultimately the root of most conflicts.[2]

We Have Different Information

Even though we might have been involved in the exact same encounter at the exact same time as another person, we both walked away from the situation with different information and experiences. This is partly due to us noticing different things. For example, consider a person who took her niece and nephew to a parade last year. During the parade, the aunt, who once played in a marching band, noticed which marching bands were in sync with each other, whether certain parts of songs were played correctly, and whether various groups marching in the parade were spaced appropriately to not interfere with each other's performances. After the parade, though, the niece just talked about the dancers and baton twirlers, and the nephew talked about all of the different types of fire trucks and horses. Even though all three watched the same parade, they each had very different information and memories about the parade afterward and were somewhat oblivious to the information the others noticed.

Similarly, we often come away from important conversations and experiences having noticed very different things and are sometimes completely unaware of elements that were especially important to another person. For instance, one person might leave a meeting furious that they were constantly interrupted by one of their colleagues and did not have the opportunity to speak, while another person might leave the same meeting happy that there was so much spirited debate about an important issue.

Additionally, we have access to information about ourselves that others do not, and others have access to information about themselves that we do not. You know more about your own previous experiences as well as the situational factors impacting your behavior in a particular moment, than anyone else does. When you are frustrated that one of your coworkers shows up to work late and is unable to focus, you might not know that they did not get any sleep the night before because they were studying for an important exam, just found out that their grandfather was diagnosed with a serious medical condition, and had a flat tire on their way to work. Your coworker might not know that you arrived early and were hoping to finish work a little bit early in order to get to an important event, and that you are wary of working with others after you have been working on a project with a partner who is not doing their part.

We Have Different Interpretations

Even if we have the same information about a situation, we might interpret that experience very differently based on our past experiences and the implicit rules we live by. We have assumptions about what the world is like and how things should be based on the families, communities, and cultures we were raised in, when in fact others might have vastly different experiences. We might have beliefs about how birthdays should be celebrated, how we should greet friends and family members, whether it's normal to go on vacation every year, how to celebrate important holidays, whether or not to arrive a little bit late for a dinner party, whether it is OK to squeeze the toothpaste tube from the middle of the tube, who in the household does the cooking or mows the lawn, or whether spanking is a normal part of child discipline.

These and many other experiences can seem like ordinary, everyday practices that we take for granted, but when we encounter others who have different sets of assumptions about what the "rules" are for everyday life, conflict can ensue. If you grew up in a community where being invited to dinner at 7:00 meant you should arrive sometime between 7:10 p.m. and 7:15 p.m. to give the host a few extra minutes to prepare, you might think your guests are being rude when they arrive at 8:00 p.m. or 6:45 p.m., instead. If you grew up in a community where it was normal to shake hands when you greet a close friend, you might feel like a friend who greets you with a kiss on the cheek is being inappropriately intimate, while that same friend might think you are being rude and standoffish to offer a handshake. Many of these implicit rules that guide our interpretations are influenced heavily by dimensions of culture, as we learned earlier in the book, while others might stem from everyday local experiences. However, our different interpretations leave us with very different emotional responses, and those differing emotional responses can result in conflict and difficult conversations.

Our Conclusions Reflect Self-Interest

We have a tendency to look for and remember information that is consistent with what we believe or want to see, and to ignore or forget information that contradicts our beliefs and hopes. This tendency is called **confirmation bias**, and it leads to overconfidence in our own beliefs, even in the presence of contradictory evidence. This tendency often occurs when we are making financial decisions, such as evaluating the appropriate price for a house or deciding which type of car to buy. It is even stronger when we are focusing on emotionally charged issues or deeply held beliefs, such as whether capital punishment should be allowed. We are usually unaware that our perception is biased and that we have been seeking information that supports our beliefs rather than evaluating all sources of information fairly. When we disagree with another person about an important issue, it is likely that both individuals are basing their argument on biased information due to our selective attention, which might make our differences seem larger than they really are. The positions we take on issues sometimes become an important part of our identity, which can heighten a difficult situation if we feel like a disagreement about an issue is also a disagreement about what kind of person we are (lovable or unlovable, kind or cruel, good or bad, etc.).

Because we have differences in what we notice, differences in how we interpret shared information, and confirmation biases that make our positions seem stronger than they might otherwise be, we often find ourselves in conflict with others, sometimes over issues that might seem fairly insignificant on the surface. If we work first, however, to understand where the other person is coming from and how they see the situation, rather than jumping to conclusions about who is right or wrong, what was intended, or who is to blame, we can often find ways to resolve seemingly difficult situations in a way that satisfies both parties.

CONFLICT MANAGEMENT

Knowing what conflict is and where it comes from is only part of the process in handling disputes in a positive and beneficial way. The other ingredient is knowing what behaviors contribute to a negative conflict communication spiral and what different strategies are available for resolving conflict. Many conflicts can either be resolved quickly or avoided altogether if people recognize the behaviors that contributed to the situation and work to change them in a collaborative way. In this part of the chapter, we will first outline four behaviors that do not help resolve conflict and even make it worse, and then we will detail the five primary strategies available for managing different conflicts.

Problem Behaviors

There are four primary problematic behaviors that create and sustain negative conflicts between individuals. In fact, these behaviors are so damaging to relationships that psychologist John Gottman was able to watch newlywed couples interact and identify which

CONFIRMATION BIAS

the tendency to look for and remember information that is consistent with what we believe or what we want to happen ones would remain married and which would divorce with more than 90 percent accuracy just by watching for these behaviors.[3] We will explore each of these four behaviors, which he refers to as the Four Horsemen of the Apocalypse, before moving on to discuss various strategies for managing conflict.

Criticism. One of the primary sources of interpersonal conflict are statements that are critical of the behavior, attitude, or other characteristics of someone else. Criticism is the expression of disapproval of someone or something based upon perceived faults in a person or behavior. Whether or not criticism makes a negative or positive contribution to a relationship depends almost entirely on the language used and the manner in which it is delivered. When criticism is focused on behaviors, then it can be constructive and helpful because people can adjust behaviors; however, when the criticism is focused on personality or character, then it can be destructive. Providing constructive criticism is a helpful skill not just for romantic partners, but also for managers who often need help changing employee behaviors without seeming to attack the individuals themselves.

Contempt. A second major contributor to negative conflict within a relationship is the expression of contempt. Contempt is different from criticism, because it is almost exclusively negative. Contempt involves the expression of insults and disdain for people, their behaviors, and their ideas. Statements exhibiting contempt often are accompanied with nonverbal behaviors that indicate a disparaging opinion of the person, such as a furrowed brow, a snarl, or even a dismissive exhale of breath. Expressions of contempt have a universally negative impact on the receiver and often function to diminish their self-esteem within the relationship. Insults and demeaning expressions can have catastrophic effects on interpersonal relationships in any setting.

Defensiveness. In the dialogic communication chapter, we introduced communication scholar Jack Gibb, who identified specific behaviors that create a defensive communication climate. Such a climate reduces listening, increases aggressiveness, and inhibits understanding and dialogue in a relationship. Recall that the behaviors that create a defensive climate include making evaluative statements about the other person, trying to control the behaviors of another or the outcome of the interaction, withholding information to get what one wants, remaining neutral and not expressing empathy or sympathy for the other person, acting superior to the other person, and not engaging in a conversation with an open mind. Defensiveness prevents a person from seeing their own roles and responsibilities in the situation and prevents parties from finding common ground when working through conflicts. In some people, this behavior becomes a part of who they are, and they ultimately view themselves as forever a victim of others and of circumstances.

Stonewalling. The final problematic behavior people exhibit that contributes to negative conflict experiences is stonewalling. Stonewalling involves withdrawing from the conflict interaction. When people stonewall, they might look and/or move away from the

CRITICISM
the expression of disapproval of someone or something based upon perceived faults in a person or behavior

CONTEMPT
the expression of insults and disdain for a person, their behaviors, and ideas

DEFENSIVENESS
prevents a person from seeing their own roles and responsibilities in the situation and prevents parties from finding common ground when working through conflicts

STONEWALLING
a complete withdrawal from the conflict, both physically and verbally

other person, and they do not make any comments themselves. Sometimes this occurs because they feel their contributions are not valued or heard, and at other times it is an expression of frustration. Most often it's because they feel overwhelmed by the conflict and use stonewalling to cope with their feelings. Stonewalling can make the situation worse if the other person perceives it as passive-aggressive, whether or not that's the intent. The presence of stonewalling should be a sign that the parties need to take a break, because without both parties present and involved in the conflict, the dispute cannot be overcome and may become worse. If one person continues trying to engage in the conflict and the other person continues to withdraw, then the conflict will likely spiral even further into negativity.

Conflict Management Styles

There are five methods for managing conflict in interpersonal settings, and each approach can be appropriate in some situations and inappropriate in other situations. Most people have a dominant conflict style they tend to use in most conflict situations, but each of us can choose to use any of the five conflict styles based on what will help both parties best resolve the conflict and maintain the relationship. Kenneth Thomas and Ralph Kilmann have developed one of the most-used instruments for identifying conflict styles (see Figure 12.1) and argue that these five conflict styles can be mapped onto two dimensions: assertiveness and cooperativeness.[4] Assertiveness is the degree to which you try to make sure your own concerns are satisfied, and cooperativeness is the degree to which you attempt to satisfy the other person's concerns. In this part of the chapter, we will examine the five strategies for resolving interpersonal conflict and address when each may or may not be the best option available.

Social Media and Expressions of Criticism

ENGAGING ETHICS

Twitter, Facebook, and other social media have made it easier for people to connect, but they have also contributed to an increase in direct expressions of criticism and contempt. People who may not know you, but see your posts on a mutual "friend's" page or Twitter thread may express disdain, name call, bully, or otherwise express contempt on something you say or post. What do you think contributes to this type of behavior? What is the impact on all three of the parties involved, and how might they respond? What happens when the conflict is between friends and family?

Thomas-Kilmann Conflict Styles

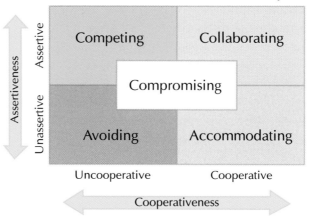

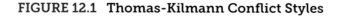

FIGURE 12.1 Thomas-Kilmann Conflict Styles

COMPETING

conflict management strategy that treats an argument like something to win, even if the other person is not happy with the outcome

Competing. The competing conflict style involves trying to win the argument or to make sure you get the resolution you want, even if the other person is not happy with the outcome. Competing treats an argument like something to win, even at the expense of the other person or any valid points they might have. In that respect, this is a win-lose approach to conflict management. There are instances when this approach can be acceptable, such as in a bid for a contract between yourself and another group, or in a job interview. When there can be only one clear winner, this may be a strategy worth employing. However, in interpersonal relationships, a competing approach often yields further discord and unhappiness between partners, because someone always feels like they lost out or were not heard, thus leading to feelings of resentment. The competing approach is best used in situations in which you care deeply about the outcome, time is limited, and a decision must be made quickly.

ACCOMMODATING

a management style defined by a person giving in to the desires and position of the other person, thereby sacrificing their own position and desires

Accommodating. This second approach represents almost the polar opposite of competing in that you give in to the desires and position of the other person. With accommodating you lose by sacrificing your position and desires to those of the other person, thus creating a lose-win scenario. This strategy may work when the issue is not something to which you are attached or on which you hold a particularly strong position. If you can let go and be satisfied with the other person winning the argument or making a decision, then this strategy may help preserve the peace. For example, if your partner cares deeply about seeing their family during a particular holiday every year, and you do not feel strongly about seeing your family during that holiday, then that might be a situation in which the best solution is to accommodate your partner's desire to spend that holiday with their family every year. However, if you care about the outcome of the conflict and are not comfortable making such a sacrifice, then accommodating is definitely not the best strategy for managing the dispute.

AVOIDANCE

conflict management strategy that involves avoiding the other person, choosing not to express or make a conflict known

Avoiding. A third strategy available for conflict management is avoidance. Avoidance is when there is a brewing conflict, but you choose not to express it and make it known, even going to great lengths to avoid the person with whom you would have the dispute. Avoidance differs from stonewalling in that stonewalling occurs during a conflict, while avoiding tries to ensure the conflict never occurs. Avoiding is a lose-lose approach to conflict management because neither side is able to address the issue and solve the problem, because they are never aware it needs to be addressed. This can lead to festering resentment and distance between two people. Avoidance is not a bad solution when neither you nor your partner feel invested in the issue, but it is not a civil way to approach disputes you or your partner care about, because it denies each of you the ability to assert your own feelings.

Compromising. Many people believe compromise is always the best solution, and this is true in some cases, but not all. Compromising represents yet another lose-lose conflict management strategy, because neither partner gets what they want completely, and they each walk away losing some desired elements. Both sides sacrifice part of what they want, while getting something they want. This strategy takes time, patience, honesty, openness, and understanding to facilitate successfully. In many negotiations, this can be an effective way to proceed, but in more complex conflicts, compromise may not be possible and may

COMPROMISING
conflict management strategy by which both sides sacrifice part of what they want while getting something they desire

Conflict Management in Intimate Relationships

MEDIATED MOMENTS

In the 2009 film *Couples Retreat*, four couples attend an exotic spa and resort in an attempt to solve issues facing their intimate relationships. Three of the couples go to support their friends, but learn while they are there that they too have issues they need to work through. As part of the retreat package, the couples do numerous activities together while also attending couples therapy sessions. It is in these therapy sessions where each couple exhibits different conflict management styles, all resulting in poor relationship satisfaction for both partners. For instance, the characters of Dave and Ronnie, played by Vince Vaughn and Malin Åkerman, engage in conflict avoidance because they never actually bring up the issues that cause stress between them. Joey (Jon Favreau) and Lucy (Kristin Davis) engage in competing conflict management, which results in quite a few screaming matches between them. Shane (Faizon Love) and Trudy (Kali Hawk), a couple with an age difference of more than twenty years, illustrate accommodating because Shane always gives in to what Trudy wants to do, even when he is exhausted or not interested. Finally, Jason Bateman and Kristen Bell play Jason and Cynthia, who initiate the trip because they have a cold and distant relationship brought about by a consistent clinical approach to conflict management that ignores the emotional elements of the relationship.[5]

Copyright © 2009 Universal/courtesy Everett Collection

not lead to satisfaction for both parties. For example, imagine you and your significant other are trying to decide where to spend Thanksgiving, and each of you wants to spend every Thanksgiving with your own family. If you agree to spend Thanksgiving alternate years so that you spend one year with your family and the next year with your partner's family, then you will have reached a compromise that allows each of you to get what you want part of the time, but that also forces each of you to sacrifice your desires part of the time.

COLLABORATION
the most beneficial of the conflict management strategies; its goal is to find a solution that allows both parties to win

Collaborating. The final strategy for conflict management is the most beneficial when used to resolve important issues that both parties care deeply about, as well as the most difficult to accomplish. Like compromise, collaboration also requires time, patience, honesty, openness, and effort, but the goal is not to identify aspects both parties can lose. Instead, when collaborating, the goal is to find a solution that allows both parties to win. Win-win scenarios are difficult to manage, and they are not always possible, but when you can employ this approach, you reap relational rewards such as increasing trust, strengthened personal bonds between partners, and satisfaction that everyone won. Collaboration requires that individuals act in good faith and with good will. The key to collaboration is to identify what each party really wants and then try to develop a solution that allows both of those desires to be met. For example, imagine that you and your partner are trying to decide how to spend your evening, and you want to go out to dinner, while your partner wants to go to a party with some friends who are visiting from out of town. If what you really want is a good meal, and what your partner really wants is to have a chance to reconnect with your friends, then through collaboration you might identify a third option that lets you both get what you want, such has hosting a dinner party with your friends or going out to a restaurant to have dinner together. The downside of collaboration is that it can take a great deal of time and can be exhausting, so it is not appropriate to use this conflict style when managing every conflict.

Too often we fall into a routine of using one particular conflict management strategy, leading to more and more irresolvable situations and damaged relationships. Instead, treat these as

Unhappy couples get into what is called a "Markov absorbing state" of negative affect, meaning that it is easy to enter and hard to exit. The reason for this "Roach Hotel Model" (they check into negative affect but they don't check out) is that repair processes fail in unhappy relationships; as good as it gets is that we all mess up communication, but only master couples can repair effectively. Effective repair requires having a "positive story of us."

—John Gottman, **Author of** *The Seven Principles for Making Marriage Work* tools in your relational repair toolkit. Not every disagreement can be resolved or managed effectively with the same approach.

DIALOGUE AND CONFLICT RESOLUTION

As you can probably tell, dialogue is most closely aligned with collaboration as a conflict management style, but its principles allow for effective and rewarding conflict management, regardless of the strategy you employ. Additionally, you may have noticed that there is an emphasis in this chapter on avoiding the creation of a defensive communication climate in conflict situations. To effectively employ dialogue in conflict, it is important to establish a supportive communication climate, and in this section of the chapter, we will provide the six guidelines identified by communication scholar Jack Gibb[6] for using good dialogic behaviors when trying to resolve a conflict with another person by doing just that.

Use Description Instead of Evaluation

Descriptive statements focus on behavior and cast no judgments regarding whether the action is right or wrong. They also do not focus on the character of the person. An evaluative statement like "You are very immature" will almost universally insult the other person and put them on the defensive. Instead, a descriptive statement would focus on the behavior, "Talking to the person next to you during a presentation is distracting to the speaker." This statement focuses on the behavior without making the person feel like their entire identity is being judged as negative, and is thus more likely to be received better.

Focus on Solving the Problem, Not Controlling the Outcome

Conflicts always occur due to some problem, and often the two parties either understand the problem differently or have different ways of solving the problem. Rather than trying to control which solution gets enacted, focus on determining which solution is most effective at solving the problem. Don't be concerned with taking credit for identifying the solution, but focus on solving the problem together. A control statement might look like this: "Let's just do this the way I suggested; we have talked it through enough." This closes down opportunities for participation by making the decision for everyone else. It results in less buy-in from the partner or group and negative feelings toward you. Instead, use statements that focus on the problem, like: "We have three potential ways forward, so let's see which one gets us to where we want to be with minimal hassle."

Be Spontaneous, Not Strategic

Strategic statements always attempt to either pressure people to do something by using leverage, or they attempt to conceal an agenda from the other party. Spontaneous statements, on the other hand, are open and allow the other person to make a pressure-free decision or contribution to the discussion. A strategic statement like "You owe me for helping you write that report when you had a family emergency, remember?" could easily be turned into something less forceful. The spontaneous version would look something like, "I have a project I could really use some help with. Are you able to spend some time with me on it?" This latter example does not leverage anything and allows the other party to make a meaningful contribution. The strategic version, on the other hand, just served to create a guilt trip for the recipient.

Express Empathy, Not Neutrality

As we established in the introductory chapter, empathy is the ability to put yourself in the shoes of the other person and try to see things from their perspective. This is the opposite of not taking sides and trying to remain removed from the situation. Conflicts always have an emotional dimension to them, and so treating them with a clinical, purely objective approach often leaves people feeling less than satisfied with the solution. A neutral statement of "I do not want to get involved with the disagreement between you and your roommate," could easily be turned into an empathic statement of "I understand that when your roommate lets the dishes pile up, it bothers you. Perhaps you should try and talk to her about it." This allows you to acknowledge the emotional dimension of the dispute without coming across as distant, and still keeps you from getting involved.

Acknowledge Equality, Don't Be Superior

In some situations, we fall back on our expertise or experience as though it makes us better or more qualified than someone else. When we point to something about us that makes us better than other people it makes them feel disrespected and defensive. Even if you do know something others do not, don't assume this makes you better than or capable of judging them. Statements like, "That was a stupid thing to do," or "Why would you go and do a thing like that?" contain an air of superiority because implicit in them is the idea that you know better than the other person. This creates a defensive climate and creates tension in conflict situations. Instead, express equality for people by developing mutual trust and an openness to their way of thinking or perception of the situation.

Be Provisional and Not Certain

PROVISIONALISM

the expression of an ability to be flexible and open to different ideas

Certain statements close off flexibility, making it appear as though there is only one way to proceed. More often than not, flexibility is possible, and when you express an ability to be flexible and open to different ideas, then it can de-escalate tensions between you and your partner. This is called provisionalism. Instead of saying something needs to be completed right now, consider softening the claim to "when you have a moment, please take care of this." This allows the other person to negotiate their time and effort and feel like there is flexibility in fulfilling the request. Provisionalism expresses good will, while certainty does not.

As you can see, creating a supportive climate takes work, but when you use supportive communication behaviors in any interaction, it becomes more likely those actions will be reciprocated by the other party, making it easier to negotiate the conflict and come to a collaborative resolution where everyone wins.

SUMMARY

Conflict is an inevitable part of human interaction, and the negative stigma that often accompanies it makes managing disputes in a positive fashion a challenge. In this chapter, we defined conflict and explored the different metaphors we use to characterize it. We also examined the various sources of conflict in relationships and identified both problematic behaviors we might use in a conflict and more effective and potentially constructive methods for managing the disputes. Finally, using the work of communication scholar Jack Gibb, we provided six guidelines for employing dialogue to create a supportive, rather than defensive, communication climate when engaging in efforts to resolve conflict.

CHAPTER 12 KEY IDEAS

- Conflict is "an expressed struggle between at least two interdependent parties who perceive incompatible goals, scarce resources, and interference from the other party in achieving those goals."

- Conflict often exists because we have different information, different interpretations, and different conclusions that reflect self-interest, even about shared experiences.

- The Four Horsemen of the Apocalypse, or behaviors that damage relationships, include criticism, contempt, defensiveness, and stonewalling.

- There are five conflict styles based on the level of assertiveness and cooperativeness of each individual: competing, collaborating, avoiding, accommodating, and compromising.

CHAPTER 12 KEY TERMS

Conflict	Competing
Hidden agenda	Accommodating
Confirmation bias	Avoidance
Criticism	Compromising
Contempt	Collaboration
Defensiveness	Provisionalism
Stonewalling	

ACTIVITIES AND DISCUSSION QUESTIONS

1. Watch Clair Canfield's TEDx talk, "The Beauty of Conflict," available online at https://www.youtube.com/watch?v=55n9pH_A0O8j. How can you use the VOCAB method suggested here to turn conflicts into opportunities for change?

2. Watch CrisMarie Campbell and Susan Clarke's TEDx talk, "Conflict: Use It, Don't Diffuse It," available online at https://www.youtube.com/watch?v=o97fVGTjE4w. How can conflict help teams become more successful? What do the speakers argue are the keys to being able to use conflict as a resource for creativity and innovation?

3. Give an example of a conflict that you have had with someone recently. Which of the three reasons that conflict exists was primarily responsible for the conflict? Were you able to resolve this conflict effectively? Why or why not? What do you think you could have done that would have helped you resolve the conflict more productively?

4. Search online for a conflict styles assessment and take the test to identify your preferred conflict style. Which conflict style was given as your primary result? Do you think that this is an accurate portrayal of your conflict style? Why or why not? In which types of situations is your primary/preferred conflict style helpful? In which types of situations is it a hindrance?

NATURE OF FORMAL PRESENTATIONS

In addition to interpersonal communication, you may also be called upon to give a formal presentation at some point during your life. Presentations may be part of a career, one that asks you to deliver a sales report or run an orientation program. The occasion might arise in your personal life, such as giving a wedding toast, eulogy, or even a roast of a friend or colleague. Even though each presentation is for a different audience, they all have some things in common. Public communication involves a presenter speaking to a group of people for an extended period of time without interruption. In formal public presentations, the speaker also typically stands in front of a seated audience.

The roots of instruction for public speaking date back to Ancient Greece and Rome. Aristotle identified three basic categories of speeches. The first, *deliberative*, involved speeches about future actions that might be taken; the second, *forensic*, included arguments about what had happened, much like you would find in a courtroom; and the third, *epideictic*, included speeches that celebrate or commemorate events or people. He also provided us with the five canons of rhetoric, or the five elements of creating and presenting a speech.

1. *Invention:* identifying the topic on which you will speak
2. *Arrangement:* determining the order in which you will address points related to the topic

DELIBERATIVE
speeches about future actions that might be taken

FORENSIC
arguments about what had happened

EPIDEICTIC
speeches that celebrate or commemorate events or people

3. **Style:** *the words and phrases you use to make the topic interesting*

4. **Delivery:** *the physical and vocal dimensions of speaking*

5. **Memory:** *remembering the entire speech (much more important during classical days than it is today)*

In this chapter, we examine the nature of public speaking using what we have learned from Aristotle through today. First we will examine the process of invention or, as we call it today, topic selection. We will then discuss how to adapt messages to audiences. Third, we will define the different types of formal presentations, and then discuss the role of the research process in speech development. Finally, we will provide suggestions and guidelines for making speeches more dialogic in nature, thus creating an environment where the audience will be more likely to listen and think about your message.

TOPIC SELECTION

When you are asked to give a formal presentation, the first and perhaps most difficult task you will need to undertake is choosing and narrowing your topic. Sometimes you will be asked to speak about something very specific, such as presenting a business report in a stakeholder meeting, but more often you will have some flexibility to choose your own topic. In these situations, you should consider several questions when evaluating potential topics for your presentation.

What is the General Purpose of My Speech?

GENERAL PURPOSE
the broad intent of what your speech should accomplish; the three types of general purposes are to inform, to persuade, and to commemorate

The general purpose is the broad intent of what your speech should accomplish. There are three primary types of general purposes: to inform, to persuade, and to commemorate. In an informative speech, you are trying to teach your audience something. For example, in a CPR class, the instructor is trying to teach their audience the steps for performing CPR effectively. In a persuasive speech, you are trying to change or reinforce your audience's attitudes, actions, or beliefs in some way. In a campaign speech, for example, a political candidate is usually trying to convince you to agree with their stance on several issues and persuade you to vote for them on Election Day. In a commemorative speech, you are usually celebrating or honoring something. A wedding toast is a classic case of a commemorative speech intended to celebrate the love and marriage of the newlywed couple.

What Topics are Appropriate for the Occasion?

If you are in a speaking situation in which you get to choose your topic, you will need to consider what types of topics are considered appropriate for the occasion. Audiences typically expect certain topics to be addressed on particular occasions. We usually expect wedding toasts to focus on the couple getting married and to perhaps include anecdotes about the couple and well-wishes for a happy marriage. We presume commencement speeches will have themes related in some way to hopes, dreams, goals, and success. We anticipate a first aid training workshop to teach us something about how to help a person during a medical emergency. In these situations, there are many potential topics you could choose that would be appropriate, but there are also many that would be inappropriate. Consider that an audience might be horrified if a speaker told a story about either the bride or groom's one-night stand with a previous romantic partner during a wedding toast, talked about genocide in a graduation address, or tried to persuade an audience to take their side on a political issue in the middle of what was supposed to be a CPR training session. When thinking about potential topics, take time to consider what types of topics might be appropriate or even expected for the occasion.

Is the Topic Appropriate for This Particular Audience?

Just as occasions carry expectations, so too do audiences. In some situations, a particular audience may be interested in or receptive to a particular message even though others might also fit the occasion. You should consider your audience's interests, needs, and level of expertise when choosing your topic, and consider how those mesh with the occasion. An audience

Hollywood Actors, Speeches, and Politics

Hollywood awards season is often an exciting time of year, when stars and directors of our favorite movies and TV shows gather to celebrate their art. Award winners are also often allotted a short period to say a few words after receiving recognition for their work. Typically these off-the-cuff remarks are a series of thank-you's to various people who contributed to their success, but on occasion some award recipients have used the opportunity to make political statements or champion social causes. For example, in 2003 director Michael Moore delivered a scathing speech against the Bush administration when his film, *Bowling for Columbine*, won Best Documentary at the Oscars. In Spring 2018 Robert DeNiro delivered a profanity-laced speech directed at President Donald Trump at an awards celebration. Where does the line exist, if it does at all, between politics and public statements? What might be some boundaries for appropriateness for award speeches? Are there exceptions to these guidelines? What positive and negative outcomes are there for making such speeches at these venues?

Credit: Featureflash Photo Agency / Shutterstock.com.

of kindergarteners is probably not interested in listening to a speech about retirement savings options, an audience of Kansans probably doesn't need to know how to protect their homes in case of a hurricane, and a group of emergency room doctors probably will not benefit from a speech on basic first aid because they already have extensive expertise in dealing with medical emergencies. Instead, you should consider what topics will be of interest to, connect with, and build upon an audience's existing knowledge in some way.

Is This Topic Appropriate for Me?

After you consider your audience and the occasion, you also should make sure your topic is appropriate for you. Is this topic something you care about? Is it a subject in which you are an expert, or about which you would like to know more? Is the topic choice one that reflects the person you want to be seen as? You will spend a significant amount of time thinking about, researching, practicing, and delivering your speech, so you should make sure the topic is one you care enough about to invest what will be a lot of time and work. A topic might be appropriate for you if you are already an expert in that area, or if you are interested in and want to know more about it. Be forewarned, some of the worst speeches happen when a speaker is just not interested in what they are talking about.

BRAINSTORM

the practice of creating a list of all the possible topics you can think of, beginning by writing down every possible idea that comes to mind, regardless of how good you think the idea is, and then afterward organizing or evaluating the ideas to help you make a decision about which to choose

Is This Topic Narrow Enough?

Once you have identified a potential topic that is appropriate for yourself, your audience, and the occasion, you will need to narrow your topic to make sure you can adequately explain your subject matter in the amount of time you have available. In a classroom presentation situation, you will probably be given a minimum and a maximum time frame. In professional contexts, the length of your presentations will vary. Sometimes you might have as little as 30 to 60 seconds to give an "elevator pitch," which is a quick synopsis of a complex issue. In these instances, your topic needs to be narrow and targeted. At other times you may have anywhere from 5 to 10 minutes, or perhaps even a full hour. When you have that much time, you can cover much more ground. If you are struggling to narrow your topic, you might find it helpful to brainstorm all of the various subtopics or components your broader, general topic contains. You could also create a concept map to help you identify the other potential areas you could cover and how they relate to one another.

CONCEPT MAP

a visual representation of all the potential areas you could cover in your speech that includes circles around topics and lines that connect related ideas; also known as a mind map

AUDIENCE ANALYSIS AND ADAPTATION

Once you have selected a topic and have begun to narrow it to fit the parameters of the speaking occasion, you should find out as much as you can about your audience so you can adapt the speech to meet its specific needs. The amount of time you will have to prepare and the amount of information you will be able to learn about your audience will vary depending on the occasion. In some situations, you will be able to collect some information about your audience's background characteristics, knowledge, and attitudes toward your topic in advance, while other times you might need to look for clues about your audience and adapt accordingly during your speech. In this part of the chapter, we will address seven different ways you can analyze an audience.

Demographics

The first way in which you can analyze your audience is by gathering information about their background. **Demographics** are categories of definable characteristics of groups of people, such as age, sex, race, ethnicity, religion, political affiliation, socioeconomic status, education level, and sexual orientation. Different types of demographic information are collected by a variety of institutions for many reasons. For example, the US Census Bureau collects some demographic data every ten years to get an overall picture of who lives in the United States. Universities collect demographic data about their employees and students to help understand who is on campus, which programs might help to meet their needs, and to track performance data by specific groups. Marketers use demographic data to better target areas where potential clients might live. As a speaker, knowing something about your audience's demographic makeup might give you some general ideas about your audience's likely experiences, expectations, beliefs, values, behaviors, and habits. This information helps you determine how best to capture their interest and appeal to them.

DEMOGRAPHICS categories of definable characteristics of groups of people, such as age, sex, race, ethnicity, religion, political affiliation, socioeconomic status, education level, and sexual orientation

Artifacts

In addition to demographics, taking a careful look at your audience and surroundings can also provide information about them. As we discussed in the chapter on nonverbal communication, artifacts, in terms of public speaking, are objects that indicate something about the values, beliefs, practices, history, and norms of a group of people. Most people have at least some artifacts that reflect things that are important to them in their offices and homes. These include everyday objects or pictures that serve as reminders of important life events or values, posters, or artwork, all of which tell you something about the person who typically occupies that space. Think about your own office, dorm room, or home. How much could an outsider learn about your experiences, knowledge, interests, beliefs, attitudes, and values from looking around for just a couple of minutes?

Similarly, you can learn a lot about a group you are speaking to by looking at the artifacts around them. Before a presentation to an organization, you might want to consider looking at its website for pictures, a mission statement, news articles, or anything else that might tell you about the group and the goals of the individuals in that group, and then show up a little early so you can pay attention to the objects in the workspace. If you are giving a speech in class, you might examine what your classmates wear, what they talk about, and what kinds of objects they carry with them, and then consider what those things communicate about your classmates' interests and values.

Informants

When you give speeches in class, you will typically know several people in your audience, but you might find yourself in other situations in which you are invited to speak to a group

INFORMANT

a contact person within the organization or group you can talk with to obtain information about the audience you will be speaking to

of people, most, if not all, of whom you do not know. In these situations, you might want to consider getting information about your audience from an informant. An **informant** is a contact person within the organization or group from whom you can obtain information about your audience. For instance, if you are invited to talk to a volunteer organization, you might ask the person who invited you to speak to tell you a little bit about the background, interests, knowledge, and needs of the audience. If you have a friend that belongs to the organization, you can also ask them to tell you a little bit about the audience and the organization.

Interviews

Contact persons are not always readily available and sometimes are not much help. In the event you do not have a contact person, you might want to consider asking the person arranging the speech to put you in touch with a few potential members of the audience so you can interview them. You can conduct interviews in person or via phone, email, or Skype to ask the individuals about their own experiences, knowledge, and interests, or ask them about the group as a whole. You can then get a general sense of the entire audience from the information you obtain from those interviews. This information can be enormously helpful in tailoring your message to the particular audience you will address.

Surveys

If you have enough time before your presentation and have the ability to reach each audience member, you can send your audience a survey to fill out and return to you before you prepare your speech. These surveys can help you gather demographic data as well as information about people's attitudes regarding specific issues. You

Understanding Appropriateness

Speeches have always had a home in all kinds of movies because of their ability to generate emotional reactions in their audiences. The 2017 film *Darkest Hour* contains a prime example of a speaker who understood his audience, the topic of his speeches, and the appropriateness of the overall message. Chronicling the early days of Sir Winston Churchill's first term as Prime Minister during the start of World War II, the film depicts excerpts of radio broadcasts and speeches made by Churchill to parliament. Celebrated British actor, Gary Oldman, delivered an Oscar nominated performance as the famed British leader, and illustrated how Churchill developed topics for his messages and then connected them with a sense of location, timing, and purpose that few speakers in history have been able to do.

could ask multiple-choice questions that give a limited number of possible responses, **Likert scale questions** that give statements and then ask respondents to circle a number that measures their level of agreement with it, **semantic differential scale questions** that ask participants to choose their position on a continuum between two polar opposites, or open-ended questions that allow audience members to give more elaborate written responses to a question.

Polling the Audience

Oftentimes, you will not have the time or opportunity to conduct a survey with your audience in advance. This does not, however, mean it is impossible to ask your audience a question. Instead, you can informally poll your audience by asking a question, or even several questions, during your speech. You can ask audience members to raise their hands if they agree or disagree with a particular statement. This can be an especially effective strategy that will help you capture your audience's attention during the beginning of your speech, while also learning something about them that you can then use later in your presentation. If you use this strategy, you should make sure you incorporate your audience's responses into your speech in some way.

Direct Observation

On the day of your speech, you will be able to learn a lot about your audience by simply observing them. During your speech, you will also be able to see your audience's nonverbal feedback, which will provide cues about how they are reacting to specific aspects of your message. You might see your audience become increasingly engaged, nod their heads, smile, make lots of eye contact, or provide other nonverbal feedback that indicates they are interested in your speech or agree with you. On the other hand, you could see your audience becoming distracted, looking at cell phones, frowning, shaking their head, looking away, or even falling asleep during your speech, which could indicate disinterest or disagreement.

Regardless of which methods of audience analysis are available—and there are always some strategies available for analyzing your audience—you should adapt your speech based on what you learn about your audience. If you find out that your audience does not know a lot about your topic, you might need to provide a little bit more background information. If your audience disagrees with your message, you might need to put in extra effort to acknowledge opposing viewpoints and provide even more evidence that supports your position using arguments that are likely to appeal to the values of your audience. If you know that specific audience members have experiences related to your topic and are open with others about those experiences, you might want to refer to them by name during your presentation. The more information you have about your audience both before and during your presentation, the better you can craft a message that will appeal to them.

LIKERT SCALE QUESTIONS

survey questions that provide statements and then ask respondents to circle a number that measures their level of agreement with the statement

SEMANTIC DIFFERENTIAL SCALE QUESTIONS

survey questions that ask participants to choose their position on a continuum between two polar opposites

CONDUCTING RESEARCH

Knowing about your audience can also help you determine which information will be most effective in delivering your message. The most time-consuming part of giving a speech is not the speech itself, but rather the research that goes into finding the information you need to make your point. Incorporating and citing research throughout your speech enhances your ability to connect with an audience, because it increases your credibility as a speaker and substantiates the claims you make. In this part of the chapter, we will identify five different types of sources you can look to for credible and useful information, describe four different types of information you will find there, and provide a way to evaluate the information you find.

Sources of Information

Despite the prevalence and utility of Google, there are a wide variety of resources for gathering information when developing a speech. Each of them has its own benefits and drawbacks, and not all will be useful for every speaking occasion. Knowing about these diverse sources of information gives you a variety of possibilities to consider when developing a presentation, adding to your ability to make an engaging and interesting message. Here are five different places you can potentially find useful information and evidence.

Peer-reviewed academic journal articles. Peer-reviewed articles are original research studies typically published in academic journals you can find in your university or college library. These studies are usually written by academic researchers, such as university professors, and are reviewed by other experts in the field before publication to ensure that the study used high-quality research methods and its results warrant the conclusions. Because the articles undergo a rigorous review process, they can provide some of the most reliable, up-to-date information, but will also usually be written with a high level of specific detail given that they are intended primarily for other experts and researchers. You can search for peer-reviewed articles by using online databases (such as EBCSO or Academic Search Premier) on your campus library website or by searching for articles on Google Scholar (http://scholar.google.com).

Books. Like peer-reviewed academic journal articles, some books are extended research reports that investigate a topic in depth. Others provide histories, background information, and overviews intended to teach you about a broad subject (such as a textbook). While other books include stories about individuals who went through a particular experience or contain completely fictional accounts. Typically, nonfiction research-based books or textbooks will be the most useful sources of evidence when you are preparing a speech, but you might find a good narrative or example in fiction books that will add some color to your presentation.

Magazines and newspapers. Magazines and newspapers are intended for more general audiences than academic journals, and they rely heavily on subscribers and advertisers to maintain profits. Some are intended to share specialized information in a particular field, some deliver current events, while others are intended purely for entertainment purposes. Depending on your topic and your audience, there may very well be valuable information in these sources. For instance, human interest stories found in certain magazines and newspapers might provide some interesting examples to help explain a point within a speech.

Web and media sources. Websites and media sources such as television shows, radio programs, documentaries, and movies can be good sources of quality information, but can also be highly unreliable. Generally, websites ending in .gov and .edu are more reliable than websites ending in .com, .org, or .net, but you will want to consider the credibility of the website providing the information in deciding whether a website should be considered an accurate source of information. For instance, www.mayoclinic.org is a highly credible source for medical information because the information is provided by the Mayo Clinic, one of the top research hospitals in the United States, while www.nationalenquirer.com gets its information from gossip magazine reports and sensationalized news stories based on rumors about celebrities. The use of Web and media sources depends largely on how you approach your topic and the connections you seek to make between that information and your topic.

Interviews with an expert or peer. For many of your speeches, it will be helpful to talk directly with an expert or a peer. An expert might be a professor who does research or teaches about the subject, or someone who has professional experience related to your topic. For example, if you are giving a speech about common running injuries, you might want to consult with a kinesiology professor who researches running injuries, a medical doctor who frequently diagnoses injuries, or a physical therapist who helps athletes recover from injuries. These would all constitute experts on the topic. Peers, on the other hand,

Evidence-Driven Research

DIALING DIVERSITY

In the library, books, journals, and magazines are often organized using one of several filing systems. You are likely familiar with the Dewey Decimal System, but the one used in most university libraries is the Library of Congress Classification System. A third system was also developed by Indian library scholar S. R. Ranganathan. In addition to a coding system, Ranganathan also is remembered for devising the five laws of library science:

1. Books are for use, not storage.

2. Every patron should be able to find what they need.

3. Every book has someone who finds it useful.

4. Use business principles to improve reader services.

5. Libraries grow, and should be prepared to handle that growth.[1]

NUMBERS
raw quantitative data

STATISTICS
quantitative reports that summarize and organize sets of numbers to make them easier to understand and visualize

EXAMPLES
instances that we use to help define or clarify concepts, draw attention to a particular feature of an experience, or elicit memories and emotions in our audience

TESTIMONY
the words of other people used to support your point

EXPERT TESTIMONY
information that you obtain from someone who has conducted extensive research on the topic, has significant experience with the topic, or holds a position that lends credibility to his or her ideas on a subject matter

PEER TESTIMONY
information that comes from someone who is in the same peer group as the audience; they are not necessarily an expert on the topic

do not possess expertise but can offer opinions or even experiences related to the topic. Instead of a healthcare provider who has expertise, you might interview a friend who injured himself or herself running. Peers provide a different type of information than an expert can, but the stories shared by peers can help your audience better understand how your topic impacts others' everyday experiences.

Types of Supporting Evidence

Each of the sources we just discussed provides information that can be used to support the points you make in your presentation. Information comes in many forms, just as it comes from many outlets. Ideally, you should use several of the following types of supporting materials in your speech to add variety, interest, and credibility to your speech.

Numbers and statistics. Numbers report raw quantitative data, whereas statistics summarize and organize sets of data to make them easier to understand and visualize. Statistics might include ratios, percentages, fractions, averages, standard deviations, or other calculations that make it easier to understand the overall impact of the data. Numbers and statistics can be especially valuable for showing the extent of a problem or the likelihood that your audience will be impacted by an issue. For example, you would be using a number if you were to say that, according to the Centers for Disease Control (CDC), 16,238 people are killed in homicides in the United States each year, but you would be using a statistic if you explained that 5.2 people out of every 100,000 will die as homicide victims each year.[2] You would be using a number if you said that according to seer.cancer.gov, 13,397,159 people are living with cancer in the US right now, but you would be using a statistic if you said that 40.8 percent of all people will be diagnosed with cancer during their lifetime.[3]

Examples. Sometimes we use a story to personalize a number or statistic. These stories are examples, which are instances that we use to help define or clarify concepts, draw attention to a particular feature of an experience, or elicit memories and emotions in our audience. Examples can be brief or extended, and they can be real or hypothetical.

Testimony. Another qualitative form of evidence you might use in a speech are statements by other people. This is also called testimony, and it involves using the words of other people to support your point. There are two types of testimony: expert testimony and peer testimony. Expert testimony is information you obtain from someone who conducts extensive research on the topic, has significant experience with the topic, or holds a position that lends credibility to his or her ideas on a subject. Peer testimony is information that comes from someone who is in the same peer group as the audience, and who is not necessarily an expert on the topic. Expert testimony would be valuable when explaining why climate change is occurring and how it will impact future weather patterns, while peer testimony would be valuable when talking about what the general student response to the new student union on campus has been. Often, but not always, testimony comes from interviews with these individuals, but there are times when you find testimony in an article you then use, despite not having done the interview yourself.

Definitions. If you are talking about a topic that might be unfamiliar to many members of your audience or are using terms that could have multiple meanings, it can be helpful to include definitions in your speech. You might choose to provide the denotative meaning of a word or phrase, which is the literal definition of that word or phrase you might find in a dictionary. Alternately, you might need to explain the connotative meaning of a word or phrase, which is the way that word or phrase is used in a particular context by a particular group of people. When using definitions, you might need to extend your definition to include the history of the word or phrase, explanations or descriptions of the thing being defined, or analogies and metaphors that help the audience understand a new concept by showing how it is similar to something that is familiar.

Evaluating Information

Once you have found a variety of sources and support materials, you will need to evaluate whether they effectively support your speech. As you evaluate your sources, you will want to make sure that they are sources your entire audience will view as credible. When evaluating the credibility of your sources, there are several criteria you should keep in mind.

How recent is the source? Typically, more recent sources will have more up-to-date, useful information. For example, an article about cancer treatments published in 1975 is not a good source of information about current cancer treatments, because a great deal of research and innovation has occurred since then that have changed the way many cancers are treated today.

Is the source in a position to know the information? If the person or organization that provided the information to the source is an expert on the specific subject, then it is probably a reliable source. For example, Dr. Sanjay Gupta, a neurosurgeon and professor at Emory University School of Medicine who is perhaps best known for his work as a CNN medical correspondent, would be an excellent source of information for a speech about brain injuries and neurosurgery, but he would not be a very credible source of information about which home building materials should be used in an area that has frequent earthquakes.

DENOTATIVE MEANING
the literal definition of a word or phrase that you might find in a dictionary

CONNOTATIVE MEANING
the way a word or phrase is used in a particular context, potentially as slang or with an implied value judgment

I think a good many people have a similar desire to be freed from the obligation to begin, a similar desire to be on the other side of the discourse from the outset, without having to consider from the other side what might be strange, frightening, and perhaps maleficent about it.[4]

—Michel Foucault

Is the source biased? If your source will gain financially, or in some other way, from convincing you to adopt a particular perspective or to purchase a particular product, you should take that bias into account when determining whether to use the information. For instance, even though LeBron James undoubtedly knows something about basketball shoes as a star basketball player for the Los Angeles Lakers, he is also a biased source because he gets paid by Nike to endorse their shoes and other merchandise. Instead, you would be better off trusting a podiatrist to help you identify which shoes might be best for you, since a podiatrist has expertise in identifying which shoes are most appropriate based on your physiology, but will likely not see any financial gain if you choose one brand of shoe over another. If you do use information from a potentially biased source, make sure the audience knows about that potential bias.

Is the information consistent with other sources? If you have a half-dozen sources that meet the previous criteria for being credible sources, and one of the sources contradicts the other five sources, it is probable that the five consistent sources are accurate, not the single source that contradicts them. Just as journalists are typically expected to have multiple sources corroborating a story before they publish it, you should have multiple sources that corroborate your claims before you try to convince your audience those claims are true.

DIALOGIC PUBLIC SPEAKING

Although many people imagine a dialogue as occurring between two people, dialogues can actually happen in the public sphere as well. Creating a dialogic environment when a large audience is involved can be difficult, and is not entirely under the control of the speaker. Nevertheless, there are some things you can do that encourage an audience to act with good will and openly exchange ideas with you as the speaker at the appropriate time. In this section of the chapter, we will provide a few suggestions for how to do this.

Identify with Your Audience

Audiences can be put off very quickly if you as the speaker do not make an attempt to connect with them in terms of their interests, values, and concerns. Demonstrate early in the speech that you tried to understand the topic from their perspective, but do so without making broad sweeping statements about "what you know about them," or being disingenuous in your attempts to connect with them.

Respect Differences

Audiences, although large and seemingly homogenous, are not made up of identical people. Even among a particular demographic group there are differences in attitudes and values, so do not make the presumption that they all know or believe something just because they are members of a certain group. There are differences among members of an audience that you should respect and appreciate.

Keep an Open Mind

Even though you may believe you know what you want to say, the evidence may take you elsewhere. Search unbiased sources first, then look to those that might be supportive of and those that may disagree with your position. This allows you to take in evidence beyond that which only supports a specific agenda. You may actually uncover information that makes you change your mind—and that is a good thing.

Strive for Audience Understanding

The tendency may be to deluge an audience with statistics or testimony in the hopes that the sheer amount of what you provide will sway them. Instead, take the information and condense it into manageable units for an audience to digest. Help them understand things the way you do, rather than force them to be convinced by quantity.

Talk with, Not at, Your Audience

Formal presentations can seem like the speaker is speaking at an audience who simply absorbs the message, but in actuality the process is much more transactional. The audience brings their own experiences, knowledge, and biases to their interpretation of your message. An effective speech retains a conversational quality that invites follow-up comments and questions when it is done.

SUMMARY

Formal public speaking presentations occur in a different communication context than interpersonal relationships. In this chapter, we explored some of the basic tenets and qualities of public speaking that make it different from a simple conversation. We first addressed the matter of topic selection, before examining how to analyze an audience for a formal presentation. We then looked at the process of researching information to use for speech construction, before offering some suggestions for making a speech to a large audience more dialogic.

CHAPTER 13 KEY IDEAS

- The five canons of rhetoric are invention, arrangement, style, delivery, and memory.

- When selecting a topic, you should consider the general purpose of your speech and whether the topic is appropriate for the occasion, the particular audience, and yourself.

- You can analyze your audience through the use of demographics, artifacts, informants, interviews, surveys, polling the audience, and direct observation.

- Five sources of information you might use to find information for your speech include: (1) peer-reviewed academic journal articles, (2) books, (3) magazines and newspapers, (4) Web and media sources, and (5) interviews with experts.

- Supporting evidence can include: (1) numbers and statistics, (2) examples, (3) testimony, and (4) definitions.

- When evaluating the credibility of a source, you should consider: (1) how recently the source was produced, (2) whether the source is in a position to know the information, (3) whether the source is biased, and (4) whether the source is consistent with other reliable sources of information.

CHAPTER 13 KEY TERMS

Deliberative	Semantic differential scale questions
Forensic	Numbers
Epideictic	Statistics
General purpose	Testimony
Brainstorm	Examples
Concept map	Expert testimony
Demographics	Peer testimony
Informant	Denotative meaning
Likert scale questions	Connotative meaning

ACTIVITIES AND DISCUSSION QUESTIONS

1. Watch this TEDx Talk presented at the University of Hertfordshire by Simon Lancaster about how to start a speech, available here https://www.youtube.com/watch?v=Bh3iM--2AW4. In the first few seconds, you'll see that he begins his speech rather unconventionally! Pay attention to the way he presents his argument, and identify what types evidence he uses to make his points.

2. You will probably be giving a speech in this class. Brainstorm several possible topics. Evaluate whether each is appropriate for you, your audience, and the occasion.

3. What are some types of evidence that you can use to support your speech? Find several sources and types of support materials that you might use in your speech. Which types of evidence will be most effective for your topic and audience?

4. Watch a live speech on your campus or in your community. If you cannot see a live speech, watch one online or on television. What was the speaker trying to accomplish? Did they use strong support materials? Did they cite their sources? How effective do you think the speech was?

ORGANIZING YOUR PRESENTATION

A common misconception people have regarding public speaking is that it is a talent you are born with and not a skill you can refine and develop. The fact is you can become better at public presentations by using and practicing certain skills. One of those skills involves organizing your main points and evidence in a way that best supports your topic and that also allows the audience to follow along. The organizational dimensions of public speaking take a significant amount of time, but the payoff is huge when you deliver an organized and coherent speech. Organization begins after you have identified your topic and gathered research on it.

While repeating information is key to organizing a presentation, there is a little bit more to developing an effective speech. In this chapter, we will talk about how to move from a general purpose and topic to a clear thesis statement. We will then examine the different parts of a speech and explain how outlining can assist you in crafting those elements. We will also provide you with tools to ensure you cite sources properly in your speech. Finally, we will provide tips for how to use proper organization of your presentation to encourage dialogue with an audience.

FROM BROAD TOPICS TO SPECIFIC PURPOSES

Before you can begin to develop your speech outline, you need to have a clear, specific goal for your presentation. It is not enough to say you are speaking about some broad topic; you must be able to lay out what your specific approach is to the topic. This is something you can only do after researching the topic and narrowing it to something that fits appropriately within the time you have to speak. In this part of the chapter, we will discuss the two steps involved in refining your topic from something broad to something specific.

SPECIFIC PURPOSE STATEMENT

a narrower version of the general purpose statement that identifies what you will talk about, what you will say about it, and what you hope the audience will take away from the speech

The first step is developing a specific purpose statement. A specific purpose statement is a narrower version of the general purpose statement that identifies the topic you will address, what you will say about it, and what you hope the audience will take away from the speech. A specific purpose statement includes both your general purpose and topic, and it is written as a declarative sentence that states what your speech will do for your audience.

Here's an example of a specific purpose statement for an informative speech.

> **Specific purpose statement:** My speech will teach my audience to do CPR by showing them how to do compressions, open the victim's airway, and give rescue breaths.

Notice that the specific purpose statement above includes the general purpose of the speech (to teach, a variation of informing), the topic (CPR), and a preview of the main points (compressions, airway, and breaths). The specific purpose statement is part of the speech development process that helps you plan your speech, but it is not something you explicitly say out loud during your speech. Instead, you will go through one final step to convert your specific purpose statement into a thesis statement.

THESIS STATEMENT

a one-sentence summary of your speech that is written the way you will say it out loud to your audience during your speech

PREVIEW OF MAIN POINTS

tells your audience how you will organize the information for that lesson or argument

A thesis statement is a one-sentence summary of your speech that is written the way you will say it out loud to your audience during your speech, and it is followed by a preview of main points. Your thesis is the statement of the primary lesson you will teach or the argument that you will make in your speech, and the preview of main points tells your audience how you will organize the information for that lesson or argument. For example, you would convert the specific purpose statement above into the following thesis statement and preview of main points.

> **Thesis:** Learning three steps of CPR can help you save a life.
>
> **Preview of main points:** Today, we will first learn to give compressions, then how to open the victim's airway, and finally how to give rescue breaths.

Notice that the thesis statement and preview of main points together include almost the same information as the specific purpose statement. Language about the audience is removed, however, since you are talking directly to them. The thesis and preview are written in two separate sentences, and the preview of main points includes signposts, or key words, that signal to the audience you are moving from one part of the speech to another. Once you have established your general purpose, specific purpose, and thesis, you are ready to develop the remainder of your speech.

THE PARTS OF A SPEECH

Every speech is different, but all good speeches contain the same three parts. They contain an introduction, a body, and a conclusion. These parts represent a modernization of the organizational structure of a speech. In Classical times, it was the *exordium*, narration, and the *peroration*—quite similar but a bit more nuanced in structure than the contemporary approach. Nevertheless, the introduction, body, and conclusion of the speech also contain certain components. Although they may sound simple, they require careful crafting to be effective. In this section of the chapter, we will explore those things that compose an introduction, a body, and a conclusion paying close attention to the introduction because, as the saying goes, "you never get a second chance to make a first impression."

Introductions

The first thing your audience hears from you is the introduction. If you do not have a clear and organized introduction, then you risk losing your audience immediately; on the other hand, a strong introduction can capture their attention for the remainder of the presentation. Introductions should be creative and memorable because they create a first impression, help to determine whether the audience will give you their attention during the rest of your speech, and set the tone for your entire presentation. They also follow a pretty standard formula. There are six parts that should be included in every introduction: the attention getter, statement of relevance to the audience, evidence of speaker credibility, thesis, preview of main points, and a transition to the body of the speech.

Attention getter. The first thing you need to accomplish in your introduction is capturing your audience's attention. You should try to engage the audience from the moment you begin to speak and make them want to listen to the rest of your speech. There are several strategies you can use to get your audience's attention, but you should carefully consider which will be the most effective for your particular audience, is most appropriate for your topic, and sets the tone you want to establish as you move forward in your speech.

The first attention-getting strategy is asking the audience a question. If done well, this strategy will engage the audience members immediately and give them an incentive to stay involved in your speech. The best attention-getting questions should solicit answers from the audience. One way to do this is to poll your audience and ask for a show of hands from those who have had a particular experience or hold a particular position on an issue that is related to your topic. If you are giving a speech advocating for adopting dogs from rescue organizations instead of from breeders and puppy mills, you might begin by asking everyone who has ever owned a pet to raise their hand. Another option is to ask a question and ask for audience answers. If you have limited time, however, you should be careful to ask questions that will have brief answers rather than questions that will lead to extended discussion. For instance, in a speech about romantic relationships, you might begin, "Psychologist John Gottman found there are four behaviors that predict if a relationship will end and called them the Four Horsemen of the Apocalypse. Can anyone guess what those four behaviors are?" Using a question as your attention getter will only be effective if it is a question that your audience can actually answer, not a rhetorical question that is not intended to be answered.

The second attention-getting strategy is sharing a surprising fact or statistic. Such data should startle your audience and make them want to know more about your topic. The information should pique the audience's curiosity, help them begin to realize how widespread a problem is, or challenge commonly held views about how things work. Be sure to cite your source for this information in your attention getter and make sure it is related to the topic on which you are speaking.

The third attention-getting strategy is beginning with a brief narrative, or anecdote. Stories help make issues come to life by connecting the issue to human experience and adding an emotional component to your speech. If you choose to use a narrative as an attention getter, you will need to be careful to keep it brief and to make sure it connects clearly to the topic of your speech.

The fourth attention-getting strategy is using a famous or inspiring quotation that relates directly to your topic. For example, if you are giving a speech about the importance of community service or a particular social issue, you might open your speech with Mahatma Gandhi's quotation, "You must be the change you wish to see in the world."[1] When you choose a quotation, you should make sure it is aligned with your topic and include a brief explanation about how the quotation relates to your topic.

The fifth attention-gaining strategy is using a joke to open your speech. Jokes can be risky, however, because they can easily be misinterpreted or distract from your speech if they are not planned carefully. If you use a joke that is appropriate for the audience and occasion, and that is directly related to the topic of your speech, the joke can be an ideal way to catch your audience's attention. But if your joke is not directly related to your topic, is offensive, or contains inappropriate language, you will quickly lose credibility and risk upsetting your audience and losing their attention before you have even reached the thesis of your speech.

Relevance to audience. After you have captured your audience's attention, you will need to provide any necessary background information and clearly establish the relevance of the topic for your audience. This is the portion of your introduction where you tell your audience members why they should care about this particular topic. This can be an especially good place to use a statistic or other source to show the overall impact of the topic before relating it directly to your specific audience.

Speaker credibility. In the third part of your introduction, you need to establish your credibility as a speaker. Explain why you are qualified to speak on this topic and why your audience should trust you. Do you have professional or work experience related to this topic? Perhaps you are qualified to speak about different types of car engines because you work in an auto repair shop and have rebuilt a couple of engines. Maybe you are qualified to speak about administering first aid because you spent five years working as a lifeguard and occasionally had to use your first aid training. If you do not have professional or volunteer experience related to your topic, then you could emphasize that you learned a lot about the area as part of your academic major or have done extensive research on the topic to prepare for the speech. Nursing majors have more expertise than most people about vaccines and how to treat common injuries, communication majors have expertise in maintaining interpersonal relationships, and computer science majors have expertise in cyber security. The key goal is to let the audience know why they should trust the information you provide on this subject.

Thesis. You should also clearly state your thesis. You learned about how to develop and write a thesis statement from your general purpose and specific purpose statements earlier in this chapter. Your thesis is a one-sentence summary of your speech that serves as an umbrella covering all of the topics you will cover. Now is the time to let the audience know what you intend to say, or what their takeaway should be from your presentation.

Preview of main points. After you state your thesis, you should end your introduction by previewing your main points. Your preview should include all of the main points you plan to cover in the order you plan to discuss them. Your preview of points is a roadmap for the rest of your speech. Your thesis statement provides the destination, while your preview tells your audience how you will get them there.

Transition to the body. After you have completed your introduction, you need a transition statement that indicates to your audience that you are ending the introduction and beginning to move into the body of your speech. We will discuss transitions in more detail, but for now just remember that you need to have a transition in order to move from the introduction to the body.

> **Transition to the body:** The first step in CPR is giving chest compressions.

Overall, the introduction of your speech should only comprise 10 to 15 percent of your total speaking time. For a seven-minute speech, this means your introduction should accomplish all six of these tasks in less than one minute, while a twenty-minute speech allows up to three minutes to accomplish these tasks. Even though your introduction will be the first thing your audience will hear when you deliver your speech, it should be the last part of the speech you write, or at least revise, because you have to decide what the body of your speech will say before you can decide how to best introduce it.

Body of Your Presentation

The body of your presentation is where you share the bulk of the information in your speech. The body of your speech should take 75 to 80 percent of the total time in your speech, so this is where you will use the most support materials and give the most detail about your topic. The body of your speech will be divided into several main points, each of which should help to support your thesis. Your main points should be separate categories of information, meaning they should not overlap and should be organized in a pattern that makes the most sense for the topic you have chosen. In most speeches, each main point should be divided into two or more subpoints that help to support that particular main point. Each subpoint should be a separate idea that does not overlap with other subpoints, and each subpoint should clearly support the main point under which it is organized rather than other main points in the speech.

Conclusions

The conclusion of your speech is your final chance to impact your audience, so it is important you make this final component of your speech memorable. The goal of your conclusion is to help your audience remember the points you have already made and leave them with a lasting impression. Your conclusion should only be approximately 10 percent of your total speaking time, and, in that brief time, you should do three things.

DIALING DIVERSITY

The Power of Clear Goals in Speeches

On August 22, 1964, at the Democratic National Committee in Atlantic City, New Jersey, an African American woman named Fannie Lou Hamer delivered a presentation on the significant challenges minorities faced when trying to vote in the South. Her talk was well organized and made several key points: she provided her own experiences trying to vote, which included being evicted from the plantation where she lived and worked because she refused to rescind her voter application, and encountering resistance at registration drives where she was beaten and ridiculed by police simply for trying to help others exercise their right to register to vote. Without proper organization and a clear thesis, her testimony would have had little impact or relevance to those to whom she spoke.[2]

Signal conclusion. After you have delivered the body of your speech, you need to indicate to the audience you are ready to begin the conclusion. You want to make sure your audience is paying careful attention during the final moments of your speech, and you can use a signpost as a signal that you are beginning the conclusion, such as "In conclusion," "Finally," "To summarize," or "To wrap up."

Review thesis and main points. After you signal that you are beginning the conclusion, you should summarize your speech by restating the thesis and main points of your speech. You might also choose to recap the highlights of your speech and pull it all together for a few final thoughts, but your conclusion should not add any new information not already presented in the body of your speech.

End with a clincher. After you have summarized your speech, you should end your speech with a clincher. A clincher is the final statement of your speech. Clinchers can use the same devices as an attention getter, such as narratives, statistics, quotations, or audience questions, and they can even refer back to the attention getter you used to open your speech. Clinchers are the last thing an audience hears in a speech and should both provide them with a sense of closure and reiterate what they should take away from the speech.

Transitions

Although not a distinct section of a speech, per se, transitional statements are the glue that holds a presentation together, and thus warrant a discussion all their own. As you have probably already gathered from the discussion of the introduction, body, and conclusion, you will need to use transitions several times during your speech. A transition is a connecting statement that lets your audience know you are moving from one part of your speech to another, and, depending on where in the speech a transition occurs, you would use one of three types of effective transitions: internal summaries, signposts, or internal previews.

- Internal summary: a statement that reviews or sums up what you just finished telling the audience

- Signpost: a word that catches the audience's attention and indicates where you are in the speech, similar to the way a road sign helps to tell you where you are and provide direction when you are driving

- Internal preview: a statement that previews what is coming up next and can even be an overview of the elements of the next main point

There are three primary places where you will use transitions in your speech: between the introduction and body of the speech, in between main points, and between the body and conclusion of the speech. The transition between the introduction and body of the speech should include at least a signpost. Transitions between main points could include an internal summary of the previous point, a signpost, and/or an internal preview of the next point. The transition between the last main point and the conclusion only needs a signpost, such as "In conclusion," since you are moving directly into a summary of the entire speech.

TRANSITION

a connecting statement that lets your audience know you are moving from one part of your speech to another

INTERNAL SUMMARY

a statement that reviews or sums up what you just finished telling the audience

SIGNPOST

a word that catches the audience's attention and indicates where you are in the speech

INTERNAL PREVIEW

a statement that previews what is coming up next and can even be an overview of the elements of the next main point

FULL-SENTENCE PREPARATION OUTLINE

an outline that includes everything you plan to say in your speech and is written somewhat like a manuscript in an outline format

KEY WORD SPEAKING OUTLINE

the outline you will put on a notecard and use during your speech; it should include only key words to remind you of your main points and subpoints, as well as source citations, statistics, and direct quotations you want to make sure you say in a particular way

OUTLINING

Knowing your thesis and the general structure of a speech allows you to then move to the next step in speech preparation: outlining. Good speeches should be carefully organized and prepared before you deliver them, and one of the most important tools for organizing your speech is an outline. There are two different types of outlines you will develop as you prepare your speech: a full-sentence preparation outline and a key word speaking outline.

The **full-sentence preparation outline** includes everything that you plan to say in your speech and is written somewhat like a manuscript in an outline format. You will use this outline to refine your speech in your early practice sessions when you are becoming familiar with the material. The **key word speaking outline** is the outline you use during your speech, and it should include only key words to remind you of the main points, subpoints, source citations, statistics, and direct quotations you want to make sure are said in a particular way. This outline is much shorter than the full-sentence preparation outline.

Signposts in Speeches

TEDx Talks have become one of the more prominent vehicles for public speaking in today's world. These talks ask experts and professionals in specific content areas to develop presentations for nonexpert audiences about their area of expertise and deliver them in usually less than half an hour. The talks are then recorded and placed online for the public to view. One of the most viewed TEDx talks was delivered in 2006 by Sir Ken Robinson, a British advisor on the arts in education to governments, nonprofits, and education and arts organizations. In the talk, intriguingly titled "Schools Kill Creativity," he lays out his presentation early on. He states his thesis clearly, indicating he wants to show that creativity is given the same emphasis in education. His main points, again illustrated early in the talk, are that we have enormous evidence of human creativity, that education and human society are unpredictable, and that children have extraordinary capacity for creativity which we squander in the current structures of education. Whether you agree with Sir Ken's thesis or argument is less relevant than his ability to organize points in a manner that maximizes the potential for audience appreciation for the case he makes. Organization is the backbone of any message, and it increases the chances it is received in the manner the speaker desires when used properly.

I.   Introduction
      A.   Attention Getter
      B.   Background and Audience Relevance
      C.   Speaker Credibility
      D.   Thesis
      E.   Preview of Main Points
      F.   Transition to First Main Point (Signpost and Internal Preview)

II.   Body
      A.   Main Point 1
          1.   Subpoint 1
          2.   Subpoint 2

Transition (Internal Review, Signpost, Internal Preview)
      B.   Main Point 2
          1.   Subpoint 1
          2.   Subpoint 2

Transition (Internal Review, Signpost, Internal Preview)
      C.   Main Point 3
          1.   Subpoint 1
          2.   Subpoint 2

III.   Conclusion
      A.   Signal Closing
      B.   Restate Thesis
      C.   Review Main Points
      D.   Clincher

FIGURE 14.1 Outline Template

As you can see in the template, Figure 14.1, outlines use symbols, labels, and indentations to help organize your speech. There are three principles, or rules, that will help to ensure you are developing an effective outline.

Subordination

The process of creating a hierarchy of ideas in which the most general ideas appear first followed by more specific ideas is called subordination. Each level of the outline has a different symbol set and amount of indention associated with it. As you can see in the example, the broadest ideas or categories of information, such as the main points, have a smaller indentation and are represented by Roman numerals. The next level of information is indented half an inch to the right and is represented by a capital letter. These lines contain the subpoints of the speech.

SUBORDINATION

the principle of outlining that creates a hierarchy of ideas in which the most general ideas appear first followed by more specific ideas

Coordination

The second principle of outlining is coordination, which is the idea that all information on the same level has the same degree of significance. Each of your main points should be equally important, and each of your subpoints should be fairly equal in importance. This is indicated by both the level of the outline and the amount of time devoted to discussing each element. Each of your subpoints should be given approximately the same length of time, and each of your main points should take roughly the same amount of time in your speech.

Division

The principle of division states that if a main point is divided into subpoints, it must be divided into two or more subpoints. If you are going to divide your subpoints into sub-sub-points, you need to divide them into at least two sub-subpoints. If you cannot divide your main point into more than one subpoint, then you are still simply stating the main point rather than explaining it further.

REFERENCES

Once you have developed the overall organization for your speech, you will need to add supporting material to substantiate your claims. Most of these support materials will come from the sources you found when conducting research. You will need to cite a source each time you use information from it in order to give credit to the original source as well as to add to your own credibility. There are three points at which you will need to refer to your sources: in your speech, in your presentation aids, and in your references page or bibliography.

Citing Sources Verbally

When you deliver your speech, you should verbally attribute the sources for any information you found while conducting research. You should give the source citation before sharing the information from it to draw your audience's attention and to enhance the credibility of what you are saying. We recommend including your source citation in your full-sentence preparation outline exactly the way you plan to say it in your speech, so you remember to attribute the source and become comfortable citing your sources while you are practicing. Each oral citation should include four components: the name of the publication or source, the date the source was published, the name of the person or organization who provided the information to the publication, and the credentials of that person or organization.

> "According to Dr. William Rawlins, an expert in interpersonal communication and professor at Ohio University, in his 1992 book titled Friendship Matters, the type and functions of our friendships change over the course of our lives."

Sometimes you will not have information about all four of these components of a citation, and in those cases, you should just include as many of these elements as possible. For instance, if a newspaper article shares information but does not refer to the source of that information, you might only be able to include the name of the newspaper and date of publication. If you obtain information from an organization's website, the organization's name might be the primary credential you need.

> "According to the Centers for Disease Control and Prevention website, last updated on May 23, 2014, diseases that are almost nonexistent today could return as epidemics if we stop vaccinating children."

In this citation, the website name also tells us the organization that provided the information, so there is no need to repeat those details multiple times.

Citing Sources in Presentation Aids

If you use an image, diagram, or other graphic in your PowerPoint presentation (or Prezi, Keynote, or any other slide deck program) from another source, you should cite that source on the slide on which the image appears. At minimum, you should include a link to the image on your slide in a small font that will not interfere with the overall impact of your slide. If the image is from an organization that lends credibility to the message (as opposed to an image that is functioning primarily as clip art), you might also want to include the name of the organization or person that is responsible for the image. In some cases, you might even want to consider including a reference to the source of the image in your speech, especially if you are also citing that source for other information you are sharing at the same time in your speech. Review Figure 14.2 for an example of how to integrate a citation into an image. Be sure to use the citation style appropriate for the occasion.

The effective wielder of public discourse, like the military man, belongs to social and political history because he is one of its makers.[3]

—Herbert Wichelns

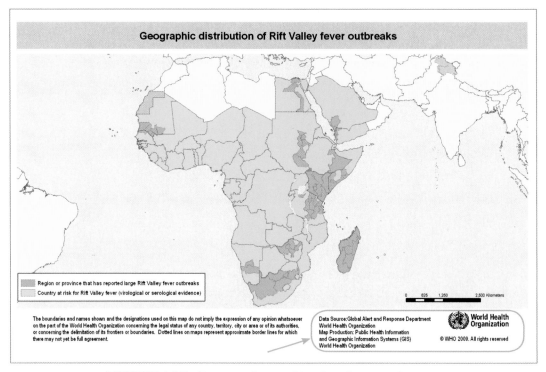

FIGURE 14.2 Integrating a Citation into an Image

Citing Sources in Your References Page

The final place you need to cite your sources is on your references page or bibliography at the end of your full-sentence preparation outline. Your instructor will probably require you to use APA, MLA, Chicago, or another format for your references section. See Figure 14.3 on the next page for an example of APA references. Citing sources in your outline and verbally attributing them in your speech helps establish and enhance your credibility as a speaker by demonstrating that you conducted research on the topic and are not just providing an opinion. If you do not have a copy of the required style manual, you can find detailed information about citing your sources at The Purdue Online Writing Lab (OWL) at https://owl.english.purdue.edu.

USING ORGANIZATION TO ENCOURAGE DIALOGUE

The goals of dialogue—encouraging people to listen and seeking to create understanding—may seem to be correlated solely with delivery, but these goals can often be achieved through the atmosphere of dialogue a speech creates. In fact, strong speech organization can go a long way toward creating a spirit of dialogue in a public setting. In this final section of the chapter, we will provide a few guidelines for organizing a speech that helps to create a dialogic environment.

APA References

Academic Journal Article (paginated by volume):

Author last name, A. A., Author, B. B., & Author, C. C. (year). Title of article. *Title of Journal, Volume number*, pages.

> Notice that the words in the article title are not capitalized, but the words in the journal title are capitalized.

Mazer, J. P., & Thompson, B. (2011). Student academic support: A validity test. *Communication Research Reports, 28,* 214-224.

> Notice that all sources that are more than one line are indented after the first line. To do this in Word, highlight your references list, click on paragraph, and choose "Hanging" in the dropdown menu under "Special." All of your references should also be in alphabetical order.

Book:

Author last name, A. A. (year). *Title of work: Capital letter also for subtitle.* Location: Publisher. Lipson, C. (2004). *Doing honest work in college.* Chicago, IL: University of Chicago Press.

Interview:

A. Last Name, personal communication, date.

L. E. Schmeidler, personal communication, March 20, 2014

> Typically an interview is cited in text, but not in the references list. For this class, though, please include your interviews in your references list.

Magazine:

Author last name, A. A., Author, B. B., & Author, C. C. (year). Title of article. *Title of magazine, Volume number* (Issue number), pages.

Bernasek, A. (2014, March 21). Life in the slow lane. *Newsweek, 1* (162), 1.

Newspaper:

Author last name, A. A., Author, B. B., & Author, C. C. (year). Title of article. *Title of Newspaper, Volume number* (Issue number), pages.

> Notice that the newspaper is the only type of source with p. or pp. in front of the page numbers.

Santos, F. (2014, March 20). Two states win court approval on voter rules. *The New York Times,* p. 1.

Website:

Author last name, A. A. (date last updated). *Title of document.* Retrieved from http://address.

National Institutes of Health. (2014, March). *Headache pain: What to do when your head hurts.*

FIGURE 14.3 APA References

Use an Interesting, Ethical Attention Getter

One common mistake made by speakers is to choose the most shocking and potentially offensive attention getter they can find to ensure the audience listens. This is not necessarily the best strategy. Instead, when creating your attention getter, try to put yourself in your audience members' places and think about what would get your interest, but not offend you, if you were them. Choosing your attention getter wisely ensures its maximum impact without risking losing the audience before you get started.

Use Personal Credibility Wisely

You may be an expert in the subject area on which you are speaking and the audience may very well not be, but this does not provide you with license to diminish their importance or abilities. Additionally, although you may know a good deal about the subject, you likely do not know everything; do not present yourself as "the authority," but rather as "an authority." If you are not an authority, but do have some knowledge, then make that clear to the audience. Be honest and modest.

Provide Credentials for All Sources

We mentioned this when speaking about references, but it bears repeating. Providing the source information to an audience is an ethical way to use information and indicates that you trust the audience members to evaluate the source veracity themselves. Giving this type of trust to an audience both enhances your credentials and also creates an environment where the audience members are invited to be active participants in the discussion of the topic.

Leave the Evaluation to the Audience

Speakers often wish to deliver content with certainty, and that is a good thing, to a point. When concluding a speech, however, particularly a persuasive speech, allow the audience to make their own decision and do not push them too hard toward a certain action or belief. Doing so can come across as suggesting to the audience "If you don't agree now then you just are not smart enough," which is the exact opposite of a dialogic and respectful environment. The discussion of the topic does not end with your speech. Instead, your speech should be treated as a contribution to a longer discursive chain that will continue well after you speak.

ENGAGING ETHICS

Credibility and Political Speaking

Political speakers from both parties often invoke support from "the people," and say things like "I have heard" and "my constituents tell me," when expressing support for their position. There is no way for the audience to understand and evaluate the credibility of this information. What ethical responsibilities should leaders have today when it comes to using public support to defend their positions? Is it enough to use these types of phrases? Why, or why not?

Acknowledge Disagreement

Disagreement exists about a great many things, and when we advise you to acknowledge disagreement, we mean for you to do so in two ways. The first is to recognize when there is contradictory research on a point you are making. You should not ignore this, but rather let the audience know there is disagreement out there and that you are siding with a particular interpretation for specific reasons. Share those reasons with the audience. Second, acknowledge that disagreements with your overall position may very well be possible. Not everyone will agree with you, and letting the audience know you are comfortable with that goes a long way toward creating a supportive and dialogic speaking environment.

SUMMARY

One of the most important parts of speech development is determining the organization of your presentation. This chapter focused on providing the tools necessary to create an organized speech. We first discussed how to turn a topic into a specific purpose and thesis. We then explored the three primary components of every speech: the introduction, body, and conclusion. Third, we covered how to cite sources and explained why that is important for you as a speaker. Finally, we provided five clear suggestions for using organization properly to create a dialogic environment for a public presentation.

CHAPTER 14 KEY IDEAS

- When developing your speech, you should move from a broad topic to a specific purpose statement, and then to a clear thesis and preview of main points.

- All speeches should include an introduction, a body, and a conclusion.

- Most introductions should include six parts: (1) attention getter, (2) statement of background and audience relevance, (3) evidence of speaker credibility, (4) thesis statement, (5) preview of main points, and (6) transition to the first main point.

- A conclusion should (1) signal the conclusion, (2) restate the thesis, (3) review the main points, and (4) end with a clincher.

- Transitions should include an internal summary, signpost, and preview.

- Outlines should follow the principles of subordination, coordination, and division.

- You should cite your sources (1) out loud in your speech, (2) in your presentation aids, and (3) in the references page or bibliography of your final preparation outline.

CHAPTER 14 KEY TERMS

Specific purpose statement	Internal preview
Thesis statement	Full-sentence preparation outline
Preview of main points	Key word speaking outline
Transition	Subordination
Internal summary outline	Coordination
Signpost	Division

ACTIVITIES AND DISCUSSION QUESTIONS

1. At this point, you have probably selected a topic that you plan to use for a speech in your class. In the space below, write the topic, specific purpose statement, and thesis statement that you plan to use for your speech.

    Topic:

    Specific Purpose Statement:

    Thesis:

2. Write two different attention getters that you could use in the introduction to your speech. Highlight the attention getter that you think is strongest.

3. Think about what you want to teach your audience. How will you organize your main points and subpoints to help your audience understand and remember your speech as much as possible?

4. Watch a speech that was given in the last few weeks. What was the speaker's thesis? Did they have clear main points? Do you think they were successful in accomplishing their goals for the audience?

5. Print an outline of a speech, cut the paper into strips, and mix up the pieces of paper. With a group, put the strips of paper in the order that they should go to form a full speech. How do you know that is the correct order? Which pattern of organization was used for this speech?

DELIVERY

The first thing most people comment on after watching someone give a speech is the delivery, because it is the most noticeable element of a speech and can be the most memorable. Speaking in front of an audience can be intimidating. Delivery is that part of speaking that makes many people turn away opportunities to share their thoughts, beliefs, and knowledge with a larger and wider audience. It is also one of the five canons of rhetoric we noted when we began our discussion of public speaking context. It has always been a point of emphasis in speech training, because sound and strong delivery can raise a presentation to new levels.

There are numerous things good delivery provides a speaker and an audience. Good delivery will help keep your audience's attention, enhance your credibility, and make your message more memorable and impactful. On the other hand, poor delivery can hurt a speech and detract from your chances of getting your message across to an audience. Poor delivery can make even the best-planned and most-researched speech easy to forget or, perhaps even worse, difficult to believe or trust. For these reasons it is important to understand the various dimensions of delivery and to practice them far in advance of delivering your presentation. You might be able to cram for a test the night before, but you cannot do the same for a presentation.

In this chapter, we turn our attention to delivery. First, we will learn about the components of delivery and the four forms of delivery. Then we will discuss a common concern for many speakers: communication apprehension or, as it is more commonly known, the fear of public speaking. We will then examine the proper ways to construct and deploy presentation aids. We will also provide strategies for practicing that will help maximize your chances of speaking success. Finally, we will discuss some ways to use delivery to create a dialogic atmosphere when giving a speech.

COMPONENTS AND FORMS OF DELIVERY

Delivery is a term that encompasses a great many parts. Just think about a speech you recently heard. Was the delivery simply verbal? Were there gestures and facial expressions that contributed to your interpretation of the message? Perhaps the inflection and emphasis placed on certain phrases or words made them more memorable for you? The fact of the matter is delivery involves many different things working together. Speeches are also delivered in different ways, resulting in different impressions of the speaker and the message. In this section of the chapter, we will discuss the components of speech delivery as well as the four ways in which people deliver formal presentations.

Cultural Variations of Speech Delivery

Photo credit: Nadezda Murmakova/Shutterstock.com

Different cultures have different expectations for appropriate attire in public speaking situations. In Western countries, like the United States, proper dress for men and women includes things like a pressed suit or dress. While hats such as baseball caps are frowned upon in such scenarios, religious headscarves are expected from certain Muslim and Hindu speakers. Women from India may wear saris when speaking, and when the Dalai Lama speaks to the United Nations or other audiences, he invariably wears his religious robes, not a suit. Understanding and appreciating the cultural backgrounds of speakers helps to identify appropriateness of dress for formal presentations. Although not wearing a pressed suit or dress, they still are wearing what they deem to be respectful and appropriate clothing for the speaking occasion when wearing religious or ethnic garb.

Vocal and Physical Delivery

Delivery can be broken into two key components: elements of speaking that deal with the voice, which we call vocalics, and elements of speaking that deal with the body, or physical delivery.

Vocal delivery. Vocal delivery includes everything that affects how your voice sounds when you speak. Even though all of them are happening at once, there are several different components of vocal delivery that you should pay attention to while you are speaking.

- Pronunciation is what a word should sound like when it is spoken according to regional rules and standards. If you mispronounce words in your speech, you might sound like you did not practice, and will thus lose credibility with your audience.

- Articulation is the process of physically shaping the sounds that make the word. Articulation errors occur when you run words together or improperly shape vowels or consonants. While this is common in everyday, casual conversation, it can hurt your credibility in a formal speaking situation.

- Volume is how loud or soft the sound of your voice is when you speak. When giving a speech, you should speak loudly enough that your audience can easily hear you.

- Pitch is how high or low your voice sounds when you speak. Lower voices tend to carry through a room more easily than higher pitched voices, so if your voice has a high pitch, you might have to work even harder to increase your volume and project your voice.

- Rhythm is the cadence or pattern of movement in your voice. Most of us have a natural cadence, but sometimes we develop a repetitive sing-song pattern when we're nervous.

- Rate is how fast or slow you speak. The typical rate of speech varies some by geographic region, but if you speak too quickly, your audience might have trouble following along. On the other hand, if you speak too slowly, you might lose your audience's interest.

- Tone refers to how variable your voice is and how "warm" your voice sounds. If you vary your voice while you speak, you will more easily convey emotions and interest, but if you speak in a monotone voice, your audience will struggle to maintain interest.

- Vocalized pauses are filler words that many speakers use when they feel like they should be saying something but do not have anything to say. Common vocalized pauses include "umm," "like," and "y'know." It is normal to use occasional

VOCAL DELIVERY
everything that affects how your voice sounds when you speak

PRONUNCIATION
what a word should sound like when it is spoken according to a rule or standard

ARTICULATION
the process of physically shaping the sounds that make the word

VOLUME
how loud or soft the sound of your voice is when you speak

PITCH
how high or low your voice sounds when you speak

RHYTHM
the cadence or pattern of movement in your voice

RATE
how fast or slow you speak

TONE
how variable your voice is and how "warm" your voice sounds

VOCALIZED PAUSES
filler words that many speakers use when they feel like they should be saying something but do not have anything to say

vocalized pauses when speaking, but too many can interfere with your speech and hurt your credibility.

By now, you have probably noticed that many of the elements of vocal delivery in public speaking include the vocalics we discussed in the chapter on nonverbal communication. As you continue, you will see that the same is true for many of the elements of physical delivery.

Physical delivery. Physical delivery, often called nonverbal delivery, can impact the way that your message is received as much as, or more than, anything else. Physical delivery includes all of the physical signals your body sends to your audience during your speech, and there are several elements you should consider.

PHYSICAL DELIVERY

all of the physical signals your body sends to your audience during your speech; there are several elements to consider

PHYSICAL APPEARANCE

includes your apparel and grooming

POSTURE

the position of your body when you are speaking

FACIAL EXPRESSIONS

the way the position and movement of your facial features convey emotion and engagement

GESTURES

the movements of your hands and arms

EYE CONTACT

looking members of your audience in the eyes while speaking

- Physical appearance includes your apparel and grooming and is the first element of physical delivery your audience will notice, even before you say a word. You should be dressed appropriately for the occasion, whether it is in class or at a wedding or funeral, but, generally, you should dress at least as formal, if not more formal, than your audience.

- Posture is the position of your body when you are speaking, and can either communicate confidence and respect or nervousness and disinterest. When you speak, you should stand up straight, in a relaxed and natural pose. While you speak, stand on both feet; do not shift back and forth from one foot to the other or cross your feet, as this will make you look unbalanced. If there is a podium, you may rest your hands occasionally as you speak, but you should not lean on the podium.

- Facial expressions convey emotion and engagement through the position of your facial features, which might include a smile, raised eyebrows, a glare, a smirk, a grimace, a frown, or many other expressions. Your facial expressions should reflect the emotional tone of the occasion and what you are saying in your speech.

- Gestures are the movement of your hands and arms and should be used to add emphasis to important points and illustrate relationships between ideas. Gestures should appear to be natural, and you should work on incorporating them into your speech when you begin practicing. Excessive or repetitive gestures can be distracting, and too few gestures can make it look like you are not engaged in your speech or failed to practice. This is especially true if your gestures are limited because you are using your hands to hold your notecards where you can read them for most of your speech.

- Eye contact is perhaps one of the most important elements of physical delivery. Establishing and maintaining good eye contact allows you to maintain your audience's attention, build rapport, and help your audience feel like you care about your speech and their response to your message. Instead of speaking to the wall in the back of the room, staring at one or two individuals through your entire speech, looking at the floor, or reading from your notes, try making eye contact with each of your audience members for a few seconds at a time. This allows you to treat your speech as many small conversations with individuals in your audience, instead of a presentation to a room full of people.

Forms of Delivery

Just as different speaking contexts call for different types of speeches, different contexts also call for different types of delivery. There are four primary types of delivery, and there are advantages and disadvantages that accompany each.

Memorized. In a memorized speech, the speaker commits the entire speech to memory and does not use any notes while delivering the speech. Memorized speeches were common in ancient Greece and Rome and are still sometimes used in public speaking competitions and during political campaigns but are rarely used in most classroom or professional presentations today. Some of the advantages of memorized speeches are that you will be able to give your speech the same way every time, and you will be able to use eye contact and gestures to their maximum effect since you will not be holding a notecard in your hand or looking at your notes or manuscript during your speech.

MEMORIZED SPEECH

a speech the speaker commits to memory and delivers without the use of any notes

However, the disadvantages of memorized speeches far outweigh the advantages for most speakers. It takes a substantial amount of time to memorize a speech, and, even if you have spent hours trying to memorize your speech, you still might forget what you intended to say. It is not uncommon for speakers who have memorized their speeches to freeze in the

Gesturing across Cultures

Every culture has its own nonverbal gestures. For example, making the "OK" sign with your fingers in the United States means "OK," while in Japan it means "money" and in France it means "zero." It is important to be careful using gestures in speeches because you do not know that everyone in the audience hails from the same culture. For example, in Great Britain during World War II Prime Minister Winston Churchill made the "V for Victory" sign with his hand, which now connotes "peace." The fact is, if that same sign is made with your palm facing in when in England it means "Up yours." Given the complexity of nonverbals, what guidelines do you think would help speakers steer clear of offensive nonverbal usage? What other gestures might be seen as problematic in your cultures? Why?

middle of their speech or forget a couple of words, causing them to completely lose their place or repeat a phrase over and over until they remember what was supposed to come next. Finally, it is very difficult to adapt your speech to the audience and occasion if you have finalized and memorized your speech far in advance.

MANUSCRIPT SPEECH

a speech the speaker writes out word for word in an essay format and delivers by reading from the manuscript

Manuscript. In a manuscript speech, the speaker writes out his or her speech word for word in an essay format and reads the entire speech from that manuscript. It is common for political speeches, news broadcasts, and many commemorative speeches to be delivered from a manuscript. Manuscripts allow the speaker to carefully word every sentence of the speech. Manuscript speeches are difficult to adapt to the audience and context, however. It is also nearly impossible for a speaker to make eye contact with individuals in the audience or to use effective gestures when reading from a hard copy of a manuscript. Finally, unless you have a great deal of experience and training in speaking from a manuscript, your verbal delivery will probably sound unnatural and choppy.

EXTEMPORANEOUS SPEECH

a practiced, polished speech that makes use of a limited speaking outline

Extemporaneous. An extemporaneous speech is a practiced, polished speech that makes use of a limited speaking outline. If you are giving an extemporaneous speech, you have practiced your speech often enough that you are familiar with the content of the speech and have nearly memorized the material, but you probably say the speech a little bit differently each time you deliver it. Speakers have a notecard with limited notes, such as a key word outline with source citations and statistics, but do not have their full preparation outline or a manuscript in front of them. Extemporaneous speeches allow you to use natural verbal and physical delivery, make eye contact with your audience throughout your speech, and adapt to audience feedback throughout the speech. An extemporaneous speech does, however, take time to prepare and practice.

IMPROMPTU SPEECH

a speech presented with little or no preparation

Impromptu. An impromptu speech is a presentation with little or no preparation. For example, you are giving an impromptu speech anytime you are called on to answer a question or elaborate on an idea in class. You will also be giving an impromptu presentation when you interview for a job. Politicians also often give impromptu speeches in response to questions asked during town hall meetings, and pageant contestants deliver impromptu speeches when they are asked on-stage questions. Impromptu speeches can be intimidating, since you cannot prepare and might not even know whether you will be speaking in advance.

COMMUNICATION APPREHENSION

COMMUNICATION APPREHENSION

the fear or anxiety associated with real or anticipated communication with another or others

For as common as communication is in our lives and as long as we have been doing it, it does generate a great deal of anxiety for many people. Communication Apprehension (CA), is defined by communication scholar James McCroskey as "the fear or anxiety associated with real or anticipated communication with another or others."[1] CA can impact people in a variety of contexts, such as speaking in one-on-one interpersonal conversations or speaking in a small meeting, but many people experience this anxiety in public speaking contexts. This is not particularly surprising; most of us have less experience speaking in front of a large group than in an individual speaking context, and research tells us that we are more likely to feel anxiety when we are being evaluated, which is usually the case in a public speaking context.

Everyone has some level of CA, ranging from very low anxiety to very high anxiety and, if you would like, you can evaluate your level of CA using the Personal Report of Communication Apprehension, also called the PRCA-24, which is located at the end of this chapter for you to take.[2] There are two components that impact the level of CA that you feel. The first is Trait CA, which is the amount of communication anxiety you were born with and naturally have due to genetics. The second is State CA, which is anxiety that is related to the context in which you are communicating. While there is very little you can do to change your Trait CA levels, the good news is that you can reduce your overall CA by working to reduce your State CA.

Some of the symptoms of communication apprehension include sweating, feeling like you have butterflies in your stomach, slightly increased blood pressure, shortness of breath, dry mouth, flushed skin, and difficulty remembering what you planned to say. While these symptoms are hard to ignore as a speaker, in most cases, your audience probably will not even notice them.

STRATEGIES TO REDUCE COMMUNICATION APPREHENSION

Fortunately, there are several strategies you can use to reduce your anxiety. The first strategy is to practice your presentation often. If you begin practicing your speech far in advance of your presentation and practice often, you will increase your comfort level with the material and therefore your confidence on the day you speak. The second strategy is to employ relaxation techniques. These might include breathing exercises, stretching and

TRAIT CA
the amount of communication anxiety you were born with and naturally have due to genetics

STATE CA
anxiety that is related to the context in which you are communicating

In the early years of the study of CA, a distinction was made between "Trait CA" (TCA) and "State CA" (SCA). TCA was seen as being a general pattern of low, medium, or high orientation of anxiety/fear across communication contexts. SCA was seen as experiencing anxiety/fear in one situation but not in others.[3]

—J. C. McCroskey

SYSTEMATIC DESENSITIZATION

the process by which a person is slowly introduced to something they fear so that each time they overcome the fear, the intensity is decreased

yoga, exercise, meditation, or any other technique that typically helps you de-stress. The third strategy is systematic desensitization, which is the process by which a person is slowly introduced to something they fear so that each time they overcome the fear, the intensity of the fear is decreased. This might involve someone who is afraid of heights going up to different floors of a tall building as they get comfortable with the height of the one they are on. The fourth strategy for reducing CA is to visualize success. Visualizing yourself being successful can help lead to the occurrence of a self-fulfilling prophecy, which is convincing yourself that something is going to happen before it does, thus leading to the occurrence of what you originally expected. The final strategy for reducing CA is to think about your speech as a conversation with one individual in the audience at a time, instead of as a presentation in front of an entire room full of people at once.

SELF-FULFILLING PROPHECY

convincing yourself that something is going to happen before it does, thus leading to the occurrence of what you originally expected

USING PRESENTATION AIDS

Decades ago, it was not uncommon to give speeches that relied almost entirely on their words to communicate messages, but today it is easier than ever to complement and reinforce messages through the use of presentation aids. Presentation aids are additional resources that engage one or more of the audience members' five senses (sight, sound, touch, taste, smell) to help them better understand the message. Depending on the topic and goal of your speech, you might choose to use one or more of the following types of presentation aids.

PRESENTATION AIDS

resources that engage one or more of the audience's five senses (sight, sound, touch, taste, smell) to help the audience better understand the message

Objects

Objects are physical items you discuss in your speech. If you bring an object to class, you bring the actual thing you are discussing into class, not a representation of it. Objects can be an excellent tool for helping your audience experience something firsthand, because an object can allow your audience to engage multiple senses at once. Using the physical object you are discussing as a presentation aid helps your audience more easily understand what you are talking about and makes it easier to visualize the processes you might be describing. In some cases, objects can also give your audience a chance to touch, taste, and smell what you are talking about; however, if you plan to use an object your audience will need to taste, touch, or smell, you should think carefully about how to best let your audience come into contact with the object, so they can experience it when you want them to during the speech. Additionally, there are some objects you should not bring when giving a speech in a class because they are banned in most university classrooms, including illegal substances, weapons, and live animals.

OBJECTS

physical items that you are discussing in your speech

Models

Models are scaled physical representations of things. Sometimes, the object you are discussing is too small for your audience to easily see, or is too large to carry easily to where you are giving your presentation. In these cases, it can be useful to have a larger or smaller representation of the object that can be easily seen or used to demonstrate the process you are trying to show. For example, most eye doctors use a much larger model of an eye to

MODELS

scaled physical representations of things utilized as presentation aids explain how the eye works and how certain conditions interfere with or damage your vision. Many architects build smaller-scale models of the projects they have designed to allow their clients to more easily visualize the building, boat, landscape, or other project.

Demonstrations

DEMONSTRATIONS
presentation aids that involve enacting the process you are trying to teach your audience

Demonstrations involve actually enacting the process you are trying to teach your audience. Demonstrations often involve using objects or models to show the audience how to do something. For example, a cyclist might bring their bike and cycling shoes to demonstrate how to clip into SPD pedals, and show how the use of clips increases the power that can be generated while cycling. Additionally, some demonstrations might primarily involve the use of the speaker's body. For example, an exercise instructor might demonstrate the proper form for a squat, a hip-hop dancer might demonstrate several common hip-hop moves by dancing for the audience, and a physical therapist might demonstrate the proper way to push off from a chair when standing by demonstrating that specific movement.

Traditional Presentation Aids

There are a variety of ways you can enhance a presentation and help an audience understand a certain concept. These can be visual, audial, or both. In this part of the chapter, we will explore some of these additions to your speech that can help an audience better understand a complicated subject.

CHARTS
visual presentation aid that shows numeric data in a series of rows and columns

Charts. **Charts** show numeric data in a series of rows and columns, as shown in Figure 15.1. Charts allow your audience to see general trends in data and are especially useful if your audience might need to be able to look up a specific value. Charts can quickly become overwhelming, however, and can be difficult to absorb quickly. If it is important to your audience to get a sense of the overall impact of the data or quickly see relationships among numbers, one of the other graphs in this section might the best choice.

Enrollment by Year[4]

Year	2011	2013	2015	2017	2019
Full-time Students	15,218	16,267	16,694	18,819	20,297
Part-time Students	13,656	13,622	14,020	13,743	12,664

FIGURE 15.1 Example of a Chart

LINE GRAPHS
visual presentation aid that uses lines along two axes to show changes in values over time

Line graphs. **Line graphs** use lines along two axes to show changes in values over time. Line graphs are especially useful for showing trends, losses, or growth, and are especially good for allowing the audience to compare trends for two or more groups over a particular time frame. The line graph in Figure 15.2 on the next page makes it easy to see that the number of full-time students enrolled increased over the last eight years, while the number of part-time students decreased during that same time frame.

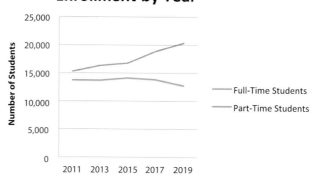

FIGURE 15.2 Example of a Line Graph

Bar graphs. Bar graphs have two axes and either horizontal or vertical bars that show the total number of items or levels of achievement in each category. Bar graphs are especially useful for helping the audience compare the levels of several different subcategories within a larger category in order to demonstrate the relative degrees of impact of each of those subcategories. The bar graph in Figure 15.3 makes it easy to quickly identify the leading causes of death in the United States and quickly shows the audience that heart disease and cancer kill far more people each year than anything else.

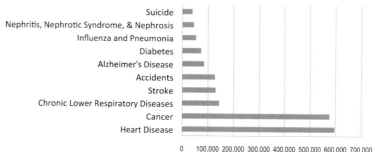

FIGURE 15.3 Example of a Bar Graph[5]

Histograms. A Histogram is a type of frequency chart that shows the proportion of individuals that obtained a certain level of achievement along a continuum. As can be seen in Figure 15.4, the horizontal axis shows categories based on ranges of achievement (sometimes called bins) in order from lowest to highest, such as grades on tests or number of items sold, and the vertical axis shows the frequency, or the number of individuals who obtained that level of achievement. Unlike bar charts, which represent discrete categories, histograms do not break between the columns because the categories are continuous.

Final Exam Scores

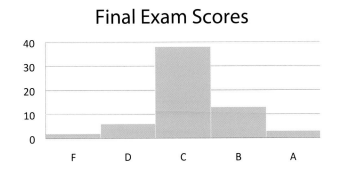

FIGURE 15.4 Example of a Histogram

Pie graphs. A pie graph is a round graph that has slices that represent how large the proportion of that particular category is compared to the whole. Pie graphs show the proportion of individuals out of 100 percent that have a particular characteristic, and are especially useful for showing demographic data or indicating preferences among a group (Figure 15.5).

PIE GRAPH

a round graph that has slices that represent how large the proportion of that particular category is compared to the whole

Favorite Fruits

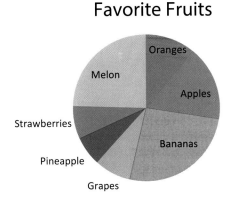

FIGURE 15.5 Example of a Pie Graph[6]

Scatterplot. A scatterplot is a graph that shows the relationship between two continuous variables. Scatterplots are useful for helping your audience understand the relationship, or correlation, between two variables. The scatterplot in Figure 15.6 has an upward slope and shows a positive relationship between height and weight, meaning that the taller people are, the more they tend to weigh.

SCATTERPLOT

a graph that shows the relationship between two continuous variables

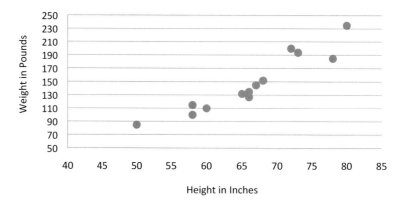

Distribution of Height and Weight

FIGURE 15.6 Example of a Scatterplot

Photographs. Photographs can also be a valuable presentation aid for showing your audience an image of something that cannot actually be brought into the classroom. You might use a photograph to show a picture of someone or an historical event, or an object you cannot easily bring into the classroom. If you use photographs or images as presentation aids, it is most effective to show the photograph or image to your entire audience at once, perhaps by using a PowerPoint slide, a projector, or a large poster. If you try to pass a photograph or image around so that each audience member can look at it closely, it can become a distraction and will not as effectively support your speech, since each audience member will see it at a slightly different time during your speech.

Videos. Many people also like using videos within their presentations. When you need to demonstrate something that is impossible for you to exhibit on your own in the classroom, a brief video clip can be an excellent way to briefly show an idea to your audience. If you plan to use video during your speech, make sure you test the video equipment in the room before you begin your speech. You should also preset the video, so all you have to do is press play when you reach that part of your speech. Have a back-up link ready to open in case someone accidentally closes your video. You should briefly introduce the video and tell your audience what to focus on beforehand, and then debrief the video for a few moments afterward to summarize what you just showed them. Finally, you should make sure the videos you plan to use are brief and do not occupy a huge part of the body of your speech.

Audio clips. Another presentation aid you might use is a simple audio clip. For instance, you might want to play excerpts from two different pieces of music to demonstrate the difference between Baroque and Romantic styles. Sound can be highly valuable in helping your audience understand that topic and others like it. The guidelines for using audio in your speech are similar to those for using video in your speech: (1) keep the audio clips brief, typically under 30 seconds; (2) test and preset the equipment, so all you have to do is press play or begin to produce the sound; and (3) preview the audio to tell your audience what to listen for, and then summarize what they heard afterward.

Multimedia Technology

PowerPoint, Prezi, Keynote, or other types of slide show presentation technologies can be highly effective ways to display presentation aids for your audience. For example, you might decide to put a chart, graph, map, or photograph on a slide so your entire audience can easily see it at the same time. You might embed a video clip or audio clip into another slide so it is ready to play at the appropriate time in your speech and then easily move on to your next graph. If used poorly, however, PowerPoint and other similar technologies can distract from your speech. For instance, many speakers put too much text on their slides, choose fonts and color schemes that make the slides difficult for the audience to read, or put extraneous information on the slides that distracts the audience from the purpose of the speech. Table 15.1 shows a few guidelines for using PowerPoint and other slideshow technologies when speaking.

Do . . .	Don't . . .
• show diagrams, charts, graphs, maps, photographs, and other visual elements that complement your message.	• fill your slides with excessive text, the outline of your speech, or entire paragraphs of writing.
• choose large (at least 28 point), serif fonts that are easy for your audience to read.	• use small, serif, or script fonts that are difficult for your audience to read.
• include blank slides in your presentation when you are not directly incorporating a slide.	• use filler slides with distracting images, animations, or anything else that takes away from your message.
• choose visually appealing color schemes and use a high level of contrast between your background and text colors.	• use colors that clash, have low contrast between the background and text, or choose colors that are commonly confused by those who are color blind.
• use animations that make images and text appear at the moment you begin to talk about them in your speech.	• use animations that introduce excessive movement, take too much time, or distract from your message.
• have a backup plan in case the technology fails, and test your presentation before you begin your speech.	• rely on extended videos or audio clips to fill time in your speech.

TABLE 15.1 PowerPoint Guidelines

PRACTICE

Practice is the final element necessary for delivering a successful speech. Public speaking is a skill that must be developed over time, and one of the best ways to become a better speaker is to do it often. In this sense, public speaking is a lot like other skills. Most basketball players shoot hundreds of baskets per week, musicians practice for several hours each day, bodybuilders do countless reps in the weight room, and most good writers spend some time writing almost every day for years. Likewise, it takes hours of practice to deliver an effective speech.

There are several ways to practice your speech. You can practice your speech by yourself in front of a mirror. This will give you a chance to become comfortable with your speech and make any needed changes while also giving you an initial opportunity to check your appearance. You can also practice your speech in front of a small group of friends or family. This is a good opportunity to get feedback from others, make additional revisions in your speech, and become more comfortable speaking in front of others. Finally, you could record a practice session of your speech and then watch it to see how you appear. This is an excellent way to identify what you are doing well and in what ways you can improve your content and delivery.

In order to make your practice sessions as effective as possible, there are several strategies you should consider. You should time yourself with a stopwatch every time you practice your speech. Your speech will be a little bit different every time you deliver it, and you will want to make sure the length stays within the expected time frame every time. Practice with your presentation aids, as you want to become as comfortable as possible using them. If practicing in front of friends, family, or others, give them some guidance about the type of feedback you would like to receive. You might give them some questions to consider as they listen, or even give them a grading rubric to fill out so they can help you make sure you are not missing any important elements. You could ask your audience to focus primarily on the organization of the ideas during the earliest stages of practice, on your support materials and arguments in the middle stages of practice, and on your delivery skills during your final stages of practice. Ultimately, effective practice sessions can and should involve more than just you.

USING DELIVERY TO ENCOURAGE DIALOGUE

Attitudes often come across through our body language more than even the content of what we say. A person's mannerisms influence the language and tenor of any interaction, whether they are noticed before engaging the party in a discussion or during the conversation. A person who looks grumpy or down might be approached (if at all) one way, while a person who is perceived to be happy or excited would be approached in an entirely different manner. With that in mind, good delivery can encourage a dialogic environment and invite audiences to engage you in a civil, yet critical, manner. There are some things you can do in terms of delivery that help to create a dialogic environment, and we will now provide you with a few of those methods.

Check Pronunciations before You Speak

Not only does pronouncing a word or name wrong damage your credibility, but it also can leave the audience with the impression you did not care enough to check the correct pronunciation, making them less interested in engaging with or even respecting you. As you practice, if you encounter names or words you are not entirely sure how to pronounce, check with a dictionary or even another person to learn how to properly pronounce the name or word.

Engage with Your Audience

A key element to creating dialogue is facing the audience and making eye contact with them. This helps create the perception you are talking with them, not at them, and thus makes them less likely to look away and more likely to pay attention. Standing up straight and looking people in the eye are signs of respect from a speaker, and so it is important to do so when giving a presentation. Even when using a visual aid, face the audience when explaining the aid instead of looking at the image.

Practice, Practice, and Then Practice Again

Unless you are delivering an impromptu speech where practice is impossible, you owe it to your audience to prepare your presentation well in advance. If you come across as having done this at the last minute, people will not feel you took them, or the topic, seriously and will be less likely to engage you during or after the presentation.

Choose Presentation Aids to Increase Understanding

Many speakers use presentation aids just because they look flashy or cool, but they serve no purpose in terms of helping the audience understand something complicated. Use presentation aids judiciously and with the purpose of helping the audience, not

"Bueller?... Bueller?..."

MEDIATED MOMENTS

In the classic comedy, *Ferris Bueller's Day Off,* Matthew Broderick stars as a high school student who skips school to go on an elaborate adventure with his best friend and girlfriend. Early in the movie, there is a scene with comedian and former presidential speechwriter, Ben Stein, where one of Bueller's teachers (played by Stein) is calling attendance and interact- ing with his class. The performance is so monotone that as the camera scans the class it highlights students sleeping and not paying attention. Although meant to exaggerate the impact a monotone voice can have on an audience, the scene underscores the importance of varying your tone of voice when trying to engage an audience.

making your speech more entertaining. To that end, if you choose to use PowerPoint or Prezi, make sure the meaning is what comes across, and that the visuals are not distracting. Also, do not feel the need to have a slide or representation for everything—only use a presentation aid for those things that may require more than words to help the audience appreciate or understand.

Choose Interesting Vocal Delivery Methods

Nothing makes an audience interested in a topic and predisposed to listen to a speaker more than a presenter who is interested in the topic and who is engaging with the audience. This excitement comes across through vocal delivery that is enthusiastic, interesting, and varied. Share your interest with the audience and they will respect you for it. Often, audiences contain people who may not care about the topic initially, but through the expression of your excitement and enthusiasm you may actually reach them and ignite an interest in them for the topic. Dialogue requires presentness, and nothing makes it easier to be present with someone than interest and enthusiasm.

SUMMARY

Delivery is often one of the most frightening elements of giving a speech, but once you understand its various components it becomes less intimidating. In this chapter, we examined the components of delivery and the four primary means by which we deliver a speech. We then explored the concept of communication apprehension, and explained how we can help manage the anxieties that accompany delivering a formal presentation. Third, we discussed various ways to use presentation aids within a speech to help an audience understand complicated material, before finally suggesting some ways to use delivery to encourage a dialogic environment.

CHAPTER 15 KEY IDEAS

- Vocal delivery includes everything that affects how your voice sounds when you give your speech, including pronunciation, articulation, volume, pitch, rhythm, rate, tone, and vocalized pauses.

- Physical delivery includes all of the physical signals that your body sends to your audience during your speech, including your physical appearance, facial expression, gestures, and eye contact.

- The four forms of delivery include memorized, manuscript, extemporaneous, and impromptu speeches.

- Communication apprehension is "the fear or anxiety associated with real or anticipated communication with another or others."

- Presentation aids can include objects, models, demonstrations, charts and graphs, photographs, video, or audio clips.

CHAPTER 15 KEY TERMS

Vocal delivery	Extemporaneous speech
Pronunciation	Impromptu speech
Articulation	Communication apprehension
Volume	Trait CA
Pitch	State CA
Rhythm	Systematic desensitization
Rate	Self-fulfilling prophecy
Tone	Presentation aids
Vocalized pauses	Objects
Physical delivery	Models
Physical appearance	Demonstrations
Posture	Charts
Facial expressions	Line graphs
Gestures	Bar graphs
Eye contact	Histogram
Memorized speech	Pie graph
Manuscript speech	Scatterplot

ACTIVITIES AND DISCUSSION QUESTIONS

1. Watch Joe Smith's TEDx talk, "How to Use a Paper Towel," available online at https://www.ted.com/talks/joe_smith_how_to_use_a_paper_towel. What type of presentation aid does Mr. Smith rely on most heavily in his speech? Which type of delivery is he using? Which tips for using delivery to encourage a dialogic environment does he demonstrate?

2. Watch David JP Phillips' TEDx talk, "How to Avoid Death by PowerPoint," available online at https://www.youtube.com/watch?v=Iwpi1Lm6dFo. Or for a shorter video, see comedian Don McMillan's "Life after Death by PowerPoint," available online at https://www.youtube.com/watch?v=MjcO2ExtHso. How can you use these lessons to develop presentation slides that will complement and enhance your presentation rather than distract from your message?

3. Find a video example of a speech online. (Hint: www.americanrhetoric.com has an online speech bank that you can use if you are struggling to find one.) Describe which aspects of verbal and physical delivery were done well and which needed improvement.

4. Think about your upcoming speech. Explain how you could use three different types of presentation aids in your speech to enhance the audience's understanding of your topic.

5. Take the PRCA-24, and calculate your scores.

Personal Report of Communication Apprehension

This instrument is composed of 24 statements concerning feelings about communicating with others. Please indicate the degree to which each statement applies to you by marking whether you: Strongly Disagree = 1; Disagree = 2; are Neutral = 3; Agree = 4; Strongly Agree = 5

____ 1.   I dislike participating in group discussions.

____ 2.   Generally, I am comfortable while participating in group discussions.

____ 3.   I am tense and nervous while participating in group discussions.

____ 4.   I like to get involved in group discussions.

____ 5.   Engaging in a group discussion with new people makes me tense and nervous.

____ 6.   I am calm and relaxed while participating in group discussions.

____ 7.   Generally, I am nervous when I have to participate in a meeting.

____ 8.   Usually, I am comfortable when I have to participate in a meeting.

____ 9.   I am very calm and relaxed when I am called upon to express an opinion at a meeting.

____ 10.   I am afraid to express myself at meetings.

____ 11.   Communicating at meetings usually makes me uncomfortable.

____ 12.   I am very relaxed when answering questions at a meeting.

____ 13.   While participating in a conversation with a new acquaintance, I feel very nervous.

____ 14.   I have no fear of speaking up in conversations.

____ 15.   Ordinarily I am very tense and nervous in conversations.

____ 16.   Ordinarily I am very calm and relaxed in conversations.

____ 17.   While conversing with a new acquaintance, I feel very relaxed.

____ 18.   I'm afraid to speak up in conversations.

____ 19.   I have no fear of giving a speech.

____ 20.   Certain parts of my body feel very tense and rigid while giving a speech.

____ 21.   I feel relaxed while giving a speech.

____ 22.   My thoughts become confused and jumbled when I am giving a speech.

____ 23.   I face the prospect of giving a speech with confidence.

____ 24.   While giving a speech, I get so nervous I forget facts I really know.

SCORING:

Group Discussion: 18 − (scores for items 2, 4, & 6) + (scores for items 1,3, & 5)

Meetings: 18 − (scores for items 8, 9, & 12) + (scores for items 7, 10, & 11)

Interpersonal: 18 − (scores for items 14, 16, & 17) + (scores for items 13, 15, & 18)

Public Speaking: 18 − (scores for items 19, 21, & 23) + (scores for items 20, 22, & 24)

Group Discussion Score: _____   **Interpersonal Score:**   _____

Meetings Score: _____   **Public Speaking Score:** _____

To obtain your total score for the PRCA, simply add your sub-scores together.

Scores can range from 24–120. Scores below 51 represent people who have very low CA. Scores between 51 and 80 represent people with average CA. Scores above 80 represent people who have high levels of trait CA.

16

INFORMATIVE
SPEAKING

Speeches can serve different purposes. One of the primary goals of some speeches is to deliver information to an audience. These informative speeches do not try to persuade an audience, though the audience may very well be persuaded; rather, they only try to convey information to an audience so they understand it. Such speeches might take place at job orientations, sales meetings, or, most commonly, in a classroom where a teacher tries to explain material to students.

Informative speeches are intended to teach the audience something new and have two key purposes: to **inform**, *which is to make the audience aware of a phenomenon, and to* **explain**, *which is to deepen the audience's understanding of that phenomenon.[1] When you are simply informing an audience, you are likely to be using the linear model of communication. Recall that the linear model treats communication as a one-way process in which a speaker gives his or her audience information, and there is no response from the audience. For example, if you are reporting the morning's headline news, sharing information about the day's stock prices, or telling someone the year you were born as part of an identity security check, you are simply sharing information with someone else. Explaining, however, goes much further than informing.*

INFORM
make the audience aware of a phenomenon

EXPLAIN
deepen the audience's understanding of a phenomenon

Speakers that seek to explain something to an audience provide deeper details about how and why something is a certain way and take care to pay attention to whether an audience accurately understands what is presented. Audience members exhibit evidence of this understanding, or lack thereof, through nonverbal reactions and their ability to accurately answer certain questions during or after the presentation.

In this chapter, we investigate informative speeches, and in doing so, demonstrate how informing and explaining share similar qualities. We will first discuss the types of information speakers typically explain to audiences. Next, we will explore different ways to explain difficult concepts, and then provide strategies for facilitating audience understanding. We will conclude by providing several suggestions for how to maintain a dialogic atmosphere when explaining material in a formal presentation.

TYPES OF INFORMATION WE EXPLAIN

There are many different pieces of information we might seek to explain to an audience. We can categorize those pieces of information into a handful of types. Knowing what type of information you need to explain to an audience helps you choose a method for arranging your points. The topic itself will often suggest the way it should be organized for the most effective explanation, but in some cases, you need to "invent" the organizational pattern. In this section of the chapter, we will explore four types of topics you might choose for your informative speech: objects, processes, events, and concepts.

DIALING DIVERSITY

Map Your Speech for Your Audience

One of the more noteworthy events during the Iraq War was the March 23, 2003 capture and subsequent rescue of US Army officer Jessica Lynch after she was abducted during the Battle of Nasiriyah. She was rescued on April 1, 2003, the first such rescue of an American POW since Vietnam, and the first ever rescue of a woman. Upon her return to the United States, she was invited to deliver her account to a committee of the US House of Representatives. In this informative presentation, she clearly states her goal, effectively organizes her information, and employs transformative explanation techniques to help correct misinformation regarding her capture, rescue, and the status of the war in Iraq.[2]

Objects

A speech about an object is a speech about a tangible item. Objects might include artifacts, mementos, souvenirs, buildings, places, or even people. For example, you probably gave speeches about objects when you stood up to do "show and tell" in elementary school. You would also be giving a speech about an object if you explained how a mortar and pestle are used to grind spices, taught your audience about Henrietta Lacks and the role her cells have played in cancer research, described several important landmarks in Seattle, explicated the significance of prayer beads in many of the world's religions, or explained the differences between types of coffee beans.

Processes

A speech about a process is a speech that explains the steps needed to accomplish something, and these presentations are usually arranged chronologically. Often, a speech about a process is a "how to" speech intended to teach the audience how to accomplish something, such as a how to create a secure password, how to change a tire on a car, or how to roast a traditional Thanksgiving turkey. These speeches can also explain processes specific to a particular industry, such as how tea leaves are grown, how plastic is recycled and then used to create something new, or how a particular marketing plan will be used to launch a new product. Furthermore, speeches about processes are often used to explain how things happen in science and medicine, such as explaining how cells divide to grow new cells, describing the steps involved in a cancer treatment plan, or helping the audience understand how climate change is leading to the rising of the ocean.

Events

A speech about an event is a speech that focuses on something that happened, is happening, or might happen at some point in the future. Speeches about events are often

"Alternative Facts"

ENGAGING ETHICS

Following the January 20, 2017, inauguration of President Donald Trump, Press Secretary Sean Spicer took to the podium at the White House and claimed the inauguration had the largest audience in history and exhorted people to look at the pictures of the crowd. This point of data became a point of contention and helped to spawn the term "alternative facts." In explaining this event, Mr. Spicer also sought to editorialize rather than inform, which helped muddy his message. What could he have done different to have a more ethical presentation of the inauguration? What responsibilities does the speaker have to the audience in this situation? Given the line between informative and persuasive speaking can be blurry at times, how might he have navigated this situation better?

organized chronologically in a way that allows the speaker to explain the event as it unfolds, but could also be arranged topically, especially when many things are happening simultaneously. For example, you might use a chronological pattern of organization to explain how the major events on Inauguration Day unfold when a new president enters office. If you are an event planner hosting a conference that has multiple elements happening at the same time, however, you might present your plan topically, with each main point explaining a different element of the conference, such as the food, the programming, and the entertainment.

Concepts

A speech about a concept explains an abstract idea instead of a concrete object. Concept speeches might include presentations about theories, ideas, religion, economics, political ideology, or laws. Concept speeches can be especially challenging because they require the speaker to take something that is abstract and intangible and make it easy for the audience to understand by using vivid description, examples, or illustrations. A physicist might drop several objects of different masses from the top of a building at the same time to demonstrate the idea that gravity pulls all objects toward the Earth at the same speed, regardless of the mass of the object. A philosopher might try to explain how John Locke's theory of mind differs from René Descartes's rationalism. Similarly, a film producer might describe the plot for a film they plan to make.

WAYS TO ORGANIZE INFORMATIVE SPEECHES

When trying to explain difficult and complex information to your audience members, the way you organize your main points is critical for helping them understand your topic. Before you begin to develop your outline, you should carefully consider which of the following patterns of organization will be most effective in helping communicate your message to your audience. The goal is to present information in the best way possible to foster understanding by the audience, and so choosing the best organizational pattern to accomplish that task is a must for any speaker.

Spatial

SPATIAL PATTERN OF ORGANIZATION

used to describe an object by explaining how parts physically relate to one another in a defined space

The **spatial pattern of organization** is used to describe an object by explaining how parts physically relate to one another in a defined space. When you use spatial organization, you might describe something in order from top to bottom, bottom to top, right to left, left to right, front to back, or in some other physical order as you visually or physically move through the thing you are explaining. For example, you might use spatial organization to explain the layout of the National Mall by first talking about the Capitol Building, which is on the far eastern end of the Mall. Next, you might discuss the Smithsonian Museums, which lie west of the Capitol building. Finally, you might end by describing the monuments and memorials on the far western end of the Mall. In another instance, a docent at the Museum of Modern

Art might describe Salvador Dalí's *The Persistence of Memory* by describing the painting from top to bottom.

Chronological

The **chronological pattern of organization** is used to describe events or processes in the order they occur in time, from earlier events to later events. Chronological organization works especially well when describing historical events, such as the events that led to the Civil War, or processes that have several steps, such as how to build a car engine. Chronological speeches can also be used to describe objects. For example, you might give a speech about the Roman Colosseum by beginning with its construction, then discussing its purposes for the Roman Republic, before discussing what state it is in now.

Cause-effect

The **cause-effect pattern of organization** is a variation of the chronological pattern of organization that discusses the causes that led to a specific event or effect. There are usually several causes that lead to each event, and each cause usually leads to several effects, and so in this kind of speech it is important not to oversimplify a cause-effect relationship by arguing that a single cause led to a single effect with no other factors involved. At the same time, your speech can easily become tangential if you focus on all of the possible causes of an event as well as all of the possible effects or outcomes. So in a cause-effect speech, you will want to choose whether to build your thesis around the causes or the effects. For example, you might decide to discuss how economic and social differences, views on state versus federal rights, and slavery were major factors that led to the US Civil War, and then discuss the overall impact of that war. In that speech, you would be focusing on the specific event (the Civil War) and talking about several causes leading to it.

Problem-solution

The **problem-solution pattern of organization** involves organizing your speech by first explaining a problem before teaching your audience about the solution to that problem. In an informative speech, the problem-solution pattern of organization might involve teaching your audience about a problem that occurred in the past and how it was solved in the past. For example, you might discuss why taking regular food into space on a space shuttle was a problem and how it was solved by developing freeze-dried food that could be rehydrated and eaten in space. Alternately, your speech might teach your audience about a common problem and teach them how to solve that problem. You might approach the problem of having nitrogen deficiency in soil and then explain how to solve the problem by adding compost, manure, nitrogen-fixing plants, coffee grounds, or chemical fertilizers to the soil. When giving an informative problem-solution speech, though, you need to be careful to make sure you are teaching your audience about the problem and possible solutions, not persuading them to adopt a particular solution.

CHRONOLOGICAL PATTERN OF ORGANIZATION
used to describe events or processes in the order that they occur in time, from earlier events to later events

CAUSE-EFFECT PATTERN OF ORGANIZATION
a variation on the chronological pattern of organization used to discuss the causes that led to a specific event or effect

PROBLEM-SOLUTION PATTERN OF ORGANIZATION
in an informative speech, used to organize a speech by first explaining a problem and then teaching the audience about the solution

Topical

TOPICAL
PATTERN OF
ORGANIZATION

used to divide your
speech into categories
or subtopics

The topical pattern of organization is used to divide your speech into categories or sub-topics. Topical organization can be used when there are specific elements of your topic you want to discuss or when your topic does not fit any of the other patterns of organization. For example, you might use topical organization in an informative speech about different types of bikes and might choose to organize your main points by talking first about road bikes, second about mountain bikes, and finally about hybrid bikes. You might also choose to give a speech about effective teaching by talking first about how students learn, second about how to manage a classroom, and finally about how to assess whether and how much students have learned. Most syllabi and schedules in college courses are actually arranged topically, providing the content focus for each particular day.

EXPLAINING DIFFICULT CONCEPTS

In many informative speeches, you will be explaining concepts that are difficult for your audience to understand, particularly if your audience is not comprised of experts in the subject about which you are speaking. There are many reasons that an idea might be difficult for an audience to understand, but according to Dr. Katherine Rowan,[3] there are three primary reasons it is hard for a nonexpert audience to understand a complex idea: (1) the language or concepts are difficult, (2) the structure or process is hard to envision, or (3) the idea is difficult to believe. When explaining difficult concepts in your informative speech, you should first identify why the concept is difficult to understand, and then choose the explanatory strategy that best helps audiences overcome that particular challenge. In this part of the chapter, we will discuss ways to overcome these three challenges to effective explanation.

Difficult Language

ELUCIDATING
EXPLANATION

an explanation that
helps an audience
understand the
definition of a term and
distinguish its essential
characteristics
from the associated
characteristics that
are only sometimes
present in that which
you are defining

When a concept is difficult to understand because the vocabulary is unfamiliar to your audience, you should use an elucidating explanation. Your goal in an elucidating explanation is to help your audience understand the definition of a term and distinguish its essential characteristics from the associated characteristics that are only sometimes present in that which you are defining. Rowan explains that elucidating explanations should include four parts: (1) a common *exemplar*, or ideal example, of the concept; (2) a *definition* that explains the essential characteristics of the concept; (3) several *examples* of the concept, along with some *nonexamples* that might commonly be mistaken as examples of the concept; and (4) opportunities for your audience to *practice* identifying examples and nonexamples of the concept.[4]

Take the case of the term "immediacy," which might be unfamiliar to some people who have not studied instructional communication or psychology. If you used an elucidating explanation to help your audience understand the concept of immediacy, you might say:

In *Dead Poets Society*, Mr. Keating, who is played by Robin Williams, seems to draw his students in and connect with them by doing things like calling on them by name, moving around the classroom, using a lot of vocal variety and gestures, using humor during class, and having a relaxed posture. All of these behaviors show that Mr. Keating has a high level of immediacy. Immediacy is "the degree of perceived physical or psychological closeness between teachers and students." Immediacy represents a set of verbal and nonverbal communication behaviors that indicate a teacher's willingness to approach and be approached by students.[5] Some examples of teacher immediacy behaviors include making eye contact with students, having a relaxed body posture while teaching, allowing for small talk, using words like "we" and "us," and using vocal variety and gestures. On the other hand, sarcastic humor, telling stories that embarrass students, and reading from PowerPoint slides are not examples of teacher immediacy.

Here you see how each of the components of an elucidating explanation are included. Not all elucidating explanations need all of these, but if you have the time, and the term is particularly hard to pin down for an audience, use as many as you can.

Difficult to Picture

Other concepts use familiar words but are difficult to understand because they are difficult to picture. Concepts or processes might be challenging to imagine because they are abstract ideas or because the process or object is microscopic and cannot easily be seen. There are two ways that something can be difficult to picture. First, it might be difficult to get an overall impression of the thing being explained, and second, it might be difficult to see the parts, processes, and interrelations of the phenomenon.

When you explain something that is difficult to picture, you should use a **quasi-scientific explanation** to help the audience better understand the phenomenon. A quasi-scientific explanation should include two key parts: (1) a graphic feature that helps the audience get an overall big picture of the phenomenon, such as a model, simplified drawing, cartoon, or diagram; and (2) verbal organizational cues that indicate the relationships among the parts or subprocesses of the phenomenon, including transitions, summaries, previews, and statements that clearly state the relationships. Some of the best quasi-scientific explanations include titles that suggest what the overall structure is, analogies that help the audience organize the information by comparing it to something familiar, and thesis statements

QUASI-SCIENTIFIC EXPLANATION

an explanation that helps the audience get an overall picture of a phenomenon and see relationships among the parts or topic sentences that suggest a model that shares similar characteristics with the unfamiliar phenomenon.

For example, it can be difficult to picture how herd immunity helps prevent the spread of vaccine-preventable diseases even when a few people cannot be vaccinated because they are newborns who are not yet old enough to receive the vaccine, or because they have a medical condition that weakens the immune system and would make getting vaccinated dangerous. To help explain how vaccinating a large proportion of a population protects those who cannot be vaccinated, you might explain that humans fighting off diseases like the measles are in some ways similar to a herd of cattle trying to fight off coyotes that prey on young calves. In both instances there is power in numbers. Along with this analogy, you might choose to provide a diagram that shows how easily diseases can spread through a population once a critical mass of people has chosen not to be vaccinated.

Difficult to Believe

TRANSFORMATIVE EXPLANATIONS

explanations that help audience members transform their everyday ideas about how something works into a more scientifically accurate understanding of the phenomenon

Sometimes concepts use simple language and can be imagined easily but are difficult to believe because they are counterintuitive. In these cases, speakers should use *transformative explanations* to help the audience change their everyday ideas about how something works into an accurate understanding of the phenomenon. Transformative explanations have four parts: they (1) acknowledge people's everyday or "lay" theory about the concept, perhaps by asking the audience to describe the concept; (2) acknowledge why the audience members' understanding seems plausible on the surface; (3) explain why their impression is incorrect and show examples that demonstrate why it is not adequate for explaining the phenomenon; and (4) explain the theory and illustrate why it is effective.

For example, when we think we see things, we are actually seeing reflected light off of the object, not the object we are looking at. This is counterintuitive because we think we are actually seeing the object that is in front of us. If you were to use a transformative explanation to help your audience understand how we see things, you might say something like this:

> Most people think when we see something, we are actually seeing the object that is in front of us. This makes a lot of sense because, in our experience, when we see something, it is really there. However, if this were true, we would be able to see everything that was in front of us all of the time. But if you have ever tripped over something while walking through a dark room in the middle of the night, you know that sometimes things are in front of you that you cannot see when there is no light. Instead, when we think we see something, we are actually seeing the light that is reflected off of the object that is in front of us.

This statement includes all the elements of a transformative explanation and illustrates how you can explain and correct a misunderstanding someone might have in a logical and civil manner.

Strategies to Help Your Audience Understand

In addition to the tips for explaining difficult content to your audience, there are several other strategies available to you as a speaker for helping your audience understand your topic and remember the key points of your presentations. These six methods may seem simple, but they go a long way in helping to ensure your audience understands and remembers the information you provide.

Use repetition. If you only say something once, your audience is unlikely to remember it. If you expose your audience to the same idea multiple times and in multiple ways, they are much more likely to remember the information. Repetition is especially helpful for aiding your audience in understanding important complicated material within your speech. Often, audiences may not completely get what you are explaining with one example. They may require another, different example—or perhaps an analogy—to help them understand the concept. Finding creative and different ways to express the same idea helps the audience achieve understanding. The more you repeat something, the greater the chance the audience will pick up on it.

Provide rewards. Your audience will pay more attention to what you are saying if they perceive they will be rewarded for doing so. Rewards can be explicit, such as giving candy to audience members who can answer questions correctly, or implicit, such as telling the audience how they will benefit from the knowledge you are sharing. When you have a choice, though, the latter works better for using rewards, because the reward lasts much longer for the audience. Creating intrinsic rewards for listening to the speech also assists the audience in investing time paying attention to you, and as we have mentioned at other times in this book, when we invest time in something, it shows we care about it. The same applies for convincing an audience that investing time in listening to your speech will reward them in numerous ways.

Developing your ability to inform and explain will assist you in many aspects of life, be those parenting, work, or recreation. Doing so will give you tools for learning complex material and sharing that material with others.

—**Katherine Rowan, George Mason University**

Show and tell. Although show and tell is a game played mainly by elementary school students, it also can play a vital role in helping adult audiences understand material. It essentially uses visual and verbal organizational cues to help your audience identify the most important concepts and understand how those concepts relate to each other.[6] Visual organization cues might include putting key words for each main point on a PowerPoint slide when you preview your main points, showing important definitions or quotations while you are talking about them, showing your audience diagrams or images that will help them visualize how concepts are related, or giving your audience a paper handout that will help them follow along during your speech. Using matrixes or other diagrams that summarize information and visually demonstrating how ideas are related can be especially helpful because the audience can more easily understand the connections between concepts.[7] Verbal organization cues include signposts, reviews, and previews that help draw the audience's attention to important concepts and help the audience understand how ideas are related. This is why the preview of main points in the introduction of your speech, transitions between main points, and the review of main points in the conclusion are so important.

Build on what your audience already knows. When explaining concepts that are unfamiliar to the audience, you can help them understand by connecting the new information to something that the audience already knows.[8] For instance, you might use an analogy or metaphor to show the similarities between something familiar and something new. One of the most effective ways of both explaining a difficult concept and identifying with an audience is to connect your topic or information to something with which they are already familiar. This helps them make the association themselves in terms they understand, making it more likely the information will be remembered.

Use humor. Incorporating humor that is related to the topic of your speech can help you capture and keep your audience's attention. You will want to be careful, however, to make sure that your humor enhances your audience members' attention to your topic rather than distracts from it. In short, humor must help them focus on the content and not you. You will also need to be careful that your humor can be easily understood by your entire audience through the use of idioms and terms you expect the audience will know. Just because a speech delivers information does not mean it needs to be boring and uninteresting.

Check for understanding. Finally, you can help your audience learn by checking for understanding periodically. Ask your audience questions or provide examples to see whether they understand the concepts you have explained so far. If you find that your audience does not quite understand the ideas, adapt your speech by explaining the ideas in a slightly different way until your audience shows they understand the concepts. To plan for this, you should prepare a few different ways to explain the same point, even if you do not end up needing all of them.

DELIVERING INFORMATION DIALOGICALLY

Helping an audience understand something is inherently transactional. You can say something, but if you do not appreciate the fact that your audience may interpret it differently, then true understanding of what you conveyed may never be achieved. Just as it is transactional, the process of informing and explaining concepts to an audience, large or small in size, can be enhanced through dialogic principles. In this final section of the chapter, we will outline a few guidelines for ensuring your delivery of information to your audience proceeds in a dialogic manner, increasing the chances of understanding and retention.

Provide Multiple Examples

When trying to explain something you know to an audience that does not know it, you must be prepared to explain the idea several different ways. Sometimes the way you learned the material will not work for members of your audience, so if you notice they do not seem to grasp the material, try another way of approaching the subject. People who are effective at explaining ideas and complicated material to others come armed to the discussion with several different examples that illustrate the same concept. The more options they have, even if they do not need them all, simply increases the likelihood that the audience will understand what they are saying.

Disseminating and Receiving Communication

Television has had a profound effect on the dissemination of information. Additionally, the advent of the 24-hour news channel concept in the 1980s has ballooned, and now there are numerous such channels domestically and internationally. This has been valuable in times of crisis because it allows for misinformation to be corrected whenever necessary. Take the 2014 Ebola epidemic in West Africa that expanded to include countries like the United States and Spain. The public, particularly in the US, had little understanding of the virus, and so numerous news channels contracted doctors and public health experts to explain the disease to the public and prevent a mass panic. One such station, the BBC, aired a 40-second report that explained how Ebola actually attacks human cells using visuals and a voice-over report. To further illustrate the impact media has on the ability to spread information, that report is now available on YouTube.[9]

Notice Audience's Nonverbal Cues

A good speaker will be able to look at audience members and determine how well they seem to understand what is being said. There will be head nods, note-taking, consistent eye contact, and other signs of listening. Conversely, a good speaker also pays attention for an audience that seems lost by focusing on lack of eye contact, confused facial expressions, head shakes, and other signs that they may not completely understand his or her message. This type of awareness depends on your confidence with and ability to deliver the material in your presentation. If you know your material, you can pay attention to others, but if you are focused on reading prepared notes, then you will not be able to pick up on the subtle, but important, cues coming from your audience.

Achieve Understanding, Not Agreement

One of the hardest things to remember with informative speaking is that the goal is not to change people's minds or get them to agree with you; rather, you simply want them to understand your point of view and why you hold it. You want your audience to understand content, not necessarily agree with it. When we focus on agreement, we delve into persuasion; speaking persuasively when the situation calls for informative speaking can have disastrous effects on our credibility and success with the presentation.

Ask Clarifying Questions

Nonverbal indicators are just one way of determining accurate transmission of information to an audience. We may also ask clarifying questions designed to see if someone understands material. Good clarifying questions are specific, not general, such as "Do you understand what I am saying?" Or "Are you following along?" These will almost universally elicit agreement from the audience. Instead, ask an audience member who appears lost to provide an example of her or his own or rephrase the definition you provided. Don't do this as a test, but rather as a check to see if your examples and speech are effectively explaining the subject matter.

Maintain Interest Throughout Your Speech

A fast way to destroy an opportunity for dialogue is to show a lack of interest in your audience or your topic. Instead, be energetic and enthusiastic when speaking and try to convey a feeling of enjoyment at the opportunity to teach, inform, or explain something to this audience. When you are interested, the audience will be more likely to be interested as well. Your interest should be both in the topic and in the audience. People are very capable of picking up on your interest in them, and if they perceive that you are not terribly interested in their understanding or reaction, they may stop listening to you.

Provide Clear Points and References

In clearly laying out the key elements of your speech in the introduction, at the beginning of each main topic, and in the conclusion, you help repeat important information for the audience. Additionally, you owe it to your audience to let them know where you gathered your information from. Citing your sources is ethical, honest, and creates an atmosphere where an audience is open to what you have to say, instead of one where they question your information and credentials.

SUMMARY

One of the primary purposes of public speaking is to explain information to an audience. That information is often complicated, and without knowing the difference between types of information and how to convey them properly, informative presentations risk failure. In this chapter, we provided the different categories of information speakers explain and explored several different ways you might organize that information when speaking to an audience. We also provided tips for delivering complicated material and maintaining a dialogic environment when trying to explain information to an audience that does not understand it.

CHAPTER 16 KEY IDEAS

- Informing involves making the audience aware of a phenomenon, whereas explaining is intended to deepen the audience's understanding of that phenomenon.

- Informative speeches can be used to explain objects, processes, events, or concepts.

- The most effective patterns of organization for information speeches include (1) spatial, (2) chronological, (3) cause-effect, (4) problem-solution, and (5) topical organization.

- Concepts might be difficult for the audience to understand because the vocabulary is difficult to understand, the concept is difficult to picture, or the idea is difficult to believe. You can use elucidating explanations, quasi-scientific explanations, or transformative explanations to help your audience understand these respective types of difficult ideas.

- To help your audience understand and remember your speech, try using repetition, offering rewards, showing and telling, building on what the audience already knows, using humor, and checking for understanding.

CHAPTER 16 KEY TERMS

Inform	Problem-solution pattern of organization
Explain	Topical pattern of organization
Spatial pattern of organization	Elucidating explanation
Chronological pattern of organization	Quasi-scientific explanation
Cause-effect pattern of organization	Transformative explanations

ACTIVITIES AND DISCUSSION QUESTIONS

1. Watch Kenneth Shinozuka's TEDYouth talk, "My Simple Invention, Designed to Keep my Grandfather Safe," available online at https://www.ted.com/talks/kenneth_shinozuka_my_simple_invention_designed_to_keep_my_grandfather_safe. Which pattern of organization was used for this speech? What was the primary type of information that the speaker tried to explain? Which strategies for helping your audience understand did the speaker use?

2. Watch Clifford Robbins's TED-Ed Animation, "What happens when you have a concussion," available online at https://ed.ted.com/lessons/what-happens-when-you-have-a-concussion-clifford-robbins. Which strategy for explaining difficult concepts was used in this video? Which pattern of organization was used?

3. What are the five patterns of organization for informative speeches? Give an example of a topic that would be ideal for each pattern (not the one used in this book) and list the three main points you would use with that pattern of organization for that topic.

4. There are some topics for which you could use different patterns of organization, depending on what you want your audience to learn. Pick a topic such as climate change or World War II. Can you develop a set of main points for that topic for spatial, chronological, cause-effect, problem-solution, and topical patterns of organization?

5. If you have an informative speech that you will be giving in this class, take a few minutes to think about what you will teach your audience. What is one concept in your speech that will be difficult for your audience to understand? Which of the three strategies for explaining difficult concepts will you use in your informative speech? Write out how you will use this strategy to explain the concept in your speech. Which other strategies for helping your audience understand could you use?

PERSUASIVE SPEAKING

Most of us try to persuade others every day. In fact, all communication is capable of persuasion to some degree; what makes a speech persuasive instead of informative, however, is its purpose. **Persuasion** involves attempting to change the attitudes, actions, or beliefs of another person. When working on a group project with classmates, you might try to convince your group mates to choose a particular topic or to do a specific part of the project. At work, you might need to convince clients that your solution will best meet their needs, motivate others to complete a project, negotiate your benefits and salary, or persuade your boss that a proposal you have developed is worth investing in. At home, you might persuade someone to watch a TV series with you, eat at a specific restaurant for dinner, or choose a particular paint color for the kitchen.

At the same time, you will be faced with numerous situations when others try persuading you, whether it is a political campaign's advertisement trying to persuade you to vote for a specific candidate, a commercial trying to convince you to use a particular kind of deodorant, or an op-ed article persuading you to support a policy. This chapter investigates how to ethically persuade others while being respectful of other perspectives. Learning how to be ethically persuasive will also help you better evaluate persuasive messages from others.

PERSUASION
attempting to change the attitudes, actions, or beliefs of another person

In this chapter, we will first differentiate between the types of persuasion. We will then provide organizational patterns for persuasive arguments. Third, we will explain how to use emotion and logic both effectively and ethically in a presentation, and then define numerous logical fallacies that should be avoided in a speech. Finally, we will provide guidelines for creating a dialogic atmosphere when trying to persuade an audience to do or believe something.

TYPES OF PERSUASION

Persuasive messages surround us all of the time, and they can be categorized into different kinds of persuasion that address certain questions. We encounter each of these questions, or categories, every day in our lives. Sometimes we are the ones trying to persuade others, but often we are the ones being persuaded to feel a particular way about an issue, idea, or topic. In this section of the chapter, we will examine the primary types of questions and forms of persuasive messages. The four types of persuasion are questions of fact, questions of value, questions of policy, and refutations.

Questions of Fact

QUESTIONS OF FACT

persuasive messages that attempt to change the audience's beliefs about something

As discussed earlier in the book, people often perceive the same events in different ways. As such, determining facts about what happened can be quite difficult. Think about court cases where lawyers argue for different interpretations of what happened in a specific instance. These arguments are prime examples of persuasion regarding questions of fact. Persuasive speeches that argue questions of fact attempt to change the audience's beliefs about something. Persuasive messages about facts are concerned with questions regarding whether something is true or false, does or does not exist, did or did not happen, or is real and not fake. For a speech to focus on a question of fact instead of being an informative

DIALING DIVERSITY

Using Speech to Stir Change

In 1851, civil rights advocate Sojourner Truth gave an address entitled "Ain't I a Woman?" Truth, who was born into slavery but eventually became a free woman and minister, used the speech—and numerous others—to raise issues of race and gender in the public sphere. This one speech was not effective at changing minds, but her efforts as a whole helped raise awareness of discrimination and the complexities of it in American society during her time. Truth's speech, relatively short by public speaking standards, addressed a question of value, but it later led to a great many persuasive attempts addressing the questions of policies toward women and minorities in the United States.

speech, it must seek to change how an audience interprets something, rather than simply teaching them or telling them about it. For example, over the last decade or so, we have often heard debates in the media about whether or not some vaccines can lead to autism and whether or not climate change is caused by humans. Participants in these debates try to provide their interpretation of the evidence supporting their answers to these questions in a way that encourages an audience to agree with them.

Questions of Value

Facts are not the only thing people debate or see differently. People also differ in terms of what they value or how much they value something. Whenever we debate priorities with a partner or an audience, or try and advocate for the "best," we present an answer to a question of value. Persuasive speeches that argue questions of value try to change an audience's attitudes toward a subject by convincing the audience whether or not a belief, object, or action is moral, ethical, important, or worthwhile. Persuasive speeches about value provide arguments about whether we should place greater emphasis on something, or value it more than we already do. For example, someone might give a speech arguing that we have a moral obligation to protect our natural resources, why it is important to develop listening skills, or why human trafficking is unethical.

QUESTIONS OF VALUE

persuasive messages that try to change an audience's attitudes toward a topic by convincing the audience whether or not a belief, object, or action is moral, ethical, important, or worthwhile

Questions of Policy

In the legislative wing of government, we often find examples of a third type of question: policy. These are often, but not always, focused on what to do in the present or future. Policies, however, need not be governmental in nature. We also might develop certain classroom policies or partners may debate a family procedure for handling bonus money from their jobs. Persuasive speeches that are questions of policy try to change the audience's

QUESTIONS OF POLICY

persuasive messages that try to change the audience's actions or convince the audience that something should be done

Student-athletes and NCAA Policy

ENGAGING ETHICS

From 2014 to 2017, members of the Northwestern University football team, led by former quarterback Kain Colter, attempted to form a union so student-athletes could argue for, among other things, better medical care, academic support, and financial assistance. Although ultimately defeated in their quest at the National Labor Relations Board, their messages and attempts to succeed represent a persuasive attempt regarding a question of policy. Not governmental policy, but NCAA policy. What forms of evidence would have been useful in their case? What information may not have helped them? How might non-student-athletes feel regarding this effort?

actions or convince the audience that something should or should not be done. You might persuade audience members that they personally should take some action or that they should support an action by another organization, group, individual, or government. For example, someone might give a persuasive speech arguing that Congress should pass a law that creates a way for undocumented immigrants who arrived in the United States as children to gain citizenship. Another person might give a speech arguing that the NCAA should honor scholarships that were offered to student athletes to finish their degrees, even if students are injured and cannot continue participating in the sport.

Refutations

REFUTATIONS

persuasive speeches in which a speaker defends his or her own position on an issue while responding to the arguments of another person

Not all persuasive efforts seek to change an audience's perspective by proposing an idea; some try to refute arguments that have already been offered by others. They are defensive and, in a way, responses to the statements of others. Persuasive speeches that are **refutations** are speeches in which a speaker defends his or her own position on an issue while responding to the arguments of another person. Refutations involve persuading the audience that your position is stronger than your opponent's or that your opponent's position is flawed. In a refutation, you will need to understand and explain your opponent's argument, address each of her or his points by showing how her or his position is flawed, and propose a more viable alternative solution. Refutations can involve questions of fact, value, or policy, and take a significant amount of time and research to prepare. Speeches of refutation are often given in political debates, campaign speeches, or when two professionals are proposing competing solutions to the same problem.

ORGANIZING A PERSUASIVE ARGUMENT

For any of the four types of persuasive speeches, you need to think carefully about how to best organize your evidence to help your audience understand the issues and your argument. Your topic and goals will help you determine which organizational pattern is most effective. In this section of the chapter, we will discuss four patterns most commonly used in persuasive speeches: problem-solution, problem-cause-solution, comparative advantages, and Monroe's Motivated Sequence.

Problem-solution

PROBLEM-SOLUTION PATTERN OF ORGANIZATION

in a persuasive speech, a persuasive pattern of organization in which you begin by explaining the problem and then discuss your solution

Persuasion is fairly common when more than one possible solution exists to a particular problem. In these cases, multiple voices provide arguments for different solutions to the problem, and the best organizational pattern for speeches attempting to contribute to this conversation is the **problem-solution pattern of organization**. This approach to persuasive speeches is similar to the problem-solution organizational pattern for informative speeches; you begin by explaining the problem and then explain your solution. Persuasive speeches that use the problem-solution pattern of organization, however, are intended to convince the audience to adopt a specific solution for an unresolved problem from among several possible solutions, whereas an informative speech teaches the audience about how a past problem was solved.

When you advocate for a particular solution in a persuasive speech, you need to explain how the solution will address the problem and why it is more effective than alternative options. For example, you might explain why there is a shortage of organs available for transplants (problem), and then propose that we switch from our current process by which those who wish to donate their organs upon death must opt in to the donor registry, to a process in which everyone is included on the donor registry by default and individuals have the option to opt out of the registry (solution).

Problem-cause-solution

In some cases, problems are merely symptoms of some larger cause that needs to be addressed. The **problem-cause-solution pattern of organization** aims to address such larger causes through its organization. This pattern is similar to the problem-solution pattern of organization, except that it adds a step to explain the causes that are contributing to the problem. After presenting the problem in the first point, you explain the underlying causes in the second point, and finally propose your solution to the causes in the third point. This pattern of organization usually helps you build an even stronger argument because it allows you to show how your solution addresses the problem as well as the underlying causes that contributed to the problem in the first place. For example, if we return to the problem of having a shortage of organs available for transplant along with a growing waiting list, we might explain that one of the causes for the organ shortage is that people tend to choose default options because those require the least effort. Since the current default option is to not be a donor, most people who might be willing to donate their organs do not go out of their way to change their preferences from the default. Thus, the solution of changing the default organ donation option addresses both the problem and the cause.

Comparative Advantages

In most cases, there are a great many ways to solve a single problem, and the real issue is determining the best and most efficient solution to the problem. This often means comparing alternative solutions to identify the better one from all the options available. The **comparative advantages pattern of organization** is used to compare two or more potential solutions to a problem in an effort to argue why the solution you support is better than another solution. This pattern of organization is especially effective for refutations. In some cases, you might convince the audience that your solution is effective, while the other is ineffective, but in other cases, you might convince your audience that your solution is better than another solution that is also effective in many ways.

When you use the comparative advantages pattern of organization for a persuasive speech, each main point articulates why your position is better than the alternatives. Your first sub-point for each main point will explain how your opponent addresses that issue, and the

PROBLEM-CAUSE-SOLUTION PATTERN OF ORGANIZATION

persuasive pattern of organization in which you present the problem in the first point, the underlying causes in the second point, and the proposed solution in the final point

COMPARATIVE ADVANTAGES PATTERN OF ORGANIZATION

persuasive pattern of organization in which you compare two potential solutions to a problem to argue why the solution you support is better than another solution that is being proposed by someone else second subpoint will explain how your solution addresses the issue more effectively. For instance, you might argue that donating money to the American Cancer Society is a more effective way to help fight cancer than donating to the Susan G. Komen foundation by comparing how many cancers each organization is trying to cure, what proportion of donations each organization spends on research, and how many lives have been saved as a result of each organization's work.

Monroe's Motivated Sequence

MONROE'S MOTIVATED SEQUENCE

persuasive pattern of organization in which you use five steps to persuade the audience to adopt a plan of action: attention, need, satisfaction, visualization, and action

The final organizational pattern for persuasive speeches is Monroe's Motivated Sequence. Monroe's Motivated Sequence uses five steps to persuade the audience to adopt a plan of action: attention, need, satisfaction, visualization, and action. In the first step, attention, the speaker captures the attention of the audience members and gets them to focus on the topic they plan to address. This is typically done in the attention getter at the beginning of the speech, using those same attention-getting devices discussed in the chapter on organizing a presentation: asking a question, sharing a surprising fact or statistic, telling a brief anecdote, using a quotation, or telling a joke.

In the second step, need, the speaker makes the audience aware of the problem, or need, that must be addressed. This step explains the broad significance of the problem, as well as why this problem is relevant to the speaker's particular audience. If audience members do not think they need to know what a speaker is talking about, they are less likely to listen. The third step, satisfaction, presents the solution to the problem by fulfilling the need established in the prior step. The fourth step, visualization, uses vivid language to help the audience members see themselves adopting the solution and satisfying the need using the speaker's preferred solution. The final step, action, calls the audience to action by reiterating the solution and telling audience members what they specifically should do to address the problem. This pattern of organization is often used in sales presentations and commercials.

To work and live together, we must, whether we like it or not, learn to talk with each other to resolve our difficulties and decide on alternatives. At the same time, we need to be able to evaluate the persuasive activities that are directed toward us as citizens, consumers, and members of social groups. The study of persuasion is, at once, one of the oldest and most important of human intellectual activities.

—Martha Watson, University of Nevada Las Vegas

USING EMOTION AND LOGIC

Effective persuasion does not depend upon organization alone. In *Rhetoric,* Aristotle argues that there are three means of persuasion, or artistic proofs, that a speaker can use to persuade an audience: *ethos, pathos,* and *logos.*[1] Aristotle called them artistic proofs because the speaker constructs them. Any effective and ethical persuasive speech or appeal requires all three of these elements to work. In this section of the chapter, we will define and describe what *ethos, pathos,* and *logos* are and how they work to enhance persuasive speeches.

Ethos

Whether or not you will believe a message from a speaker depends a great deal on how you perceive the speaker's credibility. Ethos refers to the perceived personal character, or credibility, of the speaker. In order for a speaker to have credibility, the audience must believe the speaker has expertise and experience with the topic, is a good or moral person, and has goodwill toward the audience. As a speaker, you can enhance your *ethos* by telling your audience why you should be trusted when speaking on the topic by citing credible sources, using sound logic and arguments, and showing the relevance of your topic for your specific audience. You can also enhance your *ethos* by using good delivery, appearing confident, and dressing appropriately for the occasion. Your credibility changes throughout a presentation, and could improve or decrease depending upon how you handle the speech. As you give more and more presentations and do work on a specific topic, you will gain *ethos* through your reputation in that field.

Pathos

Credibility alone cannot carry a speech, and so Aristotle also proposed an emotional dimension to persuasive appeals. Pathos is the use of emotions in persuasion, specifically the generation of an emotional attachment to your position or topic. As a speaker, you have the ability to evoke emotions in your audience members that will help them be more easily persuaded. Narratives about specific people or objects are a highly effective way to get your audience to feel emotions about the topic of your speech. They work much better than a broad statistic or sweeping generalization.

For example, opening your speech about the impact of natural disasters with a story about a family that lost everything following tornados in Joplin, Missouri, might make your audience feel sympathetic or sad. A story about a young woman who was kidnapped and became a victim of human trafficking might make your audience feel anger or horror, while a story about someone who worked hard to overcome challenges to achieve something extraordinary might evoke joy or hope in your audience. An additional way to enhance this emotional connection is through showing pictures of a single representative of the larger issue (the family, not an overhead shot of Joplin). Helping your audience members connect emotionally with your topic can help you persuade them, but you must be careful to balance emotional appeals with logic so you are not manipulating your audience. Relying

---

ARTISTIC PROOFS

Aristotle's category for credibility, emotion, and logic within a persuasive appeal; he called them artistic because the speaker creates them

ETHOS

the perceived personal character or credibility of the speaker

PATHOS

the use of emotions in persuasion

on *pathos* alone is a serious problem for a speech because it makes it seem as though the speaker either cannot locate evidence to support his or her claim, or is trying to trick an audience for personal gain.

Logos

LOGOS
the use of logic and evidence to persuade your audience

In addition to credibility and emotional dimensions of a speech, logic also is of paramount importance. *Logos* is what Aristotle termed the use of logic and evidence to persuade an audience. As a speaker, a lot of your evidence will come from the information you find while doing research for your speech, such as numbers, statistics, examples, definitions, explanations, and quotations. How you use that evidence to build logical arguments, however, is even more important. As a speaker, there are two types of reasoning processes you will use to build arguments and reach conclusions in your speech: deductive and inductive reasoning.

DEDUCTIVE REASONING
involves using general truths to reach a certain conclusion about a specific instance

Deductive reasoning. Deductive reasoning involves using general truths to reach a certain conclusion about a specific instance. The formal structure for deductive reasoning is the syllogism, which sets up a series of claims that build upon each other to reach a conclusion.

There are three parts to the syllogism: (1) the major premise, which is a statement that is believed to be true by your entire audience, (2) the minor premise, which connects the statement in your major premise to the specific instance about which you are trying to make a claim, and (3) the conclusion, which is the logical result of both the major and minor premises and is the claim you are ultimately trying to make. Figure 17.1 is an example of a syllogism.

Major premise: All dogs have tails.
Minor premise: Einstein is a dog.
Conclusion: Therefore, Einstein has a tail.

FIGURE 17.1 Syllogism

This example begins with a fact about a large category (all dogs) in the major premise, connects that fact to a specific instance (Einstein) in the minor premise, and then reaches a certain, logical conclusion about that specific instance.

INDUCTIVE REASONING
involves using several specific instances or pieces of evidence to draw probable conclusions about general truths

Inductive reasoning. Inductive reasoning involves using several specific instances or pieces of evidence to draw probable conclusions about general truths. There are four types of inductive reasoning: reasoning by cause, by example, by sign, and by analogy.

- *Reasoning by cause* is used when you claim that one event causes another. For example, you might notice that each time you eat peanut butter, you break out in hives, so you might conclude that eating peanut butter causes you to break out in hives.

- *Reasoning by example* is when you use several specific instances that are related to each other to draw an overall conclusion about them. For instance, you might observe that you enjoyed watching the movie *Superman*, loved *Guardians of the Galaxy*, and liked *Thor*, so you then conclude you enjoy watching movies that are based on comic books.

- *Reasoning by sign* occurs when you conclude that the presence of one thing indicates the presence of another. For example, when we see smoke, we usually conclude that there is a fire. When we see people walking past the window carrying umbrellas, we might conclude that it is raining outside.

- *Reasoning by analogy* occurs when you compare two similar cases in order to argue that what is true in one case is also true in the other because the two cases share similar features. For example, if an anti-bullying campaign worked well in one school, you might argue that it will also be effective in another school that has similar characteristics.

When you give a persuasive speech, it is important to carefully balance your use of *ethos*, *pathos*, and *logos* so you can effectively and ethically persuade your audience. Additionally, you should take extra care to use sound reasoning. As we are about to discover, though, not all reasoning is sound.

LOGICAL FALLACIES

Just because someone says something or presents a formal speech does not mean it is logically sound. In fact, society is rife with examples of clever arguments that make no logical sense. It is imperative that we, as speakers, avoid using such fallacious reasoning, and that, as an audience, we are able to know poor logic when we hear it. In this part of the chapter, we will identify and define eleven common logical fallacies, which are errors in reasoning that lead to invalid conclusions.

Ad Hominem Attack

In an *ad hominem attack*, a speaker tries to equate the quality of someone's argument with the quality of his or her character. This fallacy is sometimes referred to as name-calling, and it often focuses on irrelevant elements of personal history. You would be using an *ad hominem* attack if you constructed an advertisement in a campaign that labeled the other person as uncaring because they do not support immigration reform.

REASONING BY CAUSE
used when you claim that one event causes another

REASONING BY EXAMPLE
using several specific instances that are related to each other to draw an overall conclusion about them

REASONING BY SIGN
occurs when you conclude that the presence of one thing indicates the presence of another

REASONING BY ANALOGY
comparison of two similar cases in order to argue that what is true in one case is also true in the other because the two cases share similar features

LOGICAL FALLACIES
errors in reasoning that lead to invalid conclusions

AD HOMINEM ATTACK
speaker tries to equate the quality of someone's argument with the quality of his or her character by calling him or her something that would be perceived as negative by the audience

Ad Verecundiam

The *ad verecundiam* fallacy is an appeal to authority. In this fallacy, a person argues that his or her positional authority, perhaps as a parent or elected official, makes the argument correct rather than relying on logical reason to make his or her case. For example, if a child asks why he needs to brush his teeth and his mom replies, "Because I'm the mom, and I said so," his mother would be relying with an *ad verecundiam* fallacy instead of using logic to explain how brushing teeth contributes to dental health. This does not mean it is a bad idea for her son to brush his teeth, but it does mean that his mother is not using sound reasoning.

Slippery Slope

A **slippery slope** fallacy argues that once a course of action is taken, a series of other unavoidable and undesirable events will necessarily take place. It assumes that there is no way to stop or turn back once we begin moving down a particular path. If we argued that banning the purchase of some automatic guns with large magazines would eventually lead to the banning of all guns, we would be using a slippery slope fallacy because one does not necessarily mean that the other will follow.

Non Sequitur

A *non sequitur* fallacy involves making an unjustified move from one topic to another and is often a result of reasoning that is happening in the wrong order. This can often result from an inappropriate reasoning from sign. If you were to claim that someone had to be wealthy because of the type of car they drive or apartment they reside in, you would be making a logical jump not supported by the evidence. Just because someone drives an expensive car or has a nice apartment does not necessarily mean they are wealthy.

Straw Man

In a **straw man** fallacy the speaker ignores the actual position of his or her opponent, misrepresents his or her position, and then attacks that made-up position instead of the actual position. Often, the speaker oversimplifies his or her opponent's position, takes his or her comments out of context, or represents an entire group's position with bad arguments from one person in that group. Imagine that David and Chris are running for political office, and David argues that we should spend more tax money on health and education. Chris responds by saying that he is surprised that David hates our country so much that he wants to leave it defenseless by cutting military spending. In this case, Chris is using a straw man fallacy.

Hasty Generalization

Hasty generalizations involve using a small sample of evidence to draw unjustified conclusions about an entire group or category. This is a poor use of reasoning from example. If you were to ask two of your friends what their favorite television show is, and then use that as evidence that all college students love that particular show, you would be making a hasty generalization.

Either-or

The either-or fallacy, which is sometimes called a false dilemma, happens when the speaker claims there are only two alternatives when there are really many other options available. This fallacy attempts to force audience members to make a choice between two extreme positions. For instance, we often see news coverage about abortion laws label people as pro-life (opposed to abortion in all circumstances) or pro-choice (supportive of keeping abortion legal in all circumstances) when, in reality, there are many possible positions between those two.

EITHER-OR
speaker claims there are only two alternatives when there are really many other options available

False Cause

Also known by its Latin name, *post hoc, ergo propter hoc*, the false cause fallacy assumes that one event caused another unrelated event to occur because the events happened around the same time, even though the two events were completely unrelated. Put more succinctly, false cause fallacies use "after this, because of this" reasoning. False cause is the basis of many superstitions. For example, when deciding where to go for dinner, a couple rules out a restaurant at a nearby mall because "every time we go there it rains." This assumes that because they chose to go to that restaurant it will rain when, in fact, just because the events happened sequentially, it does not mean they were in any way connected.

FALSE CAUSE
speaker assumes that one event caused another unrelated event to occur

Red Herring

A red herring fallacy happens when the speaker introduces irrelevant ideas in order to distract attention away from the real issue, but sometimes tries to make them appear related to the first issue. An example of a red herring would be, "We should increase the rigor of our

RED HERRING
speaker introduces irrelevant ideas in order to distract attention away from the real issue

Logical Fallacies and . . . Cheese?

In the 2005 film *Thank You for Smoking,* advertising agent Nick Naylor (played by Aaron Eckhart) gives several presentations before various audiences trying to convince them smoking is either not bad for them or that it should not come with a warning. In a scene where he is questioned before a committee in Congress, Naylor employs numerous logical fallacies to avoid the issue of cigarettes and confuse those who are watching. For instance, he uses the *non sequitur* when asked about warning labels on cigarettes and states that if we do that, we should also put them on jet planes and cheddar cheese, because those things are also potentially harmful. His repeated performances in the movie serve to illustrate numerous logical fallacies and how convincing they sound on the surface.

classes for students. You should support this because we are in a budget crisis and do not want to be furloughed." Even though the second sentence is being used to support the first sentence, it does not address that topic. Likewise, we often see red herrings in political debates when a candidate does not want to answer a question and instead introduces a new topic that will make them appear more favorable. We sometimes refer to this as "dodging the question," "avoiding the issue," or "spin doctoring."

Begging the Question

BEGGING THE QUESTION
speaker uses a circular argument in which his or her evidence and conclusion are really saying the same thing and assume certain facts that have not yet been proven

Begging the question is the use of a circular argument in which your evidence and your conclusion are really saying the same thing, and you assume certain facts that have not yet been proven. To say, "The reason that there is such a big demand for iPhones is that everyone wants one," is an example of begging the question because the evidence used to support the conclusion is just saying the same thing in a different way. Common indicators of this fallacy include prefacing a statement with "it begs the question" and "for the sake of argument."

Appeal to Pity

APPEAL TO PITY
attempt to influence an audience by exploiting their feelings of sympathy, guilt, or desire to ameliorate suffering

Appeal to pity is the attempt to influence an audience by exploiting their feelings of sympathy, guilt, or desire to ameliorate suffering. Most commonly we see or experience this in what we call "guilt trips," where people try to make you feel guilty for asserting your own position or denying their requests. Consider a friend who asks you to help them move on a day you had planned to spend with your family. They may try to tell you they helped you before, and that if you didn't help them, they would have to do it all by themselves, thus increasing the risk they might be hurt. There is no logic to this appeal, but rather a reliance on making you feel so bad you will agree to their request to avoid the feeling of guilt.

ENGAGING IN DIALOGIC PERSUASION

Persuasion can often become contentious and uncomfortable because we tend to tightly hold to our beliefs and attitudes, not allowing ourselves to be persuaded. In fact, people may sometimes feel like being persuaded is akin to being manipulated, when that is not the case at all. Creating an environment where persuasion—true persuasion—can occur shares a number of similarities with the atmosphere needed for dialogue. In this final section of the chapter, we will provide some general guidelines for creating an open environment where persuasion can occur.

Be Open to Other Ideas

Whether you are the speaker or the listener for a persuasive message, try to put aside your personal position and allow new information to be presented. Add that new information to what you already know and see if your mind is changed. This is no small feat and requires a mutual feeling of goodwill between you and the speaker, but it is essential for creating a comfortable environment for any speaker and audience.

Don't Prejudge Speakers or Audiences

It is one thing to gather information about a speaker and an audience; it is another to judge the speaker and his or her message before they have a chance to deliver it. Believing an audience will be hostile will probably make you speak like they are, thus making them hostile. Additionally, if as an audience member you begin the presentation with the assumption you will not agree with the speaker, you likely won't.

Understand a Speaker's Perspectives

Invariably, a speaker will say something you disagree with, but that does not mean everything they say is contrary to your beliefs and attitudes. It is possible to disagree on specific elements of a position, but still agree with the overall argument. When you listen and when you speak, make distinctions between disagreements with the argument and with specific parts of the argument. This might allow you to begin to find common ground with the speaker.

Avoid Inciting Your Audience

On the one hand, you need to incorporate an emotional dimension to your speech to help your audience connect with it. On the other, you do not need to engender an extreme degree of a particular emotion in your audience. Focusing on emotion too much in a speech can increase defensiveness and aggressiveness in the audience, and that is not conducive to the exchange of ideas.

Clarify Your Credentials

When providing your experience or expertise to an audience, be clear and honest about them; do not misrepresent yourself in the hopes of appearing more credible. If you set the bar too high and then make mistakes in your address, it will damage your believability and chance to effectively persuade the audience.

Accept Disagreement

The goal of any single persuasive message cannot be to change the hearts and minds of an audience. The instances of such things happening are very difficult to find. Instead, be satisfied with an audience that simply heard and considered your ideas. Not everyone will agree with you, and if you show disdain for those that disagree, then the chances of working with those people again in the future decrease. Disagreement is good and can be the sign of a thoughtful audience. Accept that you will not win over everyone, regardless of your argument's strength.

SUMMARY

When most people think of public speaking, they think of persuasive speaking. To many, the opportunity to change someone's mind or attitude is the most enjoyable part of speech. That said, it is also a risky endeavor and, when we persuade, we must be aware of the pitfalls and traps inherent in it. In this chapter, we explored the different types of questions persuasive arguments seek to answer. We then explored how to organize persuasive arguments and how to effectively incorporate credibility, emotion, and logic into those arguments. Finally, we discussed the eleven most common logical fallacies used by speakers today and provided suggestions for creating a dialogic and supportive climate when trying to persuade an audience.

CHAPTER 17 KEY IDEAS

- The four types of persuasion are questions of fact, questions of value, questions of policy, and refutations.

- The most effective patterns of organization for persuasive speeches include problem-solution, problem-cause-solution, comparative advantages, and Monroe's Motivated Sequence.

- The three means of persuasion, or artistic proofs, are *ethos*, *pathos*, and *logos*.

- You might use both deductive and inductive reasoning to build arguments and reach conclusions in your speech. Deductive reasoning involves using general truths to reach certain conclusions about a specific instance through the use of a syllogism. Inductive reasoning involves using several specific instances to draw probable conclusions about general truths and can include reasoning by cause, example, sign, or analogy.

- You should avoid using logical fallacies—which lead to invalid conclusions—as support in your presentations.

CHAPTER 17 KEY TERMS

Persuasion

Questions of fact

Questions of value

Questions of policy

Refutations

Problem-solution pattern of organization

Problem-cause-solution pattern of organization

Comparative advantages pattern of organization

Monroe's motivated sequence

Artistic proofs

Ethos

Pathos

Logos

Deductive reasoning

Inductive reasoning

Reasoning by cause	*Non sequitur*
Reasoning by example	Straw man
Reasoning by sign	Hasty generalization
Reasoning by analogy	Either-or
Logical fallacies	False cause
Ad hominem attack	Red herring
Ad verecundiam	Begging the question
Slippery slope	Appeal to Pity

ACTIVITIES AND DISCUSSION QUESTIONS

1. Watch the TED-Ed video "How can you change someone's mind?" created by Hugo Mercier, available online at https://ed.ted.com/lessons/how-can-you-change-someone-s-mind-spoiler-facts-don-t-work-so-well-hugo-mercier. How can you use what you learned about different types of arguments to decide what will be most persuasive to a particular audience? Which types of evidence and arguments might be most effective for persuading your audience in your own speech?

2. What are some situations in which persuasive speeches are given in everyday life? Have you ever been persuaded by a speaker?

3. Give examples (not the same as the ones in your book) of a speech that would be arguing a question of fact, one that would be arguing a question of value, one that would be arguing a question of policy, and one that would be a refutation. Is it possible to try to engage in more than one of these types of persuasion in the same speech?

4. For one of the speech examples that you identified in the previous question, which pattern of organization would be most effective if you were giving a speech in which you were trying to make that argument? Why would this be the most effective pattern? What would your main points and subpoints be?

5. Find an example of a commercial that relies on a fallacy to persuade viewers. Save the link for that video or briefly describe the commercial. Explain which fallacy you believe is being illustrated and provide a rationale for that choice.

SMALL GROUP
COMMUNICATION

Human beings have depended upon groups to survive throughout their history, so it should come as no surprise that such associations are important today. Without successful and positive group associations, people would be left to fend for themselves and likely would never have survived as a species. Men and women worked together to hunt for food, develop farms, and even to raise families. Even today many of the communication situations we find ourselves in occur with groups of people, especially those tasks we complete for work. Today groups come in various forms with different names, like "units," "departments," or "committees."

Groups are fundamental to society, government, and business organizations, as each of these depends on the successful completion of group work that benefits the entire collective. The ability of any group to be successful is predicated upon the members' communication skills. Poor communication is the death knell of any group, while successful, dialogic group members can facilitate quality work and an enjoyable experience for the entire group.

In this chapter, we explore the nature and characteristics of group work. We will first spend some time defining the qualities consistent within any group before exploring a model of group development. We will then examine the different roles or tasks performed by group members in any situation before explaining the steps necessary for an effective group decision-making process. Next, we will lay out some of the common challenges and rewards to group work before finally providing some guidance on how to employ dialogue to maximize the effectiveness, productivity, and efficiency of a group.

DEFINING SMALL GROUPS

The phrase "small group" can be tricky to define, as some of the contexts we have already explored in this book might seem to fit the bill for a small group. For example, a family or even a large company may seem to constitute a group. As we will see in this section, however, the vari-

Workplace Diversity for Staff and Clientele

The workforce is becoming increasingly diverse each year, and companies recognize the importance of training employees to collaborate with diverse sets of colleagues and clients. Perhaps no industry is more attuned to this need than the hospitality industry, where guests and employees come from around the globe. Since 2002, MGM Resorts International has run a program designed to prepare its employees for working with people of diverse backgrounds. To date, more than 4,000 employees have participated in the "Diversity Champions" initiative, developing skills such as respecting differences through an emphasis on inclusive teamwork and being aware of their own reactions when interacting with people of diverse backgrounds. Employees have continually cited the value of this workshop, saying things like, "this class has brought us closer to each other." The skills in the Diversity Champions program help facilitate successful work within departments and groups of MGM Resorts International.[1] In recognition of this, and other diversity initiatives, MGM Resorts International was awarded the 2015 ExecRank Board Diversity Award. It is also important to note that this initiative is not restricted to MGM Resorts International, as numerous other companies also have instituted similar programs. In fact, a recent Boston Consulting Group survey on which diversity and inclusion policies and practices employees believe work best included efforts to eliminate diversity in day-to-day operations similar to the aims of the Diversity Champions initiative in their top-rated responses. Other effective procedures included formal sponsorship programs and individual roadmaps for advancement.[2]

ous aspects that define small groups do not apply to these scenarios, thus making them unique contexts. In this section, we will discuss six characteristics that, taken together, define a small group and illustrate how a small group differs from families and public speaking engagements.

Vary in Size

Researchers who specialize in small group communication admit there is some debate over how to define the size of a small group; however, they all concede small groups consist of between three and fifteen people.[3] To maximize the effectiveness of the group, the magic number appears to be somewhere between five and seven members.[4] It is important to note, though, that group size is not a necessary characteristic of all small groups, and that ultimately the number that allows interaction and role recognition between members should determine the size of the group. The larger the group, though, the more likely there will be subgroups, as is the case within academic departments where certain members of the department form committees to do specific work on behalf of the larger group. Although it may seem important, group size is actually not the most central characteristic of the definition of a small group.

Function as Systems

Much like families, small groups function as interdependent systems whereby something one member does impacts all other aspects of the group. When one group member does not complete something they were tasked with, it falls to another member to do so; conversely, when a member finishes a task early, they can then help someone else in the group finish another task. For small groups to function properly, members need to coordinate their efforts with each other so things are completed how and when they should be.

Maintain Task-oriented Goals

Whereas families and small groups are both interdependent in nature, small groups are task oriented, whereas families are not always so. This means that small groups focus on completing a specific action or goal and then likely disband, whereas families do not dissolve or disband when something they worked together to achieve is finished. The task can be the creation of something, the completion of a project, or the resolution of some problem, but groups are always aware they have a limited lifespan that ends when their job is completed.

Governed by Their Own Norms

Every group is different, but each expects certain behaviors from group members. Some of these norms concern the ways in which group members act toward each other, while others pertain to the processes groups follow. For instance, some groups formalize votes for important decisions with the understanding that everyone will respect the outcome, and some groups expect that members will support one another in a variety of ways when a member is in need. These are just some examples of norms that might govern the members of a group. What makes small-group norms different from the norms of families and companies is that the norms of small groups contain the force of all members and are not driven by one person's authority.

Create Their Own Identities

One way groups maintain themselves is by crafting their own identity out of all the unique quali-ties of its members. This identity serves as a boundary for membership, as it protects the group from anyone else joining and destroying its cohesiveness. Sometimes groups create codes or languages that only members know, while other times they use uniforms or physical labels. Communication scholar Ernest Bormann referred to the times when groups coalesce around a theme or particular group experience as "fantasies" and he points out that particularly strong fantasies can "chain out" and be applied to other events.[5] **Fantasies** are creative interpretations of shared events that help define a group's identity, and fantasies become so powerful that they can be used and applied to various other experiences the group may have to remind them of their common identity. In 1999, the Providence College baseball team was discontinued, but in its final season the team generated a great degree of cohesiveness by creating special warmup T-shirts inspired by the movie *Major League*. Whether it is through code languages, membership cards, or some type of apparel defining membership, the identity of the group is always pro-tected. The group identity also influences the way individual members define their own identity, making group identity a powerful internal and external influence on individuals.

FANTASIES

creative interpretations of shared events that help define a group's identity

Preserve Member Cohesiveness

The bond that links group members is ephemeral and largely depends upon each member feel-ing connected to each other. The more connected they feel, the stronger the group; the weaker the connection, the poorer the work. This form of unity represents what Gerald L. Wilson calls "a special kind of interpersonal attraction."[6] Members of high functioning groups typically like each other, but they like the group with those people in it even more. The attraction becomes less about something in the person on an interpersonal level, and more about what positive qualities that person brings to the group as a whole. In some cases, it is entirely possible to not like a person on a one-on-one basis, but truly appreciate him or her as a member of a group.

Good group cohesion comes from a sense of fairness in the group, equal opportunity to par-ticipate, the sharing of similar attitudes—especially about the task the group confronts—and the actual work being done. This latter point refers to success in accomplishing tasks and a feeling of progress throughout the experience with the group. Good groups have clear direction, specific goals understood by all members, and a plan for how each member is to act to achieve those goals. The better the group, the stronger the work, and the more suc-cessful the work, the stronger the group's sense of cohesion.

**TUCKMAN
MODEL OF
GROUP
DEVELOPMENT**

a five-stage theory of group development proposed by Bruce Tuckman consisting of forming, storming, norming, performing, and adjourning; Tuckman suggests not all groups will move through each stage depending on their tasks or goals

HOW GROUPS DEVELOP: THE TUCKMAN MODEL OF GROUP DEVELOPMENT

Even though groups are important for helping us achieve a wide variety of goals in organiza-tions and society, most groups go through a fairly predictable set of stages as they emerge and work toward accomplishing a shared purpose. This section will focus on the **Tuckman Model of Group Development**,[7] which argues that groups move through five stages in their lifespan. While it is possible that groups might be able to skip stages and still be successful at accomplishing their tasks or goals, most groups will go through all five of these stages together: forming, storming, norming, performing, and adjourning.

Stage #1: Forming

The forming stage of the Tuckman model involves group members getting to know one another and becoming oriented toward the task at hand. It is important for groups to develop cohesion in order to be effective, and the first essential step for forming cohesion is getting to know everyone in the group—their desires, their aims and vision for the group, and their understanding of the task before them. This is when group members meet and engage in conversation in an effort to learn about each other. During this stage relationships form between group members as everyone explores what their potential roles and contributions could be to the larger group task. These interactions are colored by prior knowledge of other group members and also by each individual's experiences with group work in the past. This stage also involves group members reaching a consensus on the nature of their task. In today's mediated environment, many groups go through this stage through email or perhaps virtual meetings and conference calls, but nonetheless it is important to form the group before progressing to completing the task.

Stage #2: Storming

Once group members establish a rapport, the group turns its attention to the task at hand. During the storming stage, group members might express open disagreement over what it will take to complete the task, who is best suited to what role, and what processes the group will follow to make decisions and accomplish assignments. This does not necessarily mean that negative feelings emerge, but rather that the group members examine the issues related to their task and debate the best way to move forward. The more robust the discussion about the different aspects of the task and how it might be solved, the better the group functions. The less debate and exchange of ideas at this point, the less likely the group will find the most efficient and effective solution. Some group members may attempt to bring those with different views together with a compromise, others may pose alternatives, and still others may inquire about the reasoning behind different positions taken by those in the group. The important thing at this point is to maintain a constructive approach to discussing different ideas and not take things personally or attack group members.

One of the other conflicts that emerges during this stage is about who will take on each role and how members will interact with one another. Group members might jockey for who will take on the role of the leader, and there might be clashes between individual personalities, preferred working styles, and goals that members have for the group. Some group members might try to find ways to express their individuality or feel like their identity is threatened by the direction that the group is moving, and others might voice judgments about group members who appear to be attempting to dominate the group or shirking responsibility. During the storming stage, it is essential that the group members work through these difficulties. This stage can be very destructive for groups that do not work through their differences or that allow conflicts to get out of control, but groups that do work through their disagreements constructively can emerge as strong, versatile teams that can more successfully achieve their goals.

Stage #3: Norming

During the norming stage, groups move from conflict to cohesion. During this stage, disagreements have passed, the group focuses on the task, and group roles and norms for behavior take shape.[8] This new focus on the mission of the group promotes trust, honesty, and cohesion where once there was conflict and disagreement. Groups that go through norming ultimately develop stronger bonds than those that do not.

Stage #4: Performing

Once conflict is resolved and people settle into their roles, they focus on completing the task assigned to the group. During the performing stage, group members expend their efforts in developing solutions, finishing tasks, and working together to complete their particular assignments. Individuals also become fully acclimatized to the group culture and procedures, a process that sometimes leads to what communication scholars call symbolic convergence. **Symbolic convergence** occurs when groups create a unique meaning for a term, experience, or event in the group's life that serves to further strengthen the bond between group members.[9] During the performing stage, group members report to each other on their progress, work through task and relationship challenges that may come up, and ultimately ensure the group accomplishes its objectives.

SYMBOLIC CONVERGENCE

occurs when groups create a unique meaning for a term, experience, or event in the group's life that serves to further strengthen the bond between group members

Stage #5: Adjourning

Once a group has finished its task or accomplished its goal, the group often has to decide what will happen to the group. In some cases, particularly groups that are part of a team at work, the group might simply move on to the next project and will need to keep working together. In other groups, however, the group might need to disband for a variety of reasons, including successful or unsuccessful completion of their assigned task, the end of a semester, or the need to move on to working to accomplish other tasks with other teams. In situations where the group must disband, the group enters this final stage of adjourning. This stage may be met with a variety of emotions, depending upon the experience of individual members, but whether they wish to work together again in the future likely depends upon a positive experience and feeling like their work was valued.

TASK ROLES
related to accomplishing work together as a group

MAINTENANCE ROLES
related to the development and maintenance of the relationships within the group

GROUP MEMBER ROLES: TASK ROLES AND MAINTENANCE ROLES

While working together, group members must take on several different responsibilities in order to achieve the group's goals. These roles fall into two primary categories: **task roles** and **maintenance roles**.[10] Task roles are related to accomplishing work together as a group, whereas maintenance roles are related to the development and maintenance of the relationships within the group to keep the group working together effectively. It is important for groups to balance these roles and make sure that both task and maintenance roles are being accomplished. Groups that only emphasize the task roles and do not take time for social interaction and building interpersonal relationships within the group might find that group members do not enjoy their time working together and become less productive over time. On the other hand, groups that only emphasize maintenance roles and do not balance those with task roles tend to enjoy the group interaction, but spend so much time socializing that very little work is actually accomplished.

Group members often take on multiple overlapping roles, and in many groups, a role might be taken on by several individuals. Even though groups tend to think about and prioritize task roles over maintenance roles,[11] it is important for groups to make sure that both task and individual roles are being fulfilled as the group works together. In this section of the chapter, we will examine some of the various tasks and responsibilities group members fill when working together.

Task Roles	Maintenance Roles
• Initiating	• Encouraging
• Information and opinion seeking	• Gatekeeping
• Information and opinion giving	• Harmonizing
• Evaluating ideas	• Compromising
• Energizing	• Observing and commenting
• Coordinating and elaborating	• Standard-setting
• Clarifying and summarizing	• Following
• Recording and managing tasks	

Initiating

One of the biggest challenges for groups is to simply find a way to get started. An initiator proposes ideas, ways of thinking about the problem, or ways to get organized to help the group prepare for the task ahead. This role might involve defining the task or problem, suggesting a solution or process as a starting point to solicit responses from others, or proposing ways to overcome expected difficulties.

Information and Opinion Seeking

Sometimes group members need a little bit of prodding to begin to participate in the discussion, so it is helpful to have a group member take on the task of asking others for information and opinions about the group's task. Information seeking involves asking others for facts, interpretations, and clarifications of ideas that have already been shared. Opinion seeking involves asking about group members' beliefs and opinions in order to better understand the group's values that will help to guide the work ahead.

Information and Opinion Giving

While a group needs someone to ask for information and opinions, that must also be matched with group members actually sharing information and opinions during the group's discussion. Group members might relate their experiences and knowledge directly to the group's task or problem, or they might need to find new information through research and share that information with the rest of the group. When conducting research and sharing information, it is also important for group members to share details about the quality of the sources to make sure that the information is credible and authoritative.

Evaluating Ideas

Although seemingly the complete opposite of encouraging others to share ideas and opinions, evaluating and challenging ideas brought forth by group members is another essential part of a high-functioning group. The challenges should not be aggressive or nasty, but they must be aimed at ensuring the group considers all potential aspects of an idea before it is adopted and ensuring that the group is relying on accurate information. If a member has questions regarding something the group discusses, they must feel welcome to challenge the idea and inquire about those things that give him or her pause. By evaluating ideas, each group member ensures the group does not move too quickly or lose sight of some important detail that may have been missed.

Energizing

Sometimes groups get stuck in ongoing conversation and have a hard time moving forward. Someone who takes on an energizing role prods the group to make a decision or take action, works to keep the group working productively, and keeps everything moving so that everyone is engaging in high-quality activity.

Coordinating and Elaborating

As group members share ideas with one another and evaluate those contributions, it is helpful to have someone to clarify relationships between ideas that have been shared, to expand on others' suggestions, and to envision how those suggestions might work if implemented by the group. This role might also involve coordinating the activities of the group beyond the group conversations to make sure that each person knows which tasks they are supposed to be working on and understands how their efforts overlap. This involves constant communication between group members to update one another on progress and might require planning a communication strategy for keeping everyone up to date. Without such coordination, it is entirely possible the work will be done in a vacuum and will not coalesce into a clear and consistent group effort.

Clarifying and Summarizing

As groups delve into discussion, make decisions, and divide tasks, it can be easy for members to get sidetracked from the original goal or to lose track of individual responsibilities. Each group needs someone who can raise questions about the group's direction to make sure that the discussion is related to the task at hand, to make sure that the tasks will help to achieve the overall goal, and to summarize plans to make sure that every group member has a clear understanding of what has already happened as well as the next steps that each person needs to take.

Recording and Managing Tasks

Groups often need a record of what happened and a list of decisions made at meetings, and this recording responsibility often falls to one person. Some groups officially designate a secretary or note taker to perform this role, but it is good practice for all group members to take notes and record what transpires during group meetings because even an official secretary may miss something. The record allows the group to reflect on what they accomplished and keep track of what still needs to be done and who needs to do it. Additionally, the person who takes on the responsibility of recording and managing tasks might take care of other routine details such as sending out meeting reminders, distributing materials, reserving and setting up meeting rooms, and sharing summaries or action items after the meeting.

Task Roles	Maintenance Roles
• Initiating	• Encouraging
• Information and opinion seeking	• Gatekeeping
• Information and opinion giving	• Harmonizing
• Evaluating Ideas	• Compromising
• Energizing	• Observing and commenting
• Coordinating and elaborating	• Standard-setting
• Clarifying and summarizing	• Following
• Recording and managing tasks	

Encouraging

One of the foundations of cohesiveness within groups is a feeling of support and an openness to participate in deliberations. A key way to develop this atmosphere is to make sure that everyone feels valued and welcomed in the group. A group member who is taking on an encouraging role praises other group members' ideas, has a warm attitude toward others, and indicates an acceptance of and support of others' views, ideas, and suggestions.

Gatekeeping

Another way that groups help others to feel welcome and valued is by encouraging participation by all group members. Someone who is taking on a gatekeeping role works to keep communication channels open, encourages participation from members who have not spoken up, and makes sure that everyone has a chance to be a part of the conversation. A gatekeeper might also propose ways to regulate the flow of communication to make sure everyone has an equal chance to participate by suggesting limiting the length of comments, going around the room in order to hear everyone's initial thoughts, or other processes.

Harmonizing

Disagreements and conflicts inevitably arise in most groups, and it is important for groups to find ways to reconcile those differences and find a way to move forward peacefully. A group member who is taking on a harmonizing role mediates disagreements, helps to relieve tension, and helps others explore and overcome differences.

Compromising

In additional to helping others smooth out and feel better during disagreements, groups need to find solutions that everyone is comfortable with before moving forward. A group member who is in the compromising role will offer suggestions that take everyone's perspectives into account. Someone who is part of the conflict might meet others halfway, admit an error, yield status, or give in to another's idea in order to maintain group harmony.

Observing and Commenting

In order to be successful, a group must pay attention to the processes that it is using and be intentional about the procedures being used. A group member taking on an observing and commenting role helps to keep track of and comments on group's internal processes and offers interpretations and evaluations of the group's procedures.

Standard-setting

At some point, groups must agree of the level of achievement for which they are striving. The group's standard-setter helps to articulate the standard that the group is setting for itself and helps the group to evaluate its progress toward that goal as well as the quality of the group's processes.

Following

The final group role helps to bridge the gap between task and performance roles. A group member who is following goes along with the group and passively goes along with others' ideas. The follower serves as an audience during discussions and allows others to make the group's decisions.

GROUP DECISION-MAKING PROCESS

Making sure that group members work together to fulfill all of the task and maintenance roles is an important part of creating a good group experience, but it is not enough to guarantee a successful outcome. Groups also need to pay careful attention to the decision-making process that is used in order to avoid some of the potential pitfalls of working in groups that will be described in the next section. Randy Hirokawa, Professor of Communication at the University of Hawaii at Hilo, and his colleagues[12] have developed and refined a functional theory of group decision-making effectiveness and propose five steps for group decision-making, which include the following:

Step 1: Problem Analysis

During this stage, the group needs to develop a thorough understanding of the problem. Group members should seek to understand "(a) the nature of the problem, (b) the extent and seriousness of the problem, (c) the likely cause(s) of the problem, and (d) the possible consequences of not dealing effectively with the problem."[13] As part of this process, group members will also need to identify a way to share information with one another to ensure that all group members have all of the information needed to thoroughly understand the problem. When some of the information about the problem is only known by some group members, it is often undervalued and underutilized, which can have a negative impact on group decisions.[14]

Step 2: Establishment of Evaluation Criteria

Once the group has a thorough understanding of the problem, the group must set criteria for the requirements that must be met by an acceptable choice for a solution to the problem. This must involve knowing which requirements expected by the decision evaluators (for instance, the company president) will be met by the proposed solution, as well as defining group standards for what constitutes a solution to the problem.

Step 3: Generation of Alternative Solutions

During this stage, the group should work to develop several realistic solutions for addressing the problem. The group should not discard any viable options and should come up with a number of possible choices. At this point, the group's goal is to come up with as many ideas as possible, not to make judgments about the quality of each idea.

Step 4: Evaluation of Positive Consequences of Solutions

Once the group has generated a reasonably large number of solutions, group members should evaluate the positive consequences of each choice. The group should make sure that it understands all of the possible positive outcomes associated with each option before

Developing Group Identities

Small groups are often a powerful narrative vehicle for television and movies. One such example can be found in the NBC sitcom *Community*, about a group of seven community college students from a variety of different backgrounds. In each episode of the critically acclaimed show, the group works through challenges to accomplish some sort of task, whether it is related to their college coursework, the survival of their school, or even maintaining their group. The seven individuals each have unique identities, but over the course of the show's five-year run they develop a cohesive group identity that is so powerful that other people at the school—including the dean—desperately want to join.[15]

moving on to the next stage. The group should include all of the direct and indirect effects that the solution will have, both in addressing the specific problem and in the larger impact on the overall community.

Step 5: Evaluation of Negative Consequences of Solutions

After all of the positive outcomes for each choice have been identified, it is time for the group to turn to the possible negative consequences of each proposed solution. The group should be thorough in assessing all of the disadvantages associated with each possibility. While it might be tempting to speed through this final step, this is actually the most important stage for ensuring an effective decision,[16] which means that the critical evaluating role described above might be one of the most difficult but important roles for group members to fulfill.

All five of these steps are critical to making sure that the group has all of the information that it needs before making a decision about how to solve a problem. Once a group has gone through these steps, then it can select the best path forward. After that, the group can begin to divide the project into individual tasks and decide how to implement the solution that was chosen.

THE CHALLENGES AND REWARDS OF GROUP WORK

Working in groups is not always the easiest thing to do, even when you know and like those with whom you will work. There are numerous challenges to group work that, if not managed well, can derail the work of the entire team. These challenges can involve conflicting personalities, the pressures caused by deadlines, and even in some instances groups that get along too well and do not focus on the tasks at hand. There are also tremendous rewards that can be reaped from working together in a positive manner. Working and succeeding in teams allow people to feel a sense of joint accomplishment, share common experiences with others and in some cases, to develop bonds that survive beyond the life of the group. In this section of the chapter, we will explore what the challenges and rewards of successful group work are.

Challenges to Working in Groups

There are five primary challenges groups face when conducting work. Sometimes groups encounter several of these difficulties, but other times it can be only one, or even none. Nevertheless, it is essential group members enter into the project aware of these types of pitfalls so they can work to avoid them.

Groupthink. Many groups seek, or even demand, a unanimous decision where all members agree. This can be problematic in terms of process because the pressure to conform and reach such a decision may force certain people who harbor doubts to remain silent and acquiesce in the name of unanimity. Some groups where members know each other well fail to examine ideas critically and believe in the power of their collective abilities to come to the best decision. Still other groups have members who actively prohibit seeking evidence that may change the group's course. All of these situations illustrate groupthink, or the willful seeking of unanimity despite individuals who harbor doubts.[17]

Grouphate. Scholar Susan M. Sorenson proposed a concept called grouphate, which occurs when people have strong negative feelings about the prospect of working in a group.[18] Individuals who wish to avoid working in a group, but must do so nonetheless, tend to detract from the potential cohesion and success of the group. These individuals tend to be independent people who either do what they want regardless of the will of the group, or they withdraw almost entirely from the project and do not participate.

Social loafing. Social loafing is defined as "a reduction in motivation and effort when individuals work collectively compared to when they work individually,"[19] and numerous studies have shown that most people put forth less effort when working in groups than when working alone. One of the benefits of working in groups is that members can share the workload, but oftentimes, some group members take this too far and do not do their fair share of the work. They also fail to participate in group deliberations regarding the decision-making process, assignment of tasks, or even the decision itself. As groups are systems, one member's lack of effort forces changes in other group members that include taking on additional work not completed by the social loafer, as well as developing negative feelings toward the group as a whole, thus damaging the cohesiveness of the group.

Domination. The opposite of the nonparticipant is the dominator, a person who seeks to control the discussion and the decision the group is tasked with making. Dominators speak over others, never seek input from group members, and often interrupt people when they speak. They have a vision of how to proceed and where they want the group to go and do not deviate from it. Often these people lack listening skills.

GROUPTHINK
the willful seeking of unanimity despite individuals who harbor doubts

GROUPHATE
when people have strong negative feelings about the prospect of working in a group

SOCIAL LOAFING
"a reduction in motivation and effort when individuals work collectively compared to when they work individually"

News and Cultural Groupthink

It has often been observed that news networks such as Fox and MSNBC cater their programming to one side of the political aisle. The net effect of this is a loyal viewership that tends to only get their news from that one source. This leads to cultural groupthink, as these individuals distrust and vilify those who do not agree with their perspective on the world. Conversely, people outside of this group may tend to develop poor opinions of the group and thus further polarize people, inhibiting dialogue and the possibility for collaboration and compromise. What are some ways people can prevent this from occurring? Is it possible to pierce the veil of a group like this? If so, how?

Irresponsibility. The final challenge to effective group work that we will discuss is the irresponsibility of some members. Suffice it to say, group work depends upon members trusting each other when they say they will be somewhere or do something. Sometimes that trust is violated by individuals who fail to hit deadlines, forget about meetings, or produce inferior work for the group. This irresponsible behavior is perhaps driven by a person feeling like they do not fully belong to the group, or they do not have an appropriate incentive for participating (e.g., students working on a group project may all receive the same grade, so there is no cost for irresponsible behavior). Of all the challenges to group work, this may be the hardest to deal with.

The Rewards of Group Work

Although there are numerous challenges to group work, there are also some rewards that make the effort of working alongside others worthwhile. In this section, we will briefly explore three of those rewards.

Efficiency. Groups often come together to accomplish complicated tasks that require expertise in several different areas. Other groups form simply because of the amount of work that needs to be accomplished. Properly using resources and individual talents can make the completion of a complex and difficult task much more efficient and effective. This allows people to know what their time commitment will be as part of the group and feel comfortable with what they are asked to do. Furthermore, groups often develop synergy, which means that the group can accomplish more together than the individual members could have accomplished if they were working separately. In other words, a group is often more than the sum of its parts.

Opportunity to learn from others. When people with different experiences and expertise come together to accomplish a task, there is an opportunity to broaden your understanding of various areas of specialization. Being open to the idea that expertise in different areas can

People think that communication is a "magic bullet" for group success. I like to remind people that groups can, and often do, talk themselves into trouble. The key to group success is for groups to communicate effectively about the right things—whether it be understanding the problem, evaluating alternatives, or working through interpersonal disagreement or conflict.

—**Randy Hirokawa, University of Hawaii at Hilo**

add to your own knowledge of how best to accomplish something can provide you with the chance to grow in your own sphere of work.

Exposure to diverse people. In today's global environment, groups are often composed of people in different states, regions, or even countries. One can look at this and see a challenge in that each of these people brings different cultural expectations and perspectives to the collective, but that need not be a challenge. Learning from and adapting to people with diverse backgrounds can be an enriching experience that allows you the chance to sharpen your interpersonal skills and worldview. Groups present a unique opportunity for learning about various cultures.

Group work is not easy, but it is also not something you can avoid. Whether it is during your college career or after graduation in your workplace or community, you will work with other people in a larger group. Knowing what the rewards can be from such participation and how to avoid the challenges that can accompany it will help you make the experience as beneficial as possible.

DIALOGUE IN GROUPS

Dialogic communication can help establish and maintain a positive atmosphere for small group communication. It can help facilitate the exchange of ideas, the critical examination of those ideas, and the building of strong relationships between group members. Whenever groups work together, there are bound to be disagreements and tension, but dialogic communication in these environments can turn these moments of stress into productive opportunities to advance the group goal. In this final part of the chapter, we will provide you with six guidelines for employing dialogue within small groups to help make these exchanges constructive and not destructive. They are not easy to do, but the more you make an effort at building an atmosphere where dialogue is encouraged and rewarded, the stronger the cohesiveness of the group, and the more positive the experience will be.

Allow for Non-task Talk

Building a cohesive group necessarily involves cultivating trust and comfort between the members, and the best way to do this is to allow individuals who will be working together to get to know each other. This means that the initial meeting of the group should encourage conversation not related to the group task so people can grow to feel comfortable with one another. Non-task talk also takes place during the work of the group, and it should be taken as a sign that people are working well together. A dialogic atmosphere within the group depends upon people not feeling like they are a cog in a machine, or only able to speak about certain topics, and so allowing for, and even encouraging, non-task talk is important for developing a successful group.

Paraphrase Contributions to Ensure Understanding

As we have discussed, people do not always understand and interpret statements made by other people as they were intended. In groups, it is important to ensure that everyone is on the same page, and so when comments are made, or questions asked by others, you should paraphrase what was said to make sure you interpreted it correctly. Paraphrasing statements and repeating questions to clarify the other person's inquiries help create mutual understanding and avoid miscommunication that can derail the group's efforts.

Employ Turn-taking

The risk of people talking over one another increases when several people are talking about a topic. To that end, it is essential to employ the use of nonverbal regulators to organize the conversation. It is also imperative to allow people to finish their statements or questions and not interrupt them, even when you feel like you have something important to contribute. If group members are allowed to speak over or interrupt each other, then a negative climate within the group will develop and people will be less likely to contribute in the future. Respecting the person whose turn it is to speak goes a long way toward creating a successful group.

Take Good Notes

Earlier we discussed the various tasks members of the group engage in, and we advised that all members of the group should take notes during meetings. This is a very good way to ensure the group stays on task and that everyone understands what needs to be done by whom. People cannot remember every detail of what was said during a meeting, but fewer things get lost when everyone takes notes.

Be Flexible

Everyone has his or her own talents, and good groups leverage those talents to achieve their goals. Sometimes people wish to do the same task within a group, however, and so maintaining flexibility is important when determining what you will contribute to the group's work. You may wish to take on one particular item, but when someone else is perhaps better suited to do so, you must be open and flexible to doing something else that will benefit the group. A good way to avoid conflict over these issues is to have conversations early in the group's lifespan about what needs to be done and what the expertise and desires are for those in the group. This will allow for dialogue about matching people's skills and wishes with the group's work needs.

Engage in Constructive Conflict

Every group will encounter disagreements, whether they are over the processes the group will follow, the tasks assigned to individuals, or the ultimate decision at which the group arrives. For a group to be effective, it cannot avoid these conflicts. Members must feel like they can express dissent when they have a different opinion. These disputes should be engaged constructively, with other group members seeking to identify what the reasons are behind the differing opinions and working to understand the concerns of that group member. After the group understands the rationale behind the different opinions, they can work toward bridging the gap and potentially creating a consensus. Conflict in groups should be viewed as a positive occasion, when ideas can be critically examined and improved, not as an impediment to concluding the group's work.

SUMMARY

In an increasingly global communication environment, small group communication skills are more important than ever. In this chapter, we defined small groups, illustrating how they are different from interpersonal and public speaking contexts. We examined two theories of how groups develop and explored the various tasks group members complete when working together. We then explored the various challenges and rewards of group work, before finally providing six guidelines for using dialogue to facilitate a positive and effective group experience.

CHAPTER 18 KEY IDEAS

- There are six characteristics that can be used to define small groups: (1) effective small groups range in size, (2) small groups function as systems, (3) small groups are task-oriented, (4) small groups are governed by their own rules and norms, (5) small groups create their own identities, and (6) small groups are cohesive.

- The Tuckman Model of Group Development includes five stages: forming, storming, norming, performing, and adjourning.

- Group members fulfill various group tasks, and it is important for groups to balance task- and relationship-maintenance work.

- Some of the challenges associated with working in groups include groupthink, grouphate, social loafing, domination, and irresponsibility.

- Rewards of group work include efficiency, learning from others, and exposure to diverse styles.

CHAPTER 18 KEY TERMS

Fantasies	Maintenance roles
Tuckman Model of Group Development	Groupthink
Symbolic convergence	Grouphate
Task roles	Social loafing

ACTIVITIES AND DISCUSSION QUESTIONS

1. Watch Tom Wujec's TED talk, "Build a Tower, Build a Team," available online at https://youtu.be/H0_yKBitO8M. What does the marshmallow challenge teach us about successful team collaboration?

2. Think about a recent small group or team project that you have recently been a part of (in a class, at work, as part of a team, in a social setting, etc.). Identify what happened during each of the five stages of the Tuckman Model of Group Development. In which stages did you spend the most time? Were there any stages that you skipped?

3. Which task roles and maintenance roles do you most often fill when you are working in a group? What are the benefits that these roles bring to your group? Are there other roles that you can challenge yourself to take on that have sometimes been missing in groups in which you have participated?

4. Can you think of an example in history or in a movie in which a group suffered from one of the challenges of working in a group? What happened? If you could go back in time, what advice would you have given to those group members? How might things have been different if the group had worked together more successfully?

19
LEADERSHIP

Groups of all sizes organize themselves in various ways, but one consistent component of any group is a leadership structure. In some cases, this takes the form of a small group representing the larger group, but in most cases there is one person who ultimately makes the decisions. Serving in leadership roles is something many employers look for in job candidates, and it is often an indicator that an employee is highly regarded by his or her colleagues or supervisors. It is important to understand, though, that the role of leader is one of service to the group. In effect, the leader works for the group; the group does not work for the leader. In this way, leadership is different from other roles in groups and organizations where individuals report to supervisors.

Simply having people report to you does not make you the leader, despite your oversight responsibility. A leader is different from a manager, supervisor, and even a boss in this way. A leader supplies vision, generates support for the task, and inspires a belief in others that they will take the group where they want to go. Leaders see the status quo and seek to change parts of it for the betterment of the group. Managers maintain the status quo, follow policy, conduct reviews, and do other tasks defined by the group or organization, but do not have a clearly articulated vision or mission that the members of the group understand and support. The term "manager" is a title *given to someone, while leadership is a set of qualities and characteristics displayed by an individual in a group setting. In this way, managers can be leaders, but not all leaders are managers. The same can be said for bosses and supervisors because not all of them are leaders, but they are all managers.*

Leaders are often chosen by groups based on their ability to effectively communicate with the group about their goals and how they will be achieved. In this chapter, we explore the communicative foundations of leadership. We will first identify the three primary ways groups identify their leaders. Second, we will explore the types of power that help groups recognize leaders, and which of those types leaders can also use to support the group. Next, we will examine a host of characteristics exhibited by strong leaders before exploring six leadership communication styles. Finally, we will provide a set of suggestions and guidelines for using dialogue within groups to encourage good leadership, and, perhaps, take on those responsibilities yourself.

DIALING DIVERSITY

Developing Leadership Styles to Serve Certain Groups

Much to American society's benefit, people tasked with important leadership roles in companies, governments, and schools are increasingly from historically marginalized groups. One such individual whose leadership style has been well respected at every stop in her career is Beth Ford. In July 2017, Ford became the first female CEO of Land O' Lakes, and in so doing became the first openly gay woman CEO of a Fortune 500 company. Ford made her way through the ranks of corporate America as an out lesbian, staying true to her authentic self along the way.[1] The Columbia Business School Graduate had been with Land O' Lakes in a variety of roles since 2011 before moving into this position.

LEADER SELECTION PROCESS

Despite what many people might believe, leaders are not born, nor is the role of leader something everyone wants or should take on. In fact, there are several old adages that warn of the burden leadership may place on people like, "Heavy is the head that wears the crown." Nevertheless, groups always find leaders among their members, and they do so in a variety of different ways. Sometimes these leaders are elected, and when they are it typically means they have sought the position. Other times it is less formal, and people may simply be viewed as, and thus ultimately behave as, the leader of the group. In this section, we will detail three of the common ways groups identify their leaders.

The Elected Leader

Many groups large and small use a democratic method for selecting their leaders. The larger the group, the more likely this method will be employed because it helps manage the size of the gathering much better than direct discussion. There are typical patterns groups use to elect leaders. In some groups, for example, to be elected a person has to choose to run for the position of leader, whatever the title may be (e.g., president, chairperson). Additionally, the elected leaders typically serve fixed terms before having to run for the position again. The election model has a degree of appeal because it makes the leader responsible to the group, and if they fail to live up to the needs or expectations of the organization, then they can be replaced in the next election cycle. On the other side, the election model can lead to the creation of factions of supporters within a larger group by favoring certain members over others. Additionally, the best people do not always choose to run for the leadership positions, leaving the group to choose their leader from less than ideal candidates.

The Appointed Leader

In some organizations, leaders are appointed by someone or a body outside of the group. Committees and task forces, for example, often are created with a chairperson already identified by the person who convened the group. Appointed leaders usually come with some form of expertise that qualified them to lead the group, whether it is knowledge about the task or a reputation for good group communication and management. The challenge for appointed leaders, however, is that they may not be respected by the group and may have to spend a significant amount of time generating support before they can move forward with the job the group is tasked with completing.

The Emergent Leader

The third method for leadership selection is through the emergence of a leader within the group. In these situations, there might also be an appointed or elected leader, but if that person is not providing vision or direction, then someone within the group may step forward to do so. This type of leader is identified by the group, but not officially; rather, an emergent leader demonstrates qualities that everyone else in the group sees as both needed and positive, and so they give their support to this person when they make suggestions or decisions. Emergent leaders do not typically focus on the positional benefits of being a leader and do not seek to dominate or control the group, but instead provide structure, vision, and energy to a group that needs it. An emergent leader is accepted because they are already a part of the group and were not placed in a position of authority by an outside entity; therefore, they are not beholden to segments of individuals within the group to keep the leadership position. These are leaders by example, and they treat their colleagues as equals—one of the reasons they emerge as leaders!

LEADERSHIP AND POWER

Leaders often gain their position due to a certain degree of power they either hold or are given. They also maintain their positions through the judicious exercise of that power. Leaders who abuse power will lose the respect of the group, and despite whatever title they may hold, they will lose their ability to lead the group in a certain direction. A leader's power can come from one or multiple places, and in this section of the chapter, we will explore five sources of power for leaders in a variety of different situations.[2] Keep in mind that leaders can, and often should, derive their power from several of these sources, but they need only one to be seen as the leader.

Reward Power

REWARD POWER

power linked to the ability to either provide a good thing or take away a negative thing from someone for doing a task

The first type of power a leader might have is reward power, or the ability to either provide a good thing or take away a negative thing from someone for doing a task. Some managers and bosses have this type of power over employees because they control your salary and how much of a pay increase you will receive. Teachers also employ reward power through giving good grades, extra credit, or even candy to students who do their assignments or projects well. If teachers could not give candy or provide extra credit for students, and if managers lost the ability to determine raises, then they consequently would lose power over their charges. Such is the nature of reward power; it only exists so long as an individual can give something positive (e.g., award a bonus) or take something negative away from people (e.g., decrease their workload) as a result of doing something well.

Referent Power

REFERENT POWER

power derived from the charisma of a leader, and it can be seen when people follow someone they like, admire, look up to, or otherwise are attracted to

Unlike reward power, referent power does not emanate from the leaders' ability to provide a benefit to employees. Referent power is power derived from the charisma of a leader, and it can be seen when people follow someone they like, admire, look up to, or otherwise are attracted to. When your friend is leading one of your groups, you are likely to follow her lead because you like her, thus acquiescing to her referent power over you. Referent power, though, is tricky because as a leader you may do something that even the people who like you disagree with, and if that disagreement is strong, their attraction to you may diminish, thus reducing your referent power. Referent power is also something advertisers and politicians use when they seek endorsements for their products or campaigns. Ultimately, referent power works best when it is coupled with another power source. Just think about an instructor you really admired or liked. You worked hard in their class because of that respect, and when they also issued good grades, you increased your already strong effort.

Coercive Power

Leaders who have reward power also usually have its opposite: coercive power. **Coercive power** involves the ability to introduce something negative or take away something positive from group members. Coercive power often is perceived as the strongest form of power leaders can employ, but in fact using it can be very destructive to the group and diminish one's standing as leader. Coercive power needs to exist in certain situations, however. In the military and in prisons, for example, coercive power is necessary to keep order.

COERCIVE POWER
power linked to the ability to introduce something negative or take away something positive from group members

Legitimate Power

Some power emanates from a position, and so the person occupying that position is imbued with authority that must be followed. This type of power, otherwise called **legitimate power**, is often spelled out in a governing or organizational document that delineates exactly what authorities are associated with the position. It is important to remember that legitimate power is not derived from the individual or a person's style, but rather from the position they occupy; therefore, when the person no longer occupies that position, they no longer have that authority. The classic example of legitimate authority involved President Jimmy Carter, who in the middle of his failed reelection campaign in 1979-1980 was trying to negotiate the release and return of American hostages in Tehran. President Carter was able to inquire and be briefed on the progress of efforts to return these citizens until his successor, Ronald Reagan, took the oath of office. In the limo ride following the inauguration, Carter tried to ask for an update on the hostages and was told he no longer could be briefed on their status because he was no longer president. Thus, his legitimate authority expired and transferred to the new occupant of the position.

LEGITIMATE POWER
power that emanates from a position, and so the person occupying that position is imbued with authority that must be followed

Expert Power

A final common source of power is expertise. **Expert power** comes from having specific knowledge of a topic or content area, thus providing the person with that knowledge power over those who do not have that knowledge. You may have heard someone being interviewed called "a leader in her field," or perhaps you have seen or heard of expert witnesses or expert testimony. In times of medical emergency, such as the 2014 Ebola outbreak, we defer to the CDC or other medical experts to tell the public what we need to do to avoid getting ill. These are examples of people using expert power. Within groups, sometimes we assign certain tasks to people who are experts, or at least more well versed than others in the area related to the task. This gives them expert power. Experts, however, do not always make the best leaders, so knowledge in an area alone does not necessarily qualify one to automatically become a leader.

EXPERT POWER
power gained through specific knowledge of a topic or content area, thus providing the person with that knowledge power over those who do not have it, but who need it nonetheless

LEADERSHIP STYLES AND RESPONSIBILITIES

In this part of the chapter, we will highlight six different conceptions of leadership identified by scholar Daniel Goleman, a leading expert on the concept of emotional intelligence.[3] Emotional intelligence can best be understood as the ability to manage ourselves and our relationships effectively.[4] Additionally, in this section, we will briefly explore eight responsibilities of leadership. These run the gamut from responsibilities to manage interpersonal interactions within the group to keeping everyone focused on the task at hand.

Leadership Styles

Just as there are different ways to become a leader and different sources of power and authority, there are also several unique styles of leadership. There is not necessarily one best type of leadership style; instead, each leadership style works well in some situations, but not in others. Good leaders know that the situation often dictates the leadership style that works best and adjust their leadership style to best match the needs of the situation. See Table 19.1 on pages 296-297 for these six leadership styles at a glance.

COERCIVE LEADERSHIP STYLE

a top-down approach to decision making that stifles individual ingenuity and participation and neglects motivating the group

Coercive. The first type of leadership style we will discuss actually has perhaps the most negative impact on a group. The coercive leadership style is a top-down approach to decision-making that often stifles individual ingenuity and participation, as well as destroys any type of rewards system because it is not driven by motivating group members to succeed, but rather by pushing them to do what the leader wants. The coercive leadership style often manifests in those with strong drives to achieve and desires for control. With a "do what I say" approach, the coercive leadership style can erode a group's cohesion and ability to perform.

Despite its negative qualities, Goleman believes it does have its place in certain situations. In business, he believes the coercive style can be effective in helping companies engineer turnarounds when they are underperforming or when there is a genuine emergency where discussion and group consultation are not feasible. Nevertheless, the coercive style should be used sparingly and only when its benefits are clear.

AUTHORITATIVE LEADERSHIP STYLE

comes from a place of confidence and empathy, not control and enforcement

Authoritative. On the surface this style may sound similar to coercive power because to apply coercion one needs authority, but these two styles are actually quite different. The authoritative leadership style comes from a place of confidence and empathy, not control and enforcement. This style can have a very positive impact on a group if used in the right moments, specifically when a new vision or direction needs to be supplied and workers lack motivation. The authoritative leadership style helps mobilize people toward a particular vision they lacked before.

Goleman's research found that this style is by far the most effective. Authoritative leaders provide clarity of vision in an enthusiastic way that infects the rest of the group. People who work for leaders who exhibit this style know what they do matters, and feel that their colleagues respect their participation and input. Despite its overwhelming positive impact, Goleman cautions it does not work in every situation. For instance, if members of a group are more experienced, the authoritative style can come across as condescending and over-bearing, defeating the benefits it might have otherwise achieved.

Affiliative. If the coercive leader is exacting and rigid, and the authoritative leader is inspiring, then the leader utilizing the affiliative leadership style is flexible and encouraging. By this we mean they allow risk-taking, value relationship building, and build trust with their group members. This style maximizes group harmony and generally creates a positive environment for the group to complete their work. Affiliative leaders are, in essence, people persons.

When groups encounter stressful situations or have undergone major structural changes that have caused rifts and sown distrust among the group, then the affiliative style works at its best. The risk with this style is ignoring poor performance and encouraging an atmosphere of lax work ethic, and so Goleman advises to not use this style alone, but to mix it with another leadership orientation that allows constructive criticism and clarity of expectations.

Democratic. Another positive approach to leadership is the democratic leadership style, where leaders try to build consensus and collaborate with their team or group members. To be clear, democratic does not mean everyone votes, but rather everyone has an equal share in decisions and collaborates on potential solutions. The simple truth behind this approach is that through participation, consensus can form around the best solution or way forward. The democratic approach works well when trying to generate buy-in from multiple constituencies, or when leaders want to collect input from valuable and invested employees.

This approach to leadership takes time, patience, and an open mind—it is also not always the best way to move a group forward. One of the drawbacks to this approach lies in the risk of too many meetings between parties because consensus becomes difficult to forge. It also is not as effective when group members or employees are just not knowledgeable or skilled enough to provide good feedback and input. When leaders do not know the best way forward or want a fresh perspective on their particular plan, however, the democratic style can yield substantive benefits.

Pacesetting. The fifth style of leadership Goleman identified is what he calls pacesetting. In the pacesetting leadership style, a leader is focused on setting a high standard and modeling that standard for his or her team members. It is indicative of a desire to achieve the most in the fastest time possible, and the leader expects everyone to "keep pace" with them in terms of energy and dedication. It may or may not surprise you to find this type of high-octane approach to leadership results in a negative impact on the group climate because people get overwhelmed and morale drops, but like the coercive style, it does have a place in a leader's options.

The pacesetting approach, according to Goleman's research, can be most beneficial when the members of the group are already highly motivated and very competent in their tasks. In

AFFILIATIVE LEADERSHIP STYLE
flexible and encouraging, allowing group members to take risks and work on their own to engender trust; a "people-person" leadership style

DEMOCRATIC LEADERSHIP STYLE
focused on building consensus and collaborating with his or her team or group members

PACESETTING LEADERSHIP STYLE
focused on setting a high standard and modeling that standard for his or her team members

	Coercive	Authoritative
The leader's modus operandi	Demands immediate compliance	Mobilizes people toward a vision
The style in a phrase	"Do what I tell you."	"Come with me."
When the style works best	In a crisis, to kick-start a turnaround, or with problem employees	When changes require a new vision or when a clear direction is needed
Overall impact on climate	Negative	Most strongly positive

TABLE 19.1   The Six Leadership Styles at a Glance[5]

these situations, people require little direction and work to complete tasks at a good pace. Much like the affiliative style, however, Goleman cautions to use this approach sparingly and that it should never be the sole style of any leader.

COACHING
LEADERSHIP
STYLE
focused on helping
individuals improve and
grow through training
and constant feedback

Coaching. The final style Goleman identified was the coaching leadership style, which is focused on helping individuals improve and grow through training and constant feedback. Not surprisingly, many in the business world surveyed by Goleman and his team did not employ this style because of the time commitment necessary to invest in each employee's development. The benefits of this approach include a positive group climate and an increased feeling of worth within individuals.

Despite the benefits, many in business are just not familiar with how to help people identify and improve upon their weaknesses. In fact, for the coaching style to work the leader needs to be competent enough in the areas in which they are coaching employees, and the employees need to be open to hearing constructive criticism and trying new ways to improve their weak areas. When leaders are not familiar with what they are coaching, their credibility evaporates quickly, just as it is impossible to coach the "uncoachable," or people who are not aware of, and unwilling to work on, their deficiencies.

Leadership Responsibilities

Leaders exhibit common responsibilities regardless of which style they employ in a given situation. These serve to illustrate the communication skills necessary for good leadership, whether it be democratic, coercive, or anything in between. In this section of the chapter, we will examine eight communication behaviors that serve as the foundation of leadership in many different groups and organizations.

Affiliative	Democratic	Pacesetting	Coaching
Creates harmony and builds emotional bonds	Forges consensus through participation	Sets high standards for performance	Develops people for the future
"People come first."	"What do you think?"	"Do as I do, now."	"Try this."
To heal rifts in a team or to motivate people during stressful circumstances	To build buy-in or consensus, or to get input from valuable employees	To get quick results from a highly motivated and competent team	To help an employee improve performance or develop long-term strengths
Positive	Positive	Negative	Positive

Leaders must remain well informed. Leaders are usually given information about the task and the backgrounds of group members. They are also aware of any work being done outside of the group that may impact or be impacted by their own group's work. If leaders are not knowledgeable about the task, issues, or people with whom they work, then they seek out that information. In short, leaders know more than group members.

The Pressure of Unethical Leadership

Wells Fargo, one of the largest banks in the United States, has had to answer for some very unethical and often illegal practices in recent years. They created over one million fraudulent accounts and another half million fake credit card accounts, resulting in fees being charged to people who did not know they had these accounts. Why? Because of a management push to increase revenue. When money is the goal, and people are pressured to hit certain targets, it can stretch their ethical commitments. Wells Fargo now owes billions in fines to the US government. Where in this story is the failure of leadership? How does the approach management can take trickle down to employees? What impact does unethical leadership have on morale and performance within an organization?

Leaders provide direction and structure to their group. One of the primary responsibilities of leaders is to establish the work structure for group members and assign each person his or her responsibilities. How they choose to do this is a matter of style and situational demands, but leaders must make both the structure and specific assignments clear to the group to avoid confusion.

Leaders must be flexible to the demands of the situation. Despite laying out a clear structure and delivering directions to group members, the group might need to change its approach when presented with new information or factors. Leaders must be flexible to the demands of their group and adjust as needed.

Leaders must be able to manage complex situations. The larger the group or more involved the task, the more complexity for a leader to manage. Leaders need to keep track of what is expected and being accomplished by the group, as well as how that will impact other elements not within the group.

Leaders must recognize the strengths and weaknesses of group members. One of the primary characteristics of a leader is his or her ability to recognize the skills and abilities of those in his or her group. Knowing what people can do, and what they cannot, allows leaders to place their group in the best position possible to accomplish their tasks and achieve their goals. This is also something that may invite some conflict within a group when members do not appreciate or agree with a leader's assessments.

Leaders promote group cohesiveness. Not every responsibility of the leader relates to the group task; some responsibilities also concern the maintenance of a positive communication climate and strong relationships between group members. Leaders need to stay tuned in to the atmosphere of the group and determine when to engage in activities that can help people release stress or reengage with the group's mission and identity. These non-task related functions are just as important as anything else a leader must do.

Leaders manage conflict amongst group members. A fundamental responsibility of all leaders is to adjudicate and resolve conflict between group members whenever it arises.

Leadership in a democracy depends upon the articulation of a shared goal or set of goals, and a shared willingness to make both sacrifices and compromises in pursuit of that goal or set of goals. Leadership, then, isn't something leaders do to others; it is something leaders do with others.

—Mary Stuckey, Georgia State University

Group members look to leaders to be fair, impartial, and responsible for handling disputes in a way that all parties continue to feel comfortable working with each other. Conflict management serves both task and relational purposes for the group because when individuals are fighting, they are not working to achieve the group's goal, and they also create a negative experience for everyone else. Leaders must help resolve these situations.

Leaders consider multiple perspectives. Group members have the benefit of stating their opinions, positions, and critiques whenever they wish to. Leaders, on the other hand, take all of those statements and consider them before attempting to make a decision or weighing in with the group. Even autocratic leaders make decisions by taking input from a variety of sources and perspectives, but they are the only people with decision-making authority.

Leaders are responsible for a great many things; they are not just the decision makers. Each of the eight responsibilities we discussed necessarily involve good communication skills, because without the ability to effectively communicate with the group and outside parties, then groups deteriorate and goals are not achieved. Leadership is challenging work, and both becoming and maintaining the position as leader of a group requires the ability to skillfully interact with others.

Leaders Encourage Cohesion and Communication

There are few better examples in film and television of an emergent leader than the 1957 classic film, *12 Angry Men,* starring Henry Fonda as a man who argues for reasonable doubt with his fellow jurors in what appears initially to be a surefire guilty verdict. Fonda's character, Juror 8, is not the foreman nor is he the smartest or strongest person in the room, but through encouraging others to examine evidence in a critical manner he eventually convinces them to let go of their own biases and think critically about the case. Fonda uses dialogic techniques such as asking questions aimed at understanding, not agreement, to overcome individuals who do not care about the case and simply want to leave, who are enacting their own personal biases on the defendant, and who do not wish to abandon their own initial verdicts. As the story unfolds, he moves from the lone holdout juror to the spokesperson and leader of those who see reasonable doubt in the case against the defendant. Such emergent leadership would not have been possible without his strong communication skills and calm demeanor.

LEADERSHIP AND DIALOGUE

Given the numerous responsibilities, group member personalities, and pressures that come with the position, it should come as no surprise that dialogue skills are paramount in succeeding when leading a group. In this section of the chapter, we will detail seven suggestions for effectively employing dialogue in a leadership position.

Openly Talk Through Group Processes

One of the greatest pitfalls facing leaders occurs when leaders do not discuss or detail the processes that will govern group meetings, assignments, and other functions. To be an effective leader, regardless of which style you employ, it is important that members of the group understand such things as how decisions will be made, how meetings will be managed, and how other assignments are determined. Understanding does not mean simply laying out this information, but also allowing group members a chance to ask questions and provide feedback that may improve how the group functions. Open dialogue that results in a group understanding of rules and procedures will reduce the likelihood of missteps and conflict in the future.

Encourage Alternatives, Suggestions, and Questions

Simply providing an opportunity for feedback is not enough to facilitate dialogue between group members. Effective leaders find ways to encourage participation by group members either during a group meeting or privately afterwards. It also is essential to encourage disagreement so there is a critical analysis of ideas and suggestions that hopefully results in a better decision. Leaders must take initiative in promoting participation in discussions and assignments, sometimes by directly asking individuals for specific thoughts.

Divide the Task into Manageable Units

Groups convene to confront complex issues, and any group member can feel overwhelmed by the task's complexity. To help mitigate this confusion and stress, good leaders break down the goal and task into manageable units for group members so they see the steps that need to be taken to achieve success. Leaders can turn complex tasks into simple steps, thus reducing the tension group members may feel by focusing on a large, complex task.

Continually Communicate

Even when there is information you cannot share with the group, let them know that you cannot share it instead of hiding the fact you know it. Additionally, and most importantly, maintain open lines of communication throughout the life of the group. Give opportunities for feedback, share developments that may affect the group, and give status updates about any subgroups to each member. In doing these things, good leaders must also be accessible themselves, as well as responsive. It is both respectful and a good practice for leaders to respond in a reasonably quick time frame when members make inquiries. What is challenging is knowing the most effective way to communicate information. Some messages should be delivered face to face, while other information can be relegated to email or even a text message.

Don't Let Emotions Get the Better of You

Make no mistake, being a leader does not make you more or less human. You will have emotional reactions to statements and events, but these reactions must not govern your decisions or impact the way you interact with group members. It is important to stay consistently calm when interacting with others, despite any emotions you may feel inside. This is especially true of anger and frustration, but also applies to excitement and joy. Too much of an emotional display can be read the wrong way by group members and thus may create false perceptions for those who work with you in the group. Group leaders should be stable and consistent, the rock upon which the group is built, even when they might want to erupt with emotion. Remember that emotional displays can create a defensive communication climate and are therefore inconsistent with dialogic principles.

Provide an Agenda Before Group Meetings

The next guideline for leaders who wish to effectively encourage dialogue is to provide a clear agenda in advance of any group meeting. The agenda does a number of positive things for the leader and the group. First, it demonstrates that someone is tracking where the group is headed. Second, it provides direction and structure for group members and group activities. Agendas also help focus dialogue by setting out topic areas the group will engage. This can help reduce the chances of the meeting being hijacked or going off on an unrelated tangent. There are numerous ways to construct an agenda, but they all list the order of events and topics the group will cover during the meeting, what materials are needed for the meeting, and who is expected to lead discussions on what during the gathering. This focus maximizes the time spent together and helps the leader manage the group.

Take Minutes at Every Meeting

The final guideline we will suggest for leading groups is making sure someone takes clear and detailed minutes of the meeting and that this record is kept for as long as the group works together. Minutes allow for an accurate record of who attended meetings, what was covered, how topics were discussed, what decisions were made, and who is responsible for doing what. Meeting minutes can go a long way toward solving disputes between group members by allowing people a record to examine when disagreements over decisions or assignments come up. It also promotes honesty and good behavior in colleagues when they know that what they say is being recorded. After the meeting, send the minutes to all group members so that everybody has a record of what happened at the meeting and a clear list of action items with deadlines by which they should be completed.

Tips for Successful Online Meetings

Because group members cannot always see or hear everyone who is part of a remote meeting, meetings that are held via conference call or using a web conferencing program (such as Webex or GoToMeeting) benefit from setting some additional guidelines for participation. Here are a few tips for conducting successful online meetings:

1. **Prepare your team members.** Send out an agenda and call-in information well in advance of the meeting, and include that information again in a reminder email the day before the meeting. If you plan to use PowerPoint slides during your meeting, you might also want to consider sharing your slides with your team in advance.

2. **Prepare your space.** For video conferences, you should make sure that everything that other members will see in the video will be appropriate for a professional setting. Laundry, dirty dishes, and inappropriate posters should not appear in your video frame. Additionally, you should make sure that you have a quiet space from which to join the meeting that is free of distracting background noise.

3. **Test your technology.** Well before the meeting begins, make sure that you have the appropriate software updates installed on your computer. Test your microphone, video camera, and audio to make sure that everything works properly. This is also a good time to make sure that you know how to mute your microphone. When possible, use a headset with a microphone to ensure clear audio signals and to reduce audio feedback.

4. **Establish group processes up front.** If it is the first time that your group has met online, take a few minutes to orient the group to the meeting program at the beginning of your meeting. Establish guidelines for asking questions, providing feedback, and turn-taking during the meeting. For instance, group members might be able to type in a chat box, use emoticons or a hand-raising function, or might need to verbally interject in the conversation. Remind everyone to mute their microphones when they are not speaking to help minimize background noise. When you do start speaking, unmute your microphone and announce your name before sharing your comments so that everyone knows who is speaking.

SUMMARY

Groups do not function without a leadership structure, and the success of the leadership structure depends largely on the leader's communication skills. In this chapter, we explored the power dimension of leadership, and examined the three primary ways through which groups choose their leaders. We also described the dimensions of the six major leadership styles, emphasizing that not all are appropriate all the time. We then briefly discussed some of the responsibilities that fall to leaders and provided seven guidelines for leaders to effectively employ dialogue in groups.

CHAPTER 19 KEY IDEAS

- Leaders can be elected or appointed, or they may emerge.

- The five bases of power include reward power, referent power, coercive power, legitimate power, and expert power.

- The six leadership styles that were discussed are coercive, authoritative, affiliative, democratic, pacesetting, and coaching.

- Leaders have numerous responsibilities within the group.

CHAPTER 19 KEY TERMS

Reward power	Authoritative leadership style
Referent power	Affiliative leadership style
Coercive power	Democratic leadership style
Legitimate power	Pacesetting leadership style
Expert power	Coaching leadership style
Coercive leadership style	

ACTIVITIES AND DISCUSSION QUESTIONS

1. Watch General Stanley McChrystal's TED talk, "Listen, Learn . . . Then Lead," available online at https://www.ted.com/talks/stanley_mcchrystal. Which leadership style best describes the approach he discusses in his presentation? In what types of situations is this the most useful leadership style? Are there any situations in which this might not be an effective leadership style?

2. Choose one of the five types of power and identify someone (an actual person) who you believe holds that type of power. Describe why you think they have that kind of power and how they use it.

3. Are there some types of power that tend to be used most often with each leadership style? Why or why not?

4. Which leadership style do you think you normally use when you are in a leadership role? What are the strengths and weaknesses of this leadership style? Which is it most likely to be effective? In what types of situations is it most likely to be unsuccessful?

INTERVIEWING

Of all the communication situations you will experience during your life, none combines more of the elements of public speaking, interpersonal communication, small group dynamics, and listening than interviewing. There are many different forms and several different types of interviews. Journalists interview witnesses and experts to gather information for a story, and potential clients may interview several different service providers before selecting someone to work with, but the most common interviews occur in the workplace. These can be for prospective employees, or even current employees who are going through a performance review. Interviews are important events in all of our lives.

Interviews are also an opportunity to demonstrate good communication skills. In 2016, a survey by the National Association of Colleges and Employers found that applicants' abilities to lead, work in a team, problem-solve, communicate orally and in writing, adapt to situations, and develop interpersonal relationships are some of the most important abilities to potential employers.[1] All of these can be demonstrated through a strong and successful interview, which will increase the likelihood you will be selected for the position. This is because interviews are goal-oriented communication events where both sides use question-and-answer techniques to

INTERVIEWS
goal-oriented communication events where both sides use question-and-answer techniques to achieve their ends

achieve their ends. They are, for all intents and purposes, the epitome of interactional communication where both parties are senders and receivers simultaneously throughout the engagement.

In this chapter, we examine interviewing and, although we will begin by defining the types of interviews you might encounter throughout your career, we pay particular attention to employment interviews. After defining the interview types, we will explain how an employment interview could take place through a variety of media. We will then explore the structure of an interview and the types of questions you will likely encounter when seeking a position. Finally, we will offer some guidelines for effectively employing dialogue in an employment interview to maximize your ability to succeed in getting a job offer.

Equal Opportunity Adherence in Interviews

The interview process must be an even playing field for all potential applicants. To that end there are certain questions employers cannot ask applicants at any stage of the hiring process. They cannot even find creative ways to try to obtain the information, either. There are laws interviewers must follow in an attempt to ensure the integrity of the selection process and to prevent discrimination. Unfortunately, not all interviewers adhere to these regulations and so it is important to know what can and cannot be asked in an interview. For instance, you cannot be asked about your religion, race, sexual preference, age, familial status, or citizenship status. Some examples of illegal interview questions are:

"How do you plan to handle child care while working?"

"Will you require days off for religious reasons?"

"Are you an American citizen?"

"Do you have any problems working for a female boss?"

For a complete understanding of the rules regulating the questions in an interview, see the website of the United States Equal Employment Opportunity Commission (EEOC).[2]

INTERVIEW TYPES AND FORMATS

Interviews come in all shapes and forms, and you will find yourself in any one of them at some point in your life. All interviews are goal oriented, but they have different goals for each party. For example, journalists conduct interviews to gather information for stories, while job seekers go on interviews in the hope of getting a position with a company. Additionally, interviews occur in several formats, even through different media. It used to be that all interviews were face-to-face; however, thanks to programs like Skype, interviews can now happen digitally over long distances. Interviews also do not always imply one person interviewing another—today the number of people in the room has even changed! In this section of the chapter, we will describe six types of interviews and five formats for conducting them.

Types of Interviews

Interviews are labeled and defined by the goals the particular interaction seeks to achieve. Regardless of what type of interview takes place, both parties are aware that they are in an interview situation.

Information-gathering interviews. This interview is commonly practiced by journalists, but managers and researchers also conduct these from time to time. Information-gathering interviews seek to discover facts, information, and other knowledge about a particular topic from peers, experts, witnesses, or others who may be knowledgeable about it.

Helping interviews. These interviews occur most often with counselors, psychologists, psychiatrists, and other healthcare providers. When you consult an expert in other areas, such as construction, they also are participating in a helping interview. Helping interviews take stock of a problem or challenge faced by an individual and offer informed and expert advice on how to handle it.

Problem-solving interviews. There are times when conflicts or issues arise within a company or organization that require investigation. These investigations include interviews designed to gather information but do so specifically to identify a problem's source and a solution to it. Problem-solving interviews thus operate as a form of very specific information gathering coupled with an emphasis on solving a particular problem.

Performance interviews. In most organizations, employees undergo an annual or semi-annual review of their achievements, contributions, and behavior. Often, these reviews, also called performance interviews, provide employers and managers with information used to determine raises, as well as target areas of improvement for staff. These interviews are official and are added to the personnel file of an employee. As it is an interview, the employee always has a chance to add or comment on points raised by her or his supervisor, thus negotiating the meaning of the performance period.

INFORMATION-GATHERING INTERVIEWS
a type of interview that seeks to discover facts, information, and other knowledge about a particular topic from peers, experts, witnesses, or others who may be knowledgeable about it

HELPING INTERVIEWS
a type of interview that takes stock of a problem or challenge faced by an individual and offers informed and expert advice on how to handle it

PROBLEM-SOLVING INTERVIEWS
a form of very specific information gathering coupled with an emphasis on solving a specific problem

PERFORMANCE INTERVIEWS
a type of interview that provides employers and managers with information used to determine raises, as well as target areas of improvement for staff; also called performance reviews

**EXIT
INTERVIEWS**

a type of interview
conducted by human
resources professionals
with outgoing
employees designed
to gather information
about the processes
and climate of the
organization in an
attempt to use that
information in the
future to improve

**EMPLOYMENT
INTERVIEWS**

a type of interview
in which employers
conduct conversations
with applicants for
open positions in an
effort to determine
to whom they would
like to offer a position;
the interviewees seek
information about
the company that will
influence their decision
to accept an offer,
should one come

Exit interviews. A typical practice of employers is to conduct interviews with employees who either resign or are dismissed. These interviews are conducted by human resources professionals and are designed to gather information about the processes and climate of the organization in an attempt to use that information to improve in the future. The effectiveness of exit interviews depends on the candid nature of the outgoing employee and the practical information they provide in the discussion.

Employment interviews. When people speak of having an interview, they typically are referring to an employment interview, where employers conduct conversations with applicants for open positions in an effort to determine to whom they would like to offer a position. Additionally, the interviewees seek information about the company that will influence their decision to accept an offer, should one come. Employment interviews come in several different forms, but all typically follow the same pattern and require that applicants do their homework on the company before sitting down for the interview.

Interview Formats

Thanks to today's mediated environment, interviews now take place in several different ways. In fact, you might interview for the same position several different times, each through a different medium, before receiving a job offer. Usually, but not always, interviews occur between one job candidate and anywhere from one to several members of the company. In this section of the chapter, we will discuss five different interview formats you may encounter when searching for a job.

Email interviews. In the initial stages of the job process, prospective employers may send you questions via email. Normally, these questions would only go out to people who meet the minimum qualifications for the position. The questions during this stage typically ask you to expound upon aspects of your resume or fill in other pertinent information the employer may need to further refine the applicant pool.

Phone interviews. More common to the interview process is the phone interview, where the employer arranges a time to call the job candidates with whom they wish to speak. These calls range in length, but you typically will have a day or so to prepare. It is important to make sure you know who is on the other end of the phone when interviewing through this medium, and so beginning the conversations with introductions is a good idea. Usually, the candidates chosen for a phone interview represent a "semi-finalist" approach, and some companies use these conversations to finalize their list of candidates for in-person interviews. During these interactions, employers seek to determine something about the candidate's personality, goals, and knowledge about the company.

Skype interviews. Another advancement in technology allows company representatives to interview job candidates face to face without having to bring candidates to the company's location. Digital programs such as Skype allow these conversations to happen, and they are both inexpensive and useful because you can see nonverbal reactions to questions by both parties. In some cases, Skype interviews are used instead of flying someone in because they can save substantial amounts of money; but, at other times, Skype interviews are used to see how a candidate communicates and works in a mediated environment because increasing numbers of workers are telecommuting from home offices instead of living near and working in a centrally located corporate office. Sometimes, Skype interviews are conducted in addition to phone interviews, but other times they can take the place of either the phone interview or the in-person interview.

Island interviews. A somewhat rare form of interview is the island interview, where prospective candidates are placed in a room together and asked to discuss why they believe they are the better fit for the position than the other candidates present. This type of interview format is more likely to occur when applying for graduate school, but it does happen in other professional areas from time to time. The prospective school or company watches the interaction to determine whom to select.

In-person interviews. The most common interview is the in-person interview, where finalists meet with members of the hiring committee or human resources staff. In-person interviews are often the final step in the process, but it is possible that you would have more than one in-person interview before a job offer is made. These interviews range in length from industry to industry, and could be as short as thirty minutes or as long as a full day (or even two in some cases!). Even though these interviews are conversations, the employer usually scores answers afterward to help determine to whom to offer the position. In-person interviews also occur in many different places, although most commonly they will take place where the candidate would work. Sometimes, though, they are conducted in restaurants, coffee shops, airports, and even homes.

ISLAND INTERVIEW
a type of interview in which prospective candidates are placed in a room together and asked to discuss why they believe they are the better fit for the position

INTERVIEW PROCESS

One of the advantages to employment interviews is that everyone typically knows what to expect. Most interviews follow a similar structure, though there might be slight variations. What is important to understand, however, is that in every case, the interview process begins well before you talk with the employer. First impressions are made through resumes and cover letters, although they can be enhanced or reduced based on the first face-to-face or phone interview. In this section of the chapter, we will go through the various stages of the interview process, thus explaining the structure you should expect during most job interviews.

Getting an Interview

The interview process begins with identifying the positions for which you wish to apply. This might sound easy, but examining job postings and determining your fit for these posts takes work. We will detail a few of the steps for positioning yourself well in the hopes of increasing the chances of receiving a formal interview.

Resume Dos and Don'ts

Do:

Proofread and edit your resume several times before submitting it. Potential employers will see you as lacking attention to detail if the main document representing you is not produced with care.

Use a variety of action words when describing past experiences. Words like directed, expedited, accelerated, and delivered help describe what you've accomplished and get the reader excited to know more about your potential contributions to their organization.

Quantify your impacts in previous positions, if possible. Potential employers like to know in concrete ways how you might make your mark on their company. If you can offer precise figures of how you, for example, increased sales or decreased waste, you will make a stronger case.

Don't:

Use the same resume for every position. Tailor your resume for each job you apply for.

Lie on your resume. If a lie is discovered, it could be grounds for termination. Honesty is the best policy!

Offer personal information on the resume. Potential employers cannot use information such as your marital status or non-work related affiliations to decide your employment, so leave such information off your resume.

Make sure you fit the minimum qualifications. Many applicants are removed from the pool because they do not meet the minimum requirements for the position. If the job asks for certain certifications or a number of years of experience, make sure you can reasonably make the case that you have those things. If you don't, you are wasting your time and theirs.

Determine any preferred qualifications you fit. In addition to minimum qualifications, many job descriptions contain preferred qualifications. You may still be a viable candidate without having these desired qualities, but having them will elevate your application. Make sure you find a way to highlight these for the employer.

Line up your references. Most employers today do not call references until they are ready to extend an offer; nevertheless, make sure you have spoken with the people you plan to use as references. This is both civil and professional. On a practical level, it also ensures those people will be available to field the call should it come.

Prepare your resume. All positions require a resume with a job application. Make sure yours is prepared, in a legible font and format, and contains an accurate representation of what you have done. Additionally, it is not a bad idea to bold words in the resume that match those in the job advertisement because this helps the reviewer see how you fit the position. Remember, though, that you should edit and adapt certain elements of your resume, like the lists of responsibilities and accomplishments, to the specific job for which you are applying. Don't just send the same resume everywhere—adapt it to your audience.

Write a strong cover letter. Many, but not all, positions ask for a cover letter to accompany the resume. When writing the cover letter, try to find out to whom you should address it. In the letter, do not simply detail your resume, but instead take the opportunity to elaborate on your accomplishments and explain how they fit the specific job qualifications. This is your first and most important opportunity to make an argument for why you should be considered for the position.

The Opening

The interview process continues to unfold when you are invited in to speak with representatives from the company. Not only should you arrive early for the meeting, but you should also dress appropriately. When your time arrives, the opening is your first real opportunity to make a lasting impression on the employer. Your resume gets you in the door, but your opening captures their attention and interest.

Shake hands with everyone. Although this may seem simple and possibly unnecessary, it is important to shake hands with everyone in the room before sitting down to begin the conversation. This is a sign of respect and acknowledgment, and it goes a long way toward

Falsifying Employment History

After the recession forced the closure of auto plants in Ohio in 2009, friends of one co-worker asked if he would serve as a reference for them and lie about their work history for them. Thus began the company CareerExcuse, which provides subscribers with phony companies and references for the resume.[3] The falsehoods his company purveys have been almost undetectable, and in 2013 he reported that 90% of his clients obtained jobs within 90 days. This points to a glaring weakness in today's employment arena. Despite the fact the company is illegal, it clearly is also unethical. What are some measures that can be put in place to potentially prevent this type of action being successful? Are there ways that laws should prohibit such unethical behaviors? Is this type of action a "victimless crime"?

establishing a friendly and comfortable environment. When shaking hands, remember to look the person in the eyes and use a firm handshake.

Establish a rapport with the interviewer(s). Rapport is something that should build throughout the interview, but the process of doing so begins at the start of the meeting. Good rapport is friendly and conversational. Some things that might help would be comments on the office or meeting area, compliments about the staff you have met, references to some current events related to the company, and even asking questions about the person's day. Additionally, it can be helpful to also thank the interviewer(s) for their time and recognize that their jobs are quite busy.

Introduce yourself. A common mistake during the opening is to not remember to state your name and what you prefer to be called. Some people in the room may not be familiar with you and might be meeting you for the first time, so it is always good practice to provide your name for everyone, and this can be done when shaking hands. In some cases, the people meeting with you may not have conducted the phone interview or even reviewed your resume in depth, so making sure they know your name, and how to pronounce it, is important.

The Body of the Interview

After introductions are made and rapport established, the core of the interview begins. This is when the most important work of your interview takes place. The body of the interview is the majority of the time you will spend with the prospective employer, and it functions largely as a question and answer session. In this part of the chapter, we will detail some of the types of questions you may encounter when being interviewed.

Closed-ended questions. During the initial stages of the interview process, you may be asked to answer some questions that do not require explanation. These types of questions often also have defined answers from which you will choose the best fit. These closed-ended questions are typically used to collect anonymous data about the characteristics of the pool of applicants.

CLOSED-ENDED QUESTIONS

questions that have defined answers from which you will choose the best fit

OPEN-ENDED QUESTIONS

questions that ask you to craft your best answer to the inquiry

Open-ended questions. The most common form of question in an interview is one that requires you to explain and describe your answer in detail. Open-ended questions do not provide possible answers, but rather ask you to craft your best answer to the inquiry. The remaining types of questions we will cover all fall under the category of open-ended questions.

The "tell me about yourself" question. This is often the first question asked during an in-person interview and represents the transition from the opening to the body of the interview. The question is far more complicated than it might seem because many interviewees make the mistake of providing information about their family or re-hashing their resume. In fact, employers simply want to know about your interest areas and work experiences, and how they relate to the job. Additionally, they want you to use this answer to demonstrate how familiar you are with the company and its mission. The unsaid part of this question is " . . . and how you fit this position with this company."

Resume questions. During the interview, the employer will explore your resume and will likely ask you to expand on one or two experiences you listed. Be prepared to discuss your responsibilities and accomplishments with a degree of detail that adds to the resume and doesn't simply reiterate what is on the page. If there are gaps in your resume or if you are entering a brand new field, be prepared to explain those aspects of your history.

Situational questions. Employers will ask questions designed to get you to explain how you would behave in certain situations to determine your fit for the position. Situational questions focus on what you would do if confronted with a specific set of circumstances, and the interviewer gives you the opportunity to lay out a clear approach to handling it that demonstrates your skill sets. The key is to provide as clear and detailed a response as you can to this type of question. Here are a few examples of potential situational questions.

> "How would you handle a dispute with a colleague?"

> "How would you repair a relationship with a disgruntled client?"

Behavioral questions. Whereas situational questions focus on the future, behavioral questions ask you to delve into your past experiences. There are a few principles behind this form of questioning, which is becoming more and more prevalent in the interview process. First, the idea is that to effectively answer the question, the respondent must have actually had the experience they describe because making up an answer to a behavioral question on the spot would be easy to detect. Secondly, and perhaps even more importantly to the employer, the idea is that if you behaved this way in the past, it is likely you would repeat the same behavior in similar circumstances in the future. Like situational questions, behavioral questions require details in the answer tantamount to telling a story. Additionally, oftentimes these questions ask you to talk about times when you encountered difficulty or failed at doing something. Employers want answers that focus on honesty and the ability to learn a lesson from an experience, so if you failed then say so, but follow it up with a description of what you took away from the experience so that your answer is ultimately a positive one. Here are a few examples of behavioral questions, and as you can see, they focus on the past, not the future.

> "Tell me about a time you disagreed with your boss."

> "Describe a situation where you needed to persuade someone to accept your point of view or convince them to change something."

Follow-up questions. During the course of the interview, you may provide an answer that interests the employer, and so interviewers may continue to ask you about that answer in the hopes of obtaining more detail. These follow-up questions are extremely common, especially during your answers to a behavioral question. Employers know if you get interrupted and are then asked for more detail, you will not be able to provide it if you are not telling the truth, but if you are telling the truth, these details would be easily recounted. Follow-up questions are often a sign of interest by the employer, but they are also an opportunity to correct or expound upon things you have said.

The Closing

Once the employer finishes her or his questions, the closing of the interview begins. There are a few things to keep in mind during this stage of the process because you want to make sure you leave the employer with a positive impression. This may very well be your last chance to make a strong impression in person, so be sure to make every effort to be prepared to close well.

Have questions of your own prepared. At this point, the interviewers will ask you if you have any questions, and there are a few things to remember when this opportunity arises. First, always have a few questions ready, even if you think you know the answer, because this shows interest in the company. Not asking questions makes it seem like you are not very interested in working for the company and are only looking to secure a paycheck. Second, do not tell them "you have already answered my questions," because this comes across as not having prepared any questions and thus demonstrating a lack of interest. This is also not the time to ask about salary. If the company brings up the issue of salary, then that is fine, but do not ask them first about compensation. Finally, don't ask questions that could easily be answered by looking at the company website, as this will show that you did not prepare well for the interview. It is a good idea, however, to mention something you saw on the website and ask for greater detail or clarification. Here are some good general questions that can help you in the event you don't have any specific queries about the company.

Choose your self-presentations carefully, for what starts out as your mask may become your face.

—Erving Goffman, *The Presentation of Self in Everyday Life*

"How would you describe the culture here?"

"What is a typical day for a person in this position?"

"Why did you join this company?"

"What are some of the greatest challenges and opportunities working here?"

"What is your timeline for making a decision?"

Re-establish rapport. Just as you need to establish rapport in the opening, you need to re-establish rapport in the closing to remind them of the fact you had a good experience with them and they with you. Say one or two complimentary statements about the interviewers and the company, and refer to something that occurred during the interview. You also could consider reiterating your interest in the position and company, and tying it to things you heard in the interview itself.

Shake hands with everyone. Shaking hands is not just reserved for the opening. It is just as important to conclude the interview by shaking everyone's hands and thanking them for spending their time with you during a busy time. Additionally, express to them that you enjoyed the conversation and look forward to hearing from them soon. Much like the opening hand-shake, make sure you say their names and maintain eye contact when shaking hands.

World's Best Boss

In the seventh season finale of the American hit sitcom *The Office,* the CEO of Dunder Mifflin-Sabre forms a search committee to identify a replacement for the branch manager position vacated by Steve Carell's character, Michael Scott. The episode features a parade of guest stars taking turns at making major interviewing mistakes. For example, Darryl (Craig Robinson) believes he is a sure choice for the position and is surprised when told he needs a resume and has to interview. He quickly prepares an elaborate but unsuccessful four-page resume. Nellie Bertram (Catherine Tate) also proposes eliminating office titles and creating a Zen garden for the Scranton location of Dunder Mifflin-Sabre, much to the confusion of the search committee. Robert California (James Spader), derides the company and the position to office staff before entering his interview. There are more examples, and each highlights a major interview mistake.

Following Up after the Interview

The interview process does not end when you leave the in-person interview. An important part of the process is to follow up after the interview. There are several ways you can do this, but the most effective is a "thank you" note. The thank you note is a brief statement you can send through email or postal mail that restates your gratitude for the time spent at the in-person interview, reinforces your interest in the position, recounts something you learned from the interview that makes the position attractive, and provides your contact information one more time. Thank you notes are an effective means of following up on an interview, but they should not be ornate or elaborate.

In some circumstances, it may be possible, and even worthwhile, to follow up with a phone call. When doing so, know exactly who you are calling and why. Additionally, if the person does not answer, simply leave a message about why you called and your contact information. The important thing to understand about follow-up phone calls is that you should only do them once; do not keep calling until someone answers. This can be rude and even come across as desperate—not an impression you want to leave with the prospective employer.

USING DIALOGUE EFFECTIVELY IN AN INTERVIEW

An employment interview is nothing more than a dialogue between two parties regarding a job position. Both sides seek to understand each other's expectations and needs, and they do so through the civil exchange of questions and answers. Although it is a positive outcome when each side agrees they are a good fit at the end of the interview, it is equally as positive when they understand why they were not a good fit. That said, interviews can be stressful for job candidates, and so engaging in dialogue can become difficult. In this final section of the chapter, we will provide seven tips for engaging in an effective dialogue during an interview.

Do Your Homework

Much of dialogue depends upon showing respect for the other party and demonstrating genuine interest in his or her position. One way to make this happen during an interview is to research the company and the position before arriving at the interview. This will allow you to adapt your answers to your audience, as well as determine the areas about which you want further information. Coming in prepared with knowledge about the company and job shows an interest in the company and demonstrates a respect for them that goes a long way toward creating a relaxed and supportive communication climate during your interview.

Be Your Professional Self

During the interview do not try to pretend to be someone you are not. This attempt will be noticed, and you will either not get the position or, if you do, you will likely not be happy at the company because you pretended to have different qualities, interests, and values just to get the position. Instead, be yourself and don't try to tell the interviewer what you think they want to hear. Interviewers want to hear honesty, so be honest. Just because you are yourself, however, does not mean you are among friends or can relax your professional attitude, demeanor, or language. Remain respectful and courteous throughout the interview, but do not be insincere or try to anticipate answers you think the company expects.

Use Names When Speaking to Others

Many people hear a name at the introduction stage of the interview and promptly forget it or disregard it. Don't make this mistake. When answering questions from someone, make sure you say his or her name every once in a while. It is not necessary to do so during every answer, but referencing someone's name is a sign of respect and also lets them know you truly listened at the introduction. One way to remember names is to jot them down after introductions so you can refer to your notes.

Understand the Question Being Asked

Sometimes, especially when there is more than one person conducting the interview, the questions can get confusing. There is nothing wrong with rephrasing the question back to the interviewer to make sure you know what they are asking. You can also ask interviewers to repeat the question if you feel you missed something. It is impossible to do well in an interview if you do not answer the question being asked, so it is essential that you ask for clarification if you are unclear about something.

Ensure Answers Connect to Question and Claims

Once you understand the question, be prepared to deliver an answer that you can substantiate with data or stories from your own experiences. People appreciate direct claim-data-warrant answers that provide a supported claim that you then connect to the qualities necessary for the job or why you feel that particular story reflects values consistent with your worldview and work ethic. In short, don't just tell a story, but have a point to it that employers would want to hear.

Take Notes

You will not be able to remember everything people say during the interview, so it is important to jot down a few notes you believe are important. It is also a good idea to write down the names of those who interview you in case they forget to give you business cards. As the interview progresses, the employer may reveal some things that spark questions, and by taking notes you can ensure you ask those questions when your opportunity to do so arrives. Taking notes also helps prevent you from cutting people off and illustrates to employers you are paying attention to what is going on.

Don't Interrupt Anyone

When we converse with friends and family, we sometimes like to finish sentences for other people or even cut them off to make a point or ask a question. This tendency only magnifies during an interview when we get excited about things we are being told. However, interrupting interviewers and finishing sentences for them is not a good idea and can ultimately create a negative impression of you. Let the interview follow its format and wait to ask questions until the interviewers are done speaking.

SUMMARY

An interview is one of the most common, challenging, and rewarding communication contexts. In this chapter, we differentiated between different types of interviews and the various formats in which they occur. We also explored the interview process, paying particular attention to the types of questions you are likely to encounter when on an employment interview. Finally, we discussed how specific dialogic behaviors can help you create an atmosphere more conducive to success when interviewing.

CHAPTER 20 KEY IDEAS

* There are six different types of interviews: (1) information gathering interviews, (2) helping interviews, (3) problem-solving interviews, (4) performance interviews, (5) exit interviews, and (6) employment interviews.

* Interviews might take place via email, phone, Skype, in a group "island" format, or in person.

* Interviews have an opening, a body, and a closing.

CHAPTER 20 KEY TERMS

Interviews	Exit interviews
Information-gathering interviews	Employment interviews
Helping interviews	Island interview
Problem-solving interviews	Closed-ended questions
Performance interviews	Open-ended questions

ACTIVITIES AND DISCUSSION QUESTIONS

1. Watch Anna Post's TED-Ed talk, "Put Those Smartphones Away: Great Tips for Making Your Job Interview Count," available online at https://blog.ed.ted.com/2013/05/24/how-to-nail-a-job-interview/. Which of these recommendations, if any, surprised you the most? How can you apply these suggestions in your next interview?

2. Many interviews begin with some variation of "Tell me about yourself." This is generally an invitation to give your 30–90 second "elevator speech" summing up what you think the employer should know about you, your skills, your goals, and why you believe that you are a good fit for the position. If you were asked this question in a job interview next week, what would you answer be?

3. Imagine that you are the employer and are interviewing someone for the career that you intend to pursue. What is that career? What interview questions would you ask? Write out all of the questions in the order that you would ask them during the interview.

4. Now imagine that you are the interviewee and are interviewing for your dream job. What are some questions that you would ask your potential employer when asked, "What questions do you have for us?"

GLOSSARY

Abstract
the idea that language is not tangible or concrete

Accenting
the function of nonverbal communication whereby nonverbal behaviors augment a message while it is delivered

Accommodating
a management style defined by a person giving in to the desires and position of the other person, thereby sacrificing their own position and desires

Active listening
listening with a high degree of attention to a message; we process, store, and potentially evaluate the content of the message to come to conclusions or an understanding about what was said

Active strategy
engaging in activities to learn more about the other person while avoiding direct contact with him or her

Ad hominem attack
speaker tries to equate the quality of someone's argument with the quality of his or her character by calling him or her something that would be perceived as negative by the audience

Ad verecundiam
an appeal to authority

Advising
the practice of interrupting a person to offer suggestions and opinions in an effort to be helpful even when they were not sought

Affiliative leadership style
flexible and encouraging, allowing group members to take risks and work on their own to engender trust; a "people-person" leadership style

Agreeable
remaining open to the idea that you might agree with the other person

Alliteration
the practice of using the same vowel or consonant sound at the beginning of consecutive words

Ambiguous
term that describes words as being without absolute meanings

Ambushing
the practice of focusing only on the weaknesses of what the other person is saying and ignoring the strengths of his or her position

Antithesis
the practice of placing two contrasting ideas side by side in a parallel structure

Appeal to pity
attempt to influence an audience by exploiting their feelings of sympathy, guilt, or desire to ameliorate suffering

Arbitrary
term that describes symbols themselves as having no direct connection with the things they represent

Archetypal
metaphors that use common human experiences to help describe another object

Articulation
the process of physically shaping the sounds that make the word

Artistic proofs
Aristotle's category for credibility, emotion, and logic within a persuasive appeal; he called them artistic because the speaker creates them

Artifacts
objects used to communicate information about yourself to those around you

Assertiveness
the practice of clearly, calmly, and confidently making positions and ideas known to others

Asynchronous communication
communication that occurs when the communicators are sending and receiving messages at different times

Authoritative leadership style
comes from a place of confidence and empathy, not control and enforcement

Autonomy face
the perception that we can do things on our own and our desire to avoid others making decisions for us

Avoidance stage
the couple actively avoids interacting with each other so they will not have to face each other

Avoidance
conflict management strategy that involves avoiding the other person, choosing not to express or make a conflict known

Balance
method of managing tensions that takes place when we try to find a compromise that allows us to partly fill each need while also sacrificing some of each need

Bar graphs
visual presentation aids that have two axes and either horizontal or vertical bars that show the total number of items or levels of achievement in each category

Begging the question
speaker uses a circular argument in which his or her evidence and conclusion are really saying the same thing and assume certain facts that have not yet been proven

Behavioral uncertainty
occurs when we do not know how the other person will behave in a particular situation

Bonding stage
partners make their deep commitment formal and public through an engagement, marriage, or civil union

Boundary linkage
the practice of sharing private information with another individual

Boundary ownership
the rights and responsibilities we ascribe to the person with whom we share private information

Boundary permeability
the degree to which a confidant can share private information with others

Boundary turbulence
occurs when information we believe is private and shared in confidence is broadcast to other parties

Brainstorm
the practice of creating a list of all the possible topics you can think of, beginning by writing down every possible idea that comes to mind, regardless of how good you think the idea is, and then afterward organizing or evaluating the ideas to help you make a decision about which to choose

Catfishing
the practice of pretending to have a different identity via social media in order to initiate and maintain a relationship with another person

Cause-effect pattern of organization
a variation on the chronological pattern of organization used to discuss the causes that led to a specific event or effect

Certainty and uncertainty
the internal form of the stability and change dialectic; the desire to count on things to occur and the desire to have novelty in the relationship

Channel
pathway through which the symbols travel

Charts
visual presentation aid that shows numeric data in a series of rows and columns

Chronemics
the branch of nonverbal communication that involves how people treat, value, react to, and structure time

Chronological pattern of organization
used to describe events or processes in the order that they occur in time, from earlier events to later events

Circumscribing stage
happens when the partners are primarily living different lives and their conversations are increasingly limited in scope and depth

Civility
the ability to treat others with respect so that we can have a lasting, peaceful, and positive interaction

Closed posture
the posture achieved when one shields his or her body from the other person

Closed-ended questions
questions that have defined answers from which you will choose the best fit

Coaching leadership style
focused on helping individuals improve and grow through training and constant feedback

Co-cultures
smaller specific cultures that intersect in our lives

Coercive leadership style
a top-down approach to decision making that stifles individual ingenuity and participation and neglects motivating the group

Coercive power
power linked to the ability to introduce something negative or take away something positive from group members

Cognitive complexity
the ability to recognize multiple potential ways in which a situation or message could be understood or interpreted

Cognitive uncertainty
occurs when we do not know what the beliefs and attitudes of the other person are

Collaboration
the most beneficial of the conflict management strategies; its goal is to find a solution that allows both parties to win

Commitment
the desire to make efforts to stay in the relationship regardless of what happens

Communication apprehension
the fear or anxiety associated with real or anticipated communication with another or others

Communication competence
the ability to effectively and appropriately interact in any given situation

Communication privacy management
a theory that offers a map of the way people manage private matters that are shared with others

Communicator reward value
how positive or negative we feel about a person who commits a violation

Community
refers to both a specific place where people share certain characteristics or a feeling of fellowship with others who share attitudes, interests, and beliefs

Comparative advantages pattern of organization
persuasive pattern of organization in which you compare two potential solutions to a problem to argue why the solution you support is better than another solution that is being proposed by someone else

Comparison level
our general expectations for a certain type of relationship, such as a friendship or romantic relationship

Comparison level of alternatives
expectations arising from comparing existing relationships to other possible relationships

Competence face
the effort to promote our expertise on subjects to others so they respect us

Competing
conflict management strategy that treats an argument like something to win, even if the other person is not happy with the outcome

Complementary interchange
interaction between members of a system that is based on acknowledged differences in power

Complementing
the function of nonverbal communication whereby nonverbal behavior occurring at the same time as the message displays the same content

Concept map
a visual representation of all the potential areas you could cover in your speech that includes circles around topics and lines that connect related ideas; also known as a mind map

Compromising
conflict management strategy by which both sides sacrifice part of what they want while getting something they desire

Confirmation bias
the tendency to look for and remember information that is consistent with what we believe or what we want to happen

Conflict
an expressed struggle between at least two interdependent parties who perceive incompatible goals, scarce resources, and interference from the other party in achieving those goals

Conflicting
when a verbal message says one thing while corresponding nonverbal communication indicates something different

Conformity orientation
the degree to which the family emphasizes homogeneity of attitudes, values, and beliefs

Connection and autonomy
the internal dialectical tension of integration and separation; spending time with a partner and spending time alone

Connotative meaning
meaning that comes from a set of associations a word brings to mind in a person

Contempt
the expression of insults and disdain for a person, their behaviors, and ideas

Context
the physical, emotional, and psychological environment in which the communication event takes place

Conversational orientation
the degree to which family members are encouraged to participate in unrestrained conversation about a range of topics

Coordination
the principle of outlining that states all information on the same level has the same level of significance

Critical listening
listening to evaluate a message and assess whether or not we agree with what is said; requires the most cognitive effort of any listening purpose

Criticism
the expression of disapproval of someone or something based upon perceived faults in a person or behavior

Culture
the distinctive ideas, customs, social behavior, products, or way of life of a particular nation, society, people, or period

Dead metaphors
metaphors that have lost the creative element from which they initially drew their power and now are just accepted as true terms, rather than the metaphors they are

Debate
a competitive form of communication where parties critically listen to each other with the goal of defeating the opponent's argument, not understanding the other's perspective or finding common ground

Decoding
the process of interpreting the symbols within a message

Deductive reasoning
involves using general truths to reach a certain conclusion about a specific instance

Defensiveness
prevents a person from seeing their own roles and responsibilities in the situation and prevents parties from finding common ground when working through conflicts

Deliberate confidant
a person with whom we intentionally share information meant to be kept in confidence

Deliberative
speeches about future actions that might be taken

Democratic leadership style
focused on building consensus and collaborating with his or her team or group members

Demographics
categories of definable characteristics of groups of people, such as age, sex, race, ethnicity, religion, political affiliation, socioeconomic status, education level, and sexual orientation

Demonstrations
presentation aids that involve enacting the process you are trying to teach your audience

Denotative meaning
the meaning prescribed to a sign without understanding its history of usage and application; its dictionary, or literal, definition

Dialectical tensions
tensions that occur because we simultaneously have several essential yet oppositional needs or desires within our relationships

Dialogue
a style of communication that respectfully encourages others to want to listen, while also listening in a way that encourages others to want to speak

Differentiating stage
occurs when the partners being to separate themselves from each other

Division
the principle of outlining that states if a main point is divided into subpoints, it must be divided into two or more subpoints

Egocentric
people who are completely focused on themselves and ignorant of the needs of others

Either-or
speaker claims there are only two alternatives when there are really many other options available

Elucidating explanation
an explanation that helps an audience understand the definition of a term and distinguish its essential characteristics from the associated characteristics that are only sometimes present in that which you are defining

Emotional intelligence
the ability a person has to assess, identify, and manage his or her own emotions, while also appreciating and responding to the emotions of others in a civil manner

Empathy
the ability to understand and feel the same way as another person

Employment interviews
a type of interview in which employers conduct conversations with applicants for open positions in an effort to determine to whom they would like to offer a position; the interviewees seek information about the company that will influence their decision to accept an offer, should one come

Enabling communication
interaction that is not assertive and thus allows members to continue abusive, addictive, and otherwise negative behaviors

Encoding
the process of creating a message using symbols

Entry stage
first stage of Uncertainty Reduction Theory during which we follow culturally accepted rules for interactions and politeness, including greeting one another, making small talk, and laughing at jokes

Epideictic
speeches that celebrate or commemorate events or people

Ethnicity
a group of people who identify with each other based on common experience, which might include geographic or national origin, ancestry, history, cultural and social norms, religion, race, language, ideology, food, dress, or other factors

Ethos
the perceived personal character or credibility of the speaker

Everyday talk
interaction that includes mundane, ordinary conversations across our daily experience, making up our relationships in addition to the more noticeable, "bigger" moments, such as our first big fight or a marriage ceremony

Examples
instances that we use to help define or clarify concepts, draw attention to a particular feature of an experience, or elicit memories and emotions in our audience

Excommunication
an exile from a community one belonged to whereby one is shunned into reconciliation or completely exiled; it requires no communication between the individual and the community

Exit interviews
a type of interview conducted by human resources professionals with outgoing employees designed to gather information about the processes and climate of the organization in an attempt to use that information in the future to improve

Exit stage
final stage of Uncertainty Reduction Theory during which both individuals decide whether to continue the relationship or not to pursue the relationship

Expectancy violations theory
theory that we hold expectancies for what is appropriate and/or typical for a type of person

Experimenting stage
when you engage in conversation about surface-level interests and topics with the other person to see if your interest is expanded or not

Expert power
power gained through specific knowledge of a topic or content area, thus providing the person with that knowledge power over those who do not have it, but who need it nonetheless

Expert testimony
information that you obtain from someone who has conducted extensive research on the topic, has significant experience with the topic, or holds a position that lends credibility to his or her ideas on a subject matter

Explain
deepen the audience's understanding of a phenomenon

Extemporaneous speech
a practiced, polished speech that makes use of a limited speaking outline

Eye contact
looking members of your audience in the eyes while speaking

Face threats
things that threaten to damage the image we work to present to others

Facework
the behaviors we exhibit to create and maintain the positive perception of ourselves

Facial expressions
the way the position and movement of your facial features convey emotion and engagement

False cause
speaker assumes that one event caused another unrelated event to occur

Fantasies
creative interpretations of shared events that help define a group's identity

Feedback
the various verbal and nonverbal responses to the message by the receiver

Fellowship face
an effort to fulfill the need to have others like and respect us

Forensic
arguments about what had happened

Full-sentence preparation outline
an outline that includes everything you plan to say in your speech and is written somewhat like a manuscript in an outline format

Fundamental attribution error
the tendency to overestimate the influence of internal characteristics and underestimate the influence of situational factors when evaluating someone else's behavior

Gender
a social construction that includes all of the beliefs, attitudes, actions and roles associated with being masculine, feminine, androgynous, etc.

Gender expression
ways people communicate their gender identity

Gender identity
a person's sense of self as being along a range of possibilities that include identifying as a woman, non-binary, genderqueer, agender, or a man

Gender roles
societal expectations for individuals who identify with a particular gender

General purpose
the broad intent of what your speech should accomplish; the three types of general purposes are to inform, to persuade, and to commemorate

Generalized other
a composite mental image we use to practice our potential statements or behaviors before we actually enact them

Genuineness
the act of being direct, honest, and straightforward regarding what we believe and think

Gestures
the movements of your hands and arms

Glazing over
losing complete attention with what is going on and thinking about something else entirely, often staring in a different direction than the speaker

Good manners
those polite behaviors that encourage positive relationships with others

Grouphate
when people have strong negative feelings about the prospect of working in a group

Groupthink
the willful seeking of unanimity despite individuals who harbor doubts

Haptics
the study of how touch expresses meaning

Hasty generalization
speaker uses a small sample of evidence to draw unjustified conclusions about an entire group or category

Hearing
the physiological process of capturing sound conducted by ears to the brain

Helping interviews
a type of interview that takes stock of a problem or challenge faced by an individual and offers informed and expert advice on how to handle it

Hidden agenda
goals people keep secret from other parties while working with them

High-context cultures
a great deal of meaning is derived from the nonverbal expressions, environment, and situation in which the communication is taking place, and less emphasis is placed on the words

Histogram
a type of frequency chart that shows the proportion of individuals that obtained a certain level of achievement along a continuum

Hummingbirds
seventy percent of the population who function well throughout the day

HURIER model
the six steps of listening

Hyperpersonal communication
computer-mediated communication that has a higher level of affection, emotion, liking, solidarity, and intimacy than face-to-face conversations

Identity
how we understand our own qualities, beliefs, values, and characteristics as unique or different from others

Ideology
set of ideas, beliefs, and ideals that form one's worldview and provide a basis for action

Idioms
metaphoric expressions whose meanings are not predictable from their usual use, but must be inferred from cultural markers

Image management
the process of coordinating the presentation of our self-concept with various groups in different situations

Impersonal communication
communication that occurs in order to facilitate some type of transaction; based primarily on social roles

Impromptu speech
a speech presented with little or no preparation

Inclusion and seclusion
the external dialectical tension of integration and separation; spending time alone as a couple and spending time as a couple with others

Inductive reasoning
involves using several specific instances or pieces of evidence to draw probable conclusions about general truths

Inform
make the audience aware of a phenomenon

Informant
a contact person within the organization or group you can talk with to obtain information about the audience you will be speaking to

Information-gathering interviews
a type of interview that seeks to discover facts, information, and other knowledge about a particular topic from peers, experts, witnesses, or others who may be knowledgeable about it

Initiating stage
when you take the first step to interact with someone you are interested in

Integrating stage
partners begin to develop a sense of an identity for their relationship with each other

Integration
method of managing tensions that takes place when you are able to completely fulfill both opposing forces at the same time without sacrificing part of either one

Integrity
the maintenance of a consistent application of our values in every situation

Intensifying stage
you invest more time in each other and learn more about a person's history, interests, and goals

Interactive strategy
engaging in direct contact or face-to-face conversation with the other person

Interdependence
the quality of intimate relationships whereby one person's actions influence the other and vice versa; refers to the degree of connectedness between the two individuals, including how the couple shares time and space within their home

Internal preview
a statement that previews what is coming up next and can even be an overview of the elements of the next main point

Internal summary outline
a statement that reviews or sums up what you just finished telling the audience

Interpersonal attraction
a force that draws us to someone else

Interpersonal attribution
the assumption that another person is doing something because of her or his character or disposition

Interpersonal relationships
close associations or acquaintances between two or more people; relationships might be based on love, community or business interactions, friendship, family, or some other social commitment

Interviews
goal-oriented communication events where both sides use question-and-answer techniques to achieve their ends

Intimate relationships
deeply personal bonds that we have with other individuals that are accompanied by affective communication and a sense of belongingness

Island interview
a type of interview in which prospective candidates are placed in a room together and asked to discuss why they believe they are the better fit for the position

Johari window
a four-quadrant model describing the different aspects of our self-concept based on what we and others know about ourselves

Key word speaking outline
the outline you will put on a notecard and use during your speech; it should include only key words to remind you of your main points and subpoints, as well as source citations, statistics, and direct quotations you want to make sure you say in a particular way

Kinesics
nonverbal behaviors related to the movement of the body

Larks
ten percent of the population who function best early in the day

Legitimate power
power that emanates from a position, and so the person occupying that position is imbued with authority that must be followed

Likert scale questions
survey questions that provide statements and then ask respondents to circle a number that measures their level of agreement with the statement

Line graphs
visual presentation aid that uses lines along two axes to show changes in values over time

Listening
the process of receiving and interpreting spoken and/or nonverbal messages

Listening for appreciation
listening for enjoyment; it is not high in cognitive commitment

Listening for comprehension
listening to understand and learn something new; requires a significant degree of mental effort

Listening to show support
listening to a speaker to make him or her feel valued and to show the person we care about what he or she has to say

Logical fallacies
errors in reasoning that lead to invalid conclusions

Logos
the use of logic and evidence to persuade your audience

Low-context cultures
meaning is derived mostly from the language used in an interaction, and less emphasis is placed on the nonverbal communication, environment, and situation

Maintenance roles
related to the development and maintenance of the relationships within the group

Manuscript speech
a speech the speaker writes out word for word in an essay format and delivers by reading from the manuscript

Memorized speech
a speech the speaker commits to memory and delivers without the use of any notes

Meta-communicative
communication about communication

Metonym
a metaphor that is identified by its use of tangible objects to refer to intangible things

Minimax principle
principle describing the tendency to maximize the benefits and minimize the costs in relationships

Mirror
the practice of replicating the posture of the other person to indicate mutual interest

Mixed metaphors
phrases that make use of two different metaphors that do not logically fit; compare two things that have no inherent connection with each other, creating incongruous comparisons

Models
scaled physical representations of things utilized as presentation aids

Monochronic
the category of chronemics marked by liking to do things one at a time, breaking time up into small, manageable units

Monologue
a style of communication where only one voice is respected

Monroe's motivated sequence
persuasive pattern of organization in which you use five steps to persuade the audience to adopt a plan of action: attention, need, satisfaction, visualization, and action

Morality
an inner sense of right and wrong

Multiple intelligence theory
although all individuals can access and learn about the world through each of the nine intelligences, people differ in the strength of their aptitude or preference for those various intelligences

Narrative
a story that's told when trying to explain or argue something with an audience

Narrative coherence
feature exhibited by a story with content that hangs together and makes sense

Narrative fidelity
term for describing how well a story reflects the values and beliefs of its audience

Negative
the idea that language separates things from their natural state, thus telling us not only what something is, but what it is not

Negativity bias
the tendency to focus our efforts on picking out negative information or qualities in a person or situation

Noise
anything that interferes with the receiver's ability to properly receive the message

Non sequitur
speaker makes an unjustified move from one topic to another

Nonlistening
providing the appearance of listening without actually paying attention to the message

Nonverbal communication
the elements of communication that do not involve words but nevertheless transmit messages

Numbers
raw quantitative data

Objects
physical items that you are discussing in your speech

Oculesics
the use of eye contact to send messages

Olfactics
the dimension of nonverbal communication related to smell

Open posture
the posture achieved when the majority of one's body faces the audience or other person

Open system
a system in which parts both affect and are affected by events within and outside the system

Open-ended questions
questions that ask you to craft your best answer to the inquiry

Openness and closedness
the internal form of the expression and nonexpression dialectic; refers to the degree of disclosure partners have with one another

Organization
the categorization of stimuli we select to pay attention to

Owls
twenty percent of the population who function best at later times of the day

Pacesetting leadership style
focused on setting a high standard and modeling that standard for his or her team members

Parallelism
the practice of placing related words or phrases in a pattern that highlights what they have in common

Passive listening
listening without engaging the topic in any noticeable way, trying only to absorb what is said

Passive strategy
unobtrusively observing the other person

Pathos
the use of emotions in persuasion

Peer testimony
information that comes from someone who is in the same peer group as the audience; they are not necessarily an expert on the topic

Perception
the process of giving meaning to the things we notice in the world around us

Performance interviews
a type of interview that provides employers and managers with information used to determine raises, as well as target areas of improvement for staff; also called performance reviews

Personal stage
second stage of Uncertainty Reduction Theory which we begin to explore the other person's attitudes and beliefs, while also disclosing some of that same information about ourselves

Persuasion
attempting to change the attitudes, actions, or beliefs of another person

Physical appearance
includes your apparel and grooming

Physical attraction
we are drawn to someone's physical appearance because we like the way the person looks

Physical delivery
all of the physical signals your body sends to your audience during your speech; there are several elements to consider

Physiological state
temporary condition of the body

Physiological traits
permanent enduring physical conditions that impact us throughout our lives

Pie graph
a round graph that has slices that represent how large the proportion of that particular category is compared to the whole

Pitch
how high or low your voice sounds when you speak

Politeness
the act of showing consideration for others in accordance with social expectations

Polychronic
the category of chronemics marked by trying to do several tasks at the same time and having a more fluid approach to scheduling time

Positivity bias
the tendency to highlight and overemphasize positive information and characteristics when creating an impression

Posture
the position of your body when you are speaking

Prejudging
the practice of entering an interaction with a judgment about what we believe will be said before the person has a chance to present it

Presentation aids
resources that engage one or more of the audience's five senses (sight, sound, touch, taste, smell) to help the audience better understand the message

Presentness
a commitment to the moment and the other person in the moment with us; giving your undivided attention

Preview of main points
tells your audience how you will organize the information for that lesson or argument

Primacy effect
people are prone to emphasizing the first impression of something over any subsequent impressions when forming their perception of an event or person

Principle of mutual equality
the premise that each person can make an equal contribution to the interaction

Private information
information we believe we have the right to own

Problem-cause-solution pattern of organization
persuasive pattern of organization in which you present the problem in the first point, the underlying causes in the second point, and the proposed solution in the final point

Problem-solution pattern of organization
in a persuasive speech, a persuasive pattern of organization in which you begin by explaining the problem and then discuss your solution

Problem-solution pattern of organization
in an informative speech, used to organize a speech by first explaining a problem

and then teaching the audience about the solution

Problem-solving interviews
a form of very specific information gathering coupled with an emphasis on solving a specific problem

Profanity
vulgar and irreverent language

Pronunciation
what a word should sound like when it is spoken according to a rule or standard

Provisionalism
the expression of an ability to be flexible and open to different ideas

Proxemics
how we use space to convey information

Pseudolistening
the practice of hiding our inattention by appearing to actually listen through nonverbal and verbal responses that make it appear as though we understand what is being said

Quasi-scientific explanation
an explanation that helps the audience get an overall picture of a phenomenon and see relationships among the parts

Questions of fact
persuasive messages that attempt to change the audience's beliefs about something

Questions of policy
persuasive messages that try to change the audience's actions or convince the audience that something should be done

Questions of value
persuasive messages that try to change an audience's attitudes toward a topic by convincing the audience whether or not a belief, object, or action is moral, ethical, important, or worthwhile

Race
a set of physical characteristics shared by a group of people, such as skin color, body type, facial structure, and hair color

Rapport talk
language meant to develop relationships and exchange emotional information

Rate
how fast or slow you speak

Reaffirmation
method of managing tensions that involves accepting that you cannot reconcile the contradiction and celebrate what the dialectical tension means for the couple's unity

Reasoning by analogy
comparison of two similar cases in order to argue that what is true in one case is also true in the other because two cases share similar features

Reasoning by cause
used when you claim that one event causes another

Reasoning by example
using several specific instances that are related to each other to draw an overall conclusion about them

Reasoning by sign
occurs when you conclude that the presence of one thing indicates the presence of another

Recalibration
method of managing tensions that involves reframing the contradiction so you do not see the two opposing forces as being in contradiction with one another

Recency effect
people are prone to using their most recent experience with someone as their overriding impression of the person

Red herring
speaker introduces irrelevant ideas in order to distract attention away from the real issue

Referent power
power derived from the charisma of a leader, and it can be seen when people follow someone they like, admire, look up to, or otherwise are attracted to

Refutations
persuasive speeches in which a speaker defends his or her own position or an issue while responding to the arguments of another person

Regulating
the actions that govern the course of an interaction with another person

Relationship maintenance
the work we do to keep a relationship going and in a condition with which both partners are happy

Repeating
the function of nonverbal communication whereby the physical actions that follow verbal messages reinforce what is said

Repetition
the practice of repeating words and phrases either immediately following the initial statement or in the same location in a message

Report talk
the exchange of information, solutions, and problem-solving strategies

Respect
the practice of acknowledging the inherent dignity of other people as human beings

Revelation and concealment
the external form of the expression and nonexpression dialectic; refers to what couples share with the community and what they do not

Reward power
power linked to the ability to either provide a good thing or take away a negative thing from someone for doing a task

Rhythm
the cadence or pattern of movement in your voice

Rituals
repetitive behaviors that contain a unique meaning for members, and each family develops their own traditions

Scatterplot
a graph that shows the relationship between two continuous variables

Schemas
mental frameworks for organizing information about experiences

Segmentation
method of managing tensions that takes place when we choose to privilege the parts of the dialectical pair based on different contexts

Selection
the act of choosing to attend to, consciously or subconsciously, specific stimuli in the environment

Selective listening
the practice of choosing what the main points are in a message regardless of what the speaker says

Self-concept
the image we have of who we believe we are

Self-disclosure
when one person voluntarily shares personal history and information regarding attitudes, feelings, values, and experiences with another individual

Self-fulfilling prophecy
convincing yourself that something is going to happen before it does, thus leading

to the occurrence of what you originally expected

Self-monitoring
the process of being attuned to how your actions and messages impact others

Semantic differential scale questions
survey questions that ask participants to choose their position on a continuum between two polar opposites

Semiotics
the study of the social production of meaning from sign systems like language

Sensitive
understanding and respecting diversity

Sex
one's biological classification based on reproductive function

Sexual orientation
the sex and gender to whom a person is romantically and sexually attracted

Sign
an arbitrary symbol that represents the signifier and the signified

Signified
the meaning associated with the signifier; the idea or mental construct of the signifier

Signifier
the physical thing as we perceive it in the world around us

Signpost
a word that catches the audience's attention and indicates where you are in the speech

Similes
metaphoric language devices that compare two things through the use of "like" or "as"

Situational attribution
the assumption that another person is doing something because of factors in the environment or the situation they are in

Slippery slope
speaker argues that once a course of action is taken, a series of other unavoidable and undesirable events will necessarily take place

Social attraction
we see the other person as someone with whom we would like to engage in social interaction and be friends

Social exchange theory
a theory suggesting that relationship behavior is regulated by the evaluation of perceived rewards and costs of the interaction by both sides

Social loafing
"a reduction in motivation and effort when individuals work collectively compared to when they work individually"

Social media
forms of electronic communication through which users create online communities to share information, ideas, personal messages, and other content

Social penetration theory
the process of creating and maintaining deeper intimacy with another person takes place through gradual and mutual self-disclosure

Social relationships
informal, voluntary relationships such as acquaintances, coworkers, and casual friendships

Spare brain time
the gap between the roughly 150 words a minute we can speak, and the 650 words per minute we can mentally process

Spatial pattern of organization
used to describe an object by explaining how parts physically relate to one another in a defined space

Specific purpose statement
a narrower version of the general purpose statement that identifies what you will talk

about, what you will say about it, and what you hope the audience will take away from the speech

Spiraling inversion
method of managing tensions that takes place when we alternate back and forth between attending to our needs

Stagnation stage
when couples move into the stagnation stage, they are still a couple, but primarily in name; they are neither moving forward or backward in the relationship but have hit a point when they are not relating on an intimate level

State CA
anxiety that is related to the context in which you are communicating

Statistics
quantitative reports that summarize and organize sets of numbers to make them easier to understand and visualize

Stereotyping
generalizations about groups of people that are applied to individuals we believe are members of that group

Stonewalling
a complete withdrawal from the conflict, both physically and verbally

Straw man
speaker ignores the actual position of his or her opponent, misrepresents the opponent's position, and then attacks that made-up position instead of the actual position

Subordination
the principle of outlining that creates a hierarchy of ideas in which the most general ideas appear first followed by more specific ideas

Substituting
the function of nonverbal communication whereby physical actions take the place of verbal messages

Symbolic convergence
occurs when groups create a unique meaning for a term, experience, or event in the group's life that serves to further strengthen the bond between group members

Symmetrical interchange
communication between members that seeks to neutralize the power difference and treat each person equally

Synchronous communication
communication that occurs simultaneously

Synecdoche
a metaphor that uses one part of something to refer to the whole thing

System
interdependent parts that interact with and affect one another

Systematic desensitization
the process by which a person is slowly introduced to something they fear so that each time they overcome the fear, the intensity is decreased

Task attraction
we like to work with them and can count on them to get a job done

Task roles
related to accomplishing work together as a group

Terminating stage
the final phase of relationship deterioration; couples end their current relationships and move into a post-relationship phase where they may or may not continue to have contact as separated individuals

Testimony
the words of other people used to support your point

Thesis statement
a one-sentence summary of your speech that is written the way you will say it out loud to your audience during your speech

Tone
how variable your voice is and how "warm" your voice sounds

Topical pattern of organization
used to divide your speech into categories or subtopics

Trait CA
the amount of communication anxiety you were born with and naturally have due to genetics

Transformative explanations
explanations that help audience members transform their everyday ideas about how something works into a more scientifically accurate understanding of the phenomenon

Transition
a connecting statement that lets your audience know you are moving from one part of your speech to another

Tuckman Model of Group Development
a five-stage theory of group development proposed by Bruce Tuckman consisting of forming, storming, norming, performing, and adjourning; Tuckman suggests not all groups will move through each stage depending on their tasks or goals

Uncertainty reduction theory
the idea that increased knowledge of another person improves our ability to predict future behaviors and thus reduces our own uncertainty

Unconditional positive regard
a component of dialogue originated by Carl Rogers; accepting others with a positive attitude

Unit of analysis
the item that the researcher is trying to understand or study

Valence of the violation
process of evaluation that determines how we will respond to the violation

Vocal delivery
everything that affects how your voice sounds when you speak

Vocalics
those things that contribute to the maintenance or creation of sound in your voice that help to convey meaning

Vocalized pauses
filler words that many speakers use when they feel like they should be saying something but do not have anything to say

Volume
how loud or soft the sound of your voice is when you speak

REFERENCES

Chapter 1

1. Maslow, A. H. "A Theory of Human Motivation." *Psychological Review* 50, (1943): 370-96.
2. American Cancer Society. "Find Support and Treatment." http://www.cancer.org/treatment/treatmentsandsideeffects.
3. Perry, B. D. "Childhood Experience and the Expression of Genetic Potential: What childhood neglect tells us about nature and nurture." *Brain and Mind* 3, (2002): 79-100.
4. Medina, J. *Brain Rules for Baby (updated and expanded): How to raise a smart and happy child from zero to f ive,* 2ⁿᵈ ed. Seattle, WA: Pear Press, 2014.
5. "Connected and Disconnected: Technology, empathy and loneliness." *Ashoka's Youth Venture.* https://www.youthventure.org/connected-and-disconnected-technology-empathy-and-loneliness
6. Newport, F. "Seven in Ten Americans are Very or Moderately Religious." *Gallup.com.* Accessed December 4, 2012. http://www.gallup.com/poll/159050/seven-americans-moderately-religious.aspx.
7. Schultze, Quentin J. "The God Problem in Communication Studies." *Journal of Communication and Religion* 28, (2005): 1-22.
8. Ogden, C.K., & Richards, I. A. *The Meaning of Meaning.* Orlando, FL: Harcourt Brace Jovanovich, Inc, 1923/1989.
9. Delia, Jesse, Barbara J. O'Keefe, and Daniel O'Keefe. "The Constructivist Approach to Communication." In *Human Communication Theory.* Edited by F. E. X. Dance, 147-191. New York: Harper & Row, 1982.
10. Shannon, C. E. "A Mathematical Theory of Communication." *The Bell System Technical Journal* 27, (1948): 379-423.
11. Mead, G. H. *Mind, Self, and Society from the Standpoint of a Social Behaviorist.* Chicago: University of Chicago Press, 1934.

Chapter 2

1. *Oxford English Dictionary Online*, s.v. "Culture," http://www.oxforddictionaries.com/.
2. Hofstede, G., & Hofstede, G. J. "Culture." http://www.geerthofstede.nl/culture.
3. Tannen, D. *You Just Don't Understand: Men and Women in Conversation.* New York: Harper Collins, 2001.
4. Maclachlan, M. "Indulgence vs Restraint – The 6ᵗʰ Dimension." *View on Global Working* (blog). January 11, 2013. *Communicaid.* http://www.communicaid.com/cross-cultural-training/blog/indulgence-vs-restraint-6th-dimension.
5. Hall, E. T. *Beyond Culture.* New York, NY: Doubleday, 1976.
6. Woodward, C. "Up in Arms." *Tufts Magazine,* Fall 2013. http://www.tufts.edu/alumni/magazine/fall2013/features/up-in-arms.html.
7. American Psychological Association. "Practice Guidelines for LGB Clients." 2014. http://www.apa.org/pi/lgbt/resources/guidelines.aspx?item=2.
8. Howe, N., & Strauss, W. *Millennials Rising: The Next Great Generation.* New York: Vintage, 2000.

9. Gardner, H. *Intelligence Reframed: Multiple Intelligences for the 21st Century.* New York, NY: Basic Books, 1999.

10. Woodward, C. "Up in Arms." *Tufts Magazine,* Fall 2013. http://www.tufts.edu/alumni/magazine/fall2013/features/up-in-arms.html.

11. Pew Research Center. "Religious Landscape Study." http://www.pewforum.org/religious-landscape-study/.

Chapter 3

1. Andersen, P. A. *Nonverbal Communication: Forms and Functions.* New York: McGraw Hill, 1998.

2. Burgoon, J.K.; Hale, J.L. (1988). "Nonverbal Expectancy Violations: Model Elaboration and Application to Immediacy Behaviors." *Communication Monographs.* 55: 58–79.

3. Heider, F. "Social Perception and Phenomenal Causality." *Psychological Review* 51, (1944): 358-374.

4. Ross, L. "The Intuitive Psychologist and His Shortcomings: Distortions in the Attribution Process." In *Advances in Experimental Social Psychology*, edited by L. Berkowitz, 173-220. New York: Academic Press, 1977.

5. Handa, N. and C. Power. "Land and Discover! A Case Study Investigating the Cultural Context of Plagiarism." *Journal of University Teaching and Learning Practice* 2, no. 3b (2005): 64-84; Sutherland-Smith, W. "The Tangled Web: Internet Plagiarism and International Students' Academic Writing." *Journal of Asian Pacific Communication* 15, (2005): 15-29.

6. Medina, J. *Brain Rules.* Edmonds, WA: Pear Press, 2008.

7. Hart Research Associates. "Falling Short? College Learning and Career Success." *Association of American Colleges and Universities.* January 20, 2015. https://aacu.org/leap/public-opinion-research/2015-survey-results.

8. Asch, S. E. "Effects of Group Pressure Upon the Modification and Distortion of Judgment." In *Groups, Leadership and Men*, edited by H. Guetzkow. Pittsburgh, PA: Carnegie Press, 1951.

9. Mead, G. H. *Mind, Self, and Society from the Standpoint of a Behavioral Scientist.* 1934. Reprint, Chicago, IL: University of Chicago Press, 1964.

10. Swann, W. B., P.J. Rentfro, and J. S. Guinn. "Self-verification: The Search for Coherence." In *Handbook of Self and Identity*, edited by M. R. Leary & J. J. P. Tangney, 367-383. New York: Guilford, 2003.

11. Kinch, J. W. "A Formalized Theory of Self-concept." *American Journal of Sociology* 68, (1963): 481-486.

12. Smallwood, Karl. "The Surprisingly Mysterious Life of Famed Artist Bob Ross." *Today I Found Out.* 2015.

13. Luft, J., and H. Ingham. "The Johari Window, a Graphic Model of Interpersonal Awareness." Proceedings of the Western Training Laboratory in Group Development, Los Angeles, CA, 1955.

14. van der Meulen, M. "Developments in Self-concept Theory and Research: Affect, Context, and Variability." In *Identity and Emotions: Development Through Self-organization*, edited by H. A. Bosma & E. S. Kunnen, 10-32. Cambridge: Cambridge University Press, 2001.

15. Medina, J. *Brain Rules.* Edmonds, WA: Pear Press, 2008.

16. Goffman, E. *Interaction Ritual.* New York, NY: Anchor Books, 1967.

17. Lim, T. S. and J. W. Bowers. "Facework: Solidarity, Approbation, and Tact." *Human Communication Research* 17, (1991): 415-450.

18. Cupach, W. and S. Metts. *Facework.* Thousand Oaks, CA: Sage, 1994; quoted in Em Griffin, *A First Look at Communication Theory*, 8th ed. (New York, NY: McGraw Hill), 70.

19. Ting-Toomey, S. & A. Kurogi. "Facework Competence in Intercultural Conflict: An Updated Face-negotiation Theory." *International Journal of Intercultural Relations* 22, (1998): 187-225.

Chapter 4

1. Edited and paraphrased from Pearce, W. B. and K. A. Pearce "Extending the Theory of the Coordinated Management of Meaning (CMM) Through a Community Dialogic Process." *Communication Theory* 10, 2000: 405-423); and Pearce, W. B. and K. A. Pearce. "Combining Passions and Abilities: Toward Dialogic Virtuosity." *Southern Communication Journal* 65, (2000): 161–175.

2. Poulakos, J. "The Components of Dialogue." *Western Journal of Speech Communication* 38, (1974): 199.

3. Forni, P. M. *Choosing Civility: The Twenty-Five Rules for Considerate Conduct.* New York: St. Martin's Press, 2002.

4. Johannesen, R. L. "The Emerging Concept of Communication as Dialogue." *Quarterly Journal of Speech* 57, (1971): 376.

5. Forni, P. M. *Choosing Civility: The Twenty-Five Rules for Considerate Conduct.* New York: St. Martin's Press, 2002.

6. "Maine Seeds Program." Seeds of Peace. www.seedsofpeace.org.

7. Arnett, R. C. *Communication and Community: Implications of Martin Buber's Dialogue.* Carbondale, IL: Southern Illinois University Press, 1986.

8. Goleman, D. *Focus.* New York: HarperCollins, 2013.

9. Medina, J. *Brain Rules.* Edmonds, WA: Pear Press, 2008.

10. Arnett, R. C. *Communication and Community: Implications of Martin Buber's Dialogue.* Carbondale, IL: Southern Illinois University Press, 1986.

11. Johannesen, R. L. "The Emerging Concept of Communication as Dialogue." *Quarterly Journal of Speech* 57, (1971): 376.

12. Quintilian. *Quintilian's Institutes of Oratory; Or, Education of an Orator.* edited by J. S. Watson. London: G. Bell and Sons, 1856. 12.1.1.

13. Carter, S. L. *Integrity.* New York: Harper Perennial, 1996. 7.

14. NCA Legislative Council. *NCA Credo for Ethical Communication.* 1999.

15. Gibb, J. R. "Defensive Communication." *Journal of Communication* 11, no. 3 (1961): 141–148.

Chapter 5

1. De Saussure, F. *Course in General Linguistics.* 1916. Reprint, New York: Philosophical Library, 1950.

2. Barthes, R. *Elements of Semiology.* Translated by Annette Lavers and Colin Smith. London: Jonathan Cape, 1967.

3. Kennedy, J. F. "Inaugural Address." *Americanrhetoric.com.* January 20, 1961.

4. Milton, John. *Paradise Lost.* Edited by Scott Elledge. 2nd ed. New York: Norton, 1975.

5. Fisher, W. *Human Communication as Narration: Toward a Philosophy of Reason, Value and Action.* Columbia, SC: University of South Carolina Press, 1989.

Chapter 6

1. Kappas, A., U. Hess, and K. R. Scherer, "Voice and Emotion." In *Fundamentals of Nonverbal Communication,* edited by R. S. Feldman & B. Rime, 200-237. Cambridge, England: Cambridge University Press, 1991.

2. Burgoon, J.K. "Nonverbal signals." In *Handbook of Interpersonal Communication*, edited by M. L. Knapp & G. R. Miller, 344-390. Beverly Hills, CA: Sage, 1985.

3. Ekman, P. and W.V. Friesen, W. V. *Unmasking the Face: A Field Guide to Recognizing Emotions from Facial Cues.* Englewood Cliffs, NJ: Prentice-Hall, 1975.

4. Vrij, A. Nonverbal communication and deception. In *The Sage Handbook of Nonverbal Communication*, edited by V. Manusov and M. L. Patterson, 341-359. Thousand Oaks, CA: Sage, 2006.

5.   Hall, E. T. "System of Notation for Proxemics Behavior." *American Anthropologist* 65, (1963): 1003-1026.

6.   Floyd, K. *Communicating Affection: Interpersonal Behavior and Social Context.* Cambridge, England: Cambridge University Press, 2006.

7.   Hervey, Jane Claire. "Why This Professor of Time Argued Achieving 'Work Life Balance' is Impossible." *Forbes.* July 12, 2018.

8.   Zuckerman, M. and K. Miyake. "The Attractive Voice: What makes it so?" *Journal of Nonverbal Behavior* 17, (1996): 119-135.

9.   Wolvin, A. and C. Coakley. *Listening.* Dubuque, IA: Benchmark, 1996.

10.   Pointer, M. R. and G.G. Attridge. The Number of Discernible Colors." *Color Research and Application* 23, (1998): 52-54.

Chapter 7

1.   Wilt, M.E. "A Study of Teacher Awareness of Listening as a Factor in Elementary Education." *Journal of Educational Research* 43, no. 8 (1950): 626-636; Tricia Hedge, *Teaching and Learning in the Language Classroom.* Oxford: Oxford University Press, 2000.

2.   International Listening Association, "Priorities of Listening Research: Four Interrelated Initiatives." http://www.listen.org/Resources/Documents/White_Paper_PrioritiesResearch.

3.   National Institute on Deafness and Other Communication Disorders. "Quick Statistics About Hearing." http://www.nidcd.nih.gov/health/statistics/pages/quick.aspx.

4.   Hearing Health Foundation. "Hearing Loss & Tinnitus Statistics." http://hearinghealthfoundation.org/statistics.

5.   Gardner, H. *Frames of Mind.* New York: Basic Books, 1983.

6.   Goleman, D. *Emotional Intelligence.* New York: Bantam Dell, 1995.

7.   Sargent, S.L. and J. B. Weaver, III. "Listening Styles: Sex Differences in Perceptions of Self and Others." *International Journal of Listening.* 17, no 1 (2003): 5-18. https://doi.org/10.1080/10904018.2003.10499052.

8.   Brownwell, J. *Listening: Attitudes, Principles, and Skills.* 5th ed. Boston, MA: Allyn & Bacon, 2015.

9.   Buller D. B. & and Burgoon, J. K. (1996). Interpersonal Deception Theory. *Communication Theory* 6, 203-242.

Chapter 8

1.   Maslow, A.H. *Motivation and Personality.* 2nd ed. New York: Harper & Row, 1970.

2.   Etymology Dictionary, s.v. "Community" http://www.etymonline.com/index.

3.   McCroskey, J. C. and T. A. McCain. "The Measurement of Interpersonal Attraction." *Speech Monographs* 41, (1974): 261-266.

4.   Berger, C. R. and R. J. Calabrese. "Some Exploration in Initial Interaction and Beyond: Toward a Developmental Theory of Communication." *Human Communication Research* 1, (1975): 100.

5.   Sunnafrank, M. "Predicted Outcome Value and Uncertainty Reduction Theories: A Test of Competing Perspectives." *Human Communication Research* 17 (1990): 76-103.

6.   Berger, C. R. "Inscrutable Goals, Uncertain Plans, and the Production of Communicative Action." In *Communication and Social Processes*, edited by C. R. Berger and M. Burgoon (1-28). East Lansing, MI: Michigan State University Press, 1995.

7.   Altman, I. and D. Taylor. *Social Penetration: The Development of Interpersonal Relationships.* New York: Holt, Rinehart, and Winston, 1973.

8.   Altman, I. and J. Ginat. *Polygamous Families in Contemporary Society.* New York: Cambridge, 1996.

Chapter 9

1. Stafford, L. "Measuring Relationship Maintenance Behaviors: Critique and Development of the Revised Relationship Maintenance Behavior Scale. *Journal of Social and Personal Relationships* 28, (2011): 278-303.
2. Thibaut, J. W. and H. H. Kelley. *The Social Psychology of Groups*. New York: Wiley, 1959.
3. Petronio, S. "Communication Boundary Management: A Theoretical Model of Managing Disclosure of Private Information Between Married Couples." *Communication Theory* 1, (1991): 311-335.
4. Duck, S. "Relationships as Unfinished Business: Out of the Frying Pan and into the 1990s." *Journal of Social and Personal Relationships* 7, (1990): 5-28.
5. Baxter, L. A. *Voicing Relationships: A Dialogic Perspective*. Thousand Oaks, CA: Sage, 2011.
6. Goldsmith, D. J. and L. A. Baxter. "Constituting Relationships in Talk: A Taxonomy of Speech Events in Social and Personal Relationships." *Human Communication Research* 23, (1996): 87-114.
7. Baxter, L. A. and B. M. Montgomery. *Relating: Dialogues and Dialectics*. New York: Guilford, 1996.
8. Baxter, L. A. and B. M. Montgomery. *Relating: Dialogues and Dialectics*. New York: Guilford, 1996.

Chapter 10

1. Baxter, L. A. and B. M. Montgomery. *Relating: Dialogues and Dialectics*. New York: Guilford, 1996
2. Meyer, J. J. *Sexual Life in Ancient India: A Study in the Comparative History of Indian Culture*. Motilal Banarsidass Publishers, 1989.
3. Gottman, J. M. and R. W. Levenson. "Marital Processes Predictive of Later Dissolution: Behavior, Physiology and Health." *Journal of Personality and Social Psychology* 63, (1992): 221-233.
4. Fitzpatrick, M. A. "Family Communication Patterns Theory: Observations on its Development and Application." *Journal of Family Communication* 4, (2004): 167-179; Williamson, R. N. and M.A. Fitzpatrick. "Two Approaches to Marital Interaction: Relational Control Patterns in Marital Types." *Communication Monographs* 52, (1985): 236-252.
5. Floyd, K., A. Mikkelson, and J. Judd. "Defining the Family Through Relationships." In *The Family Communication Sourcebook,* edited by L. Turner and R. West. (21-41). Thousand Oaks, CA: Sage, 2006.
6. Watzlawick, P., J.H. Beavin, and D.D. Jackson. *Pragmatics of Human Communication*. New York: W.W. Norton, 1967.
7. Ritchie, L. D. and M.A. Fitzpatrick. "Family Communication Patterns: Measuring Intrapersonal Perceptions of Interpersonal Relationships." *Communication Research* 17, (1990): 523-544.
8. Koerner, A. F. and M. A. Fitzpatrick. "Understanding Family Communication Patterns and Family Functioning: The Roles of Conversation Orientation and Conformity Orientation. *Communication Yearbook* 26, (2002): 36-68.
9. Braithwaite, D. O. and L.A. Baxter. "The Role of Rituals in the Management of the Dialectical Tension of "Old" and "New" in Blended Families." *Communication Studies* 49, (1998): 101-120.
10. Rogers, L.E. and R. Farace. "The Analysis of Relational Communication in Dyads: New Measurement Procedures." *Human Communication Research* 1, (1975): 222-239; P. Watzlawick and M. Hoyt. "Constructing Therapeutic Realities: A Conversation with Paul Watzlawick." In *Handbook of Constructive Therapies*, edited by M. Hoyt. (183-196). San Francisco, CA: Jossey-Bass, 1997.
11. Rawlins, W.K. *Friendship Matters: Communication, Dialectics, and the Life Course*. New Brunswick, NJ: Transaction Publishers, 1992.
12. Rawlins, W.K. *Friendship Matters: Communication, Dialectics, and the Life Course*. New Brunswick, NJ: Transaction Publishers, 1992.

Chapter 11

1. Carey, J. "Time, Space, and the Telegraph." In *Communication in History: Technology, Culture, and Society,* edited by D. Crowley and P. Heyer. (154-158). White Plains, NY: Longman, 1995.
2. Walther, J. B. "Computer-mediated Communication: Impersonal, Interpersonal, and Hyperpersonal Interaction." *Communication Research* 23, (1996): 3-43.
3. Ellison, N. B., C. Steinfield, and C. Lampe. "The Benefits of Facebook 'Friends': Social Capital and College Students' Use of Online Social Networking Sites." *Journal of Computer-Mediated Communication* 12, (2007): 1143-1168.
4. Ledbetter, A. M. "The Past and Future of Technology in Interpersonal Communication Theory and Research." *Communication Studies* 65, (2014): 456-459.
5. Daft, R. L. and R. H. Lengel. "Information Richness: A New Approach to Managerial Behavior and Organizational Design." *Research in Organizational Behavior* 6, (1984): 191-233.
6. Wright, K. B. and A. Muhtaseb. In *Computer-mediated Communication in Personal Relationships,* edited by K. B. Wright and L. M. Webb. (137-155). New York: Peter Lang, 2011.
7. Wright, K. B. and A. Muhtaseb. In *Computer-mediated Communication in Personal Relationships,* edited by K. B. Wright and L. M. Webb. (137-155). New York: Peter Lang, 2011.
8. Wright, K. B. and A. Muhtaseb. In *Computer-mediated Communication in Personal Relationships,* edited by K. B. Wright and L. M. Webb. (137-155). New York: Peter Lang, 2011.
9. Ledbetter, A. M., M. A. Broeckelman-Post, and A. M. Krawsczyn. "Modeling Everyday Talk: Differences Across Communication Media and Sex Composition of Friendship Dyads." *Journal of Social and Personal Relationships* 28, (2010): 223-241.
10. Nie, N. H., S. D. Hillygus, and L. Erbring. "Internet Use, Interpersonal Relations, and Sociability." In *The Internet in Everyday Life,* edited by B. Wellman & C. Haythornthwaite. (215-243). Malden, MA: Blackwell, 2002.
11. Walther, J. B. "Computer-mediated Communication: Impersonal, Interpersonal, and Hyperpersonal Interaction." *Communication Research* 23, (1996): 3-43.
12. Conner, C. "Who wastes the most time at work?" *Forbes.com.* (September 7, 2013). http://www.forbes.com/sites/cherylsnappconner/2013/09/07/who-wastes-the-most-time-at-work/
13. Sahlstein, E. "Communication and Distance: The Present and Future Interpreted Through the Past." *Journal of Applied Communication Research* 38, (2010): 106-114.
14. Sagioglou, C. and T. Greitemeyer. "Facebook's Emotional Consequences: Why Facebook Causes a Decrease in Mood and Why People Still Use It." *Computers in Human Behavior* 35, (2014): 359-363.
15. Dainton, M. and A. Aylor. "Patterns of Communication Channel Use in the Maintenance of Long-Distance Relationships." *Communication Research Reports* 19, (2002): 118-129.
16. Sahlstein, E. M. "Relating at a Distance: Negotiating Being Together and Being Apart in Long-Distance Relationships." *Journal of Social and Personal Relationships* 21, (2004): 689-702.
17. Stafford, L. *Maintaining Long-Distance and Cross-Residential Relationships.* Mahwah, NJ: Erlbaum, 2005.
18. Sahlstein, E. "Making Plans: Praxis Strategies for Negotiating Uncertainty-Certainty in Long-Distance Relationships." *Western Journal of Communication* 70, (2006): 147-165.
19. Zickuhr, K. and M. Madden. "Older Adults and Internet Use." June 6, 2012. *Pew Research Center.* http://www.pewinternet.org/2012/06/06/main-report-15/.

Chapter 12

1. Wilmot, W. W. and J. L. Hocker. *Interpersonal Conflict.* New York: McGraw-Hill, 2001.
2. Stone, D., B. Patton, and S. Heen. *Difficult Conversations.* New York, NY: Penguin, 1999.
3. Gottman, J. *The Mathematics of Marriage.* Cambridge, MA: MIT Press, 2003.
4. Thomas, K. W. "Conflict and Conflict Management: Reflections and Update." *Journal of Organizational Behavior* 13, (1992): 265-274.

5. Stuber, S. and V. Vaughn. *Couples Retreat.* Directed by P. Billingsley. United States: Universal Pictures, 2009.
6. Gibb, J. R. "Defensive Communication." *Journal of Communication* 11, (1961): 141-148.

Chapter 13

1. "Assault or homicide," Centers for Disease Control and Prevention. http://www.cdc.gov/nchs/fastats/homicide.htm.
2. "SEER Stat Fact Sheet: All Cancer Sites," Surveillance, Epidemiology, and End Results Program. http://seer.cancer.gov/statfacts/html/all.html Last Accessed: July 14, 2015.
3. Ranganathan, S.R. *The Five Laws of Library Science.* 2nd ed. Bangalore, India: Sarada Ranganathan Endowment for Library Science, 1988.

Chapter 14

1. Gandhi, M. "Mahatma Gandhi quotes." *Brainy Quotes.* http://www.brainyquote.com/quotes/quotes/m/mahatmagan109075.html.
2. Fannie Lou Hamer testimony before the Credentials Committee. http://americanradioworks.publicradio.org/features/sayitplain/flhamer.html.
3. Wichelns, H. "The Literary Criticism of Oratory." In *Readings in Rhetorical Criticism*, edited by C. R. Burghardt. (26). State College, PA: Strata Publishing, 2010.
4. Thomas, K.W. (1992). Conflict and conflict management: Reflections and update. *Journal of Organizational Behavior*, 13, 265-274.

Chapter 15

1. McCroskey, J. C. "Oral Communication Apprehension: A Review of Recent Research." Human Communication Research 4, (1976): 78-96.
2. Personal Report of Communication Apprehension (PRCA-24). https://www.jamescmccroskey.com/measures/prca24.htm.
3. McCroskey, J. C. "Communication Apprehension: What We Have Learned in the Last Four Decades." Human Communication 12, (2009): 151-171.
4. "George Mason Enrollment Trends." George Mason University. http://irr.gmu.edu/10YrEnrollTrends.pdf.
5. "Deaths and Mortality." Centers for Disease Control and Prevention. http://www.cdc.gov/nchs/fastats/deaths.htm.
6. Food Availability (Per Capita) Data System. United States Department of Agriculture Economic Research Service. http://www.ers.usda.gov/data-products/food-availability-(percapita)-data-system/.

Chapter 16

1. Rowan, K. E. "Informing and Explaining Skills: Theory and Research on Informative Communication." In *Handbook of Communication and Social Interaction Skills,* edited by J. O. Greene & B. Burleson. (403-438). Mahwah, NJ: Lawrence Erlbaum Associates, 2003.
2. Associated Press. "Former Army Private Jessica Lynch Told a House Panel Her Story of Being Rescued in Iraq Tuesday." YouTube. July 21, 2015. Accessed May 07, 2019. https://www.youtube.com/watch?v=VdMLaCug4ck.
3. Rowan, K. E. "A New Pedagogy for Explanatory Public Speaking: Why Arrangement Should Not Substitute for Invention." *Communication Education* 44, (1995): 236-250.
4. Rowan, K. E. "A New Pedagogy for Explanatory Public Speaking: Why Arrangement Should Not Substitute for Invention." *Communication Education* 44, (1995): 236-250.

5. Richmond, V.P., D.R. Lane, and J. C. McCroskey. "Teacher Immediacy and the Teacher-Student Relationship." In *Handbook of Instructional Communication*, edited by T.P. Mottet, V.P. Richmond, and J.C. McCroskey. (167-193). Boston, MA: Pearson, 2006.

6. Titsworth, B.S. and K.A. Kiewra. "Organizational Lecture Cures and Student Notetaking as Facilitators of Student Learning." *Contemporary Educational Psychology* 29, (2004): 447-461.

7. Kiewra, K.A. "How Classroom Teachers Can Help Students Learn and Teach Them How to Learn." *Theory into Practice* 41, no. 2 (2002): 71-80.

8. Bruner, J. *The Process of Education*. Cambridge, MA: Harvard University Press, 1960.

9. BBC News. "How Does Ebola Attack Human Cells?" http://www.youtube.com/watch?v=PvsKgpO9Mal.

Chapter 17

1. Aristotle. "From Rhetoric." In *The Rhetorical Tradition,* 2nd ed., edited by P. Bizzell & B. Herzberg. (179-240). Boston, MA: Bedford/St. Martin's, 2001.

Chapter 18

1. "MGM Resorts Careers". *MGM Resorts.* http://www.mgmresortscareers.com/diversity/diversity-champion-initiative.aspx.

2. Krentz, M. "Survey: What Diversity and Inclusion Policies Do Employees Actually Want?" *Harvard Business Review.* February 5, 2019. https://hbr.org/2019/02/survey-what-diversity-and-inclusion-policies-do-employees-actually-want.

3. Socha, T.J. "Group Communication Across the Lifespan." In *Managing Group Life: Communicating in Decision Making Groups*, edited by L.R. Frey & J.K. Barge, (3-28). Boston: Houghton Mifflin, 1997.

4. Cragan, John F. and David W. Wright. *Communication in Small Groups: Theory, Process, Skills.* 5th ed. Belmont, CA: Wadsworth, 1999.

5. Bormann, E.G. "Fantasy and Rhetorical Vision: The Rhetorical Criticism of Social Reality". *Quarterly Journal of Speech* 58: (1972): 396–407.

6. Wilson, G. L. *Groups in Context: Leadership and Participation in Small Groups.* 6th ed. New York: McGraw Hill, 2002.

7. Tuckman, Bruce. "Developmental Sequences in Small Groups," *Psychological Bulletin* 63, (1965): 384-389; Bruce Tuckman and Mary Ann Jensen. "Stages of Small Group Development Revisited." *Group and Organizational Studies* 2, (1977): 419-427.

8. Wheelan, Susan A. *Creating Effective Teams: A Guide for Members and Leaders.* 3rd ed. Los Angeles, CA: Sage, 2010.

9. Bormann, Ernest G. "Fantasy and Rhetorical Vision: The Rhetorical Criticism of Social Reality." *Quarterly Journal of Speech* 58 no. 4 (1972): 396-407.

10. Benne, K. D. and P. Sheats. "Functional Roles of Group Members." *Journal of Social Issues* 4, (1948): 41-49.

11. Mudrack, P. E. and G. M. Farrell. "An Examination of Functional Role Behavior and Its Consequences for Individuals in Group Settings." *Small Group Research* 26, (1995): 542-571.

12. Orlitzky, M. and R. Y. Hirokawa. "To Err is Human, to Correct for it Divine: A Meta-Analysis of Research Testing the Functional Theory of Group Decision-Making Effectiveness." *Small Group Research* 32, (2001): 313-341.

13. Orlitzky, M. and R. Y. Hirokawa. "To Err is Human, to Correct for it Divine: A Meta-Analysis of Research Testing the Functional Theory of Group Decision-Making Effectiveness." *Small Group Research* 32, (2001): 314.

14. Dennis, A. R. "Information Exchange and Use in Small Group Decision Making." *Small Group Research* 27, (1996): 532-550.

15. Krasnoff and Foster. *Community.* Los Angeles, CA, Universal Entertainment: NCB, 2009.

16. Orlitzky, M. and R. Y. Hirokawa. "To Err is Human, to Correct for it Divine: A Meta-Analysis of Research Testing the Functional Theory of Group Decision-Making Effectiveness." Small Group Research 32, (2001): 313-341.

17. Janis, I.L. *Victims of Groupthink.* Boston: Houghton-Mifflin, 1972.

18. Sorensen, S. M. "Grouphate." Paper presented at the meeting of the International Communication Association, Minneapolis, MN, 1981.

19. Karau, S. J. and K. D. Williams. "Social Loafing: Research Findings, Implications, and Future Directions." *Current Directions in Psychological Science* 4, (1995): 134-140.

Chapter 19

1. Carpenter, Julia. "A new first for LGBTQ Business leaders." *CNN Money.* July 27, 2018. https://money.cnn.com/2018/07/27/news/companies/lgbtq-ceos.

2. French, J.R.P., Jr., and B. H. Raven. "The Bases of Social Power." In *Studies in Social Power*, edited by D. Cartwright, 150–167. Ann Arbor, MI: Institute for Social Research, 1959.

3. Goleman, D. "Leadership That Gets Results." *Harvard Business Review,* (2000): 79-90. http://www.haygroup.com/downloads/fi/Leadership_That_Gets_Results.pdf.

4. Goleman, D. "Leadership That Gets Results." *Harvard Business Review,* (2000): 79-90. http://www.haygroup.com/downloads/fi/Leadership_That_Gets_Results.pdf.

5. Adapted from Goleman, D. Leadership That Gets Results." *Harvard Business Review*, (2000): 79-90. http://www.haygroup.com/downloads/fi/Leadership_That_Gets_Results.pdf.

Chapter 20

1. "Job Outlook 2016: The Attributes Employers Want to See on New College Graduates' Resumes." National Association of Colleges and Employers. 2016. http://www.naceweb.org/career-development/trends-and-predictions/job-outlook-2016-attributes-employers-want-to-see-on-new-college-graduates-resumes/.

2. "Discrimination by Type." U.S. Equal Employment Opportunity Commission. www.eeoc.gov/laws/types/index.cfm

3. Adams, Susan. "This Man's Business is Providing Fake Job Histories and References." *Forbes.com.* (December 20, 2013). https://www.forbes.com/sites/susanadams/2013/12/20/this-mans-business-is-providing-fake-job-histories-and-references/.

INDEX

low uncertainty avoidance culture, 19
low-context cultures, 21
Luft, Joseph, 43
Lynch, Jessica, 242

M

magazines, 200–201
main points, preview of, 208, 211
Maines, Nicole, 28
maintenance of intimate relationships, 147
maintenance roles, 276–277, 279t
major premise, 262
Making of Meaning, The (Ogden and Richards), 6
managing tasks, 278–279
manuscript speeches, 228
marriage practices, 149–150, 155
masculine culture, 20
Maslow, Abraham, 2, 116
Maslow's hierarchy of needs, 2, 2fig, 116
McCroskey, James, 228
Mead, George Herbert, 12, 41
media impact on relationships, 166–169
Media Richness Theory, 167
media sources, 201
mediated communication, 164–166, 170–172
mediated relationships, 163, 172–173
mediated self and others, 166–169
Medina, John, 37, 44, 53
memorized speeches, 227–228
memory, 194
meta-communicative processes, 133
metaphoric language, 71–73, 76–77
metonyms, 71–72
Miller, Terry, 78
Milton, John, 74
minimax principle, 133, 133fig
minor premise, 262
minutes, meeting, 301
mirroring, 89
mixed couples, 151
mixed metaphors, 72
models, 230–231
monochronic people, 91, 92t
monologue, 55–56
Monroe's Motivated Sequence, 260
Montgomery, Barbara, 137
Moore, Michael, 195
morality, 58
multimedia technology, 235
multiple intelligence theory, 25, 26fig
mutual equality, principle of, 54–55

N

narrative, 74–75
narrative coherence, 75
narrative fidelity, 75
Nashville, 135
national anthem, kneeling during, 86
National Communication Association, 58–59
national cultures, 18
National Institute of Deafness and Other Communication Disorders (NIDCD), 100
NCAA policies, 257
need, 260
needs, hierarchy of, 2, 2fig, 116
negative consequences, evaluation of, 282
negative quality of language, 70
negativity bias, 40
neutrality, 190
new experiences, embracing, 140
news networks, 283
newspapers, 200–201
noise, 7, 7t
non sequitur, 264, 265
nonexamples, 246
nonexpression, expression and, 139
nonlistening, 106–109
non-task talk, 285
nonverbal communication
    from audience, 252
    context and, 85–86
    dialogic, 95–96
    functions of, 86–88
    listening and, 111
    principles of, 84–86
    role of, 83–84
    space and, 90–91
    time and, 91, 92t
    types of, 88–94
    verbal messages and, 85
norming stage, 276
notes, 62–63, 286, 317
numbers, 202
Nye, Bill, 55

O

Obama, Barack, 9
objective information, 43
objects, 230, 243
observation of audience, 199
observing and commenting, 280
occupational influences, 38–39
oculesics, 90